Preaching the Old Testament

Preaching the Old Testament

A Lectionary Commentary

Ronald J. Allen
Clark M. Williamson

Westminster John Knox Press
LOUISVILLE • LONDON

Scripture quotations from the New Revised Standard Version of the Bible are copyright © 1989 by the Division of Christian Education of the National Council of the Churches of Christ in the U.S.A. and are used by permission.

Book design by Sharon Adams
Cover design by designpointinc.com
Cover art: Chagall, Marc (1887–1985). Jeremiah. *Courtesy of Réunion des Musées Nationaux/Art Resource, NY*

First edition
Published by Westminster John Knox Press
Louisville, Kentucky

This book is printed on acid-free paper that meets the American National Standards Institute Z39.48 standard. ∞

PRINTED IN THE UNITED STATES OF AMERICA

07 08 09 10 11 12 13 14 15 16 — 10 9 8 7 6 5 4 3 2 1

Library of Congress Cataloging-in-Publication Data is on file at the Library of Congress, Washington, D.C.

ISBN-13: 978-0-664-23068-5
ISBN-10: 0-664-23068-7

This book is dedicated to

Sidney Steiman
(in memoriam)

Murray Saltzman

Jonathan Stein

Rabbis who have opened the Torah, Prophets,
and Writings to us

Contents

Introduction

This volume is a companion to our two previously published works on preaching on the Revised Common Lectionary. *Preaching the Gospels without Blaming the Jews* (Westminster John Knox Press, 2004) centers on the Gospel readings in the lectionary. *Preaching the Letters without Dismissing the Law* (Westminster John Knox Press, 2006) considers the lections from the Epistles. In this book we concentrate on the readings from the Old Testament.[1] Because the lectionary does, we include comments on passages from the Wisdom of Solomon, Sirach, and Baruch. While these books are not regarded as canon by most Protestants, they are read in worship by the Episcopal, Roman Catholic, and Orthodox communions.[2]

Over the past forty years, prompted by the growing dialogue between the Jewish and Christian communities, scholars have increasingly pointed out that while the church affirms the importance of the Old Testament, preachers often neglect these books, misrepresent them, or regard their theological content as superseded by Jesus and the New Testament. Writings by biblical scholars, theologians, and scholars of preaching agree that the time is ripe for the church to rediscover the Old Testament as a vibrant wellspring of Christian faith and life.[3] This commentary encourages preachers to move in that direction.

The Old Testament Is Foundational for the Church

The Old Testament is foundational to the Christian community. In order to understand God, Jesus Christ, and the church, the congregation must understand the Old Testament. For the Old Testament contains the formative texts that reveal the nature and purposes of the God of Abraham and

Sarah, Moses and Miriam, David and Bathsheba, Ruth and Esther, Jesus and Paul. The texts of the Old Testament offer paradigms by which to identify God's presence and purposes. From the Old Testament, we learn that the God of Israel is the universal God who created the world, exercises sovereignty over it, and seeks for all its inhabitants to live in blessing.

The Old Testament, along with other Jewish writings of the Hellenistic age (circa 300 BCE to 200 CE), provided the Jesus movement with the theological concepts and vocabulary to interpret their experience of Jesus Christ.[4] Indeed, one of the permeating rediscoveries of recent scholarship is the thoroughgoing Jewishness of the New Testament. Most scholars believe that Jesus was a faithful Jew, as were his first followers. The Jesus movement regarded their turn toward the Gentile mission not as a rejection of Judaism, much less an attempt to start a separate religion, but as an outreach of the Jewish community so that Gentiles could know the blessing of the God of Israel.

From the Old Testament, Christians learn the stories, images, and values that are the raison d'être of Jesus and his followers. We find how to understand terms that are essential to Christian life—such as compassion, covenant, Gentiles, grace, Holy Spirit, judgment, justice, law, life, love, repentance, righteousness, and wisdom. Christians are immensely instructed by exploring the background of such terms in the Old Testament, in the Apocrypha and Pseudepigrapha, and in other Jewish writings of the Hellenistic age, such as the Mishnah, the Talmud, and Philo's works. Often we discover that the Old Testament background is a resonance chamber that deeply enriches our understanding of the use of such terms in the New Testament and helps the church understand itself as in the tradition of the Old Testament.

When preachers look carefully at the New Testament, they discover that the New Testament writers use the Old Testament in different ways. Sometimes the New Testament authors directly quote the Old Testament. At other times the New Testament writers allude to or echo the earlier materials, even using a single word, phrase, or image to evoke a whole story, a key value, or a pattern of feeling from the Old Testament. For example, the author of the book of Revelation says, "I saw a new heaven and a new earth; for the first heaven and the first earth had passed away, and the sea was no more" (Rev. 21:1). The reference to the "sea" is not simply a geographical reference but brings to mind the tradition—developed in the Old Testament—of associating the experience of chaos with the sea. By saying "the sea is no more," the author means that chaos will have no place in the new heaven and the new earth.

Preachers and congregations who are aware of the content of the Old Testament can appreciate the theological guidance in its own right, and can read the New Testament in full resonance with the Old Testament. In this way of thinking the Old Testament is a part of the Christian family album and reading it helps us understand our identity. Those who are unaware of the content of the Old Testament are cut off from a vital source of theological insight and can even misread the New Testament because of their lack of familiarity with how the New Testament writers presumed the Old. Indeed, congregations that do not know the Old Testament are theological orphans.

Problems in the Church's Use of the Old Testament

Despite the foundational importance of the Old Testament, the church has often misused or neglected it. Preachers misuse the Old Testament in two main ways. We summarize these problems and then explore how they sometimes come to expression in the way a preacher uses texts assigned by the Revised Common Lectionary.[5]

One common misperception is for preachers to regard the Old Testament merely as prologue to the New Testament. In this way of thinking, the Old Testament has little value in and of itself but functions to point the way to Christ and the church. The Old Testament is prophecy, preview, shadow, or antitype. Christians sometimes picture people who lived in the Old Testament period as empty, hungry, and longing for the coming of Christ. Christ is said to fulfill the prophecies of the Old Testament and human longing.

This view is undermined by two major facts. (1) The birth, life, death, and resurrection of Christ have not finally and fully brought God's purposes to completion. For example, Isaiah looked forward to a time when all people and even the elements of nature will live together in peace (e.g., Isa. 11:1–9). Christ did not fulfill that hope. War still ravages the earth. Indeed, the earliest followers of Jesus acknowledged that God's purposes are incomplete when they began to expect the second coming of Jesus. Judaism and Christianity are similar in continuing to hope for a time when God's purposes will shape every person, relationship, and event. Many recent Christian theologians reinterpret the notion of fulfillment to mean that God's work in Jesus Christ is a means whereby Gentiles are grafted into a community that witnesses to God's desire to bless all peoples. (2) Few biblical scholars in the historic Christian denominations in North America think that the authors of the Old Testament specifically intended to predict

Christ. Scholars today tend to think that where those authors articulated texts that looked to the future, they anticipated events that would take place in times much closer to their own.

Another frequent misreading of the Old Testament is to interpret it as the antithesis of the New Testament. From this point of view, the Old Testament contains theological views and suggestions for behavior that are the opposite of those in the New Testament. The Old Testament, in this line of thinking, presents an inferior view of God, and a religion of rigidity, legalism, works righteousnes, and empty ceremony with no concern for ethical living. Indeed, preachers sometimes imply that Jesus came to save people from Judaism. Congregations still hear sermons that caricature the God of the Old Testament as wrathful in contrast to the God of love and grace in the New Testament. In this way of thinking, the Old Testament and Judaism are so negative that Jesus and Christianity have superseded the Old Testament and Judaism.

The best biblical scholarship today insists that this picture of the Old Testament is a misrepresentation. When a congregation reads the Old Testament carefully, they should discover a God of love and compassion who graciously makes covenant with them. The Old instructs the community on how to love God and neighbor and otherwise how to live in the way of blessing, and what to do when covenantal community fails.

As we noted previously, these problems and others can occur in the ways preachers appropriate texts from the Revised Common Lectionary. Indeed, the lectionary itself, while not directly encouraging such theological errors, is structured in such a way as to leave the door open for them.

At the simplest level, the Revised Common Lectionary minimizes the likelihood that the congregation will encounter the Old Testament. The lectionary appoints three lessons for preaching for each Sunday. Despite the formative role of the Old Testament in the life of the church, not to mention the fact that the Old Testament is four times the length of the Second Testament, only one of the lectionary readings for preaching is from the Old Testament. (Although a psalm is appointed for liturgical use, it is not typically used for preaching.)[6]

Moreover, on the Sundays after Easter, the Revised Common Lectionary replaces the reading from the Old Testament with a passage from the book of Acts. (A psalm is retained for liturgical use.) Thus, at the theological high point of the Christian year, the lectionary ignores the sacred literature that is necessary to interpret the Jesus movement and its earliest writings.

The number of passages from the Old Testament available for preaching from the lectionary is diminished even further by the fact that more than fifty-five Old Testament passages are used more than once in the lectionary's three-year cycle.

Even more problematic than the lectionary's neglect of the Old Testament is the lectionary's use of that Testament. During the pivotal seasons of Advent, Christmas, Epiphany Day, and the Sundays after Epiphany, as well as in Lent and on Easter and Pentecost Day, the lectionary intends the reading from the Old Testament to be heard through the lens of the Gospel. In these seasons, the lesson from the Epistle is intended to amplify or draw out the implications of the Gospel. In the Sundays of Ordinary Time after Pentecost, the lectionary provides a Gospel lesson and an Epistle lesson as well as two sets of readings from the Old Testament. During this latter time of the year, congregational leaders are to choose one of these sets of readings for use in worship: either a passage from the Old Testament (and a psalm) that correlates with the Gospel lesson, or the other passage from the Old Testament (and an accompanying psalm) that presents a part of the Old Testament in semicontinuous reading. In Year A, semicontinuous readings are from the Pentateuch, especially Genesis and Exodus; in Year B they are from the Davidic covenant and the Wisdom literature; in Year C, the semicontinuous passages are from the Prophets, especially Jeremiah.

When the reading from the Old Testament is supposed to connect to the Gospels, the lectionary envisions three kinds of relationships between the readings:[7]

The first possible relationship is *parallelism*. That is, it is presumed that the material in the Old Testament passage is parallel to the Gospel reading and that the two texts present similar interpretations of God's action and human response. When both of these presumptions are accurate, the preacher can help the congregation recognize how the Old Testament reading provides the model for understanding the New Testament passage. This relationship is typically the most theologically satisfactory. For an example of exegesis and sermonic reflection on texts that the lectionary presents as having such a parallel relationship in the lectionary, see the Fifth Sunday after the Epiphany/Year C in which we note parallel elements in the calls of Isaiah (Isa. 6:1–8) and the first disciples (Luke 5:1-11).

The second possible relationship between the texts is one of *contrast* between the supposedly inferior viewpoint in the Old Testament and the supposedly superior perspective in the Gospel. Here the preacher can easily slip into viewing the Old Testament as the antithesis of the new. For an example of contrast between two texts, see our discussion of Proper 28/Year A: Zephaniah 1:7, 12–18, on the judgment on Judah because of unfaithfulness, and Matthew 25:14–24, on the parable of the Talents. Linking these two texts leaves the impression that the Jewish community portrayed in Zephaniah is similar to the one-talent servant who is condemned and thrown into outer darkness. A more complicated dimension of contrast comes when the Gospel reading pictures Jesus (and the disciples) in conflict with leaders of Judaism (e.g., Pharisees, scribes, priests). Many scholars today conclude that the Gospel writers themselves polemically created such contrasts to justify a conflict and growing separation between the congregations of the Gospel writers and some other Jewish communities after the fall of the Temple in 70 CE. This motif is at work on Epiphany 9/Year B when Mark 2:23–3:6 portrays Jesus in two conflicts with the Pharisees regarding eating heads of grain and healing a person with a withered hand on the Sabbath. After these two brief incidents, Mark says vitriolically, "The Pharisees went out and immediately conspired with the Herodians against [Jesus], how to destroy [Jesus]."

The third possible relationship between lectionary texts is *typological*. By this the lectionary means that the Old Testament reading posits a promise, prophecy, or foreshadowing that the lectionary interprets as fulfilled in the Gospel or Epistle lesson. Christian preachers sometimes intimate that the entire purpose of the lesson from the Old Testament was to predict the coming of Jesus, thus committing the errors associated with the prologue view of the Old Testament that we discussed just above. To counter this point of view, the preacher needs to encourage the congregation to recognize that the Old Testament writers did not specifically anticipate the coming of Jesus, although many ancient Jewish authors did anticipate that God would work in the future to bless Israel and the Gentiles. The preacher can help the congregation recognize that the writers of the New Testament found the ministry of Jesus to be an expression of that forward movement and can explore the idea that the Second Testament extended the promises of God to Gentiles while not negating the promises that God made to Sarah and Abraham and their descendants, promises that included Gentiles (Gen. 12:3).

The Revised Common Lectionary never allows the congregation to hear in sequence the overall story that is told in the Old Testament. During the key cycles of Advent-Christmas-Epiphany Day and Lent-Easter-Pentecost Day, the Gospel lesson sets the theme for each Sunday. Even after Trinity Sunday, when the lectionary provides for semicontinuous reading of representative passages from the Old Testament, the story is told in segments separated by almost six months. In Year A, the congregation hears narratives from the Pentateuch and hears about the entry into the promised land, but then the lectionary departs from the great story line of the Old Testament while attending to readings from Year B for Advent, Christmas, Epiphany, Lent, and Easter. In the latter half of Year B, the congregation hears the Davidic covenant and Wisdom motifs, only to be interrupted by the Advent through Pentecost readings from Year C before taking up the Prophets.

Given such fragmentation, James A. Sanders, a biblical scholar who taught for many years at the Claremont School of Theology, has proposed that the church create an alternative lectionary that is centered in telling the story of the Old Testament.[8] Such a lectionary would not follow the seasons of the Christian Year (except, perhaps, at Christmas and Easter) but would follow the story of Israel in sequence from creation through the ancestral narratives, the exodus, the entry into the promised land, the judges, the monarchy (united and divided), the exile, and return. It could also incorporate Jewish materials from the Hellenistic age.

Suggestions for Preaching on the Old Testament

Preachers can do several things to give the Old Testament a greater presence in the pulpit. The simplest action is to preach frequently from the Old Testament. While this will not work every Sunday, a preacher might set a goal of preaching at least two Sundays a month using the reading from the Old Testament as the basis of the sermon.

When the relationship between the reading from the Old Testament and the reading from the Gospel is exegetically and theologically appropriate, the preacher can bring this information into the sermon. When the readings have little relationship, the preacher might consider exchanging the assigned text from the Old Testament for one that is more appropriate, or might consider changing the reading from the Second Testament. For example, texts in the New Testament often quote or directly allude to passages from the Old Testament that help explain the material in the New Testament passage. Preachers who discover such a direct literary or theological relationship between particular texts in the two testaments might replace one of the readings in the lectionary with a passage that overtly relates to the other passage. Preachers encounter such a situation on the Third Sunday after the Epiphany/Year C, when selections from Nehemiah 8 (Ezra's sermon on the law) are paired with Luke 4:14–20 (Jesus' sermon at Nazareth). The Lukan passage actually quotes Isaiah 61:1–2 and 58:6. The preacher is well advised to replace Nehemiah 8 with the readings from Isaiah.

As noted above, the second set of readings from the Old Testament on the Sundays after Pentecost presents semicontinuous readings. A pastor can take advantage of these serial readings by developing sermon series that follow the story from one week to the next. In doing this, the preacher is practicing a form of the oldest lectionary pattern called *lectio continua*, a pattern for reading and preaching that was probably used in the synagogue by the time of Jesus.

In a similar spirit, on the Sundays after Easter, when the lectionary replaces the reading from the Old Testament with one from the book of Acts, the minister could add a reading from the Old Testament that has a literary and theological relationship with the readings from the New Testament.

Worship planners could also eliminate the duplication of lections that occurs in the Revised Common Lectionary by replacing one of the duplicate readings with another text that pairs well with the New Testament passage. And preachers should keep an open mind about whether a text from the Old Testament offers theological wisdom that is superior to a text from the New. For an example of this issue, see our discussion of Proper 17 [22]/Year B in which Mark 7:1–23 is paired with Deuteronomy 4:1–2, 6–9. It seems to us that Deuteronomy offers a better understanding of the matters shared by those passages than does Mark.

From time to time, a community's situation may be better addressed by a biblical text that is not in the lectionary or, indeed, by topical preaching that does not center in the exposition of a biblical text but in the theological interpretation of a circumstance in the congregation or world. On such occasions, a preacher should not hesitate to leave the lectionary behind and to select freely a passage (or to focus on a topic).

The Plan of the Comments

Our comments on individual passages involve three elements. (1) We always explain how a text was understood before the Common Era without any reference to Jesus or Christian doctrine. Most typically, we focus on how the final editors (such as the Deuteronomic or Priestly theologians) used the passage. (2) We often move from the significance of the passage in the world of the Old Testament to mention representative New Testament passages or themes that are informed by the older material by means of citation, allusion, echo, and resonance. (3) When readings from the Old Testament are paired with readings from the New, we often comment briefly on the relationship between the lections.

As noted previously, after Trinity Sunday, the lectionary appoints two readings from the Old Testament (plus psalms for liturgical use)—one as a semicontinuous reading from a part of the Old Testament, and the other a reading that is paired with the Gospel for the day. On each day after Trinity Sunday, we discuss the semicontinuous reading first and, following the custom in the 1992 edition of *The Revised Common Lectionary*, we indicate this reading by the use of a plus sign (+) while also adding the word "semicontinuous."[9] We indicate the readings appointed to coordinate with the Gospel by an asterisk (*) while adding the word "paired."

In recent years, a number of people in Jewish and Christian communities have rediscovered the notion of *tikkun olam*, the act of mending the brokenness of the world so that people can live together in well-being, love, peace, and justice.[10] The phrase *tikkun olam* often refers to actions of human beings to repair breaches in the divine purposes for the communities of humankind and nature.

A story from the Babylonian Talmud captures this spirit. Rabbi Beroka was conversing with Elijah regarding who has a place in the world to come when Elijah spotted two people passing by, and said, "These two have a share in the world to come." Rabbi Beroka asked them, "'What is your occupation?' They replied, 'We are jesters. When we see [people] depressed, we cheer them up; furthermore, when we see two people quarrelling we strive hard to make peace between them.'"[11]

We pray that this book and its companions will encourage a similar spirit in Christian preachers and congregations.

Year A

First Sunday of Advent/Year A

Isaiah 2:1–5

This utterly appropriate passage for the first Sunday of Advent is a future-oriented "word" (*debar*) that Isaiah "saw concerning Judah and Jerusalem" (2:1). It addresses four themes: (1) the reestablishment of Mount Zion and the Temple (tacitly understood) "as the highest of the mountains" (v. 2); (2) the claim that "all the nations [Gentiles] shall stream to it" (vv. 2–3); (3) the claim that YHWH will "teach us his ways" that "we might walk in his paths" (v. 3); and (4) the claim that "in days to come" (v. 2) there will be universal peace and the abolition of war (v. 4). This is a future-oriented "forth-telling" by the prophet; it is not necessarily eschatological or apocalyptic. It is a concrete hope for a real future that issues in a plea to the people: "come, let us walk in the light of the LORD!" (v. 5). Isaiah speaks for a God who calls on a covenant people to live into a future of blessing and well-being.

That Gentiles will learn to walk in the ways of the Lord was Isaiah's hope and an early promise to Abraham: "in you all the families of the earth shall be blessed" (Gen. 12:3). This promise was at the heart of Paul's outlook as well as that of the Gospels; in Luke, Simeon sang at the birth of Jesus that he was "a light for revelation to the Gentiles and for glory to your people Israel" (Luke 2:32). Today's passage also appears in Micah 4:1–4 verbatim with the addition of verse 5: "For all the peoples walk, each in the name of its god, but we will walk in the name of the LORD our God forever and ever."

Isaiah and Micah demonstrate openness to Gentiles, to their coming to the Jerusalem Temple, and to their receiving "instruction" (*torah*) from Zion (Isa. 2:3). The inclusion of Gentiles is a prominent theme in Isaiah

1

and in Second Temple Judaism; that it shows up prominently in Paul demonstrates his continuity with rather than his difference from this tradition. Yet, differing views on relations with Gentiles also were present throughout the Second Temple period.

Our reading is a compilation of Zion motifs that appear throughout Isaiah: (1) Jerusalem is the cosmic mountain at the center of the world, for example, 10:12, 32; 11:9; (2) the Temple is the center of Jerusalem and of the world (4:5; 8:18; 24:23, for example); (3) Gentiles will gather from all directions in Jerusalem (45:14–23; 60:1–18).

Significantly, our passage refers to the Temple as the "house of Jacob [*bêt ya'aqôb*]" (2:3, 5). The story of Jacob's exile in Mesopotamia and his return to the land of promise (Genesis 25–35) parallels the story of the Judeans exported to and returned from Babylon. Our passage indicates that the judgment passed on Judah and Jerusalem in 2:6–4:1 now lies in the past and a new hope for the future has been opened up by the faithfulness of God to the people Israel.

Part of this new promise/hope is that the "peoples . . . shall beat their swords into plowshares, and their spears into pruning hooks; nation shall not lift up sword against nation; neither shall they learn war any more" (2:4). This promise has patently not yet been fulfilled; in the twentieth century "at least 100 million human beings lost their lives in war—on average 3,500 a day."[1] Guiltily and sadly we are bound to recognize the violence that we continue to inflict on each other, on other creatures, and on the created world that God has given us as a home in which to live. Like the Judeans of old, we too need to "cease to do evil and learn to do good" (Isa. 1:17).

The lectionary subverts any triumphalism on our part. On the last Sunday before the First Sunday of Advent/Year A, it presents us with Luke's account of the crucifixion of Jesus (23:33–43), a reminder that Isaiah's vision of a world freed of violence has not yet come to pass and that the Jewish claim that the world has not yet been redeemed holds true. And it pairs today's passage with Matthew 24:36–44, where Jesus insists that "no one knows, neither the angels of heaven, nor the Son" when the coming of the Son of Man will occur. This is very much a season of Advent rather than arrival.

Second Sunday of Advent/Year A

Isaiah 11:1–10

Today's passage continues the theme developed in Isaiah 7:10–16 and 9:2–7 (please see the Fourth Sunday of Advent/Year A and Christmas Day

1/Year A): Isaiah promises a ruler in the line of David who will bring "endless peace" (9:7). Isaiah 11:1–10 in magnificent poetry announces a Davidic king gifted with all the traits that epitomize a just and righteous king. This king will look after the well-being of the vulnerable members of society. At the top of his agenda will be the central concerns of the Torah and the Prophets: "with righteousness he shall judge the poor, and decide with equity for the meek of the earth" (v. 4).

That this is to be a Davidic king is clear in verse 1: "a shoot shall come out from the stump of Jesse." The old stock of Jesse, ancestor of the Davidic dynasty (1 Sam. 16:1), will yet produce the shoot of a new tree. Other expressions in the Scriptures anticipated, after the exile, that the house of David would be restored (Jer. 23: 5–6; 33:14–22; Ezek. 37: 24–28; Amos 9:11–15; Mic. 5:1–3). (The text of Isaiah presents materials edited in ways that are hardly strictly chronological.)

On this new king "the spirit of the LORD [YHWH] shall rest" (v. 2). That is the spirit of wisdom (*chokmah*) and understanding (*binah*), character traits critical to living a life of blessing and well-being for all. It requires wisdom and understanding to arrange matters so that blessing is spread throughout the entire society and between one society and another. The way to peace (a central theme of the poem) is not by means of careless and haphazard measures. Counsel and might, the second pair of attributes, are the know-how and capacity to make sensible arrangements and effectuate them. "Knowledge and the fear [awe] of the Lord" are themes prominent in the Torah and the Prophets: wisdom and understanding are in the service of the One to whom we are ultimately committed. Rabbi Hanina ben Dosa said: "For anyone whose fear of sin takes precedence over his wisdom, his wisdom will endure. And for anyone whose wisdom takes precedence over his fear of sin, his wisdom will not endure."[2] All these gifts of the Spirit of the Lord make possible a just society.

The poem also reflects the deep scriptural aversion to killing and looks forward to a time when there will be no more killing: "they will not hurt or destroy on all my holy mountain" (v. 9) Predatory meat-eating animals will cease to kill: "the wolf shall live with the lamb, the leopard shall lie down with the kid, the calf and the lion and the fatling together" (v. 6). Poisonous snakes will not attack children: "the nursling child shall play over the hole of the asp" (v. 8). This reflects the story of Eden (Gen. 1:29; 2:16), where the human beings could eat only the fruit of trees and plants; they could not kill to eat. It echoes the covenant with Noah, which was a covenant with all the living things (Gen. 9:10). In the future as in the beginning, there is to be no killing.

We are told however that the ideal Davidic king shall "kill the wicked" (v. 4). But it is an extremely odd kind of killing: he will do it "with the breath of his lips," his words, not his weapons of war.

The contrast between this future state and the all-too-typical history of human warfare could hardly be greater than it is in this poem. In 10:32–33, describing a state of war preceding the utterance of this poem, Isaiah portrays the destruction of nature that took place in the total warfare waged by the competing powers of the region: "the tallest trees will be cut down, and the lofty will be brought low. He will hack down the thickets of the forest with an ax, and Lebanon with its majestic trees will fall." But in the new age to come, the chaos that engulfs both nature and history will itself be vanquished. The covenantal ecology of Scripture includes nature.

Romans 15:4–13 picks up on the basic biblical theme of blessing (well-being) that is to be shared in by both Jews and Gentiles and, thereby, indirectly in today's reading from Isaiah and quite directly on a number of other passages in Isaiah, for example, 49:6.

Third Sunday of Advent/Year A

Isaiah 35:1–10

Isaiah 35 has to do with the restoration of the land of Judah, following conflict with Edom, known in the Scriptures as the land south of the Dead Sea. Chapter 34 deals with the destruction of Edom subsequent to conflict between Edom and Judah (34:9). In today's reading, Isaiah looks forward to what a restored Judah, Jerusalem, and the Temple will look like.

Verses 1–2 and 6b–7 concentrate on the restored ecology of Judah: the land, rivers, living things, marshes, and rain. There is throughout Israel's Scriptures a primary concern for the well-being of all God's creatures, including the created order itself. Christians, for most of our history, have paid little attention to this biblical ecology and sometimes have even systematically eliminated it from our understanding of the Scriptures by insisting that the only proper interpretation of the Old Testament is to view everything material as a stand-in for a spiritual reality. Being concerned with the well-being of actual earthly turf was less important than understanding passages such as this one as pointing to the coming of Christ. Yet the Parousia of Christ, as Paul understood it, would also set the creation free from its bondage to decay (Rom. 8:18–25).

In Isaiah's imagined future "the wilderness and the dry land shall be glad, the desert shall rejoice and blossom" (v. 1). This would better be translated:

"let the wilderness and the dry land be glad . . ." "Desert" refers not to a natural desert but to the land whose ecology had been devastated by war. Verse 2 is better translated: "let the crocus blossom abundantly, and rejoice with joy and singing." Warfare in the ancient world was like Sherman's march from Atlanta to the sea during the Civil War: it involved total devastation of the environment, intended to deprive the enemy of resources.[3] Partly in response to widespread ecological devastation, Israelite faith laid great stress on care for all of creation. Its eschatological visions hope for a time when both nature and society will be matrixes of well-being for all their inhabitants. Isaiah 35 is part of this larger covenantal biblical ecology.

"The glory of Lebanon" and the "majesty of Carmel" with their lush environment and majestic cedars will be "given to it," that is, to Zion. "Waters shall break forth in the wilderness, and streams in the desert" (v. 6); the wadis will run with fresh water and good shepherds will have places to which to guide their sheep. The parched land will be "a pool" (v. 7) and the place where jackals roamed will be rich with reeds and rushes (a "swamp" in the NRSV). Preachers can use these hopes for a restored environment to broaden and deepen the usual understanding of what we are to anticipate at Advent, what Parousia of Christ means in its full biblical dimensions, when creation will no longer be "groaning in travail" (Rom. 8:22).

Verses 3–4 are meant to strengthen and encourage the people, who might well doubt that these promises could possibly come to pass. They are words of comfort that seek to provide the people with strength; comfort means "with strength." They encourage trust in the salvific power of the Lord. Verses 5–6a proclaim that the blind shall see and the deaf hear, the crippled shall spring up like deer and "the tongue of the speechless sing for joy." These are not metaphorical expressions; they have to do with the actual elimination of physical disabilities, removing barriers to a life of well-being, just as our other verses have to do with actual water alleviating real drought.

Verses 8–10 celebrate the return of the exiles to Zion. The "highway" is a play on the "King's highway" that ran through Edom, but this highway is "the Holy Way" taken by the exiles coming back to Jerusalem. It is "for God's people" and "the unclean shall not travel on it" (v. 8). Those traveling on it will be in a state of ritual purity on their way to the Temple in Jerusalem. Their journey will end with a triumphal entry into Jerusalem; they shall "come to Zion with singing" (v. 10). On the holy way, nature will be benign ("no lion shall be there"), and the people "shall obtain joy and gladness."

This is a marvelous vision—for Advent and for any time. Preachers could interpret it as God's invitation to the church to join the people

Israel, all peoples, and the created order on a journey toward that future for which we hope and pray.

Fourth Sunday of Advent/Year A

Isaiah 7:10–16

Isaiah 6–8 is concerned with the threat of an invasion of Judah and Jerusalem by the allied forces of Syria and Samaria around the year 734. Isaiah 7:1 refers to the fact that Rezin, king of Aram (Syria), and Pekah, king of Samaria (Israel), were planning an assault on Jerusalem. Their purpose was to coerce King Ahaz to join in their alliance against Assyria, the dominant military power in the region.

In this situation, the Lord told Isaiah to take his son Shear-jashub (whose name means "a remnant will return"), go to Ahaz, and speak to him: "Take heed, be quiet, do not fear, and do not let your heart be faint because of these two smoldering stumps of firebrands [Kings Rezin and Pekah]" (7:4). Of the threatened invasion the Lord said: "It shall not stand, and it shall not come to pass" (v. 7). That is, the attack by Syria and Samaria on Assyria will fail (which it did). In verses 8–9, the Lord adds: "If you do not stand firm in faith, you shall not stand at all." If Ahaz holds firm, either everything will turn out well or, at worst, a remnant will return from any resulting deportation. Ahaz should not go to pieces. This leads to today's exchange between Isaiah and Ahaz.

The Lord says to Ahaz: "Ask a sign of the LORD your God" (v. 10), but Ahaz refuses to "put the LORD to the test" (v. 11). The sign is to persuade Ahaz to accept Isaiah's advice. The ability to perform signs was a recognized part of prophetic activity (in first-century Galilee, Jesus of Nazareth and Hanina ben Dosa were recognized performers of signs). In spite of Ahaz's refusal to test the Lord, a sign is offered: "Look, the young woman [*almah*] is with child and shall bear a son, and shall name him Immanuel" (v. 14). Ahaz is further assured that "before the child knows how to refuse the evil and choose the good, the land before whose two kings you are in dread will be deserted" (v. 16). Syria and Samaria will no longer threaten Jerusalem.

In Isaiah 8:1–4, Isaiah went "to the prophetess, and she conceived and bore a son" (8:3). He was named "Maher-shalal-hash-baz," a name that bodes ill, meaning that the defeat of Syria and Samaria by the Assyrians is imminent.

The lectionary places our passage on the Fourth Sunday of Advent, where it has traditionally functioned in Christian perspective as a prophecy of the coming of Jesus. How can the text refer to Jesus if its plain meaning situates it in the context of a particular crisis in international conflict in the eighth century? Here is where a Jewish understanding of Scripture can help Christians. So far we have explored the *peshat* of the text—its givenness. But a text has other meanings: *remez*, its intrinsic meaning; *derash*, its interpretations, and *sod*, a spiritual meaning. Putting together the initial consonants of each term—*prds*—we come up with the term *pardes*, from which our word "paradise" is derived. The point is to recognize that the text is a *pardes* of abundantly textured meaning that describes the covenantal partnership between God and Israel and God and the church. Interpretation (*midrash*) is never of a text in itself; it is always also an interpretation of us and our experience and of each in relation to the other.

We are not required, therefore, to twist the *peshat* of today's text all out of shape in order to make it say something that it does not say in order to fit it into Advent. Nor need we fret about the fact that *almah* ("young woman") does not mean *virgo intacta*. Matthew 1:23 was in any case quoting the Greek translation, the Septuagint, not the Hebrew text. For Christians, Jesus is the decisive disclosure that God is with us. We can celebrate that and accord Isaiah's text its integrity.

Christmas Day 1/Years A, B, and C

Isaiah 9:1–7

In this comment we treat together the readings for Christmas Day (Isa. 9:2–7) and the Third Sunday after the Epiphany/Year A (Isa. 9:1–4).

In chapter 8, Isaiah, speaking to those in Jerusalem who advocate joining Syria and Samaria in war against Assyria (see the Fourth Sunday of Advent/Year A), prophesies that if they follow that course there will be war: "The Lord is bringing up against it [this people] the mighty flood waters of the River, the king of Assyria and all his glory; it will rise above all its channels and overflow all its banks; it will sweep on into Judah as a flood, and . . . reach up to the neck" (Isa. 8:7–8). Isaiah uses the imagery of Tehom, the Deep, as a metaphor for military invasion—chaos will flow over Judah.

To the opposite effect, today's reading begins on a note of hope: "there will be no gloom for those who were in anguish ['oppressed']" (v. 1). There will be a dramatic reversal of fortune. Isaiah frequently sets predictions of disaster and promises of redemption side by side (see 2:6–4:1 and 4:2–6). Verse 2 notes that "in the former time he brought into contempt the land of Zebulun and the land of Naphtali," a reference to the subjugation of these areas by the forces of Tiglath-Pileser III mentioned in 2 Kings 15:29.

In 9:2 we turn to a prophetic/messianic expression of hope for a different kind of ruler, not a war-maker but a Prince of Peace (v. 6) who in place of the chaos of war will make possible the life and well-being which are the gifts of YHWH to the people Israel and to the Gentiles. In its context, this passage speaks of the royal birth of a new ruler in the line of David (v. 7). If we try to pin down to whom the text refers, Hezekiah would be the likely candidate (it cannot have been Ahaz—see the Fourth Sunday of Advent/Year A). Much of the poem consists of throne names for the expected king (v. 6).

Our text abruptly shifts from the language of doom and gloom to that of sparkling light: "The people who walked in darkness have seen a great light . . . on them light has shined" (v. 2). Oppressive foreign rule has been thrown off. Images of servitude abound: "the yoke of their burden," "the bar across their shoulders," "the rod of their oppressors," all instruments of oppression. Then the promise comes: the "boots of the trampling warriors and all the garments rolled in blood shall be burned as fuel for the fire" (v. 5). War and oppression will cease; the conditions of Eden will return.

"There shall be endless peace" (v. 7). This is a constant in Isaiah: "nation shall not lift up sword against nation; neither shall they learn war any more" (2:4). Universal peace, including that between human beings and animals, and among animals themselves, is again the theme in 11:6–9.

Preachers could use this passage to address how Christians and Jews typically talk past each other when discussing whether Jesus is the Messiah. For Jews, the question is whether "the days of the Messiah," that "latter time" (Isa. 9:1) in which "endless peace" will arrive, have in fact yet come. Jews say "no, it has not." Christians say "yes, in Jesus we have a foretaste of it." Both are right, as is Paul when he says that "the sufferings of this present time are not worth comparing with the glory [of God] about to be revealed to us" (Rom. 8:18) in the Parousia of Jesus, who will bring the reign of God when there will be endless peace. But as there is not yet endless peace, we have much to do.

Verse 6 mentions four throne names or titles that will apply to this new ruler. "Wonderful Counselor" refers to a ruler who can develop and expand upon good plans to bring about peace and justice. "Mighty God" is a divine title applied to the ruler who will be strong to effect God's purposes. "Everlasting Father" points to the king's task to nurture the people of God. "Prince of Peace" is a messianic designation used by both Jews and Christians to refer to the Messiah; one Jewish translation is "Messiah in whose days peace [*shalom*] will be great for us." Preachers should explore what it means to follow the One who is the Prince of Peace.

Christmas Day 2/Years A, B, and C

Isaiah 62:6–12

This reading announces the coming salvation of Zion (Judea) from oppression by its opponents among the nations. The Lord promises that his steadfast love (*hesed*) and faithfulness will never allow a break with his chosen people: "I will make an everlasting covenant with them" (61:8). Not because God's people are paragons of faithfulness, but because God is the God who has graciously elected Israel, God will clothe Judea in the "garments of salvation" (61:10) and will cause "righteousness and praise [authentic worship of YHWH] to spring up before all the nations [Gentiles]" (61:11). This is a fine reading for Christmas Day, when we Christians give thanks that the light of God's revelation has also shone on us.

In this deliverance, the people Israel will be given a new name: "You shall no more be termed Forsaken, and your land shall no more be termed Desolate; but you shall be called My Delight Is in Her, and your land Married; for the LORD delights in you" (62:4). Using the metaphor of married love characteristic of Hosea, the Lord declares: "For as a young man marries a young woman, so shall your bridegroom marry you, and as the bridegroom rejoices over the bride, so shall your God rejoice over you" (62:5). The early church borrows this metaphor to talk of the church as the bride of Christ.

Our text announces that "sentinels" have been posted upon the walls of Jerusalem. Unlike ordinary sentinels, who alert the town to the approach of enemies, these sentinels are to remind God of the promises to Zion: "You who remind the LORD, take no rest, and give him no rest until he establishes Jerusalem and makes it renowned throughout the earth" (vv. 6–7). These "reminders" are directed as much to the people as to God; prayers for God's rule of compassionate justice and *shalom* remind us of that for which we are to work and pray. Like Isaiah's sentinels, we should pray and work without ceasing for the coming of God's reign on earth.

In verse 10, Isaiah reverts to his metaphor of the highway (e.g., 40:3) into the human heart by which God may come to dwell within the lives of God's people: "Say to daughter Zion, 'See, your salvation [God] comes; his reward is with him, and his recompense before him'" (v. 11). God's "reward" is not a matter of doling out to the people a prize for their good behavior; it is God's gracious deliverance of the people for whom God's love is steadfast. The people shall be called "The Holy People" (v. 12) because God, the One who is Holy, will dwell among them. They are "The Redeemed of the LORD" (v. 12), as Christians also are and which we celebrate at Christmas.

Often the good news is presented in the statement or promise that God is or will be "with us." This is why Jerusalem "shall be called, 'Sought Out, A City Not Forsaken'" (v. 12). The good news is shaped by the form of human hurt that it addresses. Often that hurt is the feeling that we are abandoned, that not even God cares about us. The Judeans—destitute, bedraggled, small, and weak—could easily have felt godforsaken. Isaiah reminds us of the good news that God never abandons God's children.

God's deliverance of and presence in Zion is to be celebrated with food and wine (vv. 8–9), a festal meal in the Temple: "those who gather it shall drink it in my holy courts." So the church celebrates Christmas with eucharistic food and wine, celebrating God's coming among us in the person of Jesus Christ.

Christmas Day 3/Years A, B, and C

Isaiah 52:7–10

Isaiah 52 exhorts Zion (the Judean people in exile in Babylon) to rejoice in the Lord's return to "Jerusalem, the holy city" (52:1). A triumphant, ecstatic exultation begins our reading: "How beautiful upon the mountains are the feet of the messenger who announces peace, who brings good news, who announces salvation, who says to Zion, 'Your God reigns'" (v. 7).

The people are still oppressed in Babylon as Isaiah indicates: "you shall drink no more from the bowl of my wrath. And I will put it in the hand of your tormentors, who have said to you, 'Bow down, that we may walk on you'; and have made your back like the ground and like the street for them to walk on" (51:22–23).

In this intense chapter, Isaiah instructs the people to dress in the clothes they would wear to a great celebration: "Put on your beautiful garments, O Jerusalem . . . for the uncircumcised and the unclean shall enter you no more" (52:1). Isaiah urges them to trust the strengthening word that he has been proclaiming since 40:1–11. He pleads with them to "shake yourself . . . loose the bonds from your neck, O captive daughter Zion!" (52:2). In verse 11, he urges them: "Depart, depart, go out from there!"

The tension comes from the fact that verses 7–10 celebrate YHWH's return to Zion "in plain sight," yet two realities persist: Jerusalem is a devastated city and the people are still under the Babylonian heel. The messenger announces peace, but peace is not a visible reality to the Judeans.

In this context, Isaiah celebrates God's victory, much as at Christmas Christians celebrate the coming into the world of Jesus, of whom the angel and the heavenly host sing "Glory to God in the highest heaven, and on earth peace among those whom he favors" (Luke 2:14). Peace, God's peace, is that to which we witness, for which we work, of which we sing at Christmas, and for which we achingly long.

Commentators have worried over the claim that the "feet" of the messenger are said to be "beautiful." Some even claim that feet are repulsive. This colossally misses the point. Any messenger who brings us the extraordinarily good news of peace and deliverance is ipso facto beautiful. Our culturally shaped notions of human beauty, those idealized photographs of surgically enhanced, botoxed and then air-brushed people noted mainly for superficiality, are in no meaningful way beautiful. But the wrinkled face of a balding, gray-haired friend who has been honest and loyal through the decades most certainly is. Isaiah's messenger has run across the rocks of the desert and the stones of city streets to announce: "the LORD has comforted his people, he has redeemed Jerusalem" (v. 9). His feet are scarred and likely bleeding. They are beautiful.

Throughout Second Isaiah, the note of universality is struck, and so here: "The LORD has bared his holy arm before the eyes of all the nations [Gentiles]; and all the ends of the earth shall see the salvation of our God" (v. 10). YHWH's intention is that Israel's well-being shall redound to all people and that all people shall live with each other in relations of peace and well-being. All people are given and called to participate. We see this in Luke 2:31–32 in Simeon's singing of God's salvation "which you have prepared in the presence of all peoples, a light for revelation to the Gentiles and for glory to your people Israel" and in the visit of the Gentile wise men from the east in Matthew 2:1–12. God is not a sectarian.

First Sunday after Christmas Day/Year A

Isaiah 63:7–9

This reading follows that from Isaiah in the second proper for Christmas Day. There Isaiah dealt with a desolated people who had returned from exile to find themselves in hard circumstances. Failure of hope sapped the energy required to rebuild Jerusalem and Judea. In today's reading, the first three verses of an expression of grief that runs through 64:12, Isaiah recalls God's gracious activities on Israel's behalf. These are all in the past, as the text points out: "he lifted them up and carried them all the *days of old*" (v. 9; emphasis ours). The people wanted to know: where is God now?

It is an almost inevitable part of the life of faith to feel abandoned by God. We do well to remember Martin Luther's insistence that our faith, hope, and trust in God are always "in spite of." We believe in spite of our unbelief, trust in spite of our lack of trust, commit ourselves to live lives of faith in spite of our sins, and we hope against hope. At Christmas we celebrate the coming into the world of the Prince of Peace in spite of the absence of peace. We love the neighbor, in spite of the fact that many of them are homeless and we seem not to notice. To lament, at its deepest level, is not to express a lack of faith. It is to confess faith in spite of the failures of faith. At its deepest level, this is one reason why it is true to say that we are justified by God's grace, not by our faith. It takes a strong faith to admit that our faith is too shaky a thing on which to hang our justification.

When the prophet gives voice to the grief and weeping of the people, he acts as mediator, interceding with God on their behalf. Frequently the roles of prophet and priest are sharply separated from each other. This is a mistake. Many figures play both roles. Moses interceded with God on behalf of the people, for example, as does Third Isaiah. And priests could speak prophetically, as we see when we note that the utterances of the prophets went into the making of the ritual and moral *mitzvoth* in the Torah.

What Third Isaiah does in this reading, for the original audience and for us, is to try to keep us committed to understanding ourselves in the only way in which, authentically, we can ever understand ourselves in any ultimately important sense: as those who are freely loved by God and given and called by God in turn to love God with all ourselves and our neighbors as ourselves. As God has acted graciously on our behalf, so we too should act graciously, particularly when doing so does not seem reasonable. Radical love is what is called for.

God's love is a relational love that calls forth love in return. God calls for us to participate as God's covenantal partners in actualizing God's purposes. So the passage begins with a piling up of terms expressive of God's grace: "gracious deeds . . . praiseworthy acts . . . great favor . . . mercy . . . steadfast love . . . savior" (vv. 7–8). The passage concludes that it was God's very presence to and among the people that saved them, not some "messenger or angel" (v. 9). This is particularly apt at Christmas when the church celebrates God's presence in the world in Jesus.

Matthew 2:13–23, describing the flight from Herod the Great and the massacre of the innocent, describes a world from which God might be thought to be absent. How else could such horrid things happen? Nonetheless, Matthew's nativity story celebrates God's presence with us in spite of stark evidence of the reign of cruelty and injustice.

Second Sunday after Christmas Day/Years A, B, and C

Jeremiah 31:7–14 or Sirach 24:1–12

The lectionary posts the readings from Jeremiah and Sirach as alternates for the First Lesson today. The two readings give the preacher a distinct choice for the direction of the sermon.

Jeremiah 31:7–14 is from the part of Jeremiah that scholars often call the Book of Consolation. It is addressed to Israel and Judah during the exile in Babylon (Jer. 30:1–31:40). Today's text is an oracle of salvation that calls the community to "sing aloud for gladness" because God will save the remnant of Israel (Jer. 31:7–8a). God will include in the great company the blind, the lame, and those with child, that is, those who need help. No one is left behind (31:8b). They walk beside brooks and on straight roads, for God is a parent who provides Israel with all it needs for a good and safe life (31:9).

God, who scattered Israel, is now reuniting the community as a shepherd gathers the flock, for God has redeemed the people from Babylon's hands, from which the people were not strong enough to break (Jer. 31:10–11). The fruitfulness of the land will be restored (31:12). Women will dance and men will be merry as God turns mourning into joy (31:13). The tithes from the land will provide abundance of food for the priests (31:14).

The season of Christmas functions similarly to this oracle of salvation in making known to today's exiles God's welcome home through Jesus Christ. The preacher might name contemporary experiences of exile and help people see how the congregation can be a community of restoration.

The book of Sirach, written about 200 to 180 BCE, brings together elements of wisdom and Torah traditions (see Proper 17/Year C). Wisdom itself is often personified as a woman who is an active agent of God.

Wisdom dwells in heaven in the presence of God (Sir. 24:1–2). She came from the very mouth of God and is thus intimately connected with God while still being a creation of God (24:3b). Wisdom dwelled in an exalted status in the heavenly world (24:4a). Wisdom "compassed the vault of heaven and traversed the depths of the abyss," meaning that she represented God as an agent in the creation of the world (24:4b–6). Wisdom sought a "resting place" on earth, a community with whom to dwell so that the human family could have her as benefit (24:7).

God chose the place for Wisdom to place her "tent" on the earth: Jerusalem. The image of the "tent" recalls God tenting with Israel during the wilderness wanderings and suggests that Wisdom has such a place in ongoing Israel. Indeed, Israel is Wisdom's inheritance, that is, the community that would embody Wisdom's teaching (Sir. 24:8). Wisdom will be omnipresent as representative of God (24:9). Wisdom is a priest of God (24:10–12). Those who partake of Wisdom "will hunger for more" and those who obey Wisdom and work with her "will not be put to shame" and "will not sin" (24:21–22).

The description of personified wisdom in Sirach is a model for understanding Jesus in John 1:1–18 and throughout the Fourth Gospel. Both Wisdom and Jesus existed in heaven before the creation of the world and served as God's agents in creation. Indeed, by the time of John some Jewish writers identified Wisdom and Word (*Logos*) (John 1:1–4). God sent both Jesus and Wisdom to "tent" and to reveal God's purposes (John 1:14, 18).

Epiphany of the Lord/Years A, B, and C

Isaiah 60:1–6

Isaiah 60 continues two themes that began to develop in chapter 56:1–8 (Fifth Sunday after the Epiphany/Year A): the ingathering of scattered Israel and the inclusion of foreigners in the Israelite community. The theological theme is God's *hesed*, God's steadfast faithfulness to the people of God. The ingathering is a major emphasis in Third Isaiah's stress on the salvation of Israel. The other major theme is the all-inclusiveness of the Isaianic vision of salvation.

Third Isaiah's vision of the return of the exiles is a point on which Second Isaiah, in his insistence that the exiles find the courage to risk returning to a desolated land, was eloquent. The change in Third Isaiah is that the group of exiles to which he was speaking has already returned to Judea. His audience was composed of them and of those who had never left, and they were anxious to know that the promises would be fulfilled. Life in Jerusalem was hardly a matter of the peace and prosperity they had been led to expect. Also, the reality was different from our usual assumption that the exiles returned from Babylon *en masse*. In fact, many did not return, and the Jewish community in Babylon flourished for a long time, eventually producing the Babylonian Talmud. Those who did return were more a trickle than a mighty stream. They awaited the fulfillment of Second Isaiah's prophecies, including the return of the rest of the exiles.

Isaiah 60 is addressed to a people in crisis. Attempts to rebuild the Temple had come to naught because of strife within the community; the economy of Judea and Jerusalem was in dire straits because of the devastation of warfare, and foreign powers (chap. 63) made incursions to loot and steal. Our passage is a word of faith and hope to a community that found its capacity for both sorely tested. It is utterly appropriate for Epiphany and the advent of Jesus, who preached and acted out the good news of the kingdom or reign of God in a time when the people Israel were again in crisis, in exile at home under Roman domination and oppressed by a kingdom ruled by a Caesar who claimed to be God.

Our passage opens with: "Arise, shine; for your light has come, and the glory of the LORD has risen upon you" (v. 1). We are reminded of Isaiah 9:2: "The people who walked in darkness have seen a great light." Darkness symbolizes adversity and suffering because of injustice, whether domestic or as a result of war. One thinks of the late scene in Melville's *Moby Dick*, when the storm is intense, the waves high, the darkness impenetrable, and the whaling boat has lost contact with the mother ship. Other ships in the vicinity, the *Rights of Man* and the *Pequod* (named for a Native American people who had been the target of genocide) have sunk. But in the whaling boat there is a candle, called "the idiot candle," that the darkness does not overcome.

What sustains the community—the only thing that can sustain us through all our crises—is the faith that we are loved by God and that we exist for a purpose that can support us in any crisis. Third Isaiah promises the people that "your sons shall come from far away, and your daughters shall be carried on their nurses' arms" (v. 4). They will be brought from far away "for the name of the LORD your God, and for the Holy One of Israel, because he has glorified you" (v. 9). The well-being of the people cannot be secured apart from their faith in YHWH, nor can YHWH be worshiped apart from the existence and well-being of a faithful people.

YHWH has always dwelt among the people and remains with them, particularly in times of crisis, and their faithfulness to YHWH is critical to the coming of the light or the rule of God. Through their commitment to worship, study, and deeds of loving-kindness, they contribute to making possible the coming of God's loving justice.

First Sunday after the Epiphany/Year A

Baptism of the Lord

Isaiah 42:1–9

This appropriate Epiphany text is Isaiah's vision of the servant of the Lord and of the mission of that servant. "Here is my servant" (v. 1), says the

Lord. But this servant is not named, leading to the long discussed question, who is this servant? The most frequently suggested answers are: Isaiah himself, the people Israel, Jesus, and Paul. Today's text suggests two answers to this question. One is that Isaiah himself is the servant, particularly since in much of his book he carries out the mission assigned to the servant, that of reminding the people that they are to be "a light to the nations [Gentiles]" (v. 7). But that answer immediately generates another: the servant is the people Israel which is to be this light to the Gentiles.

Matthew and Paul, in the readings from Matthew 2:1–12 and Ephesians 3:1–12 assigned for today, speak of Jesus' mission to the Gentiles (the wise men from the east) and Paul's mission to the Gentiles. Another answer not to be overlooked is that the servant is everybody who loves and trusts the Lord; each of us has assumed the task assigned to God's servant in this passage. Each of these answers suffices, provided that the others are also acknowledged. Isaiah, Israel, Jesus, Paul, and the rest of us are given and called to be servants of the Lord. We should read the passage as addressed to Israel and to us as those called in Christ to join Israel in serving the Lord.

Verses 1–4 address two points: who the servant is and what the servant is to do. The servant is one "chosen" by God, in whom God "delights" and who has been given the gift of God's personal presence to the human spirit. God's spirit is the wisdom of God given to the servant. Empowered by God, weak and fallible servants can do more than we imagine.

The servant "will bring forth justice to the nations [Gentiles]" (v. 1). Note the universalism of Isaiah's vision; the servant will bring justice to all people, Israel and the Gentiles. As the church has often been indifferent to whether the people Israel is treated justly, this point comes to us Christians as a critical, prophetic witness. The servant's job is not to make a lot of racket (to "cry or lift up his voice, or make it heard in the street"), but to "faithfully bring forth justice" (v. 3). He will "establish justice in the earth" and the "coastlands wait for his teaching [*torah*]" (v. 4). Justice is not yet established in the earth and many coastlands have not taken to heart this teaching; the servant's task comes to each of us as an ongoing gift and call.

The justice of YHWH is a kindhearted justice. The term "justice" requires adjectives to modify it, so that we are clear what we mean by the term. Some of the greatest injustices in history have been carried out by those in pursuit of a dream of absolute justice. Millions of people have died at the hands of those pursuing the classless society, a manifest destiny, or some idealistic political or economic vision of one kind or another. All of our religious traditions have profaned the concept of God's justice,

Christians particularly in wars that they declared either just or holy, such as the Crusades or the wars of religion from 1618 to 1648. But God's justice is justice on behalf of God's children; it is like a mother whose love for her children leads her to seek justice for them. It is the justice of YHWH's tender love.

At the same time, this is a justice for absolutely everybody. It is justice "to the nations" and "justice in the earth and the coastlands" (vv. 1, 4). All nations and peoples belong to the Lord (Ps. 82:8).

Verses 5–7 are a self-disclosure on God's part. God is the Lord who created heaven and earth and gives life (breath) and wisdom (spirit) to all people; God is the Lord who called Israel, took Israel by the hand, and kept Israel, who gives Israel "as a covenant to the peoples, a light to the nations." The covenant is never for Israel alone; it is to be shared with the Gentiles. Neither is it for Christians alone, as the church's displacement theology so long asserted. God's justice heals the sick and frees prisoners (v. 7). God does not give God's glory to idols (v. 8).

This is the task that Matthew envisaged Jesus as carrying out even in infancy, that Jesus assumed in reading this passage in the synagogue in Nazareth (Luke 4:16–21), and that Paul took on himself, all in continuity with Isaiah. It is our task as well.

Second Sunday after the Epiphany/Year A

Isaiah 49:1–7

Today's reading continues the theme of the universal salvation of the peoples of the world, Jews and Gentiles: "I will give you as a light to the nations, that my salvation may reach to the end of the earth" (v. 6). The theme is presented in the first verse: "Listen to me, O coastlands, pay attention, you peoples from far away!" God often called upon Israel to "hear!" but now God claims the attention of Gentiles. Our passage sings the gracious news of the all-inclusive love of God. God loves Israel as the apple of God's eye, but God has always intended that the descendants of Abraham and Sarah be a blessing to all the peoples of the earth and that they should be a blessing to each other and to Israel. "All the nations of the earth" were blessed in Abraham (Gen. 18:18).

The servant says of himself: "The LORD called me before I was born, while I was in my mother's womb he named me" (49:1). Jeremiah says the same and adds: "I appointed you a prophet to the nations [Gentiles]" (1:5). Paul says of himself: "But when God, who had set me apart before I was born and called me through his grace . . . so that I might proclaim him among the Gentiles . . ." (Gal. 1:15). As Israel was to serve God on behalf of the whole world, so Paul went to the whole world with his good news for Gentiles. In the Song of Simeon, Luke so interprets the significance of the birth of Jesus: "my eyes have seen your salvation, which you have prepared in the presence of all peoples, a light for revelation to the Gentiles, and for glory to your people Israel" (2:30–32).

Commentary on today's reading has often been obsessed with determining whether the servant is a particular individual or the people Israel. On one hand, the servant is sent "to" Jacob and Israel (v. 5); on the other hand, Israel is said to be "my servant Israel, in whom I will be glorified." The best answer is that both Israel and the prophet are servants of God, and indeed each of us shares the servant's task, here so beautifully sung.

Our passage makes the logic of blessing (well-being) clear. Between communities, well-being is available to Israel only if it is also available to all other peoples and vice versa. Within a community, well-being is available to some only if it is available to all. This is why, in Israel, no one was to have too little and no one too much, and why the man who built his barns bigger to hoard food while others lived in destitution did not achieve the well-being that he sought (Luke 12:13–21).

The purpose of the servant's task is that God will be glorified: "you are my servant in whom I will be glorified" (v. 3). We dare not forget in all our theologizing and preaching that we make all our witness, whether in word or deed, *ad maiorem Dei gloriam*, to the greater glory of God.

In verse 4, the servant declares: "yet surely my cause is with the LORD." The Hebrew for "cause" is often translated "justice" because *mishpat* is the heartfelt justice of a loving God; this is the order of the world as God has created it and we rely on it for all possibility of well-being in the human community and in nature. "Rabban Simeon ben Gamaliel says: On three things does the world stand: on justice, on truth, and on peace."[4]

One often hears that whereas Jesus and Paul were inclusive, Judaism was not. Frequently this is stated in terms of boundary markers; Jews had them, Jesus and Paul did not. It is time to put this pejorative contrast to rest. No group can exist without boundary markers; no congregation could identify its members. Boundary markers function as means of inclusion.

In early Judaism, there were strong inclusive tendencies. Notably the Ethiopian eunuch in Acts 8:26–40 was reading Isaiah 53:7–8. If he kept reading, he would have found Isaiah 56:4–5: "For thus says the LORD: To the eunuchs who keep my sabbaths . . . and hold fast my covenant, I will give, in my house . . . an everlasting name that shall not be cut off." Would that today's church could be as inclusive with those who are different as were Isaiah and Acts.

Third Sunday after the Epiphany/Year A

Isaiah 9:1–4

For comments on this text, please see Christmas Day 1/Year A.

Fourth Sunday after the Epiphany/Year A

Micah 6:1–8

Verses 6:6–8 of today's reading are a remarkable encapsulation of what or, as we shall see, whom God wants us to be and do. They are one of a number of summaries of "all the law" such as are attributed to Hillel, Jesus, and Paul. Verses 1–5 set up the dialogue that takes place in verses 6–8.

This is a good point at which to note the meaning of Micah's name, *Mica-el*, "who is like God?" Verses 1–6 answer the question that is Micah's name. They set forth the "controversy" (v. 2) that YHWH has with the Lord's people. The Lord demands to know "what have I done to you? In what have I wearied you?" (v. 3). God wants to know this because God is the God who "brought you up from the land of Egypt and delivered you from slavery; and I sent before you Moses, Aaron, and Miriam" (v. 4). God is the One who elected and redeemed Israel, the God of steadfast love.

Yet the people have engaged in unjust acts; "they covet fields, and seize them; houses and take them away; they oppress householder and house, people and their inheritance" (2:2). They trample on the teachings of Torah concerning the poor, the orphan, and the widow; they violate the teachings according to which the fields and houses, the boundaries of the widows and orphans, shall be respected and the vulnerable be protected from ravenous neighbors. And when the poor go to court to try to regain what is rightfully theirs, "they [the affluent] abhor justice and pervert all equity" (3:9). The rich get richer and the poor get poorer. Hence, the Lord's questions to the people.

At this point a different speaker asks: "With what shall I come before the LORD, and bow myself before God on high?" (v. 6). Micah's questioner wants to know what he or she must bring before the Lord. Should it be "burnt offerings," "thousands of rams," "my firstborn?" (vv. 6–7). The question is *what* shall I bring. The suggestions put forward spiral up to "my firstborn."

The answer comes from a different set of assumptions altogether. To begin with, the questioner is asked why she is asking. "He has told you, O mortal, what is good" (v. 8). It has been made abundantly clear in the Torah and the Prophets and the Wisdom teachings; why ask about what has been plainly disclosed?

The second difference is that what the Lord wants is not "things." The Lord's gracious offer of love finds its appropriate response in an attitude in which we love God with all ourselves and love our neighbors as ourselves. In other words, God wants us, not stuff. And the God of compassionate justice wants to see us acting out our love for the neighbor in compassionate justice for them: "to do justice, and to love kindness, and to walk humbly with your God" (v. 8). "Humbly" could well be translated "sensibly." The Scriptures are all about the "way" in which we should walk, a way for which the Torah and the Prophets are a light unto our feet and a lamp for our path. The way is made by walking, and the walking of the way of life and blessing is what God asks of us.

Fifth Sunday after the Epiphany/Year A

Isaiah 58:1–9a, (9b–12)

In our commentary on Isaiah 56:1–8, we note that it hinted at behaviors in the community of returned exiles that necessitated a reminder that doing justice and keeping the Sabbath were equally important (Proper 15/Year A). Today's reading makes clear what chapter 56 intimated. The likelihood is that Third Isaiah is criticizing the Zadokite priesthood and those most closely associated with it rather than the whole people of Judea. Those criticized seem to be sticklers for proper religious observance. They complain that in spite of all their fasting and humbling themselves, God does not notice (v. 3); they "bow down the head like a bulrush, and . . . lie in sackcloth and ashes" (v. 5), and they seem to think that doing this is the be-all and end-all of faithfulness to YHWH.

From Third Isaiah's perspective, theirs is a hypothetical faith: "day after day they seek me and delight to know my ways, *as if* they were a nation that practiced righteousness" (v. 2; emphasis ours). They are temple-treaders who never miss church; it's such a great place to gossip about the neighbors. They fail to note that they "forsake the ordinance [*mishpat*] of their God" (v. 2). "Ordinance" refers to YHWH's love acted out in justice, justice expressed as love. Instead of loving the neighbor in word and deed, they oppress their workers and fast only to quarrel and fight (vv. 3–4). Prayers like this will not reach God's ear.

Third Isaiah looks ahead to the jubilee year passage, when he asks: "Will you call this a fast, a day acceptable to the LORD?" (58:5). The "year of the LORD's favor" is a time when good news is brought to the oppressed, the brokenhearted are healed, captives and political prisoners are liberated, and all who mourn will be comforted (Isa. 61:1–2). Third Isaiah evokes the deepest dimensions of Israel's faith all the way back to the trust in God that arose from its liberation from bondage in Egypt. But now, once again freed from bondage, some Judeans are still held captive to debt and poverty, and their plight is ignored by "you who serve your own interest on your fast day" (58:3).

Verses 6–7 make up one of the most evocative passages of the entire Scriptures. They describe the kind of worship that YHWH profoundly wants to have: worship that frees people from injustice, removes their harsh burdens, frees the oppressed, shares bread with the hungry, houses the homeless, clothes the naked, and in which we do not hide ourselves away from the needs of the last, the lost, and the least. Just showing up for worship does not signify.

But neither does busying oneself with doing justice and not showing up for worship. That points to the arid moralism evident in the view that social action is sufficient and that we may sidestep the heart of the matter—the love of God for each and all and our responsive love for the One who loves all and for all those whom God loves. Being a friend of the One who is Friend of all and befriending all those whom God loves is a matter of the heart as well as of actions, as Jesus reminded his followers when he said: "I have called you friends" (John 15:15). As a rabbinical colleague sums it up: "have a good heart." Third Isaiah urges his hearers to honor the Sabbath by offering their food to the hungry and satisfying the needs of the afflicted (vv. 9–10). Worship and kindhearted justice are inseparable from each other.

This passage is placed in Epiphany because of its teaching as to what is necessary if our light is to "break forth like the dawn" and we are to know the presence of God (vv. 8–9). The prophets were concerned with society as a whole; unless it is ruled by YHWH's kindhearted justice, individuals will always suffer both from injustice and from being ignored. Individualism gets it backward in its insistence that society can go to rack and ruin as long as I am prospering. The prophets had it right: none of us genuinely prospers unless we all prosper. Blessing, well-being, has to be shared in relations of mutuality.

Today's passage interacts beautifully with Matthew 5:13–20 as well as with Paul's description of our "spiritual worship" in Romans 12, that how we throw our physical bodies into the life of the world *is* our spiritual worship.

Sixth Sunday after the Epiphany/Year A

Deuteronomy 30:15–20

Today's passage presumes Deuteronomy 30:1–14, and a postexilic setting (for background on Deuteronomy see Proper 17/Year B). The deliverance from Egypt and the making of the covenant are presented afresh to each generation (Deut. 6:20–25; 11:2–7; see First Sunday in Lent/Year C). Consequently, each generation must renew its commitment to the covenant. Many scholars think that Deuteronomy 30 contains material adapted from a covenant renewal liturgy.

This passage does not present new theological themes but compresses the theology of Deuteronomy into one short passage and puts it before the reading community as a forced choice.

Deuteronomy 30:15 makes a stark statement: the community must choose either life or death. In Deuteronomy these concepts intermingle the metaphorical and the material. Life refers to existence centered in worship of God that results in the land, progeny, material abundance, and other forms of blessing, that is, "prosperity." The path to life is obedience to the commandments recorded in Deuteronomy (30:16; cf. 10:12; 11:1, 22). Death refers to living in idolatry, which results in manifold forms of injustice as well as in diminished material quality of existence ("adversity").

Ultimately, faithfulness to God means continued existence as a people (life) while unfaithfulness leads, literally, to the death of the people (Deut. 30:18). The choice for God means a continuation of relationships that support life. The Deuteronomic theologians believe that nature can act as agent of blessing and curse. The choice against God ultimately means death.

Deuteronomy 30:19 invokes an aspect of ancient covenant practice: sealing the covenant before witnesses. This text invokes some of the most dramatic witnesses possible: heaven and earth. To choose life means to choose obedience to God's commandments. Limiting of options (walking in God's ways and forsaking others) enhances existence.

We point out elsewhere that the stark contrast Deuteronomy poses between obedience and disobedience, blessing and curse, does not account for the complexity of actual existence (see Ninth Sunday after the Epiphany/Year A and Proper 10/Year C). Life is more ambiguous than the Deuteronomists let on. However, forcing a choice often helps individuals and communities name the values that are most important to them. Choice clarifies commitment.

The Gospel lection for today, Matthew 5:21–37, neither cites nor alludes to Deuteronomy 30:15–20. Deuteronomy's emphasis on consciously choosing to serve God does have a slight reverberation with Matthew in that Matthew wants disciples to *choose* to be faithful in the ways described in 5:21–37 (e.g., seeking reconciliation) as part of the path of faithfulness that will eventuate in being included in the realm of God, the eschatological counterpart to Deuteronomy's promise of living in the land.

Deuteronomy 30:15–20 is also assigned to Proper 18/Year C, where it is paired with Luke 14:25–33, a passage with an affinity with Deuteronomy as Luke stresses the importance of making a conscious decision to follow Jesus that takes into account the difficulties that come with discipleship.

Seventh Sunday after the Epiphany/Year A

Leviticus 19:1–2, 9–18

Chapter 19 of Leviticus is an assemblage of Torah-teachings, mostly moral, directed to the people to empower them to live the life of holiness as fully as did the priests in the Temple. Today's reading provides pastors with an opportunity to communicate to their congregations the purpose of torah (way, teaching). Torah was a gracious gift from YHWH provided to make it possible for the people of God to lead lives characterized by well-being (blessing) in every respect. The God who graciously elected Israel also graciously gave Israel the *mitzvoth*.

The chapter opens with a call to holiness. The Lord told Moses to say to "the people of Israel . . . : You shall be holy, for I the LORD your God am holy" (v. 2). The rabbis interpreted this in the light of Exodus 34:6 where God characterizes God's self as "merciful and gracious, slow to anger, and abounding in steadfast love." "As YHWH is gracious and compassionate, so you should be gracious and compassionate."[5] Israel is to imitate God, as indeed Matthew and Luke call the church to imitate God (Matt. 5:48; Luke 6:36). Imitation of God is manifest primarily in responsible action toward the vulnerable: YHWH "executes justice for the orphan and the widow, and . . . loves the strangers, providing them food and clothing. You shall also love the stranger, for you were strangers in the land of Egypt" (Deut. 10:18–19).

Verse 3 reminds the people to "revere your mother and father," because elderly parents are vulnerable and have needs that their adult children are called upon to meet. This was ancient Israel's safety net—not only orphans and widows but the frail and elderly were included in it. Verse 3b says simply: "keep my sabbaths." The Sabbath was a day of rest and no mention of *doing anything* is made here. For Leviticus, ethics and ritual are not separate; we all need ritual reminders of ethical obligations.

Verses 9–10 have to do, again, with the poor and the vulnerable. A field is not to be harvested "to the very edges" and vineyards are not to be stripped clean or fallen grapes gathered: "you shall leave them for the poor and the alien." The rabbis interpreted these *mitzvoth* to mean that the furrows around the edge of the field were not to be harvested so that the poor could easily see that food was available. To harvest the entire field was regarded as robbing the poor. Gleaning programs that provide food for the poor in our society take their inspiration from these *mitzvoth*.

Verses 11–18 have entirely to do with deeds (the letter of James mentions many of these commandments). Love itself signifies deeds as much as attitudes. These are all negative commandments. As such they open up possibilities for a life of well-being; they forbid activities that destroy communal well-being. Also, they are easy to keep—one can keep them all while taking a nap. Verses 11–12 state: "you shall not steal; you shall not deal falsely . . . you shall not lie to one another," and "you shall not swear falsely." The ancient rabbis said: "If you have stolen, you are likely to deny, then to lie, and end by taking a false oath."[6] Such behavior destroys community; those who are members of one another do not lie to each other.

Verse 13 adds that people should not "steal" from one another and should not hold back a laborer's wages until morning; the verb in the latter *mitzvah* means to "oppress" or "extort." To withhold until tomorrow the pay of the poor is tantamount to stealing, to holding on to money gained illegally. In Matthew's parable of the laborers in the vineyard, the laborers were paid at the end of the workday—in accordance with Torah.

Verse 14 again is concerned with the vulnerable, the deaf and the blind. That we should not curse the deaf or put obstacles in the way of the blind is followed by: "you shall fear your God." The deaf cannot hear a curse nor the blind see obstacles, but while they do not know who insulted or hurt them, God knows and they are under God's protection. Congregations that make their buildings accessible to the handicapped have corrected the ways in which they had placed obstacles in the way of the vulnerable.

Verse 15 addresses matters of injustice and indifference. It is concerned with just judicial procedures. Judges should be neither partial to the poor nor deferential to the important. In our times perhaps we should say that the poor should be provided with lawyers as able as those whom the rich can afford. Verse 16 forbids slander, which obviously destroys community. Slander, the rabbis said, kills three persons: the slanderer, the person who believes the slander, and the person who is slandered.

Verse 16 adds: "you shall not profit by the blood of your neighbor." This is also translated as: do not stand idle when your fellow human being is in danger.[7] If we can help someone who is in trouble and fail to do so, according to Torah we have committed a serious crime. We are obligated to help, but not to the extent of losing our own lives.

Verse 17: "you shall not hate in your heart anyone of your kin." Verse 18: "you shall not take vengeance or bear a grudge against any of your people." "Kin" refers to all those of one's "kind." Our awareness of kindness derives from this origin. That we are to love the stranger as we love ourselves shows that this *mitzvah* does not place a limit on our responsibility. "Reprove your neighbor" means that disagreements are to be worked out person-to-person, in community, so that we do not bear grudges against one another.

Verse 18: "you shall love your neighbor as yourself," quoted by Jesus as part of the greatest commandment (Matt. 22:34–40), should be paired with Leviticus 19:33–34: "you shall love the alien as yourself, for you were aliens in the land of Israel." The commandment to love the stranger is repeated thirty-six times in the Scriptures of Israel. To the extent that repetition is significant, it is the most important commandment in the Torah. Love the neighbor and the stranger!

Eighth Sunday after the Epiphany/Year A

Isaiah 49:8–16a

Today's reading immediately follows Isaiah 49:1–7, discussed on the Second Sunday after the Epiphany/Year A. There the servant of YHWH was given the dual task to be "a light to the nations" (49:6) and "to bring Jacob back to" Judea and Jerusalem. Verses 8–13 continue to stress the return of the exiles to Judea, while verses 9–16a speak to the continued weeping of the exiles over their predicament in Babylon.

The Lord reiterates the point that the people's "salvation" is at hand: "In a time of favor I have answered you, on a day of salvation I have helped you" (v. 8). The occasion of Israel's exile is now in the past, a point that bears repeating to a community that laments its situation. Isaiah had proclaimed that the people had served its term, that its penalty was paid (40:2). But they had not taken this to heart. The facts of their weakness and Babylon's strength, obvious to their *eyesight*, prevented them from sharing the prophet's *insight* into the deeper realities of their situation.

Verses 8–13 are a word not of assurance but of reassurance, offered to the community when its faith was badly shaken; it re-presents the good news. God reminds Israel that "I have kept and given you as a covenant" (v. 8). God promises that the land will again be established and those in captivity will be told "come out" (v. 9). There will be food along the way, hunger and thirst will not be a problem, and "springs of water will guide them" (v. 10). They will be joined by others returning "from the north and from the west, and from the land of Syene" (v. 12). The heavens, the earth, and the mountains will sing for joy "for the LORD has comforted [strengthened] his people, and will have compassion on the suffering ones" (v. 13). God's compassion does not deny difficulties, but can see us through them.

Nonetheless, the people respond with a lament (v. 14): "The LORD has forsaken me, my LORD has forgotten me." Reasons for the lament are not hard to find. No change had yet taken place in the military and political arrangements of the world. YHWH's people were still dispersed at considerable distance from home. In the prevailing theology of the ancient world, these facts made a strong case for the claim that YHWH had forgotten the people.

In the Lord's response, Isaiah refers to the "destroyers" of the people, their "waste and . . . desolate places," their "bereavement," and the fact that they were "prey" and "captives" (vv. 19–20, 24). The lament has made a point that God does not deny but takes to heart. And the people voice their lament to God; they do not "dress up" their prayer in a false piety; they are honest.

God replies, first, by restating God's compassion: "Can a woman forget her nursing child, or show no compassion for the children of her womb? Even these may forget, yet I will not forget you" (v. 15). God's compassion (*rachamim*, womblike love) is perfect, unlike human compassion, which even in the best cases can fail. Second, there will be a rebuilding of Judea; "your builders outdo your destroyers" (v. 17) and the people will be joined by fellow Israelites from other places (v. 22).

Here we find the God of Israel to be, not an impassible deity, but a responsive, empathetic God who engages in the contest for the human heart amid the anguish and conflict of real life. God's maternal compassion for God's people (and for all people) is real but not squishy; it is backed up by God's conviction that considerate justice will prevail in the ways of the world. That is something for which to work and pray.

Ninth Sunday after the Epiphany/Year A

Deuteronomy 11:18–21, 26–28

The authors of Deuteronomy wrote after the exile using stories from the era of the wilderness wanderings to explain why the exile happened and to persuade their later generation to follow God's instruction (see Proper 17/Year B). The reading for today reinforces these motifs.

The literary context of today's lection begins at Deuteronony 10:12–13, where the authors ask a question that sounds as if it came from a liturgy, "What does the LORD your God require of you?" The answer: to revere God, to walk in God's ways, to love and serve God with all the community's heart and soul. Deuteronomy 10:14–11:17 recalls the congregation's experience of God's salvific work, and the importance of serving God and not turning from God (11:16). The consequences of turning away are summarized in 10:17.

Echoing Deuteronony 6:4–9, the passage for today helps the congregation develop a practical plan for nurturing obedience and minimizing the likelihood of serving other gods. The community is to put "these words of [Moses]" in their heart and soul, that is, to internalize the teaching of Deuteronomy and to become a community that persistently teaches the ways of God (see Proper 26/Year B).

The Deuteronomic Moses sets before the community a fundamental choice. On the one hand, the community can obey God and be blessed. On the other hand, the community can disobey and be cursed (Deut. 11:26–28; 26:16–27; cf. Josh. 24). The blessings and curses concern individual existence, communal life, and even the relationship of humankind and nature. Every aspect of life is affected.

Preachers sometimes object that Deuteronomy takes a wooden and over-simple approach to the relationship of obedience and disobedience, blessing and curse. Preachers rightly point out that obedience, Deuteronomy-style, does not always result in material blessing, and disobedience does not always end in curse. The righteous sometimes suffer innocently while the wicked not only go unpunished but prosper. At one level we agree. At another level, people get through life better when they seek to walk in God's way, for even in the midst of difficult material circumstances, the awareness of divine presence can sustain and empower. Indeed, God hopes for people to experience as much blessing as any set of circumstances allow, even as God seeks to help each set of circumstances make possible a greater degree of blessing. Inversely, when people do not attempt to walk in God's way, the community is diminished. To be sure, particular individuals and groups may actually prosper as a result of turning away from covenantal design (love, justice, mutuality, and abundance), but such forces erode community and set in motion forces (e.g., greed) that eventually undercut quality of life for all.

Deuteronomy 11:18–21, 26–28 is paired with Matthew 7:21–29 on Proper 4/Year A. While Matthew does not make direct reference to Deuteronomy, Matthew presumes a Deuteronomy-like atmosphere. The word that the New Revised Standard Version translates as "evildoers" (*anomia*) in Matthew 7:23 could better be rendered "lawless ones," that is, those who do not live according to Torah. Matthew speaks of "acting on" Jesus' words in a way reminiscent of Deuteronomy's emphasis on actively walking in the way of God. Matthew puts a choice before the reader between acting on the words of Jesus (leading to a house built on rock) and not acting on them (leading to the fall of the house) in a way that is similar to the choice that Deuteronomy puts to the reader.

Last Sunday after the Epiphany/Year A

Transfiguration Sunday

Exodus 24:12–18

This is an apt passage for Transfiguration Sunday. It is part of a chapter in which the Sinai covenant is inaugurated in an act of worship of YHWH. In verse 1 the Lord said to Moses: "Come up to the LORD, you and Aaron, Nadab, and Abihu, and seventy of the elders of Israel, and worship at a distance." The emphasis of Exodus 24 is not on the Torah-instructions themselves (the *mitzvoth*) but on the Lord who gives them and with whom Israel is in personal relationship. In verse 12 the Lord makes clear with the pronoun "I" that it is the Lord who has given "the law and the commandment . . . for their instruction." In faithfully hearing (*shema*) and doing the *mitzvoth*, Israel is responding in love to God's love. The people willingly accept the teachings of the Lord, saying "All the words that the Lord has spoken we will do" (v. 3), a commitment they repeat in verse 7.

Verses 3–8 relate a rite of consecration similar to the consecration of Aaron to the priesthood, a rite also followed by a meal (Exod. 29:19–21, 32–33; Lev. 8:22–31). In the rite "young men of Israel" present burnt offerings and sacrifice oxen "as offerings of well-being to the Lord" (v. 5). Moses takes half of the blood, sprinkles it on the people and says: "See the blood of the covenant that the LORD has made with you in accordance with all these words" (v. 8). Half of the blood is "dashed against the altar" (v. 6), in recognition that all life is a gift of God and that blood belongs to God (one reason why killing is a crime—it is the shedding of blood that is not ours to shed).

Exodus assumes that Israel is already in covenant with God; they do not become covenanted with God at Sinai. At Sinai they learn what their calling is as God's people. The consecration celebrates being at one with the Lord (atonement is the usual term) as well as Israel's task within the covenant that goes back to Abraham and Sarah. Israel's response to the rite is to say again "All that the LORD has spoken we will do" (v. 7).

Then Moses and the rest go up the mountain. In the lead-in to today's reading they see the God of Israel: "under his feet there was something like a pavement of sapphire stone, like the very heaven for clearness" (v. 10). And "they beheld God, and they ate and drank" (v. 11). The event achieves its pinnacle in a communal feast of companionship that is a communion with YHWH and each other, an event of life-giving elation.

This is but one time among many in the First Testament where we are reminded that YHWH is holiness-in-community with the people, that God dwells with the people. It is immediately followed by a story (chap. 25) in which the Lord instructs Moses on the building of a sanctuary "so that I may dwell among them" (25:8).

Today's reading is sandwiched between these two stories; its meaning is interwoven with what precedes and follows it. Again, the Lord summons Moses to come up the mountain where, this time, he will receive "the tablets of stone, with the law and the commandment, which I have written for their instruction" (v. 12). Here Moses will receive the instructions for the sanctuary in which the Lord may dwell with the people.

As at the burning bush, which was not consumed, so here Moses is exposed to the glory of God "which was like a devouring fire" (v. 17). But Moses is not devoured by the fire, as the bush was not. Moses is with God in glory and remains there for forty days. The presence and communion with God that took place on Sinai in these stories is also the theme of the transfiguration.

Ash Wednesday/Years A, B, and C

Isaiah 58:1–12 (Alternate)

For comments on this passage, please see the Fifth Sunday after the Epiphany/Year A.

Joel 2:1–2, 12–17

The book of Joel opens with a word of the Lord: "Hear this, O elders, give ear, all inhabitants of the land! Has such a thing happened in your days, or in the days of your ancestors? Tell your children of it, and let your children tell their children, and their children another generation" (1:2). Joel proceeds to describe a plague of locusts (1:5–2:17) that devastated Judah. "The vine withers, the fig tree droops. Pomegranate, palm, and apple— all the trees of the field are dried up" (1:12) and the people are called to a fast. In a dire crisis, the one thing that we can do is return to the Lord in trust and hope. That is the larger context for today's reading.

In 2:1–2, Joel is instructed to "blow the trumpet in Zion; sound the alarm on my holy mountain! Let all the inhabitants of the land tremble, for the day of the LORD is coming, it is near." The "day of the LORD" in Joel could be a time of judgment and punishment for Judah (see 2:11) or one of deliverance from disaster and devastation (see 2:31; 3:14). In today's passage it is the former, but we should keep in mind that for Joel "the LORD is a refuge for his people, a stronghold for the house of Israel" (3:16).

At first glance, it might seem that the imminent disaster is military: "a great and powerful army comes. . . . Fire devours in front of them, and behind them a flame burns. . . . They have the appearance of horses, and like war-horses they charge" (2:2–4). Yet because the book opened with a long description of an outbreak of locusts, it seems clear that the devastation wrought by the locusts is being compared to that wreaked by an army as it destroys the environment (which armies regularly did).

Verses 12–17 describe the fast to which Joel calls the people of Judah. This is an appropriate text for Ash Wednesday and the beginning of the Lenten period of reflection. To understand the situation faced by the people of Judah, it is helpful to recall the "dust bowl" of the American Southwest during the Depression. The dust bowl was caused not by locusts but by destructive farming practices that stripped the topsoil from farmland plus a drought that wiped out all crops and enabled the wind to blow thick clouds of soil everywhere. America's "dust bowl" was commemorated in John Steinbeck's novel, *The Grapes of Wrath*, which shows that the cost to community and human life was overwhelming. That was the situation in Judah: "What the cutting locust left, the swarming locust has eaten. What the swarming locust left, the hopping locust has eaten, and what the hopping locust left, the destroying locust has eaten" (1:4).

Someone once said that prayer is what is left to do when there is nothing else that we can do. A calamity of major proportions that spreads previously unseen devastation in its wake, like a hurricane or tsunami, leaves us profoundly humbled before the destructive power of nature. The point of a fast is to ritually act out our humility before the Lord. A fast does not mechanically produce the desired results (such as the restoration of the Gulf Coast after Hurricane Katrina in 2005), nor is it a way to appease an angry God. Joel does not say that the Lord brought about the plague of locusts; instead he cries out to the Lord because "fire has devoured the pastures of the wilderness . . . [and] even the wild animals cry to you because the watercourses are dried up" (1:19–20).

The whole people is asked to an assembly, including infants and children (2:16). They are to fast, weep and mourn, rend their hearts and not their clothing (2:13), because God "is gracious and merciful, slow to anger, and abounding in steadfast love [*hesed*]" (2:13). In the next reading from Joel, the Lord will answer their prayer.

First Sunday in Lent/Year A

Genesis 2:15–17; 3:1–7

Genesis 2:4b–14 describes the first human being living in a paradise. The close relationship between the human being and the natural world is evident in the fact that God made the human being (*adam*) from the earth (*adamah*). God places the human being in a lush garden from which flow four rivers that water the whole world. The human being works, but the work is meaningful and satisfying (Gen. 2:5, 15). This is a theology of work: joining with God in making the world a garden. Only in Genesis 3:19 does labor become negative (Proper 5/Year B).

The human being can eat freely of every tree except the tree of the knowledge of good and evil (note: as in Gen. 1:29, the human being is a vegetarian). The phrase "good and evil" (and similar phrases) occurs only a few times in the Bible, usually in reference to making decisions that can lead to good or bad consequences (Deut. 1:39; 2 Sam. 19:35; 1 Sam. 14:17, 20). Limitation meant optimum freedom and blessing, for by respecting the limitation that God placed on the tree, the human being could have forever enjoyed God's original design to live in a world that was like Eden. Genesis 2:17b and 3:14–19 spell out the most dramatic consequences of eating of the tree.

Genesis 3:1–7 tells the story of how the first couple came to eat of the tree. The serpent here is a creature that God made, albeit a creature "more crafty" than others. Interpreters infer from Genesis 3:14 that the serpent had legs when it was in the garden. The serpent's craftiness is evident in the fact that it does not directly tempt the woman but takes the indirect approach of asking a question to which she knows the correct response (Gen. 3:1–3).

The serpent then reveals how creatures sometimes become misguided. It offers the woman as a good something that is actually bad by promising that the couple will not die but that their eyes will be opened and they will "be like God, knowing good and evil" (3:4–5). The woman wants things that she believes are good: nourishing and good-tasting food, beauty, and wisdom, but she thinks that to get them she must cross a boundary that God has set (3:6a). Had the couple turned the snake away, they would have had the very things with which the snake tempted them.

The woman is sometimes blamed for taking the forbidden fruit. However, the man was present, did not resist, cooperated freely in the eating, and is therefore equally responsible. To make humorous remarks about the woman and the fruit only reinforces a negative caricature that damages women.

When they ate, the serpent's prophecy came partly true. Their eyes *were* opened, but instead of seeing the serpent's promises fully realized, they immediately beheld their nakedness and became ashamed. Moreover they received decision-making power that could now curse as well as bless. They did not lose the capacity to participate with God in blessing, but henceforth, individuals and communities have had to attempt to discern the way of blessing from the way of curse, and suffer the consequences of the latter.

The readings for today explain why the world is not the superabundant realm of natural fertility, covenantal community, and justice pictured in both Genesis 1:3–2:4a and the Edenic world of Genesis 2:18–24 (Proper 22/Year B): creatures presumed for themselves roles belonging to God. The story of Genesis 2 is a paradigm of how temptation operates in the world: by offering us as blessing (good) things that really lead to curse (evil). The latter story presses a pastoral question. How do we creatures today encounter the serpent's lure to claim for ourselves things that rightly belong to God?

These latter qualities make a thematic connection between this story and that of the temptation in Matthew 4:1–11. For while the serpent of Genesis is not the devil of Matthew, both are creatures who offer Jesus (and us) penultimate possibilities in the guise of the ultimate.

Jewish reflection in the Hellenistic age sometimes identified the serpent with Satan (e.g., Wis. 2:24; Rev. 12:9–15; 20:2; Lev. R. 26; Fathers

According to Rabbi Nathan 1), but Genesis knows nothing of this association. Nevertheless, the preacher could help the congregation trace the development from serpent-as-misguided-creature to serpent-as-devil as a way of helping the congregation recognize how tradition changes over time. Other passages in the New Testament allude to this text, for example, 2 Corinthians 11:3; 2 Timothy 2:14; and Revelation 12:9–15; 20:2.

Second Sunday in Lent/Year A

Genesis 12:1–4a

Genesis 1–11 is primeval history focusing on God's attempt to work with all peoples at once to bless the human world. In Genesis 12:1–3, God works with one family as a model for others. In Genesis 12–16, the ancestral couple is known as Sarai and Abram but in Genesis 17 God changes their names to Sarah and Abraham to represent the divine promise.

Sarai and Abram had moved from Ur to Haran, the latter roughly five hundred miles from Canaan (Gen. 11:27–32). God's call to Sarai and Abram is an act of sheer grace, unmerited favor. Nothing suggests that God chose them because they had merit. The couple is to go from Haran to the as-yet-unnamed land that God would show them. They separate from their family, an act that was dramatic in antiquity.

The promise to Sarai and Abram contains six parts: (1) God will make of them a great nation. Their influence is not self-serving but is in the service of blessing. Because of the circumstances of the ancestral couple (Abram was seventy-five years old and Sarai was barren, Gen. 12:4; 11:30), this part of the promise seemed unlikely. (2) God will bless Sarai and Abram. Blessing, here, refers to total quality of life: material security, supportive community, shalom. (3) God will make their name great so that they will be a blessing. As we learn from the changes in names in Genesis 17:5–6 and 15–16, this promise is not for the self-glorification of the two human beings but is missional, for their names and their life story point to God's power to bless. (4) God will bless those who bless Sarai and Abram. But (5) God will curse the one who curses Sarai and Abram. (6) In them, "all the families of the earth shall be blessed."

By immediately beginning the journey, Sarai and Abram model how a person or a people should respond to God's call. In Genesis 12:7, God indicates that the land of Canaan is the land that God will give them. A morally troubling point is that God eventually took the land away from the Canaanites to give it to the descendants of Sarai and Abram.

Sarai and Abram were chosen not for special privilege but for witness. God chose them to be *conduits* of the knowledge of blessing to the wider human community. This story is a paradigm for subsequent generations. Given the age and circumstances of Sarai and Abram, it seemed unlikely that these promises could come true. Yet, these two responded by doing what God said, and discovered that God could bring about the promise. Where, in our world, do possibilities for blessing seem unlikely? How can we respond like Abram and Sarai by moving in response to the divine leading?

Genesis 12:1–9 is not organically related to either John 3:1–17 or Matthew 17:1–9. However, Romans 4:1–5, 13–17, is a Pauline exegesis of the story of Sarah and Abraham. While Paul does not directly quote from Genesis 12, the preacher can call attention to a theme that is fundamental both to the Priestly theologians and to Paul in Romans 4: to show that through Sarah and Abraham God intended to bless Gentiles. Other passages refer to Genesis 12, often with emphasis upon God blessing Gentiles, for example, Acts 3:25; Galatians 3:6–9, 16; cf. Acts 7:4–5; Hebrews 11:8–12.

Third Sunday in Lent/Year A

Exodus 17:1–7

In the previous passage in Exodus (Proper 20/Year A), the Israelites complained to Moses because of their hunger in the wilderness of Sin: "you have brought us out into this wilderness to kill this whole assembly with hunger" (Exod. 16:3). Now they demand: "Why did you bring us out of Egypt, to kill us and our children and livestock with thirst?" (17:3). The apparent absence of God's care in the lack of the necessities without which life and well-being are impossible, leads to a loss of trust in God. God's liberation of the people does not look so good when the result is an agonizing thirst.

The key to today's passage is in verse 7: Moses "called the place Massah [test] and Meribah [quarrel], because the Israelites tested the LORD, saying, 'Is the LORD among us or not?'" Interpretation is made difficult because we face what appears to be a dilemma. On the one hand, it is difficult not to empathize with people whose throats are parched and whose strength is sapped because there is no water to drink. This is a perilous condition, especially in a desert. On the other hand, it is inappropriate for the people to stake out the conditions that God must meet if they were to recognize that God was, indeed, present with them. This is a failure to trust God to do for us those things which only God can do. We must admit that we are all prone, in the midst of deep crisis, to do the same.

There is testing of another kind going on in this passage—God is still testing the people Israel (16:4). In today's passage, the people still have difficulty trusting God and understanding that God's purposes are not identical with theirs. So they put God to the test, in the fashion of those prayers we sometimes hear that regard God as our cosmic fetcher, the One who is to deliver to us whatever we ask for.

But God does not respond with anger to Moses' plea, "What shall I do with this people?" (v. 4). Instead, God instructs Moses to take the elders of the people and the staff with which he struck the Nile, making the water in the Nile unfit to drink (Exod. 7:17–18), and go to Horeb and strike the rock "and water will come out of it" (17:6). This water is life-giving.

Horeb is Sinai, where Moses will receive the Torah from God. Both Torah and life-giving water are received from God at Sinai. In Deuteronomy 30:19, after having given the Torah to Israel, God declares: "I have set before you life and death, blessings and curses. Choose life, so that you and your descendants may live." Torah is not an arbitrary compilation of laws foisted upon the people for the purpose of subjecting them to an authoritarian rule. The recurrent themes of Torah are the treatment of the stranger whom we are to love as we love ourselves, the plight of orphans and widows, the oppression of the poor by the rich, the cruel and unjust behavior of the powerful. The vulnerable other is the one whose voice speaks through the Torah. The Torah is God's instruction as to how the people of God are to live if they are to receive life and well-being. Not living by Torah, committing idolatry, theft, murder, breaking up families by lusting after our neighbors' spouses, is to bring curse and death upon ourselves as a consequence of our decisions and behavior.

Our passage relates life-giving water to life-giving Torah. One is essential to our physical well-being, the other to our personal and communal well-being; without either, we die. Jesus, too, gives us living water (John 4:10–15).

Fourth Sunday in Lent/Year A

1 Samuel 16:1–13

This lection presupposes the Deuteronomic theology (see Proper 17/Year B), especially the Deuteronomic editing of the books of Samuel (see Proper 2/Year B) and the request of the elders to change Israel from a confederacy living in covenant under the leadership of judges and prophets to a monarchy. Although Samuel warned against such a course (1 Sam.

8:1–20, Proper 5/Year B), they persisted. Samuel anointed Saul, but, just as Samuel warned, the monarch was disobedient and was deposed (13:1–15a; 15:10–34). The narrator says plaintively that God was sorry for making Saul ruler over Israel (15:34).

God tells Samuel to take a horn to the home of Jesse, grandchild of Ruth (Propers 26/Year B and 27/Year B), who lived in Bethlehem (about six miles south of Jerusalem), to anoint a ruler for Israel whom God had designated from Jesse's children (1 Sam. 16:1). Monarchs were appointed by anointing with oil, which functioned similarly to a sacrament as an outward sign of a deeper reality.

When Samuel feared that Saul would kill him if Saul learned the purpose of Samuel's mission to Bethlehem, God instructed Samuel to carry out a ruse: the prophet was to invite Jesse to sacrifice a heifer. God would then show Samuel whom to anoint (1 Sam. 16:2–5). The ruse raises the question of when one can trust the word of a prophet.

Samuel reviews the children of Jesse in 1 Samuel 16:6–13. That the venerable prophet misperceives Eliab—not only the eldest (hence the most likely candidate) but also tall and handsome—as the new ruler should caution readers in every age to heed God's corrective to Samuel to look as God does, not "on outward appearance" but "on the heart" (16:6–8).

Seven of Jesse's children passed before Samuel (1 Sam. 16:8–10). The youngest, however, was keeping the sheep, so that Jesse had to call him from the field (1 Sam. 16:11–12). Shepherds stayed with the sheep, led them to food and water, protected them from animals and thieves, tended their injuries, and disciplined them. Because of the similarity of this role with that of the sovereign, people in the ancient Near East sometimes referred to the national sovereign as a shepherd. The fact that David was a shepherd was thus prescient of his service as sovereign. The question always in the back of the mind of the reader is the degree to which David (or any monarch) was a faithful shepherd. Though the presence of God "came mightily" upon David (v. 13), David did not always respond to that Spirit in an optimum way.

On the one hand, that the anointing of David takes place while Saul is still on the throne suggests that God is often providentially active even before others are aware of need. On the other hand, the secrecy is troubling; it seems hardly fair to Saul for Samuel (and God) to anoint a successor to Saul without Saul's knowledge.

David later sometimes behaved in ungodly ways.[8] He led Israel to heights of political achievement never equaled in Israel's history but did not shepherd the nation into embodying the covenantal life described in Deuteronomy. In only a few years, the united monarchy divided into two nations that collapsed and their leadership was exiled. The editors thus imply that the community reading this text while rebuilding the nation after the exile (when the Deuteronomic history was given its present form) should be less interested in a Davidic model of political success and more interested in a common life that embodied covenant.

The relationship of 1 Samuel 16:1–13 with the Gospel and Epistle lessons for today is a puzzle. John 9:1–41 and Ephesians 5:8–14 have no exegetical or theological connections with the reading from Samuel.

Fifth Sunday in Lent/Year A

Ezekiel 37:1–14

Ezekiel 37 is one of the best-known passages in the Bible. Ezekiel prophesied during the exile (see Proper 9/Year B). The lection for today comes from the strand in Ezekiel's preaching that affirms that God will end the exile and regenerate the community in the promised land. While Christians sometimes think that Ezekiel 37 anticipated the resurrection of individuals from the dead, a closer reading shows that the prophet speaks of the restoration of Israel by ending the exile. Indeed, resurrection is inseparable from the restoration of the people Israel from exile.

The spirit puts Ezekiel in the middle of a valley of dry bones. The bones are void of skin and ligaments and are disconnected from one another (Ezek. 37:1–2). When God asks Ezekiel whether the bones can live, the prophet is agnostic: "You know" (v. 3). God indicates that the bones will come to life as the prophet speaks God's message. Although scholars debate whether the term breath (*ruach*) here is better rendered wind or spirit, the essential point is that God will infuse the bones with new life (vv. 4–6).

When Ezekiel prophesied as God instructed, the bones began to come together, and ligaments and flesh appeared, but they did not have breath (vv. 7–8). God told the prophet to direct the breath into the bones so that they "stood on their feet, a vast multitude" (vv. 9–10).

In 37:11, the author reveals that the bones are "the whole house of Israel." The community as community is as dead as the bones in the valley. However, God is opening the graves and returning them to their own soil, where they will recognize that God has acted and will live accordingly (vv. 12–14).

Preaching here is the means of restoration. Through preaching, the breath of God enters the bones. An implication is that pastorally sensitive prophetic preaching can play a key role in revitalizing community.

This text speaks to congregations and other communities who are in situations similar to that of dry bones. The preacher can help such congregations identify points at which the Spirit is trying to move through them. How can the congregation be ever more receptive to that movement? Some preachers do face a hermeneutical difficulty, for the health of some communities is so diminished that coming alive seems impossible. To hold out the vision of Ezekiel 37 to such communities may only prolong the dying and use up large amounts of resources (human, fiscal, ecological—electricity, gas, heating oil). A preacher might note that while individual congregations die, the breath of God can infuse the congregation's remaining resources with fresh life in other settings.

The Gospel lesson appointed for today is John 11:1–45, Jesus raising Lazarus from the dead. The lectionary here brings together two texts that are connected more by catchword than substance. As just noted, the passage from Ezekiel is not about the resurrection of individuals from the dead but about the social restoration of the whole house of Israel by ending the exile and regenerating the community and the land. Nevertheless, both passages affirm the power of God to bring life out of difficult situations. A preacher could call attention to the similarities and differences, as well as to the importance of respecting the particularity of what biblical texts invite readers to believe and do. A preacher could use these different texts as a starting point for a sermonic conversation on different ways of thinking about God and hope for the future in this life and beyond.

Palm/Passion Sunday/Years A, B, and C

Isaiah 50:4–9a

Today's reading is the third Servant Song in Isaiah. It has to do with Second Isaiah's relations to the Lord and to those among his people who react negatively to his proclamation by hitting, insulting, and spitting on him. It asks how we manage to stay faithful to the Lord, to find the heart to remain steadfast, when the consequences of speaking the truth are personal hostility directed against us.

The servant introduces himself as one to whom God has given "the tongue of a teacher" (v. 4). Since this is a text for Passion Sunday, it is appropriate to note that Jesus is called teacher (*didaskalos* or *rabbi*) more than forty times in the Gospels. What the Servant Song says of second Isaiah is also true of Jesus and, for that matter, of every servant of the Lord who tries, with genuine humility, to speak the truth to those who may well not want to hear it. Although the truth is a comforting word, it is also a word that often discomfits those who most need to hear it.

God gave the servant the tongue of a teacher so that he might "know how to sustain the weary with a word" (v. 4). This is a remarkable concept and well states a key function of ministry—to sustain the weary with a word, to speak the apt word that gives us courage in the face of anxiety and fear, that brings reconciliation out of estrangement, that opens up the possibilities of authentic community in the face of isolation, that gives hope in a time of despair and strength to the weak and overburdened.

In order to do this, God had to give the servant an ear that could "hear" (*shema*) the word of a compassionately just God. God "opened" Isaiah's ear so that he did not "turn backward" in the face of adversity. Those who speak need to be excellent listeners, to God and to those to whom they speak. We need an open ear when we listen to God in our prayers, in our studies, and in our attempts to live out in word and deed the faith that is ours. Too often in prayer all we do is talk. There is a Jewish saying that study is a higher form of worship than prayer, because in studying we listen to God while in prayer, the only thing about us that is open is our mouths.

Part of what Isaiah learns, according to this passage, comes from his suffering. This does not mean that suffering is necessarily redemptive. Much of it is simply destructive of life and well-being, like the suffering of the thousands of children who die of starvation every day. Yet there are people who have endured intense suffering and gone on to become inspiring figures with tremendous ability to spread the love of God and neighbor in the world. The writers of this book know a survivor of Auschwitz. His entire extended family died there; only he survived. When we got to know him he was carrying the message of resisting prejudice and loving the neighbor throughout the public schools as an unpaid ambassador on behalf of gentleness and compassion. He had walked through the valley of dark shadows but, like Isaiah, "did not turn backward."

In answer to the question, how did you do this? Isaiah says simply: "The Lord God helps me" (v. 7). All servants of the Lord need a listening ear so that they, too, may receive a word that sustains the weary and suffering.

This reading is paired on Passion Sunday with Philippians 2:5–11, the Christ-Wisdom hymn in which Christ "did not regard equality with God as something to be exploited, but emptied himself, taking the form of a slave [servant] . . . and became obedient to the point of death" (vv. 6–8). The "servant" could refer to any of God's faithful servants. Paul so uses it here to refer to Christ as the servant in whom God's love is clearly disclosed, to the end that God's name should be confessed ("the name that is above every name" being the name of God, YHWH). The last line of the hymn, "to the glory of God the Father," may not be overlooked. The Matthew readings from the passion narrative correlate with Philippians 2:5–11.

Good Friday/Year A

Isaiah 52:13–53:12

Today's reading is the fourth Servant Song found in Isaiah 40–55. At one time, scholars pondered whether the servant to which Isaiah refers was an individual or the community of Israel. Today a wide-ranging scholarly opinion is that the servant refers to the community. The Servant Songs answer the question, What is the vocation of the people Israel when the community is in exile in Babylon? Earlier songs confirm that Israel is called by God to be a light to the nations (i.e. the Gentiles), that is, Israel is to model for the idolatrous Gentiles how the God of Israel (the universal God) seeks for people to live together. For development, see our commentary on the other Servant Songs: Isaiah 42:1–9 (First Sunday after the Epiphany/Year A); 49:1–7 (Second Sunday after the Epiphany/Year A); and 50:4–9a (Palm/Passion Sunday/Years A, B, and C).

Within this purpose, Isaiah 52:13–53:12 deals with a problem that vexed people in Isaiah's day and that continues to vex congregations today. God had promised Sarai and Abram blessing on their descendants (Gen. 12:1–3). Blessing included land, security, and material resources so that all could live in covenantal community. The exile, and the suffering that went with it, challenged the trustworthiness of this promise. The reading for today asserts that God will restore Israel (vindicating the divine promises), and will use the suffering of the servant community to help the Gentiles recognize the trustworthiness of the God of Israel and turn to God for blessing.

The prophet begins by assuring the listeners that God will restore Israel. God will cause the community to prosper and be "exalted" (Isa. 52:13). Many Gentiles looked down on Israel because of the community's disfigured state, but the restoration will startle the Gentiles (52:14–15a). The reversal of Israel's circumstances will show the Gentiles the regenerative power God (52:15b).

Isaiah 53:1–3 compares the life of the people Israel to the figure of a young person growing up like a tender plant and who, in maturity, was despised and rejected by others, and who suffered by going into exile as a result. To Gentile onlookers, Israel appeared to be a very ordinary community. Indeed, the suffering of the people caused the Gentiles to perceive Israel as being "of no account." What could such a people offer the Gentile world? Isaiah 53:4–12 responds to this question.

Scholars and preachers sometimes use complicated theories of sacrifice to explain Isaiah 53:4–9. What happens to Israel is itself a model for the Gentiles to ponder. Though Israel sought to be faithful to God, Israel was often treated unjustly by larger and more powerful nations. Israel itself turned away from the faithful life, took up with idols, and practiced injustice, thus prompting God to exile the community. The prophet describes Israel's bitter circumstance in a variety of images, for example, stricken, wounded, punished, oppressed, afflicted, like a lamb before the slaughter, cut off from the land of the living, as in a grave, crushed with pain, and anguished. To Gentiles, Israel's situation looks hopeless.

However, as the opening part of the song promises, God uses Israel's bitter circumstances as occasion to demonstrate how God can restore even the most broken community. God will bring forth offspring for the people and will prolong their days; God's purposes (seemingly dormant in the exile) will again prosper through the nation (Isa. 53:10). God's righteousing activity through Israel will cause others to embrace the God of Israel and thereby share in righteousness (that is, in living covenantally in the way of blessing). The community will bear the iniquities of the Gentiles who will see the suffering of the community and will want to live covenantally so as to avoid bringing such suffering on themselves (Isa. 53:11). By going into exile, Israel was treated as a transgressor, yet the suffering of the community functions to bear the sin of many (especially Gentiles) and as intercession for other transgressors (53:13b) for it gives God, in the restoration, the opportunity to give the battered Israel a portion with the great, and for Israel to divide the spoil with the strong, thus pointing Gentiles to the God of Israel as the source of the restorative life. Despite their wounded, diminished appearance, the life of Israel points to God who can bring blessing to all.

Since this reading occurs on Good Friday, preachers and congregations often assume that the servant was Jesus. On the one hand, a preacher needs to help the congregation recognize that, from Isaiah's perspective, the servant is Israel. On the other hand, the Suffering Servant of Isaiah provides a model for interpreting the death and resurrection of Jesus (e.g., Matt. 8:17; Luke 22:37; John 12:38; Acts 8:32–33; Rom. 10:16; 15:21; Phil. 2:5–11; Heb. 9:28; 1 Pet. 2:22, 24). The death of Jesus, like the situation of the servant in Isaiah's day, appeared to demonstrate weakness and defeat. Yet, God raised Jesus from the dead, and thereby, gave a sign that God has the power to resurrect all in the divine realm. The death and resurrection of Jesus do not supersede the Suffering Servant of Isaiah 52:13–53:12, but re-present that theology for the time of the Roman Empire. The implicit hope of the earliest writers of the Jesus movement is that those outside the community will see that the God of Israel still seeks to restore the broken world, and will repent and turn to that God for the path to restoration.

Easter Day/Year A

Jeremiah 31:1–6

The lectionary proposes Jeremiah 31:1–6 as an alternate reading to Acts 10:34–43 as the First Reading for the day. If Acts is read and Jeremiah is not, then, on the defining day of the Christian year the voice of the Old Testament is completely silent. We strongly recommend, therefore, that the congregation read from Jeremiah on Easter Day.

The middle part of the book of Jeremiah dates from the exile when the prophet offered hope that God would return the exiles. Today's passage contains such an oracle of salvation. The language of Jeremiah 31:1 is the language of covenant and indicates that the promises in the oracle are God keeping faith with the divine promises. Israel and Judah may have broken the covenant, but God did not.

In the oracle itself, language from the exodus tradition points out that those who were not killed in the escape from bondage in Egypt found grace (*hen*) in the wilderness. Jeremiah has earlier compared the exile to wilderness (Jer. 4:22–28; Proper 19/Year C). When Israel needed rest in the wilderness, God appeared (Jer. 31:2). God assures Israel that God loves the community "with an everlasting love" and God continues to be "faithful" (*hesed*) (31:3, cf. 32:18; 33:11; Deut. 7:7–13; 10:15). Jeremiah wants to be sure the community interprets the exile not as a denial of God's love but as God's covenantal discipline (Jer. 31:18; cf. 7:28; Deut. 4:36; 11:2; 21:18).

Earlier the prophet spoke of the community as a harlot (Jer. 2:20; 3:1–8). However, when promising to rebuild the community, God now compares Israel to a virgin, a person innocent and full of promise. God will rebuild Israel (Jer. 31:4a). Some scholars hear a marital echo here similar to Hosea 2.

The restored Israel will be like Miriam leading the procession of dancers celebrating the exodus from Egypt (Jer. 31:4b; cf. Exod. 15:21). Israel will plant vineyards in the mountains of Samaria and eat the fruit (31:5). Indeed, the day is coming when Israel and Judah will be reunited and all will worship in Jerusalem (31:6).

The lectionary today provides alternate Gospel readings telling different versions of the revelation of the resurrection: Matthew 28:1–10 and John 20:1–18. Neither Matthew nor John directly allude to the passage from Jeremiah. However, the general theme of God's faithfulness does underlie both Jeremiah and the Gospel readings. The readers of Matthew and John, and the congregation today can believe that as God proved faithful to Jeremiah and to the exiles, so God will prove faithful to the promises of the resurrection.

Easter Evening/Years A, B, and C

Isaiah 25:6–9

Please see Easter Day/Year B for commentary on this passage.

Day of Pentecost/Year A

Numbers 11:24–30 (Alternate)

This passage also occurs in the lectionary on Proper 21/Year B; since the latter reading tells the whole story of Numbers 11, we treat it here in its larger context. Today's story presents us with a conundrum. In the book of Exodus, when the people complain because of a lack of water to drink and food to eat (Exod. 15:22–26; 17:1–7), YHWH provides food and water. Numbers 11:1–3 mentions an unspecific complaint, but this time YHWH's "anger was kindled [and] . . . the fire of the LORD burned against them, and consumed some outlying parts of the camp" (v. 1). The second complaint (11:4–6) is specific: "If only we had meat to eat!" (v. 4). The Israelites recall an excellent list of foods in Egypt (a recall incompatible with the Exodus 1–2 account) and compare the manna that God provides unfavorably with it: "now there is nothing at all but this manna to look at" (v. 6). Again, the Lord "became very angry, and Moses was displeased" (v. 10).

How are we to understand this dramatic change from a compassionate divine response in Exodus to anger and punishment in Numbers? The complaints in Exodus preceded the granting of the covenant at Sinai (Exodus 20); the complaints in Numbers follow the granting of the covenant. Previously the people were merely beginning to come to terms with what it meant to be followers of YHWH, but now they are supposed to understand what it means to trust in and rely upon the Lord. Yet they complain.

This may account for why it is "the rabble among them" (v. 4) and not the whole people who "had a strong craving" for the better food available in Egypt. Yet they prod "the Israelites" to "weep again" (v. 4). The complaint is that manna is, well, just manna (as to "manna," see Proper20/Year A). This time, the complaint is directed against God's gracious gift of manna. This yields a significant homiletical theme: how many ways can we find fault with God's gracious gifts to us?

This introduces a third complaint, that of Moses to God: "Why have you treated your servant so badly? Why have I not found favor in your sight, that you lay the burden of all this people on me? Did I conceive all this people? Did I give birth to them . . . ?" (vv. 11–12). (Note that here God is discussed with female imagery.) In Exodus Moses interceded with God on behalf of the people; in Numbers Moses wants out of his leadership role, to the point of asking to be "put . . . to death at once" (v. 15). Moses says that he does not want to "see my misery" (v. 15). He laments: why did I get stuck with this dysfunctional bunch?

YHWH's response to Moses is to give YHWH's spirit to the seventy elders that "they may share the burden of the people along with you so that you will not bear it all by yourself" (v. 17). Moses does as God commands; God blesses the elders with God's spirit and they begin to prophesy (vv. 24–25). Like Moses, pastors too can use some help in dealing with congregations. That such help can be found in the congregation is what the passage suggests. Surely there are some wise heads out there.

Two of the people, Eldad and Medad, who were not among the seventy, also begin to prophesy (v. 26). Joshua asks Moses to stop them but he answers: "Would that all the LORD's people were prophets, and that the LORD would put his spirit on them!" (v. 29). Moses' complaint is the only one on which God looks favorably.

One underappreciated point of the book of Numbers is its focus on organization. Its authors and redactors were aware that organization is necessary to serve God's purposes. There is no split here between spirit and organization, a point that we should take seriously. In Mark 9:38–50, the exorcist who cast out demons and was not a follower of Jesus is a parallel figure to Eldad and Medad. Like Moses, Jesus affirms him.

Trinity Sunday/Year A

Genesis 1:1–2:4a

Although this passage tells the story of the world's first moments, the passage was given much of its present shape by the Priestly theologians in and after the exile. According to the prophets, Israel had become unfaithful and unjust, and, consequently, God allowed the Babylonians to invade and conquer the nation, and take many of Israel's leaders into exile in Babylon. To some Israelites the gods of the Babylonians appeared to be more powerful than their own God. When many of the leaders returned from Babylon, they found the infrastructure of Palestine in disarray, and the returnees often came into conflict with residents who had remained in Palestine during the exile. Israel's life was a kind of chaos.

Genesis 1:1–2:4a asserts the sovereignty of the God of Israel over all other deities. The Babylonian story of creation, *Enuma Elish*, told the story of creation as a fierce battle between Tiamat, ruler of the watery deep, and the god Marduk, in which the world was created when Marduk slayed Tiamat and split Tiamat's carcass in half to form the upper and lower parts of the universe. The God of Israel, in contrast, creates by nothing more than speaking. Furthermore, Genesis implies that objects that were often deified in the ancient Near East—such as sun, moon, stars, and animals—are simply creatures. People commit idolatry by worshiping such things.

The Priestly account critiques the Babylonian story by indicating in Genesis1:1–2 that before God began to create, the universe was a "deep," the Hebrew word for which (*tehom*) is related to the name Tiamat. The "deep" was a primeval sea that existed before the words of creation. Preachers sometimes envision "order" and "chaos" as opposites, but here chaos is a force field whose parts do not work together to serve God's purposes. The act of creation reshapes the elements of chaos and brings them into cooperation with the divine purposes that are spelled out in Genesis 1:3–2:4a.

Such motifs are intended to persuade the community to trust God and to live faithfully in God's ways. The text assures the community of the reliability of divine power. The God who created the world could permit the exile and could be trusted to restore the life of the community upon return from exile.

Although the text does not use the words "covenant" or "justice," Genesis 1:3–2:4a depicts the character of a just, covenantal community. According to Genesis 1, God intended the created world to be a community in which each element has its own integrity while living in mutually supportive relationships with all other elements (including nature). This world is so absent of violence that neither animals nor human beings kill in order to eat but are all vegetarian (Gen. 1:29–30).

Human beings are created in the image of God (Gen. 1:26–27). This image is the capacity to exercise dominion in the way that God does, that is, by ruling in limited human spheres in the ways that God does in the cosmic world. To exercise dominion is not to have license to do whatever one wants (such as despoiling the earth) but is to help the various elements of creation live together in covenantal community. The female and the male are equally created in the divine image. This passage implies egalitarianism with no sense of hierarchy.

This passage is important to the New Testament. For the apocalyptic theology that is a part of many of the New Testament writings contends that the end time (the eschatological world, the realm of God) will be like the beginning times (the world at creation and before the fall). The ministries of Jesus and the church thus witness to God's intent to remake the fallen world into the quality of life depicted in Genesis 1 and 2. Furthermore, the Scriptures often directly cite or allude to this passage (e.g., Matt. 19:4; Mark 10:6; Acts 17:29; Rom. 14:2; 1 Cor. 11:7; 2 Cor. 4:6; Eph. 4:24; Col. 3:10; 1 Tim. 4:4; Heb. 4:4, 10; Jas. 3:9; 2 Pet. 3:5).

While the hope of apocalyptic re-creation has not come to pass, the preacher can point out that Genesis 1 can be for us, as for the early Jesus movement, a paradigm of God's purposes for cosmic community. The generativity with which God imbued the world at creation is still at work in the creation to create and re-create.

Genesis 1 is assigned to Trinity Sunday because of the plural, "Let *us* make humankind in our image" (Gen. 1:26). While Christian exegesis has sometimes interpreted this pronoun as a reference to the Trinity, in its exilic or postexilic context the plural undoubtedly referred instead to the members of the heavenly court, the heavenly beings alongside God, a common motif in ancient Near Eastern literature.

Proper 4 [9]/Year A

Genesis 6:9–22; 7:24; 8:14–19+ (Semicontinuous)

This reading is the first of a series of semicontinuous readings from Genesis and is the only one from the primeval history (Genesis 1–11). This history explains why God called Sarah, Abraham, and their descendants. God had sought to bless the whole world directly through creation and re-creation, but human beings so violated God's purpose of living in mutual support that God decided to attempt another means of blessing the world: by using one human family (Israel) as a model of the way all could be blessed.

Today's passage is a semicontinuous telling of the flood, the complete text of which is Genesis 6:1–9:17 (see First Sunday in Lent/Year B). This story is similar to other ancient Near Eastern tales of floods destroying the world (e.g., Gilgamesh). The biblical writers reshaped a common cultural motif to serve the God of Israel.

One of the most poignant lines in the Bible is Genesis 6:6, in which the narrator says that God was sorry for making humankind (cf. 6:7). Whereas God intended humankind and nature to live together in mutually supportive community, the earth had become corrupt (spoiled, ruined) and filled with violence. Noah, however, was "righteous" (that is, lived in right relationship with God and with other creatures).

The Hebrew word "ark" (Gen. 6:14) is the same one rendered "basket" in Exodus 2:3. This small detail points to larger themes in this story: the faithfulness God showed to Noah is the same as the faithfulness God shows to Israel, and the faithfulness God shows to Israel demonstrates the faithfulness that God will show the whole human family. This motif intensifies when God declares in Genesis 6:18 that God will make a covenant (*berith*) through Noah with all people and with the "living things" (8:22–9:17). God, then, is in covenant with all people and all other living things; therefore, we are to live covenantally with all God's other people and creatures to experience blessing.

With rain from the sky and waters from the subterranean deeps, God reduces the earth to the chaotic deep of the universe before creation (Gen. 1:1–2). In the same way the preexilic generation had reduced the social world to chaos, so they are now themselves destroyed by chaos (exile), the very means by which they violated God's aims.

Most boats in antiquity were open but the ark is covered (thus providing more protection from the water). It is unimaginably larger than the typical vessel and shelters representatives of all living things. The ark is thus a manifestation of grace and a symbol to which Israel and other peoples could later turn when threatened.

Upon disembarking, one of Noah's first acts is to build an altar epitomizing the fundamental purpose of life: to serve God. God, in turn, pledges not to destroy the world again by flood, an assurance meaningful in the Near East where tremendous rains fall during certain times. More importantly, in 8:22, God makes an unconditional promise to all: God will forever maintain the structures of creation that support life. No matter how degenerate and violent life becomes, the possibility for blessing remains because life itself "shall not cease."

God re-created the world so that all its future inhabitants have the opportunity to live in ways that resemble the covenantal world of Genesis 1–2. Indeed, 8:17 contains the same command as 1:28. However, 8:21 reminds the reader that the inclination to evil is deeply embedded. Noah himself immediately betrayed God's design (Gen. 9:18–28), and in only a few generations Noah's descendants built the tower of Babel (11:1–9). Subsequently, God turned to Sarah and Abraham to be a blessing to all other families.

To Israel's neighbors, this story is an assurance that the God of Israel seeks to bless them while it simultaneously challenges them to want to live in the ways of the God of Israel as the path to blessing. To Israel, this story offers a similar assurance of blessing while also reminding them that their God is the universal God of all peoples, and that they have a special mission to witness to that God.

In the Hellenistic age, some Jewish apocalyptic theologians viewed the flood as a paradigm for the apocalypse (*1 En.* 54:7–10; 65:1–66:13; 83:1–11; 89:1–9; 106:1–107:13). To such writers, the old must be destroyed before the new can take effect. Passages in the New Testament resonate with themes from the story of the flood, such as Matthew 24:36–39; Luke 17:26–27; 1 Peter 3:18–22; 2 Peter 2:4–10; 3:5–7. Hebrews 11:7 uses Noah as a model of the faith of Hebrews.

Deuteronomy 11:18–21, 26–28 (Paired)*

For comments on this passage, please see the Ninth Sunday after the Epiphany/Year A.

Proper 5 [10]/Year A

Genesis 12:1–9+ (Semicontinuous)

For comments on this text, please see the Second Sunday in Lent/Year A.

Hosea 5:15–6:6 (Paired)*

For the historical context of today's reading, please see Proper 12/Year C. The period when Uzziah was king in Judah and Jeroboam king in Israel (Hos. 1:1) was one of peace. After Jeroboam's rule, things fell apart under a series of inept rulers. Eventually Israel and Syria initiated war with Judah. Hosea 5:8–7:16 addresses this period of discord and struggle. In 5:8–14, the Lord pronounces judgment and punishment on Israel and Judah for this covenant-violating conflict that is destructive of God's commitment to peace. The promises of peace and disarmament with which our last reading from Hosea ended (Eighth Sunday after the Epiphany/Year B) have been contravened by the outbreak of war and calamity.

The Lord commands that a distress signal be sounded: "Blow the horn in Gibeah, the trumpet in Ramah. Sound the alarm at Beth-aven [Bethel]; look behind you, Benjamin! Ephraim [Israel] shall become a desolation in the day of punishment.... The princes of Judah have become like those who remove the landmark; on them I will pour out my wrath like water" (5:8–10). War always brings death and destruction, and the Lord vows, "I will be like a lion to Ephraim, and like a young lion to the house of Judah. I myself will tear and go away; I will carry off, and no one shall rescue" (v. 14).

We should think about how to deal with passages that depict God as bringing death and destruction as punishment. Often Christians fall into the trap of describing YHWH as a God of wrath and judgment unlike the God of grace and love of the New Testament. This is a Marcionite mistake and reflects a Gnosticism that seeks to escape the rough edges of history. God is a covenantal God of compassionate justice, a God who relationally seeks the cooperation of God's covenant partners. They and we always face the question whether we will choose the way of life and blessing which God gives and calls us to or the way of death and destruction that is its alternative. After giving the Torah to Israel, God declares: "I have set before you life and death, blessings and curses. Choose life so that you and your descendants may live" (Deut. 30:19). If we choose death and curses, we get death and curses. The desolation wreaked on Israel and Judah in this passage is not the Lord's doing; it is the result of human folly and stupidity.

Consequently, our passage includes a call to repentance: "Come, let us return to the LORD; for it is he who has torn, and he will heal us; he has struck down, and he will bind us up" (6:1). The people confess that they have not known the Lord and the Lord's ways: "Let us know, let us press on to know the LORD; his appearing is as sure as the dawn; he will come to us like the showers, like the spring rains that water the earth" (v. 3). God's grace and presence are "as sure as the dawn." God is not the problem.

As is typical in Hosea, the Lord responds to this cry of penitence out of the Lord's heartbroken distress and travail with God's people, wondering "what shall I do with you, O Ephraim? What shall I do with you, O Judah?" (v. 4). The people's love for God, like our love for God, is erratic and vacillating, "like a morning cloud, like the dew that goes early away" (v. 4). The Lord is agonized and drained, like a parent fretting over a child who makes bad decisions (11:1–4) or a spouse over a wayward loved one. What the Lord desires of us is "not sacrifice" but "steadfast [loyal] love ... the knowledge of God rather than burnt offerings" (v. 6).

God does not want temple-treaders or churchgoers who wage war. This passage should be preached for its importance. Its relation to the story of the call of Matthew and the story of a girl restored to life and a woman healed is not obvious (Matt. 9:9–13, 18–26) except that Jesus carries out the will of God in serving life rather than death.

Proper 6 [11]/Year A

Genesis 18:1–15, (21:1–17)+ (Semicontinuous)

The readings for today fall into four literary-thematic units. Each unit has its own theme.

First is the practice of hospitality as welcoming the divine (Gen. 18:1–8). Sarah and Abraham were camped by the oaks (or terebinths) of Mamre (near Hebron, about twenty miles west of the Dead Sea). In the heat of the day, when people would not ordinarily be out, three unnamed visitors approached. Some Christians claim they were the three persons of the Trinity but that idea is not in the text (and did not emerge formally until the second century CE). More likely, in accord with similar stories from the same time, they are the Deity and two attendants. Sarah and Abraham embody the spirit of hospitality, which called for them to provide strangers with welcome, safety, refreshment, drink, food, and conversation. As the text unfolds, the nomadic couple (and the readers) realize that by welcoming these strangers, they have welcomed life-transforming presence. A preacher could explore with the congregation how we, today, could similarly be hospitable to strangers and, perhaps, encounter a similar presence.

The second thematic unit is the promise of God to Sarah (Gen. 18:9–15). Sarah was ninety years old and her menstrual cycle had stopped (v. 11). Nevertheless, one of the visitors announced that Sarah would have a child (v. 10). Sarah, who was in the tent, laughed, a resonance with the name Isaac which means "laughter" (v. 12; cf. 17:17). The visitor, now identified as God, asked whether anything was too wonderful for God to do (v. 13). Sarah denied laughing, but that lie that did not stop God from keeping the promise. The preacher might ask, "When do we laugh at possibilities for blessing that seem as unlikely to us as ninety-year-old Sarah giving birth?"

Writers of the New Testament regarded Genesis 18:1–15 as an important text, as we can see by the fact that they refer frequently to it, for example, Matthew 19:26; Mark 10:27; Luke 1:18, 37; 7:44; Acts 3:25; Rom. 4:13; 9:9; Galatians 3:6–9; Hebrews 11:11; 13:2; 1 Peter 3:6.

The third significant motif in the readings for today is the birth of Isaac, demonstrating God's faithfulness and power (Gen. 21:1–7). In 12:1–3, God promised that the old couple would be the parents of a great nation. In 15:1–6, God promised that the heir would be a biological child. In 17:16–21, God promised that Sarah would be the mother. Now, the promise has come true. On the eighth day after birth, Isaac was the first person circumcised (21:4). Isaac's name means "laughter" and the birth transformed Sarah's laughter from that of incredulity to affirmation and amazement (vv. 6–7), thus showing that the divine power can transform a situation. Sarah said, "Everyone who hears [my transformed laughter] will laugh with me." Subsequent generations in situations like that of Sarah—with limited potential as in the exile—remembered God's faithfulness and power in keeping promises, and could live through discouragement in hope.

In the fourth thematic unit, God authorizes Abraham and Sarah to send away Hagar and Ishmael (Gen. 21:8–17). In Genesis 16:1–15, when a biological heir seemed unlikely, Sarah arranged for her servant Hagar to give birth to Abraham's child (Ishmael), who was to be treated as Sarah's and would be heir to the estate. But, after Isaac's birth, when Sarah saw Isaac playing with Ishmael, Sarah asked Abraham to send away Hagar and Ishmael so that Isaac alone would receive the couple's estate (21:10). By freeing the slave and her child, the child would lose his share of the property.[9] Abraham was distressed at the prospect of sending away Hagar and Ishmael, his son, but he did so. Let us be clear: sending Hagar and Ishmael into the wilderness was a morally repugnant action. Although Abraham abandoned Hagar and Ishmael to the wilderness, God did not do so. God promised to make a nation of Ishmael (21:13). When Hagar and Ishmael were threatened with dehydration, God caused a well to flow (21:19).

Paul interprets the stories of Sarah and Hagar by means of allegory in Galatians 4:1–7, 21; 5:1 to undercut not Jewish people and the Torah but *Gentiles* in Galatia who *misunderstood* and *misused* the Torah.[10] In Romans 9:6–18 (esp. v. 7), Paul uses Genesis 21 to help Gentile readers see that the Jewish people are children of the promise as much as are Gentiles. Genesis 21 is also in the background of Matthew 1:2; Luke 3:34; Acts 7:8; and Hebrews 11:11, 18.

Exodus 19:2–8a (Paired)*

Chapter 19 is the last piece of narrative before the giving of the torah (way, instruction) begins in chapter 20. From now on in the Torah, passages of story will alternate with passages in which law, or instruction, is given.

Law and story interact throughout the Torah and law changes in response to incidents that show the inadequacy of prior law. As important as law, torah, is to Israel, equally important is the recognition that the purpose of torah is that the people may have lives of blessing and well-being. As a result, when the orphaned daughters of Zelophehad complain to Moses and Aaron that they cannot inherit their father's property because only sons could inherit (and Zelophehad had no sons), the Lord said to Moses: "The daughters of Zelophehad are right in what they are saying; you shall indeed let them possess an inheritance . . ." (Num. 27:1–7). Torah in Israel and postbiblical Judaism has not ceased developing even today.

Torah is the gracious gift to Israel from the God who loves Israel. In today's reading this point is stressed with YHWH's remark: "You have seen . . . how I bore you on eagles' wings and brought you to myself. Now therefore, if you obey my voice and keep my covenant, you shall be my treasured possession out of all the peoples" (19:4–5).

The image of God as a mother bird is strikingly gracious. Deuteronomy 32:11–12 puts it this way:

> As an eagle stirs up its nest,
> and hovers over its young;
> as it spreads its wings, takes them up,
> and bears them aloft on its pinions,
> the LORD alone guided him [Israel].

This is a frequent image in the Scriptures: "Hide me in the shadow of your wings," prays the psalmist (Ps. 17:8). "All people may take refuge in the shadow of your wings" (Ps. 36:7). "In the shadow of your wings I will take refuge" (Ps. 57:1). "Like birds hovering overhead, so the LORD of hosts will protect Jerusalem" (Isa. 31:5). Matthew 23:37 and Luke 13:34 attribute to Jesus the statement: "How often have I desired to gather your children together as a hen gathers her brood under her wings . . ." The Gospels owe this image to Israel's Scriptures.

In a supersessionist way of thinking, Christian commentators have too often emphasized the "if" in the statement "if you obey my voice and keep my covenant, you shall be my treasured possession." They stressed that Israel's covenant with God was conditional and that Israel lost the covenant through disobedience. We reject this reading as tendentious and ideologically motivated by a desire to assert that Christians displace Jews in the covenant. Such a reading is works-righteous, turning the graciously given covenant into a condition apart from which God cannot be gracious.

Instead we note that Exodus all along assumes that Israel is in covenant with God. Israel inherits the promises given to the ancestors (Exod. 3:15–17; 6:4) and God remembers this covenant (Exod. 2:24; 6:4–5) originally made with Abraham and his descendants, the Israelites (Gen. 17:17). The covenant at Sinai is a second and more detailed covenant within the prior and utterly gracious covenant.

The point of the "if" is not that Israel might lose the covenant. The question is if Israel will carry out its vocation in the covenant: to be a witness to the Gentiles and to be YHWH's people by following the way of life about to be given to them. They can only follow it if they "hear," *shema*, understand it. To "hear" God's voice *is* to obey God. The "if" also has to do with the reality that Israel must do this freely—it must "choose" life and blessing and not death and curse (Deut. 30:19).

Proper 7 [12]/Year A

Genesis 21:8–21+ (Semicontinuous)

For comments on this passage, please see Proper 6/Year A.

Jeremiah 20:7–13 (Paired)*

Prior to the exile, the young Jeremiah prophesied to Judah that God would deliver the land and its people into the hands of Babylonian invaders because the community had turned to idolatry, wicked alliances, and injustice (see Fourth Sunday after the Epiphany/Year C). Several times Jeremiah says that his prophecy has caused some people in the community to turn against him, persecute him, and even to plot his death (Proper 20/Year B).

The priests, prophets, and civil officials of Jeremiah's day were complicit in the idolatry and these other behaviors, and Jeremiah confronted them with a stinging word of judgment. In Jeremiah 20:1–2, a priest named Pashur placed the prophet in stocks to express his displeasure at Jeremiah's sermon. Jeremiah countered, saying that God named Pashur "Terror-all-around" (20:3). God then solemnly said that God would give Judah to Babylon, and Pashur and his cohort would go into captivity (20:4–6).

The text for today is Jeremiah's lament over what happened to him in the exercise of his prophetic ministry. Some scholars think that Jeremiah 20:7 is much stronger in Hebrew than in English with the word "entice" meaning something more like "deceive" or "seduce" and the word "overpower" referring to rape, so that Jeremiah means that God deceived and overpowered the prophet.

Jeremiah explains his dilemma. While he cries out that *God's* violence and destruction are coming as a result of Judah's unfaithfulness, people nonetheless reproach *him*, Jeremiah (20:8). Yet, if he decides not to speak in God's name, he experiences something like an interior conflagration that wearies him as he tries to contain it, and it cannot be contained (20:9).

The people say about Jeremiah (as Jeremiah said about Pashur), "Terror is all around." They experience terror when they hear Jeremiah's preaching, and it makes them so uncomfortable they want to take revenge on the prophet (20:10). Ironically, what the people experience as terror (Jeremiah's preaching of judgment and repentance) is actually the pathway to blessing. What they experience as security (idolatry) is actually the route to destruction.

However, Jeremiah believes that God is present like "a dread warrior" and will cause Jeremiah's persecutors to stumble. Indeed, God will shame them and "their eternal dishonour will never be forgotten" (Jer. 20:11). The prophet is confident that God will do these things because God tests the heart and mind to determine who is righteous and who is not, and distributes retribution and reward accordingly (20:12). Consequently, Jeremiah praises God for saving the prophet's life (20:13).

A preacher can assure the congregation that we can be as straightforward with God as Jeremiah in voicing frustrations with our ministries and with God. In the midst of such honesty, the prophet continued to be faithful and discovered, in the process, a sustaining Presence.

This text is paired with Matthew 10:24–39 which is part of Matthew's pastoral encouragement to the community to endure in their witness much as Jeremiah did. The preacher might take a similar tack.

Proper 8 [13]/Year A

Genesis 22:1–14+ (Semicontinuous)

The reading for today is sometimes called the "akedah" from the Hebrew word *akad*, which means "to bind," as in "the binding of Isaac." The emphasis, however, is less on the binding of Isaac and is more on the mutual faithfulness of Abraham and God. The reading should be 22:1–19, for verses 17–19 state the purpose of the story in its context in Genesis. The narrator gives no information about the emotional or psychological states of the characters, but the stark telling of the story evokes feeling in the listener. An underlying theme is to deny that human sacrifice has a place in Israel.

The narrator says simply that God "tested" (*nasab*) Abraham (Gen. 22:1). Almost all commentators point out that while God and the reader are aware that this event is a test, Abraham is not. The horrific divine command is stated in verse 2. If Abraham carries out the directive to make Isaac a burnt offering, then the promises, repeatedly affirmed in chapters 12, 17, and 18, are rendered void because Sarah and Abraham would no longer have an heir.

With haunting economy of language, the text describes Abraham, Isaac, and the traveling party preparing for the journey and making their way to the place God had shown them (Gen. 22:3–6). When they neared the place of sacrifice, Isaac realized that they had no lamb (v. 7). Abraham announced solemnly that God would provide.

Abraham was faithful in building the altar, laying the wood, binding Isaac, and raising the knife, but he says nothing. "The intensity of the anguish is beyond the ability of words to express."[11]

The angel interrupts the action, "Abraham, Abraham." The test is over. God knows that Abraham is faithful (Gen. 22:11–12). As Abraham had said in verse 8, God provided (Gen. 22:13). Yet, as J. Gerald Janzen has written with insight. "Isaac *has* been truly sacrificed—truly given up and given over to God. The life [Isaac] will go on to live is truly God's, and Abraham no longer has any claim on it."[12] By naming the place, Abraham also made explicit a penultimate meaning of the story, "The Lord will Provide."

The ultimate point of the story is in verses 16–18, as God reaffirmed the promise to bless the children of Sarah and Abraham and through them to bless other human families (as was promised in Gen. 12:1–3). God reinforces the reader's confidence in God's promise-keeping will and power by swearing an oath.

This heartrending story has significant pastoral purpose: to encourage later generations to remain faithful even in the face of circumstances that seem to deny the promises of God. The narrator wants readers (especially the exiles) to believe that the God who provided the ram can also provide for them.

At the same time, the story raises a searching theological issue. It is one thing to say that the *story* as story has for listeners the pastoral function just stated. It is another to think that God *actively* creates circumstances to *test* individuals and communities. Even if God has the power to do so, it would hardly express unconditional love if God *creates* circumstances of pain and suffering, even in the name of helping those suffering develop a deeper faith. From a theological point of view, we believe that while difficult circumstances sometimes challenge faithfulness, the circumstances result from the brokenness of the world and not from divine personal directive. Within such circumstances God remains faithful so that people can discover, as did Abraham, the divine trustworthiness, and can emerge more confident in their own faithfulness.

New Testament writers use the story of the binding of Isaac in three ways: (1) to call attention to the event as a demonstration of God's trustworthiness to keep the promise to Sarah and Abraham (e.g., Gal. 3:6–8; cf. Luke 1:55, 73–74; Acts 3:25; Heb. 6:13–14); (2) to present Abraham as a model of human faithfulness (e.g., Heb. 11:17–19; James 2:18–25); (3) to help readers understand the depth to which God went in giving up Jesus to death as a part of the movement from the old, broken age into the coming eschatological world (Rom. 8:31–32).[13]

Jeremiah 28:5–9 (Paired)*

After Babylon had conquered and exiled many leaders (see Propers 16–20/Year C), those who remained in Judah disagreed about how to respond to Babylon. Some wanted to revolt against the conquering nation from the east, but Jeremiah believed that path would lead to national annihilation and that God wanted Judah to remain a viable entity by submitting to Babylon. To demonstrate this message God told Jeremiah to wear a yoke representing submission. Jeremiah was not counseling selling out to Babylon but recognizing that God is absolute sovereign of history and had temporarily given Judah to Babylon (Jer. 27:1–7). The people did not need to try to liberate themselves but should wait for God to act in their behalf. Jeremiah delivered this message to the monarch and priests with a warning not to listen to the words of prophets who were counseling revolt (27:8–22).

Hananiah, a false prophet, opposed Jeremiah in the Temple, claiming to have a message from God that God had broken the yoke of Babylon and within two years would return to Jerusalem from Babylon all the treasures from the Temple and exiles (Jer. 28:1–4).

Although Jeremiah wished that Hananiah was right (Jer. 28:5–6), two things persuaded him that Hananiah was wrong. First, the true prophets focus mainly on judgment by prophesying war, famine, and pestilence. One work of the prophet is to help the congregation recognize points at which it is failing to live up to the covenant and to announce potential punishment as a way of motivating the community to repent or to understand why judgment has fallen upon them (28:7–8). Second, as in Deuteronomy 18:15–20, the word of a true prophet, whether a word of judgment or salvation, comes true (Jer. 28:9). The latter criterion worked fairly quickly in Jeremiah's favor. After a face-off, Jeremiah predicted that Hananiah would die "within this year," and sure enough, "in the seventh month, Hananiah died" (28:12–16).

In retrospect, it is easy to villainize Hananiah and lionize Jeremiah. However, had today's congregation been in the Temple, they might have had difficulty deciding which message to believe. We consider criteria for distinguishing true and false prophets in Proper 15/Year C.

The calling of the prophet was to assess the relationship of the behavior of the community to God's purposes revealed in the covenant, and to speak a word of challenge or judgment when the community was falling short of those purposes. The prophet could speak a word of salvation when the community doubted that God would ultimately fulfill the promises that God had made to Sarah and Abraham. Although Jeremiah is right that, on balance, the classical prophets spoke more of judgment than of salvation, there are times when a community's failure is not moral turpitude but failure to believe the promises of God. The prophet speaks a word of hope to the latter community.

The text from Jeremiah is paired with Matthew 10:40–42. The context of the latter text is conflict between the followers of Jesus and those who oppose the idea that Jesus and the disciples are harbingers of the divine realm (Matt. 10:16–39). Matthew 10:40–42 shifts focus to those who welcome followers of Jesus (especially missionaries). Those who welcome prophets receive a prophet's reward. The prophets here are community members who receive and transmit messages from the risen Jesus concerning how to live from the perspective of the realm of God. The prophet's reward is to live in that realm.

Proper 9 [14]/Year A

Genesis 24:34–38, 42–49, 58–67+ (Semicontinuous)

As Genesis 24 opens, the promise to Sarah and Abraham is imperiled because Isaac, the only heir, does not have a spouse. Abraham sent a servant to Canaan to find a spouse for Isaac (but not a Canaanite spouse) (Gen. 24:1–9; cf. Deut. 7:1–6; Josh. 23:12–13).

With an angel for providential guidance, the servant went to Canaan with a bride price as well as gifts, and waited at a well. The woman who would give a specific response to the servant's request for water would be not only the spouse but a means whereby God showed steadfast love (*hesed*) to Abraham (Gen. 24:12, 14). J. Gerald Janzen points out that a meeting at a well is often a type-scene of promise and generativity (e.g., Rachel and Jacob, Zipporah and Moses, the Samaritan woman and Jesus).[14] Rebekah appeared at the well and exhibited hospitality toward the servant similar to that of Sarah and Abraham toward the visitors at Mamre (Proper 6/Year A), reminding the reader of the theological potential of welcoming strangers, and revealing Rebekah to be made from the same stuff as the ancestral couple (Gen. 24:10–33).

The servant emphasized Abraham's impressive holdings while interpreting the events that led to the servant seeking Rebekah for Isaac (Gen. 24:34–49).When the brother (Laban) and father (Bethuel) agreed that God made the arrangement, the servant gave impressive gifts beyond the bride price (24:50–54).

Nevertheless, when the servant was ready to return with Rebekah to Isaac, her family wanted her to remain a few days. When asked her preference, Rebekah said immediately "I will [go]" (Gen. 24:58), exhibiting the spirit of Sarah and Abraham, who responded similarly to God's invitation in Genesis 12:1–3. As the story of Rebekah unfolds, readers recognize that God works through women as active participants in keeping the promise. Indeed, in 24:60, a blessing is pronounced over Rebekah that she will be the mother of myriads who will gain possession of land, the same promise given to Sarah and Abraham in Genesis 22:17b. Her actions are part of the way God keeps the promise.

A compelling dimension in the saga told in Genesis 12–50 is that the promise God made to Sarah and Abraham (Second Sunday in Lent/Years A, B, and C) did not come to complete fulfillment in one easy moment but encountered multiple challenges over generations. Consequently, readers recognize that the promises of God may be fulfilled after periods of time during which the readers need to be faithful and patient.

Janzen notes further that the notion of divine "steadfast love and faithfulness," so important in the life of Israel (e.g., Exod. 34:6) and to Paul in Romans 9–11, is given formative expression in Genesis 24. Here we see that "the problem of existence" turns not just on human sin and divine forgiveness but "equally—if not more—on the question of divine faithfulness to a needy world."[15]

Rebekah and Isaac are only once jointly cited in the New Testament (Rom. 9:6–10; Isaac only, Gal. 4:28). Isaac is mentioned several times: as part of the genealogy of Jesus (Matt. 1:2; Luke 3:34); as a central figure in the eschatological realm of God (Luke 13:38), even as one of the hosts of the eschatological banquet (e.g., Matt. 8:11), and as one whose life verifies God as life-giver and promise-keeper (Matt. 22:32; Mark 12:26; Luke 20:37; Acts 3:13; 7:8; 7:32; Heb. 11:17–18). Hebrews refers to the story of Isaac (and Jacob) living with their parents in tents in the land of promise as an example of faith (11:9; cf. v. 20).

Zechariah 9:9–12 (Paired)*

A contemporary of Haggai (Proper 27/Year C), the prophet Zechariah spoke to the same situation. Those who returned from exile were a small community of destitute people suffering from hunger and drought. "You have sown much, and harvested little; you eat, but you never have enough . . . and you that earn wages earn wages to put them into a bag with holes" (Hag. 1:6). "The heavens above you have withheld the dew, and the earth has withheld its produce" (Hag. 1:10).

Zechariah is concerned that the people no longer trust and hope in God. Their faith has been taxed to the limit and threatens to fade away. Leading up to today's reading are eight visions of hope and promise. Zion's cities "shall again overflow with prosperity; the LORD will again comfort Zion and again choose Jerusalem" (1:17). God will "strike down the horns of the nations" that assault Zion (1:21). God will be a protective wall of fire around Zion (2:5) and remove the guilt from Judah (2:9). All the Gentiles will join with the people of God; they "shall join themselves to the LORD on that day, and shall be my people; and I will dwell in your midst" (2:11; see 8:20–23).

In today's reading Zechariah tells another vision of hope: "Rejoice greatly, O daughter Zion! Shout aloud, O daughter Jerusalem! Lo, your king comes to you; triumphant and victorious is he, humble and riding on a donkey" (9:9). Because kings were anointed in Israel, this passage speaks of a messianic (anointed) king. The triumph is over the enemies of Judah who have frequently marauded it, but it is YHWH who has achieved this triumph over Damascus, Tyre, Sidon, Ashkelon, Gaza, and Ekron (9:1–8). The coming king is triumphant because God has won the victory.

The messianic king is "humble," signified by the fact that he will ride on a donkey, not a warhorse, against which prophets frequently inveighed. Isaiah regarded Israel's warhorses as symbols that it had "forsaken the ways" of God: "their land is filled with horses, and there is no end to their chariots" (2:6, 7). "Alas for those who . . . trust in chariots because they are many and in horsemen because they are very strong" (Isa. 31:1). It is also the case, however, that the king will be humble because he will know that it is God's glory that dwells in the midst of Israel (Zech. 2:11).

This anointed king will be an actual ruler who brings peace to Israel and the entire world. "He will cut off the chariot from Ephraim and the war horse from Jerusalem; and the battle bow shall be cut off, and he shall command peace to the nations; his dominion shall be from sea to sea, and from the River to the ends of the earth" (9:10). Christians often say that Jews were expecting a military messiah, but here Zechariah speaks of an anointed one who comes in peace after God has been victorious over all of Israel's enemies and who, in turn, brings peace to Judah and the nations from sea to sea. He will eliminate the warhorse and bring about disarmament "to the ends of the earth."

The reading ends on a note of hope: the Lord will set Judah free from what has been its prison; they will return to their "stronghold" as "prisoners of hope" and God will restore everything to them "double" (vv. 11–12).

The lectionary pairs this reading with Matthew 11:16–19, 25–30, for reasons that are unclear. It would be a better reading for Palm Sunday, with which it has an obvious fit. There were two "triumphal" entries into Jerusalem at Passover in the year 30. The other was Pilate's from Caesarea Maritima, down the coast and up to Jerusalem from the west, mounted on his warhorse at the head of the Tenth Legion. Jesus came from Galilee to Jericho and up to Jerusalem from the east, to the Mount of Olives and across the Kidron Valley riding on a donkey, a parody of Pilate's military entrance.

Proper 10 [15]/Year A

Genesis 25:19–34+ (Semicontinuous)

Many stories in Genesis are etiologies, stories that explain origins. Today's lection interprets how Jacob took precedence over Esau, while explaining the relationship of Israel and the Edomites. The text also reinforces the idea of God's faithfulness in keeping the promise while negatively interpreting Edomite culture.

Although Rebekah had been told that she would be the mother of "thousands of myriads" (Gen. 24:60), she remained barren. In response to Isaac's prayer, God caused Rebekah to conceive. The story thus speaks hope to all who are in situations of barrenness.

In antiquity, the law of primogeniture assumed that the firstborn received a greater share of inheritance and social power than others (the birthright). Rebekah's fetuses struggled in the womb, perhaps over who would be born

first. The conflict was so intense that Rebekah expressed regret at the preg-
nancy (Gen. 25:22). God stated that Rebekah carried not only two infants
but two nations, and, furthermore, by divine decree, the law of primogeniture was reversed in this case: the elder Esau would serve the younger Jacob
(Gen. 25:23).[16] Israel and Edom are thus blood siblings and their tensions
are sibling rivalry. In the background, God seeks to bless both.

The names of the twins reveal their character. The first to emerge from
the womb "came out red" with a hairy body. The word red (*'admoni*) is a
play on the word Edom (meaning red or ruddy) and probably refers to
ruddy skin. The hairy quality anticipates Genesis 27:11–24. In some circles in antiquity, excessive body hair was regarded as crude, a detail that
makes a social comment on Edomites (Gen. 25:25).[17] The younger comes
from the womb holding to Esau's heel, which the narrator associates with
the name Jacob to mean that the younger twin sought to supplant the
older. The picture of Jacob as supplanter and struggler become very
important in Genesis 26–32.

Esau was a hunter and Jacob a farmer (Gen. 25:27–28). Given the biblical editors' aversion to killing (Gen. 1:26–28; 9:3–4), this is an implicit theological comment not only on the twins but on the communities descended
from them. The Edomites and those like them are descended from a people with an inclination to violence, whereas Israel comes from stock that, at
its best, lives in covenant with other elements of creation. However, the
notion of covenant is not idealized, as we see in the next verses.

In Genesis 25:29–34 the narrator exposes both twins as living short of
divine purposes. Jacob was cooking a stew when a famished Esau appeared.
Esau saw the stew simply as "red stuff," a play on "Edom" (vv. 29–30), evidently not knowing, as a person living in community should, that the
dish was lentil stew (v. 34). He was so undisciplined that he gave up his
birthright to satisfy his immediate hunger. Jacob lived out the interpretation given him in 25:26 by seizing Esau's weakened state to supplant the
older twin. This pattern of behavior characterizes Jacob in the next chapters, and presages aspects of Israel's later life when the community practices other forms of injustice.

The biblical redactors use these associations to explain the irascible
behavior of the Edomites in later centuries (e.g., Isa. 11:10–16; 34:1–17;
Jer. 49:7–22; Ezek. 35:1–15; Amos 1:6–11; 2:1; Obad. 1–21; Mal. 1:2–4).
However, some biblical writers preserve positive pictures of the Edomites.
For example, the characters in the book of Job are Edomites (assuming
Uz was in Edom), and the Deuteronomic theologians welcome Edomites
(Deut. 23:8).

This text asks today's congregations haunting questions. How are we, like Esau, willing to sell our birthrights to satisfy immediate hungers? How do we, like Jacob, exploit others, even taking from them means of blessing (such as the birthright)?

Paul regarded the birth of Esau and Jacob as evidence of God's desire (and power), as an act of grace (Rom. 9:11), to bless both Gentile and Jewish worlds (Rom. 9:10–13). Further, in Romans 9:12 Paul quotes Genesis 25:23 to show that the Jewish people (the younger) play a special role in God's work in comparison to the Gentiles (the elder), and in Romans 9:13, Paul stresses that God chose Jacob (the Jewish community) as the means of blessing. The children of Esau should, therefore, honor the children of Jacob (cf. 11:20; 12:16–17). Both Matthew and Luke place Jacob in the genealogy of Jesus (Matt. 1:2; Luke 3:34).

Isaiah 55:10–13 (Paired)*

Although the lectionary lists today's reading as Isaiah 55:10–13, we treat all of chapter 55 because it is one literary unit as well as the conclusion to Second Isaiah. In this remarkable chapter in which many central motifs of Second Isaiah appear, the reading opens (vv. 1–2) with an extraordinary invitation to "delight . . . in rich food," "wine and milk without money and without price." It is extraordinary, addressed to "you that have no money." The only condition is that those invited must be the destitute, the hungry and the scruffy of society. Christians will note the echo of this passage in the Magnificat: "he has filled the hungry with good things, and sent the rich away empty" (Luke 1:53). In Isaiah this banquet is related to the new Temple to be built in Jerusalem when, typically, a banquet would be held. It later becomes the eschatological banquet celebrated upon the arrival of God's realm of compassionate justice. It is a free banquet, open to those who have no money and to all willing to sit at the same table with the poor.

Verses 3–5 are a promise, introduced with the command: "Incline your ear . . . to me" (*shema*, hear). "I will make with you an everlasting covenant, my steadfast, sure love for David." Christians in their displacement mode have claimed that the covenant with Israel was intended to be temporary. But "everlasting" does not mean "temporary." There is a transformation of the Davidic covenant here. Now God says of David "I made him a witness to the peoples . . . nations that do not know you shall run to you" (vv. 4–5).

In spite of the sins of Israel's kings in leading the people into injustice, resulting in the exile, the promises of the covenant with David, of blessing, well-being, peace, economic sufficiency for all, and compassion to the vulnerable, were indispensable to God and to Israel. Second Isaiah has been at pains to say that everything had happened according to God's intent, that Israel's ignoring of justice could not be ignored by God, and that God had remained faithful to Israel. Now this everlasting covenant is broadened to make explicit its intent, that the children of Abraham be a blessing to the Gentiles. All those "nations that do not know you" shall be included, and the light to the nations will be composed of all of God's faithful. Paul will be an apostle to these Gentiles (Gal. 2:2).

Verses 6–9 call the people to "seek the LORD while he may be found, call upon him while he is near" (v. 6). Just as the kingdom or reign of God "has come near to you" (Luke 10:9), the presence of God is available to people provided that they turn to God. The problem Israel faced was of its own making. Returning to God is always a possibility; the gates of prayer are always open. It takes resilience of character in any relationship to face the fact that the problem is with us, the responsibility on our side of the relationship. But, says God, "my thoughts are not your thoughts, nor are your ways my ways" (v. 8). Unlike us, God "will abundantly pardon" (v. 7).

Verses 10–11 beautifully articulate God's redeeming grace. God's word is like "the rain and the snow [that] come down from heaven . . . making it bring forth and sprout" (v. 10). We human beings do not bring rain and snow into being; they come down from heaven. Similarly, God's word comes from God's mouth and it "shall accomplish that which I purpose" (v. 11). It is a free gift, given out of God's unfathomable love for Israel.

Verses 12–13 proclaim the joyous return of the people to Jerusalem: "you shall go out [from Babylon] in joy, and be led back in peace" (v. 12). All nature will participate in the return and its joy: "the mountains and the hills . . . shall burst into song, and all the trees of the field shall clap their hands" (v. 12). Living in harmony with all living things was a reality in Eden, a hope for Isaiah, who proclaimed a time "when they would not hurt or destroy on all my holy mountain" (11:9), and a promise for Second Isaiah, for whom all of creation will return to a state of well-being in the event of redemption.

Isaiah 55 is an ever-pertinent word at Easter and on all the other occasions when this text is assigned by the lectionary.

Proper 11 [16]/Year A

Genesis 28:10–19a+ (Semicontinuous)

As Jacob came down the birth canal after Esau, he gripped Esau's heel so as to supplant his twin, thus, according to the narrator's etymology, explaining the name "Jacob" as "one who supplants" (Gen. 25:26; Proper

10/Year A). From that moment on, the events of Jacob's life were consistent with the meaning of his name: he repeatedly deceived and supplanted. In today's text, he is fleeing Esau. With no safe place to spend the night, he placed a stone near his head and lay down (Gen. 28:11). While Christians often think that Jacob used the stone for a pillow (not very comfortable!), more likely he placed it beside his head so as to provide protection in case a thief should try to whack Jacob's head with a stick in the night.

While asleep, Jacob dreamed. Although the NRSV describes the content of his dream as a "ladder," it was actually a ramp that extended from earth to heaven. Angels, a part of the retinue of heaven, were ascending and descending (Gen. 28:12). God came down the ramp and repeated to Jacob the same promise that God had made to Sarah and Abraham and to Rebekah and Isaac—they would have many descendants. God emphasized that the divine presence will not leave Jacob (Gen. 28:13–15; cf. Second Sunday in Lent/Years A, B, and C, and Proper 6/Year A).

Jacob awoke and interpreted the significance of what had happened: God had been with Jacob on the journey, yet Jacob "did not know it" (Gen. 28:16). Overcome, Jacob declared that spot to be "the house of God" and "the gate of heaven," that is, points at which the community could come into contact with the divine (Gen. 28:17). By creating a pillar and placing oil on it, and naming it Bethel (*beth* = house; *el* = God; "house of God"), Jacob marked the place as one where people could encounter God. The pillar helped Jacob and others remember the divine promise and presence.

The story of Jacob foreshadows aspects of the postexilic community that gave this story the form it has now. They understood themselves as somewhat like Jacob: having violated the covenant, they left their homeland and, so to speak, paid the price of exile for the injustice and idolatry that brought about national collapse. Jacob did not seek this dream, nor did his conduct merit it. Rather, at the very moment that Jacob was fleeing his home to pay the price for deception and supplanting, God gave him the dream as an assurance. The promise that God made to Jacob was still in force for the exiles, and, indeed, for all of Jacob's descendants.

A preacher might explore ways that, figuratively, God opens a ramp from earth to heaven in order to reassure the congregation when, like Jacob, their world is disrupted, especially when it is disrupted by Jacob-like deception and supplanting. What stones have previous generations set up that have become Bethels for us?

The unvarnished way in which the Bible presents so many of its main characters is one reason for taking it seriously. Characters like Jacob are not placed on a pedestal and held up as impossible ideals but are presented in their raw humanity. We can identify with them and can believe that the God who worked through them can also work with us.

The New Testament seldom overtly refers to this story. The writer of the Fourth Gospel has Jesus say, "You will see heaven opened and the angels of God ascending and descending upon the One from Heaven" [NRSV: "Son of Man"] (John 1:51). In Hebrews 13:5, the author admonishes the congregation not to love money and to be content with what they have because God said that God would never leave or forsake them (Gen. 28:15). Paul alludes to the promise of Genesis 28:14 in Galatians 3:8.

Wisdom of Solomon 12:13, 16–19 (Paired)*

On Proper 8/Year B we discuss the historical circumstance and overall purpose of the Wisdom of Solomon. The reading for today offers a rationale for the conquest of Canaan by the Israelites. It is part of a larger retelling of significant aspects of the story of Israel to show that just as wisdom (often personified as a woman) accompanied and guided the community through many decisive events of its past, so wisdom would guide the community of the Wisdom of Solomon through the difficult times in which it lived.

The author recounts the sins of the Canaanites. These include sorcery, unholy rites, slaughter of children, feasting on human flesh and blood, and parents murdering children, sins for which God could have destroyed all the people in the land (Wis. 12:3–7). God chose to judge them "little by little," however, so that seeing the judgment upon them they would have opportunity to repent (12:8–11).

Wisdom 12:12 asks, who can question or resist God's judgment? No one can accuse God of unfairly destroying them, since they violated God's requirements. No one of sober mind can plead as an advocate of the unrighteous before God the Judge (12:13) for God is fair and just toward all (12:14). Monarchs cannot say that God punishes unfairly, for God only condemns those who deserve punishment (12:15). God will in complete righteousness spare those who do not deserve annihilation (12:16). Though God has the power to do whatever God wants, God's mildness and forbearance keep God's exercise of condemnation in check. Indeed, that gives the human family opportunity to repent.

The only real point of connection between this passage and Matthew 13:24–30, 36–44, is that each portrays God as righteous judge of the world. Where the Wisdom of Solomon asserts that God judges "with mildness" and governs with "great forbearance," the parable concludes that God throws all evildoers "into the furnace of fire, where there will be weeping and gnashing of teeth." Wisdom repeatedly emphasizes that God will punish the wicked (e.g., 3:10–13; 4:20–5:23; 11:15–12:2; 12:23–27), but the punishment is much less severe than being cast into a furnace of fire. In this respect, the Wisdom of Solomon portrays God as a little more gracious than does the Gospel of Matthew.

Isaiah 44:6–8 (Alternate) (Paired)*

Second Isaiah spoke to the people in Babylon surrounded by the local gods and their worshipers. Like us, they lived in an idolatrous culture. What made matters worse was that the gods of Babylon appeared to be quite successful in the eyes of many members of the exilic community. It was widely assumed that a deity's majesty rose and fell with the success or failure of that deity's city-state. This was not the case with YHWH, who could use other nations and their armies to bring about judgment on YHWH's own people, but it was nonetheless a widely shared assumption in the ancient world.

In this context, Marduk appeared to a defeated people as powerful indeed, while YHWH looked like a deity defeated at the hands of Babylon. These displaced Jerusalemites would have been regularly exposed to celebrations of Marduk's destruction of Jerusalem and the Temple. Marduk's temples were magnificent; YHWH's lay in ruins. The problem facing Isaiah was that Marduk-worship seemed to "work" while bitter doubt could easily beset those who had put their reliance on YHWH. Hence, today's reading is a proclamation that "there is no god besides" YHWH (v. 8) followed by a lengthy argument against idolatry; verses 9–20 satirize idols and idol manufacturing.

Verses 6–8 and 21–23 frame this section of Isaiah. The Lord is creator and redeemer of Israel, the first and the last, the rock (the salvation) of Israel; God formed Israel as God's servant, swept away Israel's sins and redeemed Israel. God is the God of creation and redemption who will be praised by the heavens and the forests and who will be glorified in Israel.

Verses 9–19 describe the process of making idols and then worshiping them, lampooning the idea of giving ultimate devotion to things that we have made—those who do this do not have the sense to see that "this thing in my right hand [is] a fraud" (v. 20).

Two issues arise for today's church from this passage. One is posed by verses 9–20. Statues, images, stained-glass windows, Torah scrolls, Bibles, Communion ware—all are created by human hands or technological processes of manufacture. This does not make them "frauds." All religions make use of finite realities to point to the divine and ultimate. We cannot verify that members of another religion necessarily confuse their symbols with that which they symbolize. Any uncomprehending outsider could ignorantly think another religion worshiped its symbols.

We know that idolatry is real, not because other people are guilty of it, but because in our hearts we know that we are. We know that we are more committed to storing up treasures on earth than to storing up treasure with God. Every religious tradition is an ambiguous mix of faithfulness and idolatry, as is every religious life. Claims of idolatry are not a helpful way to describe the difference between one religious tradition and another. Christians have idolized many things, most notably the Bible. Any religious tradition can make frauds of its symbols.

The other issue is how we should understand the relation between God and "the gods." Second Isaiah is not saying that our insights, discernments, concepts, and metaphors for God are on target, that only we know God, and that all people who differ commit idolatry. The prophetic critique against idolatry is for the most part directed against the people Israel itself. Christian readers should see the prophetic critique of idolatry directed primarily at themselves, not some alienated "other" or scapegoat.

YHWH is the One who will be who YHWH will be (Exod. 3:14). Hence, all our metaphors, concepts, and models are fallible. The only knowledge of YHWH that is remotely adequate is that made evident in deeds of loving-kindness and kindhearted justice for all people. All the rest is hot air.

Matthew's parable of the wheat and the weeds urges his community not to impatiently identify and uproot sinners; be patient and let the Lord sort it out. At the deepest level, Matthew could be read as arguing that it borders on idolatry to readily identify the sinners among us. The greatest sinner most of us will ever see is in the mirror.

Proper 12 [17]/Year A

Genesis 29:15–28+ (Semicontinuous)

In Genesis 29:1, Jacob arrives in the land of Laban. There are similarities and differences between the stories of Isaac uniting with Rebekah and of Jacob's marriages. Among the ironic differences: whereas Isaac's envoy went with a vast bride price, Jacob, who had stolen Esau's birthright and blessing, arrived with nothing. Jacob suffered the consequences of the injustice he perpetrated upon Esau.

At a well—a symbol of generativity and a place where couples met one another for the first time (Proper 9/Year A)—the shepherdess Rachel appeared. Women were seldom shepherdesses in those days, so we realize that she exercised unusual agency, like many other women in Genesis. Rebekah, for instance, acts as decisively as Abraham in responding to the possibility of going to the promised land (Proper 9/Year A). When Rachel realizes that the newcomer is her cousin, she tells her brother Laban, who receives Jacob (Gen. 29:9–14).

Commentators are divided on the meaning of Laban's questions in Genesis 29:15. Does Laban express genuine concern for Jacob? Or does he fake concern with an eye toward taking advantage of Jacob's remarkable strength and skill (Gen. 29:10)? Or does Laban degrade Jacob to the place of a hired laborer? Regardless of the interpretation of that issue, it is soon clear that Jacob pays the price for the deception that he visited on Esau and Isaac.

The Bible seldom mentions romantic love between women and men, and previously has only spoken of such love between Isaac and Rebekah (Gen. 24:67). Thus the reader recognizes the depth of feeling Jacob has for Rachel when the text says simply, "Jacob loved Rachel" (Gen. 29:18; cf. v. 20). Jacob, not having a bride price, agreed to serve seven years for Rachel. Here is another irony: Jacob, who was accustomed to other people serving him, agreed to *serve* for Rachel.

At the end of seven years, a wedding occurred. Jacob spent the night with the bride and in the morning was dumbfounded to find "it was Leah" (Gen. 29:25), Rachel's older sister. While contemporary folk may not undersand how Jacob could have made this mistake, the narrator either assumed that ancient people would be familiar with how such a thing could happen (the bride wore a veil; it was night) or was not concerned about such details. The point is that Jacob has been duped in the way that he duped Esau and Isaac.

When Jacob protested, Laban noted that in Haran the older daughter was married prior to the younger. Jacob, the younger brother, has now been supplanted by custom. Jacob then worked another seven years for Rachel.

Leah suffered an indignity when Jacob expressed a preference for Rachel, and the text ends on the plaintive note that Jacob "loved Rachel more than Leah" (Gen. 29:30). Ironically, Rachel was initially barren while Leah gave birth to Levi and Judah (from whom descended the priests and the Davidic line) as well as Reuben, Simeon, Issachar, Zebulun, and Dinah, and Leah's maid bore Gad and Asher. Rachel's maid gave birth to Dan and Naphtali, and eventually Rachel herself bore Joseph and Benjamin.

In an era when deception is commonplace in business and politics, a preacher could use the story of Jacob to indicate the consequences of deception. Even if deceivers are not personally exposed, the practice of deception undermines community. In a culture that celebrates immediate gratification, Jacob's commitment to serve fourteen years for Rachel is a model of how to respond to disappointment and delay, and how to commit long-term to participating with God in activities of blessing. The text continues to demonstrate that God can work with all manner of circumstances (including dishonesty) to help keep the divine promise. Indeed, while Jacob was disappointed to find himself married to Leah, she was responsible for ten of Jacob's twelve children, who became the twelve tribes. Could God work with circumstances that seem disappointing to the congregation in order to effect blessing?

As far as we know, the writers of the New Testament neither cite this passage nor allude to it.

1 Kings 3:5–12 (Paired)*

For commentary on this passage, please see Proper 15/Year B.

Proper 13 [18]/Year A

Genesis 32:22–31+ (Semicontinuous)

People in ancient times believed that a name often indicated a person's character or purpose. At birth Jacob was given a name that described his life through the middle years: one who (through deception) supplants others. In today's lection, Jacob received a new name that signals both an aspect of this identity as well as that of the people Israel.

After marrying Leah and Rachel (Proper 12/Year A), Jacob continued to behave in ways consistent with his name by fleecing Laban out of Laban's best sheep (Gen. 30:25–43). The resulting confrontation contains an ironic and humorous dimension as the deceivers made mutual accusations (31:1–42). They covenanted not to harm one another, and marked it with a pillar, Mizpah ("watchpost"), praying "The LORD watch between you and me, when we are absent one from the other" (31:48–50). Christians often overlook the fact that this prayer calls for God to see that Jacob will not mistreat Laban's people and that Jacob and Laban not cheat one another (31:51–32:2).

Jacob's relationship with Esau was still unresolved and, hence, inconsistent with God's purpose that people live in community. According to ancient Near Eastern custom, a thief should make restitution. While seeking to do so, Jacob learned that Esau was coming, which aroused Jacob's fear. In an irony, Jacob instructs messengers to tell Esau that Jacob is Esau's servant (Gen. 32:3–21).

The night before Jacob was to meet Esau, Jacob sent the traveling party across the Jabbok and slept alone (Gen. 31:22–24a). The Jabbok is a small stream feeding into the Jordan about halfway between the Sea of Galilee and the Dead Sea. Jacob faced reunion with a potentially violent Esau; on this reunion hung the future of Jacob and the blessing of the nations. Esau could destroy Jacob and his family.

In the night, a figure wrestled with Jacob until almost daylight. Initially neither Jacob nor the reader knew the identity of this intruder. A thief? Esau? A water spirit? The struggle was intense, and the newcomer could not wrestle Jacob into submission (32:24b–36).

The key moment in the narrative occurs in verse 28. God changes Jacob's name to Israel, which means "one who struggles with God." This passage interprets the story of Israel as a community struggling similarly with God. As the struggle closed, God blessed Jacob (v. 29). However, he is marked by this encounter: he limped because of a blow to the hip (v. 31).

In the next episode the assurance communicated in 32:22–32 is fully seen. Jacob had struggled to reunite with Esau, and they are reconciled (Gen. 33:1–17). The struggle for community, fearful as it is, brings blessing.

This story is a narrative foreshadowing of the ways in which Israel struggled with God as a part of the mission of being a conduit to the blessing of the nations. The text does not romanticize struggle in general but calls our attention to struggle in behalf of discerning and following God's purposes. The passage is an assurance. In the face of overwhelming odds (Esau, the powerful stranger) God is present and will work inexhaustibly to provide opportunities for God's purposes and blessing to prevail.

To be sure, just as Jacob walked away with a limp, Israel would sometimes suffer (and still does). The passage assures the community that even when blessing does not immediately result, God is present and doing all that God can do to bring it about. Indeed, struggle with God is not only constitutive of the identity of Israel but can become a means of grace.

Jacob did not realize immediately that he was wrestling with God. Is it too much to think the same may be true of people today? A sermon on this text could be a haunting occasion on which to help the congregation become Jacob in struggle with God regarding the present and future of the blessing of some aspect of the world.

This text is not specifically mentioned in the New Testament. However, in a broad sense, the theme of struggling with God about the pathway to blessing is an undercurrent in the New Testament. The Synoptic Gospels picture Jesus wrestling in Gethsemane with God in a way reminiscent of Jacob (e.g., Matt. 26:36–46; Mark 14:32–42; Luke 22:40). Paul struggles to explain how the reluctance of some in Israel to acknowledge the validity of the Gentile mission is eschatologically resolved (Rom. 9:1–11:36). To be Christian is to be grafted into wrestling with God regarding how blessing can come to all.

Isaiah 55:1–5* (Paired)

For comments on this passage, please see Proper 10/Year A.

Proper 14 [19]/Year A

Genesis 37:1–4, 12–28+ (Semicontinuous)

The saga of Joseph is a bridge from the ancestral stories in Genesis to the bondage and deliverance in Egypt. Throughout, God's providential hand preserves Israel and keeps alive the possibility of blessing for all.

According to Genesis 37:1–4, Jacob loved Joseph more than the other children. Jacob made Joseph a "long robe with sleeves." While an older translation is the memorable "coat of many colors" the meaning of the Hebrew is unclear but may be kin to a long-sleeved robe associated with the royal court (2 Sam. 13:18). While preachers sometimes suggest that the siblings hated Joseph because he was spoiled, the text itself does not say that. Joseph is innocent but surrounded by enemies.[18]

Joseph had two dreams in which he had authority over other family members which increases their dislike (Gen. 37:5–11). Dreams were regarded as a means whereby the Transcendent communicated with people on earth. Joseph's dreams not only anticipate subsequent events, but bespeak the active agency of divine providence through Joseph.

Jacob sent Joseph about fifty miles to Shechem (and thence to Dothan), to gather a report on whether the siblings and the flock were living in peace (Gen. 37:12–17). When the siblings saw Joseph coming, several of them plotted to kill him, and throw his body into a pit. Such pits were common in the area and were typically cut from rock at depths up to twenty (or more) feet to store water during the rainy season. The brothers try to turn the pit, which was made to sustain life, into an instrument of death. In this, they would bring a double dishonor upon themselves by first murdering and then by not giving Joseph an honorable burial (a very important practice in the ancient Near East). Their plan was to lie to Jacob, saying that a wild animal had devoured Joseph (Gen. 37:18–20).

While the siblings follow Reuben's voice of moderation by taking the robe and throwing Joseph into the pit without killing him, they still violate prescripts of family loyalty, and this violation intensifies when they eat near Jacob in the pit (Gen. 37:21–23). Given the pattern established in Genesis that sin begets consequences consistent with the sin, the reader is not surprised when the survival of the family is soon threatened. Where do congregations today encounter similar violations of community?

When a caravan of Ishmaelites came with gum, balm, and resins—materials used in Egypt for perfume, religious rites, and the care of the body—Judah negotiated with the siblings to sell Joseph instead of killing him. Ishmaelite and Midianite traders are mentioned, a fact that may reveal simply an awkward intermingling of two traditions, but that might indicate two groups of traders so that the siblings bargained to get the better price.[19] As God provided for the outcast Ishmael when Ishmael and Hagar were sent to the wilderness, God used Ishmael's descendants to provide for outcast Joseph.[20] A preacher might explore how, in our context, communities that are analogous to Ishmael can provide saving guidance for those entrenched in social power.

Twenty pieces of silver was the price of a slave. In another ironic twist, the slavery of Joseph later became a means of provision for the desperate family.

Returning to Jacob, the siblings dipped the robe in goat's blood and took it to Jacob who cried out that a wild animal had devoured Joseph who was "without doubt torn to pieces." Jacob tore his garments and mourned Joseph according to the expressive customs of the times and with heightened grief (Gen. 37:29–36).

The New Testament brings up Genesis 37 only once. Luke recalls this story (and other incidents from the narrative of Joseph) in Stephen's recitation of themes in the history of Israel that demonstrate both God's providence and the stiff-necked character of Jewish people (e.g., the jealousy of the brothers). Luke uses this reading both to justify tension between the Jewish community of Luke's day and to assert continuity between Jewish tradition and Luke's community. As God was present through Joseph, so the writer of the Third Gospel believes, God is present in Luke's community (Acts 7:9–16). According to Matthew, Joseph the husband of Mary descended from Joseph (Matt. 1:2).

1 Kings 19:9–18* (Paired)

For comments on this passage, please see Proper 7/Year C.

Proper 15 [20]/Year A

Genesis 45:1–15+ (Semicontinuous)

Since the events of the text discussed in Proper 14/Year A (Gen. 37:1–4, 12–28), two major things have happened that set the stage for today's reading. First, Joseph demonstrated remarkable administrative skills (Gen. 39:1–6a), integrity (Gen. 39:6b–23), and an ability to interpret dreams that made sense of life (Gen. 40:1–41:36). Pharaoh recognized these abilities and made him chief overseer of Egypt (41:37–45). By the time of Genesis 45, Joseph was one of the most powerful people in Egypt.

Second, Joseph had dreamed of a famine and prepared Egypt by storing grain (Gen. 41:46–57). When Jacob heard that Egypt had food, he sent all of Joseph's siblings except Benjamin to buy some (Gen. 42:1–5). Joseph recognized his family but they did not recognize him. Joseph imprisoned them, prompting them to think that they were paying the penalty for selling Joseph. Joseph kept Simeon but released the others to take abundant amounts of grain to Canaan on the promise they would return with Benjamin (42:5–25). On the trip, they discovered that the money they had used to buy the grain was in their bags and became fearful (42:26–38).

Reluctantly Jacob permitted them to take Benjamin. To their surprise, Joseph received them in his own house with a feast (43:1–34). Joseph ordered grain for them, but also he hid a silver cup in Benjamin's bag so Joseph's officers could find it and accuse the siblings of theft (44:1–13). The siblings protested their innocence, but Joseph enslaved Benjamin while releasing the others to Canaan (43:14–17). Judah pleaded for the release of Benjamin on the grounds that Jacob would go down to Sheol in unrelieved suffering over the lost Benjamin (44:18–34).

Respect for previous generations was a core value of ancient Near Eastern society. Moved by Judah's description of Jacob's plight, Joseph could no longer keep his secret but emptied the room of Egyptians and said, "I am Joseph. Is my father still alive?" The siblings were dumbfounded (Gen. 45:1–3).

Joseph recalled the wrongful act of which the siblings were guilty. They stand accused. Yet, in the next sentence, Joseph offered a pastoral word as a theological interpretation of what had happened among them. "Do not be distressed or angry with yourselves because you sold me here; for *God sent me before you to preserve life*" (Gen. 45:4–5, emphasis ours). According to the theologians who shaped this narrative, God used the events of Genesis 37–44 to prepare provisions through Joseph in Egypt for the family during the famine. Readers in later generations could thus have confidence that the sovereign God of Israel could ultimately work through any circumstance for blessing.

The reader must also conclude that God used Joseph's remarkable administrative ability to prepare Egypt itself for the famine. In this way, Joseph's service in Egypt was a life chapter fulfilling the promise to Sarah and Abraham that through their descendants, the other families of the earth would be blessed (Gen. 12:1–3).

Because the famine would last five more years, Joseph instructed the siblings to bring Jacob to the land of Goshen (an area in the eastern part of Egypt) where it would be easier for Joseph to provide for them (Gen. 45:6–15). Pharaoh is so moved by the reunion, that he sends wagons to help the family move and declares, "Give no thought to your possessions, for the best of all the land of Egypt is yours" (45:16–28).

One function of this text is to assure readers that God can work for good through any circumstance, no matter how bitter. However, the preacher needs to handle this claim with care. It is theologically inconsistent with the affirmation that God is unconditionally loving to think that God would directly *cause* events that brought such *pain* to Joseph, Jacob, and the siblings, even in the name of long-term good. Because God is omnipresent trying to help each event in life reach the highest potential available, the community can affirm that God is ever at work in events such as those in Genesis 37–44. God tries to help every event achieve as much blessing as possible. When good does result from difficulty, we can give thanks for the good without thinking that God orchestrated the difficulties.

Christians typically have negative associations with Pharaoh and Egypt. While Exodus exposes pharaonic repression, the Priestly writers who redacted Genesis with their universal theology portray Egypt and the pharaoh here as instruments of providence and recipients of blessing. This presentation cautions us against caricaturing others. It presses us to ask, "Where might Egyptians today function as agents of blessing?"

Luke alludes to this passage (and others from Genesis 37–50) in Acts 7:9–16 in ways described on Proper 14/Year A.

Isaiah 56:1, 6–8* (Paired)

The first chapter of Third Isaiah beautifully articulates themes that come to prominence in the New Testament. We deal here with the first eight verses of the chapter; in omitting verses 2–5, the lectionary drops part of the text that could help the church think about some contentious issues it faces today.

The Lord who speaks in this chapter is "the Lord GOD, who gathers the outcasts of Israel" (v. 8). The people Israel has been scattered in exile and the prophet seeks to shore up the faith of those who had returned to Jerusalem that their fellow Jews still in exile would yet be brought home. Luke, in the Pentecost story about "devout Jews from every nation under heaven" (Acts 2:5), stresses God's faithfulness to scattered Israel, prior to developing the case for the admission of Gentiles to the community of Jesus-followers.

Our passage begins with a dual emphasis on justice and salvation: "Maintain justice, and do what is right, for soon my salvation will come, and my deliverance be revealed" (v. 1). The Hebrew word translated as both "justice" and "deliverance" is God's love freely given. God frees us to respond with love of God and the neighbor, a love acted out in deeds of justice and loving-kindness. Together, they effect salvation. We are tipped off that there is something about the common life of the returned community that calls for an emphasis on doing "what is right."

Verse 2 emphasizes the importance both of keeping the *Shabbat*, "not profaning it," and avoiding evil. The temptation to conform to the religious and political norms of the surrounding societies of the Persian world was strong. This temptation remained after the return and brought with it the danger that the witness to YHWH's kindhearted justice might be altogether lost. Sabbath keeping is an identity marker, but before we dismiss identity markers as exclusivist, we should note that Israel's identity markers were its most profound rituals and behaviors: worship, study, and deeds of loving-kindness. The church's most obvious identity markers are its sacraments: Baptism and the Eucharist, and its commitment to spreading the love of God and neighbor.

Verse 3 shows that identity markers need not be exclusivist: "Do not let the foreigner [the resident alien, the stranger] joined to the LORD say, 'The LORD will surely separate me from his people.'" Verse 6 picks up the theme of foreigners again: God will bring to God's "holy mountain," Zion, those foreigners who "love the name of the LORD . . . who keep the sabbath . . . and hold fast my covenant." Their sacrifices will be accepted in the Temple, "for my house shall be called a house of prayer for all peoples" (v. 7). In Jesus' time, the court of the Gentiles was by far the largest court at the Temple.

This stance is a change from the requirements of Torah, which stipulated that we should love the alien as we love ourselves but otherwise barred aliens from full participation in Israel's worship (e.g., Exod. 12:43). For Third Isaiah, membership in the Jewish people is important, particularly in light of the danger threatened by assimilation, but membership is redefined so that Sabbath keeping and worship become means of being a part of the people Israel.

Sandwiched inside this discussion of foreigners is Third Isaiah's startling announcement about eunuchs: "To the eunuchs who keep my sabbaths . . . and hold fast my covenant, I will give, in my house [temple] and within my walls, a monument and a name better than sons and daughters . . . an everlasting name that shall not be cut off" (vv. 4–5). This is inclusive Judaism with trumpets blaring. Eunuchs were definitely strange in the heterosexual culture of their time and would be even more so in ours, because they fall outside all such current categories as gay, lesbian, or straight. But as Philip came up with no reason not to baptize the Ethiopian eunuch (Acts 8:26–40), Third Isaiah understands God's love to be all-inclusive. Today's church seems to be of a considerably divided mind and heart on this matter; the lectionary even drops these verses. Including them might help produce a more thoughtful and compassionate church.

Third Isaiah's breadth of outlook and universalism with regard to foreigners are strikingly presented in Matthew 15:21–28 as a position of which the Canaanite woman persuades Jesus!

Proper 16 [21]/Year A

Exodus 1:8–2:10+ (Semicontinuous)

Behind Exodus lies Genesis with its themes of blessing and the inclusion of Gentiles in God's economy of blessing. YHWH said to Abram: "I will bless you, and make your name great, so that you will be a blessing. I will bless those who bless you, and the one who curses you I will curse; and in you all the families of the earth shall be blessed" (Gen. 12:1–3). Blessing is inclusive well-being: care, protection, a safe place, health, children, God's presence, economic sufficiency, hospitality for the stranger. In the story of the birth of Moses, these themes are central.

A new pharaoh arose in Egypt who "did not know Joseph" and feared the people Israel (1:8–10). This unnamed king acts on the basis of his ignorance and fear of the stranger and violates the hospitality typical of ancient societies, such as that which the Hittites extended to Abraham (Gen. 23:4–6). Pharaoh's ignorance led to the oppression of the Israelites and God's curse upon Pharaoh and Egypt. The absolutely powerful God-King (Pharaoh's designation) was stupid. Power makes one stupid; absolute power makes one absolutely stupid. Pharaoh will learn with whom he is dealing.

In 1:11–22 we see Pharaoh's tactics at work. First, he imposes harsh conditions of "forced labor" on the people Israel, in spite of which "they multiplied and spread, so that the Egyptians came to dread the Israelites" (v. 12). In addition, the king ordered the Hebrew midwives to kill all boys born to Israelite mothers (v. 16). "But the midwives feared God; they did not do as the king of Egypt commanded them, but they let the boys live" (v. 17). Because the midwives were agents of God's blessing in bringing these boys safely to birth, God "gave them families" (v. 21), blessing those who blessed Israel. The king responded by ordering all his people to toss every Israelite boy into the Nile (v. 22).

When Moses was born (2:1–2), his mother "saw that he was a fine baby," that he was "good," a reverberation from Genesis 1: "and God saw that it was good." She hid him as long as possible, put him in a basket and "placed it among the reeds on the bank of the river" (2:3). Pharaoh's daughter saw the child and sent a maid to bring it to her. The maid, Moses' sister Miriam (Exod. 15:20), pulled a fast one on Pharaoh's daughter and turned the baby over to Moses' mother for nursing until "the child grew up" (2:10).

Moses' mother cares for Moses until he is grown and then returns him to Pharaoh's daughter, who "took him as her son" (2:10). "She named him Moses, 'because,' she said, 'I drew him out of the water.'" His name, *mes*, is the Egyptian for "son," one who is drawn out of a mother's womb.[21] He will draw his people out of Egyptian oppression.

All the critical roles in this story are played by women—the midwives, Moses' mother, his sister Miriam, and Pharaoh's daughter. Their actions make possible the rest of the narrative of the people Israel. Without them and their actions, the rest of the story does not happen. That a woman, Mary, is the first in the Gospel story to trust in the Holy Spirit's strange announcement is not a brand-new thing in the scriptural narrative. Did Pharaoh's daughter act knowingly? Or did she act solely out of compassion for an abandoned child? The text throws no light on this intriguing question. But through such compassion, YHWH can work to bring about blessing among YHWH's children.

The story of Jesus' birth in Matthew, like that of Moses' birth in Exodus, features an imperial ruler (Herod the Great, who was Caesar's appointed king of Judah) who operated out of fear (Matt. 2:3) and followed the way of curse and death rather than that of life and blessing. Each ruler killed many children, but Moses and Jesus escaped to lead the people Israel or all the lost sheep of Israel out of bondage.

Isaiah 51:1–6* (Paired)

In today's reading, the prophet (who is also servant and teacher) addresses "you that pursue righteousness, you that seek the LORD" (v. 1). In the prior reading from Isaiah, the Lord gave his servant "the tongue of a teacher, that I may know how to sustain the weary with a word" (50:4; see Palm/Passion Sunday/Years A, B, and C). Today, it is the "weary" people to whom Second Isaiah speaks. However they may understand themselves, in his eyes they are those who "seek the LORD."

In this long iteration of the blessings that await God's people upon their return to the land of promise (the passage runs through 52:12), Isaiah encourages them to remember who they are. Wise pastors are aware that calling the people of God to remember whom God gives and calls them to be is always pertinent.

"Listen!" (*shema*, hear!) says Isaiah: "Look to the rock from which you were hewn, and to the quarry from which you were dug. Look to Abraham your father, and to Sarah who bore you" (vv. 1–2). Memory is the essence of identity and knowing who we are. Those of us whose loved ones have struggled with Alzheimer's disease learn hard lessons about what loss of memory entails. When your mother asks who you are and why you're here, your heart sinks. Robbed of memory, everyone is a stranger to us and we are strangers to ourselves. A forgetful community is no longer aware of what it is about, what its purpose is, or whom it loves.

Second Isaiah wants its readers to remember Abraham, of whom God made a people (v. 2). The story of the Jewish community rested on a primordial act of loving grace and gracious love, God's utterly gratuitous covenant with Abraham and Sarah. Did they know themselves to be a despairing, desolated people in exile in a new Egypt, without hope or prospects and overwhelmed by the powerful of their time? They were to remember Abraham and Sarah of whom God made a people dedicated to be "a light to the peoples [Gentiles]" (v. 4). Were they living on the bottom rung of Babylonian society? They were to remember Eden and know that "the LORD will comfort Zion; he will comfort all her waste places, and will make her wilderness like Eden" (v. 3). Their memories enabled them to look forward to joy, gladness, and song (v. 3).

The all-inclusiveness of God's grace rings out in Second Isaiah. "A teaching [*torah*] will go out from me, and my justice for a light to the peoples. . . . The coastlands wait for me" (vv. 4–5). The mission given to the exiles is to carry the message of God's compassion, justice, and truth to all peoples. Israel's covenant with God was to be a light and blessing to all peoples.

God's "salvation will be forever, and my deliverance will never be ended" (v. 6). Such bold promises of redemption from captivity still met with skepticism and doubt among Second Isaiah's listeners, evident in verses 7–16, which follow today's reading. It is important to note this because listeners to today's sermons may well harbor unspoken doubt about God's promises. Second Isaiah evokes God's power by reassuring the people that God will lead them in safety to the land of promise: "You have forgotten the LORD . . . who stretched out the heavens and laid the foundations of the earth" (v. 13).

It is when God's power is far from evident, God's people defeated and in exile, that the Scriptures speak of God's power. They do it to reassure the people that faith and trust are feasible because God is ultimately reliable. It is like Martin Luther King Jr., going along a dusty road in the middle of the civil rights movement, asking his followers: "How long?" And answering: "Not long!" When things look bad, messages of a powerfully gracious and compassionate God reassure us that as God made "many" from Abraham and Sarah (v. 2), so God can do great things with us.

The lectionary pairs this passage with Peter's declaration about Jesus in Matthew 16:13–20. At Jesus' time, with Judea under Roman occupation, the people were in exile in the land of promise. Roman soldiers patrolling the Temple at Passover when Jews celebrated liberation from oppression had replaced Babylonian soldiers oppressing the people in exile outside the land of promise. In such a situation, Jesus' messiahship, confessed by Peter, was lived out. And it brought him into conflict with Rome.

Proper 17 [22]/Year A

Exodus 3:1–15+ (Semicontinuous)

In verses 1–6 of today's reading, the first important image is the blazing bush that was not consumed (v. 2). The burning but not burned-up bush has long puzzled interpreters. We receive great help, however, from J. Gerald Janzen, who points us to the many ways in which images of the bush (or tree) and fire are used in Scripture. Isaiah 65:22 likens the dispirited people in exile to a tree that becomes a symbol of hope: "Like the days of a tree shall the days of my people be, and my chosen shall long enjoy the work of their hands" (Gen. 21:33; 49:22–26; Ps. 128:3; and Ezek. 17:24 are a few of many examples). Fire symbolizes both the adversities of the people Israel and God's saving of them from those adversities: "the LORD has . . . brought you out of the iron-smelter, out of Egypt, to become a people of his very own possession, as you are now" (Deut. 4:20). Psalm 66:10–12 prays: "For you, O God, have tested us; you have tried us as silver is tried. . . . we went through fire and through water; yet you have brought us out to a spacious place." Under Egyptian tyranny, the people Israel burned; because of God's love for Israel, Israel was not consumed.[22]

The second important theme involves God's command to Moses to "remove the sandals from your feet, for the place on which you are standing is holy ground" (v. 5). To be invited to remove one's sandals was to be welcomed. Moses is welcomed into relationship with God as God simultaneously draws an ultimate respect from Moses. Moses is no longer an "alien" (Exod. 2:22) but a guest. Preachers might link this passage with Jesus' washing of his disciples' feet in John 13:1–11. There, Jesus, the "sent one" of God, acts as his Father had acted with Moses.

The rest of today's reading is one of the most important passages in the Scriptures; in it God reveals to Moses God's "self-given name."[23] The God who discloses God's name to Moses is the One who heard the cries of the people Israel (3:7), the One who had been "with" Israel in the iron-smelter of Egypt and promises Moses and Israel "I will be with you" (v. 12) in the exodus from Egypt, and who responds to Moses' request for a name with "I AM WHO I AM" (v. 14). Because the verb *'ehyeh*, when God is the subject, always means "I will," and not "I am," the better translation of *'eheh 'asher 'ehyeh* is "I will be whoever I will be."

If knowing the name of a deity was supposed to give some power over that deity, "I will be whoever I will be" names the God of whom all our images, symbols, metaphors, models, and concepts are forever inadequate. All our ideas of God's will are similarly fallible. This name deepens the mystery of God even as God self-discloses Godself. In disclosing Godself, God retains the sovereignty not to be defined by a name. Israel and the church may address God, but may never possess God.

Because of their reverence for God's name, Jews ceased saying it and instead used circumlocutions to speak of God. In Judea *adonai* was substituted for YHWH and among Hellenistic Jews *kyrios* was substituted when YHWH appeared in the text. They would use other expressions such as

Ha-Shem, "the Name," *Ha-Kadosh Baruch Hu*, "the holy One," *Shechinah*, "the Presence," or *Ha-Rachaman*, "the compassionate One." One well known to Christians is *Shamayim*, "heaven." The *Malchut Shamayim*, "kingdom of heaven" or "rulership of God," is consistently used by Matthew.

Jesus teaches his followers to pray "Our Father in heaven, hallowed be your name" (Matt. 6:9; Luke 11:2). Notice that this is stated in the passive voice; there is no mention of the One who will bring about the hallowing of God's name. Jesus' own speech of God, throughout the Gospels, regularly uses the passive voice to refer to God's action; to the paralytic whom he healed he said, "your sins are forgiven" (Matt. 9:2; Mark 2:5; Luke 5:20), not "I forgive you . . ." Use of the "divine passive" indicates that God is the actor. Examples are far too numerous to cite, but note briefly: "they will be comforted" (Matt. 5:4), "they will be called children of God" (Matt. 5:9), "she will be saved" (Luke 8:50), "after I am raised up" (Matt. 26:32). Jesus also hallows it by reverentially not pronouncing it. In John's Gospel, "I am" is the name of God and Jesus' mission is to make God's name known, and so he prays toward the end of the Gospel: "I have made your name known to those whom you gave me from the world" (John 17:6).

Jesus' own name (*Joshua* when transliterated from Hebrew, *Yeshua* from Aramaic) means "YHWH [*Adonai*] saves." His name proclaims God's name. Understanding this will yield profound interpretations of all passages about Jesus' name, such as Acts 4:12: "there is no other name under heaven given among mortals by which we must be saved." This passage is often used to affirm a Christian exclusivism with regard to salvation. Appropriately read, it should not be so used.

When we encounter a statement about God's name in the New Testament, we should ask whether Exodus 3 is being evoked. For example, when Paul says, in the christological hymn in Philippians 2:9–10, that God gave to Christ Jesus "the name that is above every name, so that at the name of Jesus every knee should bend," do we recognize that it is the name of God, YHWH, that is "above every name"? In Isaiah 45:23, "the LORD" says: "To me every knee shall bow, every tongue shall swear."

Jeremiah 15:15–21 (Paired)*

In today's passage Jeremiah reminds God that he has suffered on God's account (Jer. 15:15). Jeremiah has "eaten" God's words and made them a part of the fabric of the prophet's being to the point that God's message became a joy to Jeremiah and the prophet is "called by [God's] name." Jeremiah in

Hebrew means "YHWH exalts" (15:16). Because of Jeremiah's call, the prophet leads an isolated existence (15:17). Jeremiah's life is like an incurable wound (15:18a). His deepest lament is that *God* deceived him. Instead of being a living fountain (2:13), God is a "deceitful [untrustworthy] brook," or "waters that fail" (15:18b; cf. 2:31). Unfortunately Jeremiah does not specify *how* God is deceitful, but some commentators speculate that Jeremiah feels abandoned, even overwhelmed by opponents.

God responds with a statement that may catch today's congregation off guard. "If *you* [Jeremiah] turn back [repent], I will take you back" (Jer. 15:19a). Jeremiah has done something serious enough to compromise the prophet's vocation and God calls for repentance. While the text does not specify what he has done, 15:19b suggests that Jeremiah may have uttered something "worthless," perhaps that God deceived the prophet (15:18). The people (who complained about God's faithfulness, Proper 25/Year C) are to turn to Jeremiah for help; the prophet is not to speak in their mistaken ways (15:19c).

If Jeremiah returns, God will make Jeremiah as a "fortified wall of bronze," that is, immensely secure. No matter how contentious his enemies, they will not prevail because God has sealed the promise (Jer. 15:20). Jeremiah can count on God for deliverance from the wicked (15:21; cf. Proper 20/Year B).

On the one hand, this passage can serve as a pastoral warning that prophetic ministry—either individually or as a community—can arouse opposition and suffering kin to that experienced by Jeremiah. The suffering Jeremiah has in mind is not general suffering but comes about as others oppose prophetic evaluation of their situations. The sermon can prepare the congregation for such encounters and can help the congregation develop resources to sustain them through such confrontations. On the other hand, the preacher does not want to speak glibly of such intense difficulties, nor to encourage neuroses around suffering. The preacher might even raise the question whether the congregation is challenging today's idolaters with enough voltage to inspire opposition.

This passage also reminds today's congregation not to idealize Jeremiah (or other biblical characters). Jeremiah evidently lost sight of his vocation for a time so that God had to *invite the prophet to repent*, that is, to return to faithfully enacting his calling. Perhaps that awareness can help ministers be a little more patient with themselves and their congregations in similar circumstances.

The text also encourages humility on the part of would-be prophets. Not everything that Jeremiah said proved to be prophetic. The fact that

Jeremiah could misinterpret God's purposes ought to provoke today's preachers not to *assume* that we are always right but to engage in continual reflection and be willing to change as needed.

The reading from Jeremiah is linked with Matthew 16:21–28, the first prediction of Jesus' passion (Matt. 16:21–23) and with the teaching that following Jesus involves denying oneself and taking up the cross (16:24–28). Although Matthew does not here draw directly on Jeremiah, the reading from Jeremiah represents a Jewish tradition of the faithful witness who, like Jeremiah, encounters opponents who cause the witness to suffer.

Proper 18 [23]/Year A

Exodus 12:1–14+ (Semicontinuous)

Today's text tells of the first Passover celebrated by the people Israel, the feast that Jesus of Nazareth went to Jerusalem to celebrate many years later. It is the feast of liberation from bondage and oppression. As the first Lord's Supper or Eucharist was observed under the shadow of Roman occupation and oppression, the first Passover was observed "hurriedly" (v. 11), because shortly the people would have to escape from Pharaoh. Pharaoh is one of the "gods of Egypt" (Pharaoh did claim to be god) from whom YHWH will free the people and on whom YHWH "will execute judgments" (v. 12).

Our text begins with a comment about the calendar: "The LORD said to Moses and Aaron in the land of Egypt: This month shall mark for you the beginning of months; it shall be the first month of the year for you" (vv. 1–2). "Time," says Abraham Joshua Heschel, "is the heart of existence."[24] Human beings can presume to control things in space, but time is beyond our control and manipulation. Time in the Scriptures is where we encounter holiness; certain days, such as the Sabbath, are called "holy," but no object in space ever is. Time is where we meet God.

Our text brings us face to face with the most important transformation in the history of the Israel of God with the God of Israel—the conversion of cyclical agricultural festivals into festivals of historical events. Passover is the first—a spring festival becomes the celebration of the exodus from Egypt and of God's involvement in history. With this change comes another: the people Israel becomes a "congregation" (v. 3). Previously, they were identified by tribes, but for the first time in Scripture they are described as a congregation. The early church will refer to itself as an "ecclesia," a community called out from among the various peoples of the world.

Each family eats the Passover in its home, as Jews still do. Parents, children, grandparents, cousins, aunts and uncles in the extended families of ancient Israel gathered for the celebration. Observing the Passover in this fashion means that the experience of the children is shaped by ritual prior to their becoming adults. The Passover and its rich meaning becomes part of them. God's redemption of Israel and of all people from bondage shapes the character and outlook of a people. In the Passover the participation of children is highlighted and brings great joy.

We note, also, that Passover is a "means of grace," given by YHWH, and it is also the people's response to YHWH's unconditional love. Not a commandment, the keeping of which will justify Israel, it is a gift from YHWH who has already elected Israel.

Preachers should be disturbed by verses 12–13, in which YHWH says "I will strike down every firstborn in the land of Egypt, both human beings and animals." What do we make of a destroying God? First, let us not minimize the destructiveness of the plagues inflicted (at least in the narrative) on Egypt—not only Pharaoh and others responsible for Israel's suffering were hit by the plagues, but all the little people who had no say about the system of absolute dictatorship in which they live. And when the plagues are described as killing all the fish in the Nile (7:21), ruining the land (8:13–14), killing all the livestock and wiping out all the vegetation (10:17), and slaying every firstborn, we know they faced a widespread disaster.

Yet, all this made no difference to the powers-that-be in Egypt, as the story of the exodus makes clear. Why did God do it (if God actually did)? Recall that when Moses and Aaron said to Pharaoh "Thus says the LORD, . . . 'Let my people go,' . . . Pharaoh said, 'Who is the LORD, that I should heed him and let Israel go? I do not know the LORD, and I will not let Israel go" (5:1–2). The question is: Who is sovereign in history, Pharaoh or YHWH? Pharaoh's stupidity is noted more than once in the text.

Perhaps the best way to read the plagues account is more as a historical parable than a strict recording of events, a parable with a lesson: the fate of authoritarian dictatorships hostile to freedom and well-being is always destruction. The New Testament tells many stories of destruction. There are banquet parables in Matthew which result in people being thrown into the outer darkness to weep and gnash their teeth (Matt. 8:12; 13:42; 22:13; 25:30, for example). And we have Luke's parable of the nobleman who gave ten pounds to each of ten slaves to "do business with" while he was gone, and who said to those who failed to succeed in this task, "but as for these enemies of mine who did not want me to be king over them—bring them here and slaughter them in my presence" (Luke 19:27).

In each testament, God is associated with destruction. The authors of this book do not believe that God acts to destroy. We believe that the alternative to God's way of life and well-being (blessing) is death and destruction and that our choice is between the two.

Ezekiel 33:7–11 (Paired)*

In today's passage Ezekiel reflects on the prophet's role in the community. In the background is the awareness that most of the prophets (and priests) of Judah and Israel prior to the exile failed to carry out the prophetic task of alerting the community to the fact that the people were violating the covenant and therefore inviting curse upon themselves. This reading not only explains what the prophets did not do, but indicates why many of them are in exile. The text also implies that Ezekiel and prophets who do what he does are trustworthy and can point the community toward restoration.

Ezekiel compares the work of the prophet to that of a sentinel who was responsible for watching over a city and alerting the population to dangers. The prophet puts forward two scenarios reflecting on the work of prophet as sentinel. In Ezekiel 33:2–5, the sentinel sees a sword (that is, disaster) about to come upon them and blows the trumpet. Those who hear the trumpet but do not heed its warning are responsible for the disaster that befalls them. Had they taken warning, they could have been saved. In a second instance, the sentinel sees the sword coming but does *not* blow the trumpet and disaster befalls the community (v. 6). "Their blood," God says, "I will require at the sentinel's hand" that is, the sentinel has committed a capital offense.

The sentinel is not responsible for the decision that the people make when they hear the trumpet. But the sentinel *is* accountable for sounding the trumpet, and when he does not, the sentinel is indicted for criminal neglect which carries with it the consequences of a capital crime.

God appointed Ezekiel (and other prophets) as sentinels whose work is to watch over Israel, to gauge where they are failing to live according to the covenant, and to help them recognize the consequences of their behavior. Ezekiel stresses the role of the prophet in *warning* the community. When the prophet recognizes violations of covenant that will invoke curse and remains silent, God will punish the prophet (Ezek. 33:7–8). This explains why the prophets of the preexilic community are in Babylon. When confronted by a prophetic warning, the community may want to know whether they can anticipate a renewed future or whether they will waste away (Ezek. 33:10). In strong language, God says, "I have no pleasure in the death of the wicked." God is not a sadist but rather wants the wicked to "turn from their ways and live" (33:11).

This passage raises a searching question for the preacher. Am I doing all that I can do to warn the congregation and the larger culture about the multitudinous violations of God's purposes taking place in our idolatrous, racist, self-absorbed, exploitative culture?

The passage from Ezekiel is joined with Matthew 18:15–20, a passage instructing leaders of the Matthean synagogue in how to approach members who have sinned against others in the community. While this Matthean passage does not draw from today's reading from Ezekiel, the Matthean text does call attention to the role of leaders in the community, actually taking the lead in a manner similar to that prescribed in Ezekiel in helping the community name and deal with a situation disrupting the community's ability to live out its purpose.

Proper 19 [24]/Year A

Exodus 14:19–31+ (Semicontinuous)

The first two paragraphs of today's reading (vv. 10–18) are the context for verses 19–31. The whole begins and ends on the note of "fear" (vv. 10, 13, 31). The Israelites were "in great fear," because they were trapped between the sea in front of them and Pharaoh's army behind them. They demanded of Moses: "Was it because there were no graves in Egypt that you have taken us away to die in the wilderness?" (v. 11).

There is nothing wrong with fear and there are times when any sane person will be afraid. Our awareness of danger is a life-preserving way to help us avoid injury and death, part of the goodness of creation. The Israelites had sufficient reason to fear and to let Moses know about it. Nor was Moses calm and unruffled in this dilemma; God asks him, "Why do you cry out to me?" (v. 15).

But Moses said to the people: "Do not be afraid, stand firm, and see the deliverance that the LORD will accomplish for you today" (v. 13). This expression, "do not be afraid, fear not," occurs frequently in the Scriptures. Psalm 23 gives voice to it: "I fear no evil; for you are with me; your rod and your staff—they comfort me" (v. 4). Jesus frequently addresses it to his disciples, as in the storm-tossed boat on Galilee: "Why are you afraid? Have you still no faith?" (Mark 4:40).

Moses shifts the people's attention from Pharaoh to God: "see the deliverance that the LORD will accomplish for you today" (v. 13). Fear can make us move out of danger. But sometimes we are so gripped by it that we freeze, trapped in hopelessness. Moses gets his people to "see" things differently. Like many of us—parents, pastors, or people responsible for others in a frightful situation—Moses too has to hear "do not be afraid." Faith in God is the answer to pathological fear and anxiety; it is courage (from the French *coeur*, heart) in the middle of a problematic situation. That situation might be Pharaoh's army or Pilate's executioners or the emptiness felt after the crucifixion. In all such cases the word is: take heart in God the deliverer.

God tells Moses to say to the Israelites "go forward" (v. 15), that is, into the sea! And they did, which shows that they had taken heart (which in this situation is itself something of a miracle), because the parting of the waves is not yet known to them. So they do, and the angel of the Lord and the pillar of cloud move behind them, blocking the Egyptian army from catching up with the Israelites. Was this an obvious miracle, visible to all, or the way the Israelites and Moses felt about the situation? We do not know, of course, but we do know that when someone describes the day a loved one died as "a dark, cold day," we are not just getting a weather report.

Moses "stretched out his hand over the sea" (v. 21) and the waters were driven back, enabling the Israelites to cross "on dry ground" (v. 22). The Egyptian army rushes into the parted waters; their chariot wheels bog down, Moses stretches out his hand again, and the waters close upon the Egyptians. Of the entire army, "not one of them remained" (v. 28). Here we recall part of the Haggadah for the Passover Seder where the story is told that the angels laughed at the slaughter of the Egyptians and God reprimanded them: "My children are dying, and you laugh?!" This story testifies to the Jewish affirmation of life and blessing for all. Liberation should not have to be at such a cost.

The story concludes saying that in this way YHWH "saved" Israel (v. 30) and Israel saw the "great work" (*hoshia*), a term related to the name *yehoshua*, "Joshua" in Hebrew, *yeshua* ("Jesus") in Aramaic. The term means "YHWH saves."

After these events, "the people feared the LORD and believed in the LORD and in his servant Moses" (v. 31). Fear of God is not dread, but awe; it is tensively related to belief, trust; Israel stands in awe of a trustworthy God. Fear has been transformed.

Exodus 15:1b–11, 20–21 (Responsive)

Although the lectionary indicates that this passage, the song of Miriam, is to be used responsively, pastors might well use it as the text of a sermon. It is a hymn/poem on the theme of YHWH's salvation of the people Israel at the sea, which scholars long ago concluded was one of the oldest pieces of literature in the Old Testament. Verses 13–15 deal with themes pertaining to the settlement of Israelites in the land of promise and the peoples of Edom, Moab, and Canaan whom they encountered there. These obviously date from a later time.

One theme of the song, the rulership of YHWH, the reign or kingdom of God, is central to the Gospels' presentation of the ministry of Jesus; the song of Miriam celebrates a time when God was the ruler of Israel, when Israel had no human king and God ruled in justice and equity for all. YHWH is praised for having led the people "to your holy abode" (v. 13), the land of Israel where God dwelt among the people. YHWH is holiness in community with the people. God's "holy abode" in Israel is the "sanctuary . . . that your hands have established" (v. 17). This part of the hymn ends with the promise "the LORD will reign forever and ever" (v. 18).

Although the song of Miriam occurs at the end of today's reading (vv. 20–21), scholars have long thought that the song of "Moses and the Israelites" (v. 1) was prompted by the song of "Miriam . . . and all the women" (v. 20). Let us look at some of the reasons for the claim that Miriam's song prompted that of Moses.

First, the preceding verse, 19, begins with "for" (as the older RSV translation has it). That way of beginning indicates that the hymn in verses 1–18 is accounted for by what is now to be described. Second, the NRSV puts a period at the end of verse 19, although when we see that the verse begins with "for," it is an incomplete sentence and should not have a period after it. So verses 20–21 are included in the explanation of the singing of Moses and the Israelites. The "them" to whom Miriam sings in verse 21 is a masculine plural, not a feminine plural as it would be if the text wanted to convey that the women sang only to each other. The reading that most makes sense of this is that Miriam and the women, with their dancing and tambourines, led the singing of Moses and the Israelites.[25]

The song of Miriam concludes the first long section of Exodus. We recall the central role of women in God's actions of blessing and deliverance in the first two chapters of Exodus—the midwives who refused to kill baby boys born to Hebrew women, the Levite woman who sought safety for Moses by placing him in a basket lined with bitumen and putting it "among the reeds on the bank of the river," the daughter of Pharaoh who had the baby brought to her, Moses' sister and her action in returning Moses to his mother for nursing, the daughters of the priest of Midian who provided hospitality to the adult Moses.

This section of Exodus begins and ends on the note of the critical role of women in the story of Israel. Like the women who are the first to visit the tomb of Jesus, the first to speak to the apostles about his resurrection, Miriam is the first to testify to God's deliverance of Israel from the sea and Pharaoh, the first to call attention to God's *hesed*, "steadfast love" (v. 13).

She is not the last woman in Scripture to sing of God's casting down the mighty (Pharaoh) and lifting up the nobodies (Israelite slaves). Another Miriam (Luke 1:46–55) sings of the Lord who "has brought down the powerful from their thrones, and lifted up the lowly" (v. 52). These two songs might well be considered together, in a departure from the usual lectionary placements of them.

Genesis 50:15–21 (Paired)*

In antiquity the last actions and words of a human being often capsulate fundamental and long-lasting dimensions of meaning. Genesis 50 consists of three interrelated scenes that summarize main themes from the ancestral saga and prepare the congregation for the book of Exodus.

In the first scene, Jacob wanted to be buried in the cave in the field of Machpelah, the family burial site that Sarah and Abraham had bought. Consequently, when Jacob died in Egypt, Joseph had the corpse embalmed. This detail may seem innocuous to the early twenty-first century congregation, but the Hebrew people did not typically practice it; embalming was an Egyptian religious custom and this is the only reference to embalming in the Bible. Nahum Sarna stresses that the writers of Genesis accord no religious meaning to the embalming.[26] However, embalming Jacob's corpse made it possible for Jacob to be joined with his ancestors in the promised land. Here, the universal God worked through the Egyptian custom of embalming to make it possible for Joseph to return the body of Jacob to the land of promise (Gen. 50:1–14). Is the universal sovereign working today through customs outside of Judaism and Christianity to lead communities toward qualities that fulfill the divine intention for human life?

J. Gerald Janzen points out that the size and intensity of the Egyptian retinue who accompany Joseph on the journey to Jacob's final resting place is further testimony to the blessing of God flowing through Sarah and Abraham into other families.[27] The Egyptians themselves recognize that the God of Israel has blessed them.

In the second scene, at Jacob's death, the siblings feared that Joseph would then take revenge against them for selling him into slavery. They appeal to Joseph not as family members who have claims on one another but on the basis of a statement, not otherwise recorded (did they make it up?), attributed to Jacob, imploring Joseph to forgive them for the crime they committed. They offered to become slaves to Jacob (Gen. 50:15–19).

Jacob forgives them because, as he makes clear, God intended the things that happened for good, indeed, "to preserve a numerous people as [God] is doing today." For Jacob to act vengefully would be for Joseph to assume the role of God by reinterpreting those events (see Proper 15/Year A). Janzen notes that Joseph "relieves the crushing burden of their guilt by placing it within the horizon of God's providential care for the whole human family."[28] To forgive is to create the possibility that the family may become a community of blessing on the model of Genesis 1, a community that honors the integrity of the individual elements while they live together in mutual support.

In the final scene, Joseph assures the siblings that God will bring them into the land that God swore to give to Sarah and Abraham (Gen. 50:24). This would prove true for the Israelites later enslaved in Egypt, and for the exiles in Babylonia. The reader is implicitly invited to believe that God is faithful in keeping other promises, too.

Genesis 50:15–20 is paired with Matthew 18:21–35, the parable of the Unforgiving Servant. Both texts share the goal of encouraging forgiveness in community. However, the approach of Genesis 50 is theologically superior because it lures readers toward the practice of forgiveness by helping them imagine a community restored by forgiveness. Matthew threatens that God will not forgive members of the community who are themselves unforgiving. For citations of the end of Jacob's life in the New Testament, see Acts 7:15–16 and Hebrews 11:22.

Proper 20 [25]/Year A

Exodus 16:2–15+ (Semicontinuous)

We include the latter half of chapter 16 in our discussion because its themes are important to contemporary Christians. For the fifth time, the Israelites are referred to as a "congregation" (four times in chapter 12 and in 16:2, 9, 10, and 22). This points to the new reality that the people Israel is a congregation created by God's act of liberation, not just an assembly of tribes. But Israel's sense of itself has not kept pace with this development: they "complained against Moses and Aaron in the wilderness" (v. 2). They misunderstand themselves and they misremember their past under Pharaoh's oppression where they now claim that "we . . . ate our fill of bread" (v. 3).

God responds to Israel's murmuring not with anger but with a promise: "I am going to rain bread from heaven for you" (v. 4). God graciously responds to Israel's plight, as God had earlier heard their cries of oppression and responded.

Their hunger in the wilderness has led to Israel's loss of faith in God's project and in the leadership of Moses and Aaron. We who are well-fed need to recognize that nothing erodes confidence faster than hunger. Their question is whether God, who performed the extraordinary deed of liberation, can provide ordinary food and drink. If we look for God only in the "mighty acts" of history, we will be unable to see God in the simple realities of daily life, such as food, the kindness of neighbors, the love of family, and the gift of children.

Exodus 16 returns to basic themes of Genesis: life and blessing (well-being). These are found in the regular workings of worldly reality. Manna (vv. 4–8) and quails (vv. 8, 13) are natural phenomena in the Sinai Peninsula. The fruit of the tamarisk tree when perforated by plant lice emits a whitish substance that in the cool morning thickens into a ball. Loaded with sugar and carbohydrates, it can be baked into a bread; indigenous people in Sinai still eat it and call it "manna."[29] As to the quail, migrating birds sometimes fall to the ground worn-out by strong head winds and can be captured by hand. These are gifts from God who works in the ordinary processes of nature and not only in the epic deeds of history. God's purpose in providing the ordinary gifts of food is that the people "shall know that I am the LORD your God" (v. 12).

Much of chapter 16 is concerned with the rhythms of time, of days, weeks and Shabbats, days of rest. Under Pharaoh's demanding governance, the Israelites had to gather straw for making bricks every day in order to meet their production quota. In the wilderness they gather not straw but food that nourishes. In Egypt there was no day of rest; they were required to toil every day, year round. In the Sinai every sixth day is followed by "a day of solemn rest, a holy sabbath to the LORD" (v. 23). Nothing is said of the Sabbath as a day of worship; it is simply a day of rest, rest which is essential to human well-being. The Sabbath in Exodus 16 is like that of the creation story—a day built into the created order of things. Moses instructs the people to eat a Sabbath meal (v. 25); it is a day to be enjoyed, in contrast to the absence of all such days under Pharaoh. Observant Jews still keep the Sabbath as a day of rest and joy, a temporal sacrament reminiscent of Eden and pointing to the days of the Messiah still to come. The rest of us, caught up in the grind of producing and consuming, would do well to recover it.

Exodus 16 calls to mind the Lord's Prayer—"give us this day our daily bread." Appreciation of God's graciousness in the ordinary is essential, if we are to see God anywhere at all. The accounts of the feeding of the five thousand and four thousand deliberately evoke today's passage with their repeated emphasis that Jesus fed the hungry "in a deserted place."

Jonah 3:10–4:11 (Paired)*

Although the story of Jonah is told as if it took place in the eighth century BCE, the book was written after the exile when Palestine was a colony of Persia. The writer uses the earlier setting to send a message to the community under Persian rule. Jewish people pondered how to live in relationship with the relatively friendly but still powerful Persians and with the growing fact of Jewish Diaspora—Jewish people living in other parts of the Mediterranean basin. Using satire, the book of Jonah calls the community to continue the vocation of Genesis 12:1–3, to be a nation through whom other nations come to blessing. Even if the entire book of Jonah cannot be read in worship, it is a single story and the preacher should tell the whole.

God called Jonah to call the wicked city of Nineveh (on the Tigris River approximately 450 miles northeast of Jerusalem) to repent, but Jonah refused the call and fled on a ship for Tarshish (perhaps located near present-day Spain). In response, God sent a great storm and the sailors threw Jonah overboard to quiet the sea. God provided a great fish to swallow and thereby protect the prophet (Jonah 1:1–2:10).

God sent Jonah a second time to Nineveh, where he preached that the city must repent or be overthrown. The people believed Jonah. The Ninevites fasted, and in an apparent spoof on how Gentiles sometimes misunderstand Jewish practices, covered the animals with sackcloth (a sign of mourning and repentance). When God saw that Nineveh repented, God did not bring calamity upon them. (Jonah 3:1–10.)

But Jonah was angry that God expressed grace, mercy, and steadfast love toward Nineveh. He sat down outside the city to see whether, in fact, God would destroy it (Jonah 4:1–5). God caused a bush to grow and shade Jonah, but the next day God sent a worm to wither the bush and then sent a merciless sun and a hot wind so that Jonah wished for death (4:6–8).

Jonah confessed to being angry about the bush. God closes the book by means of an argument from the lesser to the greater: if Jonah was concerned about a single bush (that came and went without Jonah's labor), should not God also be concerned about the 120,000 people in Nineveh "who do not know their right hand from their left" (i.e., who do not know how to live in the way of blessing), not to mention their animals? (Jonah 4:9–11).

Preachers sometimes speak of the universalism of Jonah. But this is a myopic understanding, for Jonah does not offer a thoroughgoing universalism (the notion that everyone will be saved). Rather, he presumes repentance on the part of Gentiles. Nevertheless, in league with a deep current in the Old Testament, Jonah testifies to the concern of the God of Israel for the welfare of all peoples, even Persians and others in the growing Diaspora. Through repentance, God provides means whereby all can be blessed.

The preacher might take a clue from the fact that the book closes with a question with which the community hearing the story must wrestle. Does the congregation agree with the God of the book of Jonah? If today's congregation is similar to Jonah, reluctant to seek the welfare of communities who are different from it, the preacher might help the community welcome latter-day Persians who repent. Going beyond, the sermon might help the congregation recognize how God seeks to bless these others and identify ways the congregation can cooperate with such efforts.

The reading from Jonah is paired with Matthew 20:1–16, the parable of the laborers in the vineyard. While the parable does not cite Jonah, the lectionary wants the congregation to recognize through Jonah that concern for welcoming repentant Gentiles is not an innovation of the Matthean community but comes from deep within the Jewish tradition. For the Third Sunday after the Epiphany/Year B, Jonah 3:1–5, 10 is paired with Mark 1:14–20. Though the Gospel passage does not refer to Jonah, in Mark 1:14–15, Jesus calls people to repent. The selection from Jonah illustrates the effectiveness of repentance. For other references to Jonah in the New Testament, see Matthew 12:28–32; 16:1–4; Luke 11:29–32.

Proper 21 [26]/Year A

Exodus 17:1–7+ (Semicontinuous)

For commentary on this passage, please see the Third Sunday in Lent/Year A.

Ezekiel 18:1–4, 25–32* (Paired)

As noted in connection with Proper 9/Year B, Ezekiel prophesied during the exile with the twofold purpose of interpreting the reasons for the exile and offering hope that God would return the community to the *eretz Yisrael* (land of Israel). Today's reading is weighted toward the first of these purposes.

Ezekiel cites a proverb that summed up a widespread way of thinking in Israel. "The parents have eaten sour grapes, and the children's teeth are set on edge" (Ezek. 18:2), meaning that the sins of the parents will besmirch the lives of those who come after them. According to Ezekiel 18:3, this proverb will no longer apply in Israel. Instead, "Because all lives are mine" (because God controls all generations), "it is only the person who sins that shall die" (Ezek. 18:4). Each generation will be held responsible for its sins and be punished accordingly.

In Ezekiel 18:5–24, the prophet brings forward the case of four generations that demonstrate the truth of the proverb (Ezek. 18:5–9, 10–13, 14–18, 19–24). He then puts the listeners on the spot by asking whether God's ways are unfair, or whether the congregation itself is unfair in its complaint against God (18:25). When the righteous sin, they are punished, but when the wicked repent, they are saved (18:26–28). How can Israel claim that God is unfair?

While God will judge the community according to its ways, God pleads with Israel to repent (Ezek. 18:30). God wants the people to cast away their transgressions and "get yourselves a new heart and a new spirit." Here Ezekiel sounds very much like Jeremiah 31:31–34 (see Fifth Sunday in Lent/Year B) where the "new covenant" means not replacing the old one but a fresh mode of implementation. God does not want the people to die, but pleads for them to "turn, then, and live" (18:31–32).

Ezekiel has aspects of this subject both right and wrong. It makes theological sense that only the generation that sinned should *directly* pay the price for that sin. However, in real life the relationship between cause and effect among generations is not so neatly demarcated. A generation that despoiled a river in the name of industrial progress may leave behind an ecological disaster that affects generations to come. Generations far removed from those who committed a particular sin may be affected negatively by it. A better way to nuance Ezekiel's concern is to think that the presence of distress in a generation does not *necessarily* mean that the affected generation committed the sin that caused the distress. God is present to help the community deal with the distress.

The lectionary pairs this reading with Matthew 21:23–32. Matthew uses these texts to portray the Jewish leaders in a bad light (Matt. 21:23–27) and to suggest that these Jewish leaders might not enter the realm of God (Matt. 21:28–32). The picture of the obdurate Jewish people in Ezekiel reinforces the similar picture of the Jewish leaders in the Gospel and suggests that they get what they deserve. This combination of readings has the effect of reinforcing anti-Jewish tendencies. The preacher should explain the consequences of the pairing and repudiate them.

Proper 22 [27]/Year A

Exodus 20:1–4, 7–9, 12–20+ (Semicontinuous)

Jews refer to the Ten Commandments as the "ten words." Protestants traditionally call them "commandments," stressing that they are laws which we cannot keep but which drive us to seek grace. For Jews the first "word" is: "I am the LORD your God, who brought you out of the land of Egypt . . ." (v. 2). It is grace.

The ten words are formed by this opening reminder of who God is— a God of love graciously given—and by Israel's responsive love (the rest of the words). Torah-instruction (a better term than "law") is shaped by a mutual love: God's unfathomable love for Israel and Israel's very fathomable love for God. "Law arises out of gospel."[30]

Eight of the ten words begin: "you shall not." People often speak of negative commandments as off-putting "do nots" that constrict life. We can imagine experiences that may lead people so to think. But that misconstrues the negative instructions in the Torah. First, we can keep all of them while taking a nap. That's hardly burdensome. Second, negative *mitzvoth* deal with the parameters of behavior. They do not specify what we should do, simply what we should not do. They name the actions that cancel all possibility of living with others a life of well-being (which can only be lived *with* others). Killing, adultery, stealing, bearing false witness, and coveting a neighbor's spouse or property destroy communal well-being. Torah is given that we may have life and well-being.

"You shall have no other gods before me" (v. 3): "Other gods" were plentiful in Israel's environment. They are no longer around (in their explicit form), but we too must deal with many "so-called gods in heaven or on earth" (1 Cor. 8:5). Anything or anyone that is proximate and relative may be regarded as ultimate and absolute and thereby become an "other god." Today's other gods include the cult of self-fulfillment, excessive wealth, nationalism, religious obscurantism, and the ultimate value of the "bottom line."

"You shall not make for yourself an idol" (v. 4): Images of "other gods" are forbidden for the same reason as having other gods—worship of the finite winds up being destructive of life and well-being (witness Nazi worship of the "Volk"). Images of YHWH are forbidden because *'ehyeh 'asher 'ehyeh* cannot be imaged. No images, ideas, concepts, models, or metaphors are adequate to the God who is always ahead of us. But note that YHWH is not only the One who acts on others; YHWH is also the One who interacts with them, is acted upon by them, "hears" their prayers. Images cannot do this. Banning images protects God's communion with us as much as it does God's transcendence.

"You shall not make wrongful use of the name of the LORD your God" (v. 7; see commentary on Proper 17/Year A for discussion of the name of God). We petition this in the Lord's Prayer: "hallowed be your name." To hallow is to honor as holy. The ways in which we make wrongful use of God's name are hardly limited to cussing when we hit our thumb with a hammer. The way in which presidents wrap themselves in God's name when in political trouble or trying to build up support for a war come to mind. Empty talk, cheap grace, easy religion, self-interest parading as piety: the church should speak against all wrongful use of the name of God.

"Remember the sabbath day, and keep it holy" (v. 8). We Gentile Christians have lost the idea of the Sabbath. On Shabbat all work is banned, that of yourself, your family, your employees, your livestock, even that of strangers (think of migrant workers) in the vicinity. Here Shabbat is grounded in the creation—"for in six days the LORD made heaven and earth . . . , but rested the seventh day" (v. 11). Strangers and animals are to keep it. It is a gift, a day of systematic loafing, a limit on our constant striving and attaining. If we were to cease driving cars one day a week, we could give the environment a rest.

"Honor your father and your mother" (v. 12). This *mitzvah* is directed to adult children and has to do with their older parents; it expresses the concern of the Torah for the vulnerable. In their old age we are to see to it that our parents' needs are cared for. Israel's social policy was to guard and protect the aged. Can we say that of our social policy?

"You shall not murder" (v. 13). Whether the translation should be "murder" or "kill" is much debated. Leviticus 17:11 and Genesis 9:6 stress that all life is God's and that we may not engage in the "shedding of blood" (Jer. 22:17; Ezek. 22:6, 27). "Kill" seems to be the better translation.[31] A negative instruction opens up into its affirmative side, as "you shall have no other gods before me" (Exod. 20:3) opens up into Deuteronomy 6:5: "You shall love the LORD your God with all your heart . . ." So "you shall not kill," opens up to "you shall love your neighbor as yourself" (Lev. 19:18). The ease with which we kill today, especially with the instruments of warfare, is opposed to God's intent for the world, that it attain a life of well-being for all.

"You shall not commit adultery" (v. 14). In ancient Israel adultery was patriarchally understood: for men having sex was adultery only when it was with a woman married to another man. For a woman it was having sex with any man other than her husband. In one sense, adultery was a property crime. Any contemporary understanding of this commandment has to break out of a patriarchal framework. More deeply, what is at stake are the relationships of loyalty, compassion, and faithfulness that constitute any healthy family (and not only any heterosexual family). How are children to grow up into adults who can sustain relationships of compassion and faithfulness if the most intimate place where they can drink deeply of those values is lacking them? Israel's God is deeply committed to the well-being of families; they are a central part of God's concern that we live and live well.

"You shall not steal" (v. 15). If you have ever had anything stolen or your home burglarized, you know the feeling of having been violated. Biblical faith understands stealing as "a violation of a person, not just a person's wealth."[32] Other provisions in the Torah deal with the punishments for stealing. They involve repayment of what was stolen, in multiples, for example: "five oxen for an ox, and four sheep for a sheep" (Exod. 22:1). The underlying principle is that "all who act dishonestly are abhorrent to the LORD your God" (Deut. 25:16). This instruction leads us to reflect on what constitutes stealing. Is it stealing to reward executives with $150 million golden parachutes when thousands of children per day die of starvation?

"You shall not bear false witness against your neighbor" (v. 16). This instruction had to do with testifying in court, because life in a just society is impossible if courts of justice are corrupted. More broadly biblical faith is concerned with the sins of speech—all misleading, libelous, defamatory, malicious talk about others is condemned (Hos. 4:2; Lev. 19:16). One of our greatest lies is against language itself when we abuse it and talk pejoratively of others. We usually sin with words before we sin with deeds. Verses 12–16 are picked up in the story of the rich young ruler (Matt. 19:16–30; Mark 10:17–31; Luke 18:18–30).

"You shall not covet" (v. 17). Here the Decalogue turns to internal urges and desires. We are not even to want our neighbor's house (and so to steal it), our neighbor's wife (and so to commit adultery). If the tenth word had only to do with so-called "externals," it would add nothing to the first nine because not stealing and committing adultery have already been addressed. A major educational task of the Christian community is to educate the feelings and desires of its members, to help the community practice being the people it is given to be.

Isaiah 5:1–7 (Paired)

Isaiah's "vineyard song" follows the prophet's description and denunciation of social and moral chaos among the people of God (3:1–4:6), which contextualizes today's reading. The vineyard song is aptly paired with Matthew's parable of the wicked tenant farmers who are responsible for the vineyard that is the people Israel (Matt. 21:33–46); taken intertextually, the two texts interpret each other. The image of the people Israel as a vineyard occurs frequently (Jer. 2:21; 12:10–11; Ps. 80:9–17; Ezek. 15:1–8).

Although today's passage has long been referred to as a "song," the actual song comprises only verses 1b–2; the rest of the passage consists of the word of the prophet to the "inhabitants of Jerusalem and people of Judah" (v. 3). There are ways in which this passage is perplexing; paying attention to its complexities will help avoid a too-easy interpretation of the text. Ostensibly a love song sung to a vineyard, the passage shows us before it is over that it is, instead, a parable (*mashal*) together with its interpretation (*nimshal*), as indeed is Matthew's parable that is paired with it. How the everyday, mundane language of much of the parable qualifies as a love song is a perplexity; how a vineyard can be held to account for producing a poor crop is another. Are the people of Judah the vineyard or those held responsible for it or both? And why is God impatient to destroy the vineyard, to "make it a waste" (v. 6)?

The outline of our passage is clear: the love song (vv. 1–2b) precedes an appeal to the people to "judge between me and my vineyard" (v. 3) in an implied setting of a court of law, which is followed by the passing of a verdict on the vineyard (vv. 5–6). No advocate for the vineyard is present to speak up on its behalf. In other places in the Old Testament, such an advocate does intervene with God on behalf of the people (e.g., Exod. 32:30–32) and elicits from God a recognition that God is gracious (Exod. 34:6–7). The last verse provides the interpretive key for the passage, identifying the vineyard as "the house of Israel and the people of Judah."

Our passage is less a love song than an indictment and conviction of Israel in which the inhabitants of Jerusalem and Judah, who are the vineyard, are asked to pass judgment on themselves, after which the verdict is announced! Isaiah's theology is uncomfortably Deuteronomic in its quick move to the language of curse: the vineyard will be "devoured," "trampled down," made "a waste"; "it shall be overgrown with briers and thorns" and the clouds will "rain no rain upon it" (vv. 5–6).

The basic premise is that the people will get their just deserts. If we are faithful, we will not be devoured (by ravaging armies or by drought and famine); if we are not faithful, all the blessings of life and well-being will be denied to us. Things seem to be that simple. Job will pose severe questions to Deuteronomic orthodoxy. More deeply, the theological critique is that faithfulness to God's grace on our behalf is never a matter of getting what we deserve. We receive abundantly more than we deserve by way of God's grace. In our honest moments, most of us are relieved to know that God's mercy tempers God's judgments and that we receive less than we deserve for our unfaithfulness.

Isaiah is best understood in the light of the concern with the geopolitics of his time. That the vineyard is to lose its fence and hedge, leaving it vulnerable to predators and thieves, clearly points to Assyrian invasion, the basic concern of chapters 6–12. The people are to understand this invasion to be God's doing on account of their unfaithfulness and failure to do justice: "he expected justice, but saw bloodshed; righteousness, but heard a cry!" (v. 7). Nonetheless, we are presented with Deuteronomic theology. By comparison, Matthew's vineyard parable criticizes those who tend the vineyard and prophetically threatens only to replace them with other vintners who will take proper care of the vineyard. Each should be read as prophetic self-criticism, not as a criticism of "them" on which we are given a pass.

Proper 23 [28]/Year A

Exodus 32:1–14+ (Semicontinuous)

Today's reading illustrates covenantal faith in God in which we are expected not only to trust God but also to question God. Radical trust in God evokes an audacious faith; it not only permits but requires questioning. Moses exhibits precisely this kind of faith; he has the chutzpah to question even God, an audacity to confront God over God's intent to "consume" the people Israel (v. 11), as Abraham had confronted God over the fate of Sodom and Gomorrah (Gen. 18:16–33).[33]

Our story opens with a crisis. Moses' presence among the people has assured them of the presence of the God who saw them out of Egypt. But

Moses has been on the mountain a long time; his return was "delayed" (v. 1), and having no one to "go before" them, they take matters into their own hands, whereas the initiative in the exodus story had been from YHWH. In their fear they demand of Aaron "make gods for us, who shall go before us; as for this Moses . . . we do not know what has become of him" (v. 1). They ask Aaron to make an image, forbidden by Exodus 20:4 because the personal, interactive God cannot be replaced by an impersonal, impassible object.

"Go before" elsewhere in Exodus is used only of YHWH or Moses (e.g., 14:19; 23:23). Now the people seek a god made by human hands to go before them. They do not request a "calf"; but this is what Aaron fashions from the gold that he collects. The calf (or bull) served in the ancient world as a symbol of fertility and military power. Because of the fertility connections, their celebration (v. 6) has often been interpreted as a sexual orgy. But "burnt offerings and . . . sacrifices of well-being," eating, drinking, and being joyous, are all proper activities in the worship of YHWH. The only matter that is not is the calf, which is important in today's story for protection against feared attacks. The people want something to stand in the place of the absent Moses and the absent God (since Moses had represented God's presence, Moses' absence represents God's presumed absence). They failed to trust God and they put their trust in something that they could manipulate—an image.

It is a sign of YHWH's relationality and vulnerability, that YHWH's "wrath" (v. 10) burns hot against the people for so quickly (v. 8) turning away from the obedience they had promised (Exod. 24:7). When we feel anger at our children for their self-destructive behavior, it is only because we care very deeply; we should appreciate that God does, too.

God says to Moses: "Now let me alone, so that my wrath may burn hot against them and I may consume them; and of you I will make a great nation" (v. 10). God proposes displacing the people Israel and replacing them with another people! Christians will later take up the displacement/replacement theme and claim that this is precisely what God has done in Christ: replace sinful Israel with the obedient church (Barnabas, Justin Martyr, Irenaeus, Tertullian, Augustine, and Chrysostom among many others persistently rang the changes on supersessionism).

What far too many Christians rejoiced in, Moses rejected. He intercedes with God on behalf of the people: "Turn from your fierce wrath; change your mind and do not bring disaster on your people" (v. 12). Moses makes three arguments with God. First, he points out that God has just brought Israel out of Egypt (v. 11); what kind of sense does it make to follow that up so quickly with their destruction? Second, what will the neighbors think? How will the Egyptians react? Will they decide that you acted out of malice toward Israel? And third, don't you remember your promise to Abraham and Isaac, "I will multiply your descendants like the stars of heaven" (v. 13)?

"And the LORD changed his mind" (v. 14).

This passage could well be paired with Romans 9:1–5 where Paul argues that he would wish himself "cut off from Christ" for the sake of his own people (9:1, paraphrasing Exod. 32:32) and stoutly denies that Israel has been rejected by God (11:1). Arguing with God in prayer is a theme in the parable of the Unjust Judge (Luke 18:1–8). Our text relates ironically to the banquet parable appointed for today (Matt. 22:1–14). In it, the king was so angered at those who were invited but refused to come that "he sent his troops, destroyed those murderers, and burned their city" (v. 7). Whereas Moses talked God out of consuming Israel, the invitees in Matthew's parable have no one to intercede for them.

Isaiah 25:1–9* (Paired with Gospel)

Please see Easter Day/Year B for commentary on this passage.

Proper 24 [29]/Year A

Exodus 33:12–23+ (Semicontinuous)

In today's reading, Moses continues to manifest the chutzpah to argue with God. In a passage left out of the lectionary, Moses had said to God on behalf of the people: "But now, if you will only forgive their sin—but if not, blot me out of the book that you have written" (Exod. 32:32). Paul paraphrases this comment in Romans 9:3 where, speaking on behalf of members of the people Israel who do not believe in Jesus Christ, he says: ". . . I could wish that I myself were accursed and cut off from Christ for the sake of my own people, my kindred according to the flesh." Later he asks, "Has God rejected his people?" and answers, "By no means!" (Rom. 11:1). God may be angered, but never forgets that God's own character is that of steadfast love and grace.

The opening verse of today's reading finds Moses still raising objections to God's intentions. God had said to Moses (33:1–2) that Moses and "this people" should leave "this place" and go to the land of promise and "I will send an angel before you." Whereas previously God had gone before

Israel, now God promises only that "an angel" will go before the people. Moses objects. He wants, instead, God's very own presence: "If your presence will not go, do not carry us up from here" (v. 15). Moses shows a lot of chutzpah, twice speaking in the imperative to God. First he says, "See, you have said to me, 'Bring up this people'; but you have not let me know whom you will send with me" (v. 12). "See" means "look!" Moses wants God to stop and think and says so. In verse 13 he again demands: "Consider too that this nation is your people." God has been willing to deal with Moses but, in spite of having had a change of heart, still does not want to be personally present to the people. Moses twice insists that God consider what God is proposing. He is an effective priest, mediator, on behalf of the people.

In verse 16 Moses questions God: "how shall it be known that I have found favor in your sight, I and your people, unless you go with us?" In this long story of his intercession, Moses takes the initiative. Remarkably, God patiently hears Moses out and responds favorably. Moses' prayers are answered. God is affected by Moses, and Moses' prayers open up possibilities for the relationship between God and Israel. God promises Moses: "I will do the very thing that you have asked; for you have found favor in my sight, and I know you by name" (v. 17). This is neither the first nor the last time in the Scriptures of Israel that God responds favorably to being questioned. Perhaps God wants us to question.

To all of which, Moses makes yet another demand: "Show me your glory, I pray" (v. 18). Moses wants to see God clearly, as he and Aaron and seventy of the elders had in 24:9. But this time God shunts Moses' question in a new direction; rather than God's glory, God will show Moses "all my goodness" and "will proclaim before you the name, 'The LORD'" (v. 19). God wants to convince Moses of God's faithfulness, more than God's presence, of which Moses can hardly be unaware, having been engaged in prolonged conversation with God.

Having previously promised that God's presence would go with Israel (v. 14), God now makes a further promise and statement about God's character: "I will be gracious to whom I will be gracious, and will show mercy on whom I will show mercy" (v. 19). It is an awesome, momentous matter to know that God is gracious, more significant than seeing God. God answers Moses' prayer to "see" God by meeting Moses' deeper need; God gives us what we most need, not always what we most want.

The passage ends with YHWH's saying to Moses that he may see God's back but not God's face. Since Moses and others had clearly already seen God, the point is not that it is impossible to see God; rather it is that after so great a sin it is gracious and merciful of God to free us from having to look God in the face.

Isaiah 45:1–7 (Paired)*

Second Isaiah faced the difficult prospect of convincing an exiled people that YHWH would restore Israel to life and blessing in the land of promise. But how to do this in a situation that was under the control of Marduk and his Babylonian worshipers? (See the Seventh Sunday after the Epiphany/ Year B and the First Sundays after the Epiphany/Years A and C.)

Isaiah had proclaimed that Israel had learned from its hard experience of exile: "comfort my people, says your God . . . and cry to her that she has served her term, that her penalty is paid" (40:1–2). Now, God will act redemptively on Israel's behalf. Today's reading is the Cyrus prophecy and begins with 44:24: "Thus says the LORD, your Redeemer, who formed you in the womb . . . who says of Jerusalem, 'It shall be inhabited,' and of the cities of Judah, 'They shall be rebuilt'" (vv. 24–26). God says of Cyrus: "He is my shepherd, and he shall carry out all my purpose" (v. 28).

The key to today's reading lies in YHWH's purpose to bring about kindhearted justice for all peoples and particularly for Israel. Militarily victorious, Cyrus conquered Croesus of Lydia in 546 CE and combined Persia and Media into a united kingdom. As a progressive ruler he understood that it was in his interest to see to the well-being of other peoples. Although Cyrus worshiped Marduk, he served YHWH's purpose of considerate justice. "For the sake of . . . Israel my chosen, I call you by your name . . . though you do not know me" (45:4).

The Lord starkly announces that Cyrus is "his anointed," that is, his *messiah* (45:1). "Messiah" means "the anointed one," and Isaiah identifies Cyrus as God's messiah to restore the people Israel to the land of Israel, *eretz Yisrael*. This messiah is about the business of doing this-worldly things: returning Israel to its land, financing that return, and reconstructing its infrastructure and institutions, including the Temple. Jerusalem "shall be rebuilt" and the "foundation [of the Temple] shall be laid" (44:28).

For Second Isaiah, YHWH could use foreign rulers who did not know YHWH to carry out YHWH's purposes, to discipline Israel, and to restore the people. Second Isaiah was sophisticated, quite aware that Cyrus was not a faithful servant of YHWH. Without knowing it, Cyrus was carrying out God's purposes with respect to the people Israel. Isaiah prompts us to ask whether other peoples and their leaders are, in God's providence, trying to teach us lessons that we need to learn.

The Lord uses Cyrus for God's universal purposes: "that they [all peoples] may know, from the rising of the sun and from the west, that there is no one besides me; I am the LORD, and there is no other" (v. 6). God's purpose is that all peoples shall be a blessing to each other. They shall share that blessing only in relations of mutuality with and difference from each other. Cyrus is different from the people Israel—they are the Lord's but Cyrus does not so understand himself. Yet in serving the Lord's purpose, he is nonetheless also the Lord's. He, too, is one whom God created.

Our reading ends with a verse on which much ink has been spilled: "I form light and create darkness, I make weal and create woe; I the LORD do all these things" (v. 7). This is often interpreted to mean that the omnipotent God does all things good and evil. Whatever happens, God is directly responsible for it, every great instance of peace and every atrocity of war, every self-transcending act of justice and every drive-by shooting.

We take it differently, noting that if we seek to determine God's will by referring to whatever happens, then we have no need of the revelation of God in the history of Israel, in the Torah and the Prophets, and decisively in Jesus Christ, to be clear about what God's will is. We simply have to point to the general run of stupidity and happenstance and say "There! That's God's will."

Rather, we think that God has created a world in which blessing and well-being are possible, provided that we accept them as gracious gifts rather than seeking to hoard them for ourselves and provided that we allow others to receive them as well. Blessing has to pass through many hands. If we do not live so as to make well-being possible, we set up the conditions that make for curse and death, and we receive our share of these.

God is not in control of the decisions and actions of finite but free agents such as ourselves. If God were, the world would be a much happier place and 15 million children per year would not die of starvation. All each of us has to do to discern that God is not in control of our lives and behavior is to examine our lives and behavior.

What links the Cyrus prophecy to the account in Matthew 22:15–22 of the question about paying taxes to Caesar lies in Isaiah 45:5: "I am the LORD, and there is no other; besides me there is no god." Coins with Caesar's image on them proclaimed the Caesar-theology of the Roman Empire, that Caesar was God or the Son of God or pontifex maximus or showing Caesar's spirit ascending to heaven to join the other gods. Unlike Cyrus, Caesar was decidedly not pursuing an enlightened program of considerate justice.[34]

Proper 25 [30]/Year A

Deuteronomy 34:1–12+ (Semicontinuous)

The lectionary places Deuteronomy 34 as a bridge between the readings about the deliverance from Egypt (and the covenant at Sinai) and the entry into the promised land (in Joshua). The lectionary thus jumps from the departure from Sinai in Exodus 33 to the edge of the promised land (Deuteronomy 34) with little attention to the wilderness wanderings so important to Israel's identity. Moreover, today's lesson presupposes the first thirty-three chapters of Deuteronomy. To honor the text, the preacher needs to alert the congregation to the change in theological worlds from Exodus to Deuteronomy.

The death of Moses took place on Mount Nebo, a peak a little over 2,600 feet high located across the Jordan about forty miles east of Jerusalem. On the mountaintop, Moses saw the promised land (Deut. 34:1–4a). However, God forbade Moses to enter the land (Deut. 34:4b). Deuteronomy offers two explanations for this decision, both of which are theologically disturbing.

In the first, God commanded the people to take the land (Deut. 1:6–8; cf. 1:19–21). However, after a report from spies, the people refused to go forward, saying that God "hates us" and "has brought us out of the land of Egypt, to hand us over to the Amorites to destroy us" (1:22–28). Moses was faithful and pled with the people to obey the divine command (1:29–33).

God declared that no one from that generation, other than Caleb, Joshua, and the children would enter the land. The others would wander forty years in the wilderness (Deut. 1:34–40; cf. 1:46–2:8a; 8:1–10; 29:2–10). Moses entreated God for permission to enter the land but God again denied it. God did permit Moses to see it, but told the prophet never to speak of these matters again (3:25–29). Moses continued to be faithful by instructing the people to be obedient upon entering the land (4:21–24; cf. 32:52). Although Moses faithfully represented God's will to the community, God held Moses accountable for the failure of the people and punished Moses. This decision by God is hardly fair.

In the second explanation, perhaps added by a Priestly editor, God refused Moses entrance to the land because Moses "broke faith with me among the Israelites at the waters of Meribath-kadesh in the wilderness of Zin, by failing to maintain my holiness among the Israelites" (Deut. 32:48–52). This statement refers to Numbers 20:1–13 (cf. Num. 20:22–29; 27:12–23) when the people were thirsty and God commanded Moses and Aaron to bring forth water from a rock. The text is not clear as to *how*

Moses "broke faith." Consequently, scholars offer several different interpretations, none of which warrant a recrimination as severe as exclusion from the land.[35]

The Deuteronomic theologians use God's punishment of Moses to illustrate that disobedience brings curse. From today's perspective, the punishment seems disproportionate. The preacher may want to join the book of Job in raising a theological protest against viewpoints such as this aspect of Deuteronomism.

Moses died at the age of 120 but only by God's command. Indeed, until death Moses was the epitome of vigor (34:5, 7). According to Deuteronomy 21:13, households mourned thirty days for a parent. By mourning, the community acknowledges Moses as head of the house, one who represents the family's most important values and identity (34:10–12).

In a moving pastoral touch, Deuteronomy 34:5 implies that God personally buried Moses (Deut. 34:6). Despite denying Moses the promised land, God sees that Moses is accorded a proper burial (with attendant respect) according to ancient custom.

By stating that Moses laid hands on Joshua, the narrator assures readers that they can trust Joshua's leadership because Joshua was Moses' legitimate successor.

Deuteronomy 34:10–12 implies that Deuteronomy is *the* set of theological criteria to evaluate community life. This text buttresses "the authority of Deuteronomy against versions of God's teaching that were inconsistent with the book."[36] Communities do need clear core values by which to evaluate possibilities for community life. Yet, making the teaching of Deuteronomy absolute makes it an idol. Moreover, today's congregation should be theologically and morally uneasy with aspects of Deuteronomy, such as the demand to execute people who worship sun or moon (Deut. 17:2–7).

Leaders are sometimes called, like Moses, to lead congregations toward promises the leaders will never themselves realize. What theological resources sustain people under such circumstances? Furthermore, a sobering realization is here. Faithful leaders sometimes bear the fate of unfaithful communities.

Leviticus 19:1–2, 15–18 (Paired)*

For comments on this passage, please see the Seventh Sunday after the Epiphany/Year A.

Proper 26 [31]/Year A

Joshua 3:7–17+ (Semicontinuous)

The book of Joshua tells the story of Israel's entry into the promised land and the fulfillment of the promise God made to Sarai and Abram (Second Sunday in Lent/Year A). Although the book of Joshua tells the story that took place when Israel entered the land, the book was given its present form by the Deuteronomic theologians to speak to a community after the exile (Proper 17/Year A). The stories in the book of Joshua dramatize the power of God to keep promises, and confirm the main claims of Deuteronomy.

Deuteronomy closed with the people camped at the edge of the promised land and leadership transferred from the dying Moses to Joshua (Deuteronomy 34; Proper 25/Year A). Joshua 3:1–6 gives instructions to the people encamped at the Jordan. The people are to sanctify themselves (including adopting the practices of warfare in Deut. 20:1–9; 21:10–14; 23:9–14). They are to follow the ark of the covenant, a physical representation of the divine presence and power. Commentators often note that the Jordan is more than a geographical location; it is an important symbol of boundary between two qualities of life: between being landless and landed, wandering and settled, being disciplined and being blessed. The divine presence, represented by the ark, facilitates such crossings.

God invested Joshua with the power that was manifest through Moses thereby both assuring the community that the quality of leadership associated with Moses was still among the people, and indirectly asserting that the Deuteronomic interpretation of the tradition beginning with Moses should be authoritative (3:7–8). Joshua predicted two signs that would demonstrate that God was among them. First, when the feet of the priests carrying the ark touched the water, the Jordan would stop flowing. Second, the people would drive out the inhabitants of the land (3:9–13).

When crossing the Jordan, the people followed Joshua's guidance. The crossing itself took place just as Joshua said, thereby reinforcing the reader's confidence in Joshua and in the theology of Deuteronomy. The priests with the ark preceded the people, and when the feet of the priests touched the edge of the river, the water stopped in a heap upstream, and the people crossed over on dry ground.

This event obviously echoes the crossing to the sea at the exodus, reminding the reader that just as God opened the sea, so God can continue to work in the world. What God is pictured as doing at the Jordan, God did again in Babylon: brought the exiled (homeless) people into the land of promise. These motifs invite the preacher to ask, Where is God, figuratively speaking, leading people across the Jordan today?

In Joshua 4:1–9, the people set up stones to mark the event. People who see the stones would not only remember the event but also recollect the continuing power of the "God of all the earth." It might be interesting for the preacher to reflect with the congregation on the monuments (small and large) that are important in the congregation's world. What memories and promises do these monuments bring to mind and heart?

In the Gospel of Matthew, John the Baptist refers to Joshua 4:1–9 in a way that connects to the Gospel lesson for today, Matthew 23:1–12. While calling people at the Jordan to repentance and baptism in preparation for the apocalypse, John says to some Pharisees and Sadducees, "Do not presume to say to yourselves, 'We have Abraham as our ancestor'; for I tell you, God is able *from these stones* to raise up children to Abraham" (Matt. 3:9, emphasis ours). Matthew uses this reference to caricature and discredit some Jewish leaders in Matthew's own time. Beyond that caricature, however, in the spirit of Deuteronomy Matthew recognizes that each generation is responsible for its own witness. Stephen mentions Joshua 3:7–17 in Acts 7:45.

Micah 3:5–12* (Paired)

Micah was active in Judah, in the latter half of the eighth century (Micah 1:1). He spoke to a situation in which inequality and wrongdoing abounded. The prosperous increased their holdings of land by driving small farmers off land that they had inherited. "They covet fields, and seize them; houses, and take them away" (2:2). They deprive widows and orphans of their homes: "The women of my people you drive out from their pleasant houses; from their young children you take away my glory forever" (2:9). The "heads of Jacob and rulers of the house of Israel [the political leaders] . . . hate the good and love the evil" (3:1–2).

The topic of today's reading is that the prophets, seers, and priests of Jerusalem actively collude in this total violation of the Mosaic covenant. Micah describes the behavior of the leaders of Jerusalem graphically: "you heads of Jacob . . . tear the skin off my people, and the flesh off their bones . . . [you] chop them up like meat in a kettle, like flesh in a caldron" (3:1–3). When these same leaders turn to the Lord in time of crisis, "he will not answer them; he will hide his face from them at that time, because they have acted wickedly" (v. 4).

Now Micah turns his attention to the preachers, priests, biblical scholars, professors, and evangelists. He hears nothing from them about all this devastation of widows, orphans, the destitute, and the homeless. When what is needed is the Word of God, Micah encounters silence. They are wayward shepherds. Greed and covetousness unite them with the political and business leaders. "Its rulers give judgment for a bribe, its priests teach for a price, its prophets give oracles for money" (3:11). One need only think of the Rolex-flashing televangelist claiming to be evangelical while making a case for war or "mainline" pastors opposing war who do not clearly speak against it. The religious leaders have put their truthfulness up for sale to the highest bidder. They "cry 'Peace' when they have something to eat, but declare war against those who put nothing into their mouths" (v. 5). These seers, priests, and prophets "shall be disgraced, and . . . put to shame; they shall all cover their lips, for there is no answer from God" (v. 7). God will be silent when the evildoing rulers turn to God (v. 4), and God will be silent when the wayward shepherds pray to God for a word to say.

The religious professionals' infatuation is with money, not with YHWH. They have lost their ardor for God and their love for the neighbor, and when it comes time to say something significant they are empty. The concordance has been thumbed, the commentaries consulted, the manuals revisited, the systematic theology texts considered, and the preacher is silent. To these professionals "it shall be night to you, without vision, and darkness to you, without revelation" (v. 6).

Verses 9–11 recap the criticism of rulers, prophets, and priests that Micah has already articulated and point out their false piety: in spite of their unjust behavior "they lean upon the LORD and say, 'Surely the LORD is with us! No harm shall come upon us.'" Micah disabuses them of this illusion: "because of you Zion shall be plowed as a field; Jerusalem shall become a heap of ruins" (v. 12).

Prophetic critique of religious leaders is always apt; it reminds us of the compromises we make and of how we fail to be faithful to our obligation to proclaim the truth in season and out. If we read the diatribe of Matthew's Jesus against the scribes and Pharisees in that sense, as self-criticism to take to heart, it makes the same point that Micah makes. If we read it in the tradition of Christian anti-Judaism, as justifying God's reputed rejection of Israel, we distort it and again fail to serve God's purpose of compassionate justice.

Proper 27 [32]/Year A

Joshua 24:1–3a, 14–25+ (Semicontinuous)

In ancient literature a major figure's last words and actions were often of great significance. Joshua began these final words by reminding the community that God has been faithful: to the original ancestral families (Josh. 24:2–4), at the exodus (vv. 4–7a), during the wandering in the wilderness (v. 7b), and when the people occupied the promised land (vv. 8–13). God's promise-keeping was altogether a work of grace (note esp. v. 13).

Each generation is responsible for renewing its own loyalty to YHWH and for living accordingly. Joshua indicates that the community is to revere (that is, obey) God and to serve God (that is, to worship liturgically and to follow in the divine ways) by putting away other gods. Joshua 24:15a presumes an ancient viewpoint: by definition everyone serves a god. The question is, which deity will Israel serve? And which deity will the reader serve?

Joshua 24:15 contains one of the most famous expressions in the Bible, one much used by preachers: "Choose this day whom you will serve . . . but as for me and my household, we will serve the LORD." The people remember God's gracious and powerful efforts in their behalf and immediately join Joshua's affirmation (Josh. 24:1–18).

In 24:19–20, the interaction between Joshua and the people takes a surprising turn. The leader suggests that the people will find it difficult to honor the commitment they have just made, so that God will "turn and do you harm, and consume you, after having done you good" (v. 20). Prior to the exile, many in the community had turned to other gods (e.g., Jer. 1:16; 2:11, etc.). This language interprets the exile as the consequence of that decision, with this text intended to motivate the postexilic congregation to serve God alone and thereby avoid a repeat disaster.

Today's congregation may have difficulty understanding verse 19b: when the text says that God "will not forgive your transgressions or your sins." By this, the passage does not mean that God will forever reject the community if they violate the commitment they have just made. It means simply that their infidelity will inevitably have a consequence (exile). The postexilic congregation recognizes that they have a fresh opportunity to revere and serve God and to lead a life of blessing.

When the people insisted that they would serve YHWH, Joshua declared that they were themselves witnesses to their commitment (Josh. 24:21–23). This language is very strong for it means that they are to testify against themselves in the event that they turn to other gods. It is especially urgent since despite what they have just said, foreign gods are among them even as they speak, perhaps a reference to the fact that even with the memory of the exile hanging on their hearts, some who have returned to the land are already trafficking with lesser gods (v. 23). Nevertheless, the people reaffirmed their loyalty to God, and Joshua made a covenant and a record of it (vv. 24–26a). Joshua erected a stone at Shechem as a witness and reminder: if the people turn to other gods and do not witness against themselves, other witnesses will accuse them (vv. 26b–28).

In the Sixth Sunday after the Epiphany/Year A, we discuss the values of helping congregations make a forced choice. In choosing between God of Israel and other gods, the choice is not simply which deity will be the focus of the community's liturgical acts of worship; the choice will determine the total character of the community's life. Choosing YHWH is choosing a life of blessing. Choosing other gods is choosing harm. A community becomes like the deities it worships. Whom does the congregation revere and serve?

Human finitude being pervasive, such a choice is not a one-time affair. Over time, good intentions can fade and commitments can drift into compromise. From time to time, preachers need to help congregations recall and return to their deepest commitments. Moreover, making a choice for God is not as simple as Joshua's stark alternative. In North America our personal and communal lives are inextricably entwined with the values and behaviors of the gods. The preacher can help the congregation live with this ambiguity by attempting to discern in every situation how to revere and serve God as fully as possible while confessing its complicity with the gods.

Stephen mentions two passages from Joshua 24 in his sermon in Acts 7. In Acts 7:16 he recollects Joshua 24:32 and in Acts 7:45 he refers to Joshua 24:18. Regrettably, Stephen's sermon is constructed by Luke to portray certain Jewish people in Luke's own time in a bad way in order to serve Luke's polemical purposes (Acts 7:51–52). The congregation needs to understand that this choice includes renouncing caricatures such as those found in Acts 7. John 4:5 echoes Joshua 24:32 by pointing out that the place where Jesus encountered the Samaritan was Sychar (Shechem). This detail reinforces the woman's comment that salvation comes from the Jewish people (John 4:22). For the Fourth Gospel, the divine power that was at work in the days of Joshua continues to work through Jesus.

Amos 5:18–24 (Alternate) (Paired)

One of the most famous passages from the Prophets, today's reading is often quoted in sermons dealing with issues of justice. Following Amos's lament over the sins of the northern kingdom (see Proper 23/Year B), today's prophecy was likely uttered at Bethel and precipitated the action of Amaziah, the priest of Bethel, in exiling Amos from the northern kingdom (7:10–11).

Verses 18–20 strike a note that began in 5:16–17: the future will be grim for Israel if it does not turn and worship the Lord appropriately, in authentic worship that expresses and reinforces the considerate justice that the people are to be actively engaged in doing as their grateful response to all that God has graciously done for them. Amos broaches the topic with a discussion of the "Day of the Lord," a prophetic expectation of a time (frequently referred to as "that day") when the Lord would put things right between all people and between them and the created order. The Prophets could speak of the day of the Lord as a day of great expectation or a day to be dreaded. Amos does the latter, likening it to "darkness, not light" (v. 20). God's putting things right will not be a happy time for the rich who oppress the rights of the poor, the orphan, and the widow.

Amos launches into a full-blown critique of the worship at Bethel (vv. 22–23). He censures every kind of worship in which Israel engages. The "festivals" were the yearly observances of Passover, Pentecost, and *Sukkoth*, or Booths. "Solemn assemblies" were weekly services of worship and sacrifice. "Burnt offerings" were those in which the entire victim was offered to God, totally burned on the altar with its smoke rising to the heavens. "Grain offerings" were offerings of grain (often for the sake of the poor in place of the more costly animal or bird offerings), and "offerings of well-being" (or "peace offerings") involved a meal (offerings and meals obviously continued to characterize the worship of Israel and the church). The "noise of your songs" and the "melody of your harps" refers to musical worship in the sanctuary. Amos will have none of it; all of it is rejected, utterly.

The language of rejection is spoken by YHWH in the first person and is also unreserved. The Lord utters six rejections: "I hate . . . I take no delight . . . I will not accept . . . I will not look upon . . . Take away from me . . . I will not listen" (vv. 21–23). Yet the larger context puts this in Amos's perspective. What he rejects is worship without the active practicing of considerate justice. "Seek good and not evil . . . establish justice in the gate" (5:14–15). It is not enough to "come to Bethel—and transgress; to Gilgal—and multiply transgression; bring your sacrifices every morning, your tithes every three days . . . for so you love to do, O people of Israel!" (4:4–5).

We sense that worship had become empty. Genuine worship reflects and reinforces an active faithful life of doing justice. Worship without practical ethics is empty, about this Amos is clear. We may assume that he also thought that ethics without worship is blind, but speaking to a dire situation, he was concerned with righting the listing ship, not with framing a comprehensive view.

Rather than this empty worship, he proclaims famously, "let justice roll down like waters, and righteousness like an everflowing stream" (5:24). It is said that the prophets expressed grand visions and the rabbis wrote contracts, as though there were some great chasm between these two. But it was Amos who called for justice to be done in particular cases—"in the gate"—indicating that the concern for cases and contracts was at the heart of the prophetic message. Letting justice roll down like waters will require much attention to particulars if justice is ever to be done anywhere.

This reading is paired with Matthew's parable of the Ten Bridesmaids; it would be more appropriately paired with his parable of the Last Judgment.

Wisdom of Solomon 6:12–16 (Paired)*

On Proper 8/Year B we note that the Wisdom of Solomon was written during the Hellenistic age when Gentiles, probably in Alexandria, were harassing the Jewish community. This book intends to strengthen its readers to maintain fidelity to their heritage even when harassed. In the reading for today, one strategy of the writer is to continue the wisdom tradition of Israel while grafting into it some ideas from popular Hellenistic philosophy in order to show that those who possess wisdom can live confidently in the present because wisdom brings them immortality. In the Jewish wisdom tradition, Wisdom is one of God's closest agents, who was active in creation and who continues in the world to help the community live according to divine design. Wisdom of Solomon adds to this notion the idea that Wisdom will guide the soul to the goal of life, which is to live after death in the immediate presence of God. This is what it means to be immortal.

Much like Proverbs 1:20–33 and 8:22–31 (see Proper 19/Year B and Trinity Sunday/Year C), Wisdom 6:12–16 personifies Wisdom as a woman. She is radiant (illuminating) and unfading (immortal). The key point is that those who love Wisdom and seek her (especially members of the community) can discern her and find her (Wis. 6:12). Wisdom *wants* to be known, and those who arise early can find her sitting by the gate, that is, in a public place ready for discourse (6:13–14). Those who fix their thoughts on Wisdom can live through the harassment of the community "free from care," that is, aware that the discomfort is not the ultimate value of life (6:15). Wisdom actively seeks people and is graciously omnipresent with them (6:16).

Wisdom 6:17–20 is a syllogism, a common device in Greek rhetoric in which each element builds on the previous one until the argument reaches a conclusion. In this six-part syllogism wisdom begins with the desire for instruction, which, in this Jewish context, means instruction in the ways of Wisdom and Torah. Instruction leads to love of Wisdom that, in turn, results in "the keeping of her laws," that is, living in the Jewish way. Heeding her laws assures one of immortality, which achieves the goal of life by "bringing one near to God," that is, into the unmediated presence of God. The "desire for wisdom leads to ruling [NRSV: "a kingdom"]," that is, to ruling in the manner of Wisdom 3:8 (see All Saints/Year B).

This reading from Wisdom occurs with the parable of the Ten Bridesmaids, in which five of the bridesmaids wisely prepare for the coming of the eschatological realm of God and five do not (Matt. 25:1–13). Wisdom, for these maidens, is the capacity to perceive that the present world is about to end in an apocalypse and that they need to be prepared (see Matt. 7:21–27).

Proper 28 [33]/Year A

Judges 4:1–7+ (Semicontinuous)

The book of Judges continues the Deuteronomic retelling of the story of Israel that we described on Proper 17/Year B. Judges repeatedly demonstrates that faithfulness results in blessing while unfaithfulness invokes curse. The book sets forth a typical pattern: unfaithfulness, consequent difficulty, cry for repentance, and deliverance. However, as the book lengthens, the seasons of blessing are fewer while those of curse are more numerous until the book ends with the land in chaos. A judge during this period of Israel's history presided over judicial cases but could also be a more general military and community leader who operated under the impetus of divine inspiration.

Today's text assumes the Deuteronomic viewpoint (Judg. 4:1–3; cf. 2:11–3:31). The people had done "evil in the sight of God," that is, they had violated the covenant of Joshua 24 by worshiping baals (e.g., 2:11; see

Proper 27/Year A). Consequently, for twenty years they had lived under the heel of the Canaanites, whose armies were commanded by Sisera with his nine hundred chariots of iron. The mention of iron is significant, for iron was a technological advance the Israelites did not have. The Israelites repented and cried to God for help. God was faithful and responded through Deborah—judge and prophet.

While women could rise to positions of leadership in Israel (e.g., Miriam), it is still surprising to find a woman in Deborah's position of prominence. Some scholars think that, as a way of maintaining male superiority, male editors excised from Israel's sacred literature memories of women who functioned in authoritative positions. However, stories like that of Deborah were so vibrant they could not be expunged.

Deborah received a message from God to direct a military campaign against Sisera. The commander of her army, Barak (a male), was to take ten thousand warriors to Mount Tabor (about ten miles west of the Sea of Galilee). Deborah would draw Sisera's force to the Wadi Kishon, just west of the mountain where Barak's army would crush Sisera's.

Barak, however, is hesitant and agrees to go only if Deborah goes with him. The reason for Barak's reluctance is not clear. Is he afraid? Does he distrust the word of a woman? Does he question the military plan? Is this a case of Joseph R. Jeter Jr.'s observation, "There are some things one just does not want to do alone"?[37] Deborah promises to go with Barak, but with the proviso that Barak understands that the glory of the victory will reflect not on him but on "the hand of a woman" (Judg. 4:8–10). When Barak obeys, success follows.

The story unfolds just as Deborah said. Of Sisera's army, the text says, "No one was left" (Judg. 4:11–16) save Sisera, who had fled on foot. In one of the most grizzly scenes in the Bible, Jael (a woman from whom Sisera sought shelter) killed Sisera by driving a tent peg through the general's head (Judg. 4:17–23).

The lectionary does not appoint the Song of Deborah (Judg. 5:1–31a) as a part of the reading for today, but most scholars consider it one of the oldest (and most evocative) pieces of poetry in the Jewish tradition. The hymn, which offers a different version of the story told in Judges 4, celebrates God as divine warrior, tells an even more brutal version of the death of Sisera, celebrates the fact that Sisera's mother will never see her son again, and concludes by wishing the same fate on all Israel's enemies. The song describes Deborah as "a mother in Israel," language that puts Deborah on the same plane as the male prophets who are described as "father" in Israel (e.g., 2 Kgs. 13:14).

The sermon could look for analogies to the situation of Israel and to leaders (and realities) like Deborah and Barak. Where are individuals and communities snared by the consequence of their disobedience today? What persons or ideas promise renewal through a return to faithfulness in the manner of Deborah? Given Deborah's gender, the preacher should identify feminine agents of renewal. Are there ways in which some of us are like Barak—wanting to be a part of the movement toward renewal yet wanting to feel the support of others in the process? Perhaps the preacher can point to some supportive others—especially women—who are as unexpected in our setting as was Deborah in ancient Israel.

The savagery in Judges 4–5 invites a reflection on the relationship of violence to the divine aims similar to the one proposed on the Fourth Sunday in Lent/Year C.

Since relatively few lections feature a woman as the central character, Judges 4 could become a starting point for a sermon that explores reasons for the diminished representation of women in leadership in the world of the Bible, that lifts up other women who appear in similar roles, and that uses such materials as part of a theological rationale for actualizing the leadership of women.

The New Testament does not refer to the story of Deborah.

Zephaniah 1:7, 12–18 (Paired)*

Zephaniah worked in the latter half of the seventh century in Judea in a period when Jerusalem and Judah were under the oppressive dominance of Assyria. Just as in the time of Jesus Roman dominance meant the presence of Roman religion in the temple that Herod the Great built to Roma and Caesar in Caesarea Maritima, so in Zephaniah's time Assyrian dominance of Jerusalem brought with it the presence of Assyrian deities and their associated worship practices.

Manasseh, according to 2 Kings, "did what was evil in the sight of the Lord, following the abominable practices of the nations that the Lord drove out before the people of Israel. For he rebuilt the high places that his father Hezekiah had destroyed; he erected altars for Baal, made a sacred pole . . . worshiped all the host of heaven, and served them. He built altars . . . for all the host of heaven in the two courts of the house of the Lord" (21:1–5; see 23:4–14).

Zephaniah's lead-in to his proclamation of the fearful Day of the Lord that is to come in judgment on Judah is a response to three sins committed in Judea. One was idolatry: "I will cut off from this place every remnant of Baal and the name of the idolatrous priests; those who bow down on the roofs to the host of the heavens; those [who] . . . swear by Milcom" (1:4–5). Milcom was an Ammonite deity (2 Kings 23:13), to whom Solomon had built a high place. Another was syncretism: idolatry is bad enough but the leaders brought these deities and their rites into the Temple, perhaps seeking to appease their oppressors. Third, in all this the Judeans forgot the Lord.

Along with this negligence with regard to YHWH came a parallel negligence toward the Torah and the Prophets, particularly the commitment of both to active justice on behalf of widows and orphans. Zephaniah seems mainly concerned with the three sins mentioned above, but in verses 10–11 the Day of the Lord first hits the business district of Jerusalem: the Fish Gate, where fish were bought and sold, the Second Quarter, a commercial area, and the Mortar wail: "for all the traders have perished, all who weigh out silver are cut off." God's judgment will begin, as it were, with Wall Street.

The Day of the Lord will not start with the Temple, but given what Zephaniah has said (vv. 4–6), it will doubtless get there. The Lord will scour Jerusalem "with lamps," casting light into all its dark corners, punishing "the people who rest complacently on their dregs" (an allusion to bad wine that is undrinkable), judging those who hold the view that "the LORD will not do good, nor will he do harm" (v. 12). If this is a saying that was current, apparently there were people who had come to view God as irrelevant, either not willing to act or incapable of acting, the practical atheists of their time.

Zephaniah's harshest criticism is directed at the comfortable: "Their wealth shall be plundered, and their houses laid waste . . . though they plant vineyards, they shall not drink wine from them" (v. 13). God will wage war against Judah (vv. 14–18) and, eventually, "will utterly sweep away everything from the face of the earth" (1:2). God is sorely grieved at the behavior not only at Judea but at all its enemies (2:1–15). They are, after all, to be a blessing to each other, but instead they visit curse and death upon each other. Hence, curse and death they shall receive.

There are grave questions to be asked regarding God as a God of war, even if in the case of the prophets this is not their ultimate way of thinking (Zeph. 3:14–20). In the hands of less thoughtful interpreters, such a depiction can slide easily into a deification of war, a fact to which the testimony of history is abundant. We suggest that God's wrath and anger indicate how deeply God is pained by sin and destruction because of God's great love for God's people.

Today's text is paired with Matthew 25:14–30, the parable of the Talents, with which it has little in common except for the master's judgment on the "worthless slave" who is thrown into the "outer darkness," a darkness like that of the Day of the Lord.

Proper 29 [34]/Year A

Reign of Christ

Ezekiel 34:11–16, 20–24* (Paired)

The first part of the reading for today concentrates on the role of the monarch in helping (or not helping) the community live according to God's purposes in covenant. People in the ancient Near East often spoke figuratively of national leaders as shepherds and of communities as flocks.

By omitting Ezekiel 34:1–10, the lection overlooks an important point: the exile resulted in no small part from the failure of monarchs (and priests and prophets) of Israel. Instead of seeing that all in the community had the resources to experience blessing (with a special eye on the poor), the rulers failed in significant regards. They not only fed themselves instead of feeding the sheep but fed themselves *on* the sheep (34:2–4). Consequently, the sheep were scattered through exile, becoming prey to wild animals (34:5–9). God is now against the shepherds and will dethrone them (34:10).

God becomes the shepherd who will rescue the scattered sheep, return them from exile to Palestine, and take care of the flock by providing good pasture, tending to their injuries, getting them to lie down (rest) and maintain a vital flock (34:11–16).

Many members of the flock have taken some of the good pasture for themselves while treading down the rest of the pasture and fouling the clean water. The entire community does not behave in this way: some remained faithful ("*my* sheep"). God will judge between fat sheep and lean and will create a flock in which the faithful sheep will "no longer be ravaged" (Ezek. 34:20–22). The fat sheep became fat and the lean sheep became lean because of the behaviors described in Ezekiel 34:17–19. As the practical means for doing so, God will bring forward a shepherd (ruler) from the line of David. God will work through that shepherd/leader to create a flock/community in which people live according to the covenant in blessing.

This text underlines the importance of both leadership and participation on the part of regular members in maintaining a vital community. A message could reflect on the qualities of leadership on the part of ministers and lay leaders that are important to helping the community live in accord with God's purposes. It could also reflect on how others in the congregation can share pasture and clear water. The preacher could project these concerns onto larger screens: what kinds of leaders and participants can move the nation or world toward values, relationships, and practices to make life a blessing for all? The preacher may need to name false and true shepherds and fat and lean sheep. What needs to happen for the congregation or the larger community to become a healthy flock?

This lection from Ezekiel is paired with Matthew 25:31–46, the parable of the apocalyptic judgment of the sheep and the goats. Both Ezekiel and Matthew speak of separation between the faithful and unfaithful members of the community. Ezekiel focuses on separation of true and false shepherds (i.e., monarchs and leaders) as well as fat and lean sheep (community members). Inexplicably, the lectionary omits Ezekiel 34:17–19, in which Ezekiel refers to separating rams and goats. In the parable Matthew speaks of sheep (and goats) in reference to typical participants in community, though elsewhere Matthew warns of false prophets (shepherds) (7:15–20). The false shepherds of Ezekiel neglect covenantal responsibilities to the poor—persons much like those whom the goats neglected in Matthew's parable (Ezek. 34:3–4; Matt. 25:42–44). Ezekiel has in mind restoring a community in Palestine whereas Matthew has the final apocalyptic judgment in view. Nevertheless, these two texts in their different nuances call attention to the importance of enacting essential Jewish values of living in covenant in community as leader and participant—or facing the consequences.

Thanksgiving Day/Year A

Deuteronomy 8:7–18

While the passage assigned for today is a good beginning for a Thanksgiving sermon, the wider context raises theological problems that dampen the thanksgiving mood (for background on Deuteronomy, see Proper 17/Year B). Deuteronomy 6:10–15 presumes that God will remove the current inhabitants of the promised land and give Israel "large cities that you did not build, houses filled with all sorts of goods that you did not fill, etc." Such displacement is hardly just. Deuteronomy 7:2 commands Israel to "utterly destroy" the inhabitants of the promised land. On the surface, such a command is morally repugnant and is inconsistent with a God of unconditional love. The preacher can critique these notions while pointing out the intent of these texts on another level. Deuteronomy 6:10–15 aims to stress the land as an act of grace. Deuteronomy 7:2 stresses that Israel cannot compromise itself with false values (especially idolatry and injustice). In any event, commentators note that the strategies of 7:3–5 *assume* that the command to "utterly destroy" was not carried out with the thoroughness prescribed by the text.

In 8:1, the Deuteronomic Moses stresses the importance of the community observing "the entire commandment" so they may "live and increase and go in and occupy the land." Deuteronomy 8:2–6 reminds the community that God's faithfulness in the past is reason for observing the commandments today. God made the people hunger in the wilderness but then provided manna to help them see that "one does not live by bread alone but by every word that comes from the mouth of [God]," that is, on the basis of what God commands. Their clothes did not wear out; their feet did not swell. They have seen in the past that what God says comes true.

Consequently, Deuteronomy 8:7–20 indicates that what God will do in the future is further reason for obeying the entire commandment. If they live as God wishes, they will revel in the land described in 8:7–10 with its ever-flowing water, abundance of grain, fruit, vegetables, as well as raw materials such as iron and copper.

A fear of the Deuteronomic theologians is that "prosperity can lead to complacency and forgetting one's dependence on God." Thus, the text "warns that the effects of satiety are liable to be exacerbated with the passage of time when Israel's own labors yield further prosperity, and it credits that prosperity to its labors alone."[38] To guard against this malady, Deuteronomy 7:11–18 counsels the community neither to exalt itself nor to forget that blessing comes from God and not solely from its own achievement. According to 7:18a, God does not simply give the community its prosperity but rather God "gives *you* power to get wealth" (v. 18a). The community has actual power that it can use in cooperation with (or resistance to) God's purposes.

The passage closes with the threat that forgetting God and worshiping idols will result in national collapse (8:19–20). To a congregation around the time of the exile, this threat is not hypothetical but will be (or has been) realized in their own history.

Preachers sometimes caricature today's passages as a self-serving "gospel of wealth." However, the theme of material prosperity in Deuteronomy is more mature. Existence is a material affair. While blessing cannot be exhausted by material concern, fullness of blessing is more than a nonmaterial feeling. Deuteronomy reminds us that God intends for life to manifest the divine purposes, which include a material world of peace, security, and abundance. Obedience to the commandments does not magically create such a community. Human beings and nature can do things that interrupt blessing. However, walking in God's ways optimizes the possibility of material blessing, especially as community members express solidarity with the marginalized by sharing material goods (e.g., Deut. 14:28–29; 15:7–11; 16:9–12; 24:10–22; 26:12–13). On the one hand, the preacher needs to warn against crude materialism. On the other hand, the preacher can help the congregation give thanks for the opportunity to walk in God's ways, which includes working for a world of material security for all.

Deuteronomy 8:7–18 appears today with the story of Jesus healing ten lepers (nine Jewish and one Samaritan) only one of whom (the Samaritan) returns to give thanks to Jesus (17:11–19). The texts from Deuteronomy and Luke are not organically connected. The focus of the Gospel reading is only secondarily on the motif of thanksgiving. Luke uses the figures of the nine in a way consistent with other passages in the Third Gospel and Acts to contribute to the discrediting of some Jewish people. Luke overlooks the fact that the nine going to the Temple would give thanks to God as a part of the ritual of cleansing. Luke uses the Samaritan as a part of Luke's strategy to encourage the Lukan congregation to welcome Samaritans and Gentiles into the eschatological community. To the degree that thanksgiving is a theme in Luke 17:11–19, the Samaritan rightly gives thanks to Jesus, but Luke could have made that point without befouling the Jewish companions. For developing a sermon with a thanksgiving theme, then, Deuteronomy 8:7–18 offers a better option than Luke 17:11–19.

The Gospel writers cite Deuteronomy 8:3 in the temptation of Jesus (Matt. 4:4; Luke 4:4) while Paul makes a very different use of the same text in 1 Corinthians 8:3.

Year B

First Sunday of Advent/Year B

Isaiah 64:1–9

In our commentary on Isaiah 63:7–9 (First Sunday after Christmas Day/Year A), we noted that 63:7–64:12 laments God's apparent absence from the Judeans in their time of disillusionment after their return from exile. They asked, Where is God? "Where is the one who brought them up out of the sea . . . ? Where is the one who put within them his holy spirit?" (63:11). "Where are your zeal and your might?" (v. 15).

Continuing the lament, our reading begins with a plea: "O that you would tear open the heavens and come down . . . to make your name known to your adversaries, so that the nations might tremble at your presence!" (v. 1).

The prophet pleads with God to make God's presence known to the people and confesses on their behalf, recognizing that responsibility for the strained relationship with God lies with the people who had been controverting God's will for them. "We have all become like one who is unclean, and all our righteous deeds are like a filthy cloth. We all fade like a leaf, and our iniquities, like the wind, take us away" (64:6).

The people can open themselves to God's blessing and salvation by turning to God (*shuv*). Sometimes Third Isaiah addresses splits within the people, but in 64:5b–7 he conducts the whole people in an acknowledgment of their sin. Reflecting the Jewish view that the gates of repentance and reconciliation with God are always open, he enables the people to become responsible for facing themselves (which only they can do) and once again open to themselves the possibility of relying on God's

123

faithfulness to Israel rather than on the futile notion that they can perfectly well take care of themselves, which in Third Isaiah's time showed itself to be patently untrue.

The prophet appealed straight to the heart of God: "Where are the yearning of your heart and your compassion?" He ends the confession of sin with a confession of faith: "Yet, O LORD, you are our Father; we are the clay, and you are our potter; we are all the work of your hand" (v. 8).

In today's reading we see the true role of the prophet. For as much as Third Isaiah has hauled the people of Judea over the coals, he profoundly loves his people and in no sense rejects them. He is moved by empathy for their suffering and identifies with them in pleading with God: "After all this, will you restrain yourself, O LORD? Will you keep silent, and punish us so severely?" (v. 12).

Throughout this lament, Third Isaiah has given voice to God's unconditional love for Israel; he recalls God's gracious deeds, great favor, mercy, steadfast love, and God's presence to and with the people (63:7–9). Because God is a God of *hesed*, the prophet can plead with God as he does.

This passage is apt for Advent, when we long for the coming of light and peace into a world of darkness and conflict. Isaiah does not make cheap promises that all our troubles are over, that we need not worry about the homeless, AIDS victims, and mentally ill people who wander the streets of our cities. He offers a change of perspective, from hopelessness in the face of adversity in a world of indifference, and calls upon us to look to the only One who can, in an ultimate sense, help. We are reminded: God is indeed our caring parent and God's reign of compassionate justice will assuredly come. Mark's Gospel is as clear as Isaiah that "about that day or hour [when God's rule will come] no one knows" (Mark 13:32). He is equally clear that we should "keep awake" for it (v. 35) and live toward it.

Second Sunday of Advent/Year B

Isaiah 40:1–11

God's imminent arrival to the people Israel is announced in today's reading. The people of God are in exile in Babylon, coping with the fact that they have lost everything—their land, their city, their Temple with its psalms and offerings, and their institutions. They despair in God's ability to keep the promises made to them and are tempted by the success of the Babylonians and their god Marduk in bringing about victory and prosperity. How can they continue to trust and rely on the Lord?

But ever since the Lord promised Abraham and Sarah a land and people and well-being to be shared by all, and since the exodus, the faith of Israel was tied up with historical and political events; it is a this-worldly faith in concrete blessing and redemption. In keeping with this faith, Second Isaiah speaks a prophetic word to the people. He does not ignore the reality they face. The prophets did not look away from history to proclaim cheap grace; they looked deeply into history to find genuine grace. Preachers can use today's reading to do in our times what Isaiah did in his: proclaim the good news of God within the terrors of history.

There are three divine commands in today's reading. The first (vv. 1–2) is: "Comfort . . . comfort my people." Say to her "that she has served her term, that her penalty is paid, that she has received from the LORD's hand double for all her sins." An appropriate relationship between the people and the Lord is possible because of God's forgiveness. Under exile the people have suffered disastrously, realized the consequences of their sin, turned, and opened themselves to God's word. The word of God is contextual. As God afflicted the people when they were comfortable, committed injustice, and did not rely on God, now God comforts the afflicted; God commands the prophet to "speak tenderly to Jerusalem." God remains steadfastly committed to the covenant relationship with the people Israel.

The second command (v. 3) is: "In the wilderness prepare the way of the LORD, make straight in the desert a highway for our God" (see the Third Sunday of Advent/Year A for treatment of the "Holy Way" for God's people to return to Jerusalem). This is a way that God will travel. God is not handing out instructions to the department of transportation on how to build a highway. This is a parabolic highway prepared for the Lord who created heaven and earth and is the God of "all people" (v. 5). It symbolizes God's return to dwell again within the people of God, God's re-entry into the life of the exiles. When this highway is completed, "the glory of the LORD shall be revealed, and all people shall see it together" (v. 5). That Christians see it indicates that this forth-telling has at least partially come to pass. God's glory will also be seen when scattered Israel is returned to the *eretz Yisrael* (43:7).

The third command is "Cry out!" (v. 6). Isaiah asks: "What shall I cry?" He receives an answer about human finitude: "All people are grass, their constancy is like the flower of the field. The grass withers, the flower fades, . . . but the word of our God will stand forever" (vv. 6–8). How does this answer speak to the situation of the exiles? It shocks us into awareness of our limits and future deaths, but how does it speak forth hope to the oppressed? This is how: it reminds them that their harsh overlords will not be around too long. To God the inhabitants of earth "are like grasshoppers" . . . "princes . . . and . . . rulers of the earth are as nothing" (40:22–23).

God's advent comes with the announcement: "Here is your God!" (v. 9). The Lord "comes with might" to the salvation of Israel from oppression. "He will feed his flock like a shepherd . . . and gently lead the mother sheep" (v. 11). Faced with the horrors of history—far from home, dealing with the great power of the day, its army and its king—Isaiah directs the people to understand themselves in relation to the One who is God. The God of steadfast love and forgiveness will "carry them in his bosom."

In the apocalyptic statement of Mark 13:24–37, Jesus forth-tells the advent of the "Son of Man coming in clouds" who will "gather his elect from the four winds" (13:26–27). As Isaiah pointed the people in the direction of the future that God had in store for them, a world re-created from the chaos brought by armies and militarism and restored to God's purposes for it, Jesus points us ahead to the time when what we pray for, that God's rule may come on earth as it is in heaven, will be the case. He invites us to live toward that day.

Third Sunday of Advent/Year B

Isaiah 61:1–4, 8–11

Today's reading applies to more than one servant of God in the Scriptures. The description that Second Isaiah provided of the Lord's servant, that the Lord has "put the Lord's spirit upon him" (42:1) is said of a new servant of the Lord, one who comes with a word to the oppressed (61:1b). Luke 4:18 will tell of Jesus reading this passage and saying, "Today this scripture has been fulfilled in your hearing" (Luke 4:21). In Isaiah the servant was sometimes an individual, sometimes a group within Israel, and sometimes the people Israel. Scholars have puzzled over the identity of the servant in Isaiah, but to worry about that question is to miss the larger point, that the fact that the servant is not named is deliberate. Many within Israel could be the servant in different times, places, and circumstances; it is utterly appropriate that Jesus is so regarded.

The early communities of Jesus-followers knew many people who claimed that the Spirit of the Lord was upon them. Some were authentic figures, but enough were charlatans that 1 John 4:1 advises us: "Do not believe every spirit, but test the spirits to see whether they are from God; for many false prophets have gone out into the world." We should heed

1 John's counsel. Today's text provides us with the criterion by which to decide whether a particular claimant to the Lord's spirit passes muster: the true servant acts out the understanding of salvation at the heart of YHWH's purpose: "the LORD has anointed me . . . to bring good news to the oppressed, to bind up the brokenhearted, to proclaim liberty to the captives, and release to the prisoners; to proclaim the year of the LORD's favor" (61:1–2). This is the jubilee year of Leviticus 25.

Isaiah promises that those who were in exile and now are in a bad way in Judea will yet wear "a garland instead of ashes, . . . the mantle of praise instead of a faint spirit" (v. 3). Their redemption will be expressed in tangible ways: they will rebuild what has been ruined and restore the devastated cities (v. 4). We should imagine them as like contemporary survivors of a natural disaster, a tsunami or hurricane, which has destroyed towns, cities, and countryside, wiped out the infrastructure, destroyed houses, leveled everything. Redemption is never merely spiritual, except for gnostics. It involves physical life in all its dimensions. Jesus actually fed the hungry, instead of only talking to them about the bread of life. What the people of Judea needed was to be able to live a reasonably safe life in a functional society.

In verses 5–7, we find two emphases characteristic of some strands of Second Temple Judaism. The first is the welcome to strangers and foreigners (v. 5) that repeatedly marks the universalism and openness of the Isaiah tradition. Another is the shift in emphasis, later characteristic of the Pharisees, from the Temple priesthood to the people themselves as the priests of YHWH in this new situation. "You shall be called priests of the LORD, you shall be named ministers of our God" (v. 6). The Pharisees regarded the table in every home to be as holy as the Temple altar, and all Jews as priests (an early version of the priesthood of all believers); Isaiah stressed that the people themselves are the priests of the Lord. This idea has been around since Exodus 19:6: "you shall be for me a priestly kingdom and a holy nation."

Our passage ends on the note of God's considerate justice: "For I the LORD love justice, I hate robbery and wrongdoing." The kind of justice involved cares for the oppressed, the brokenhearted, the captive, the mourners, the homeless. God is steadfast to the covenant, and if the people also remain faithful to that covenant, being true to the gift of considerate justice, the long hoped-for return of well-being will take place.

The heart of today's reading is beautifully given voice in the Magnificat (Luke 1:47–55), assigned for today.

Fourth Sunday of Advent/Year B

2 Samuel 7:1–11, 16

David actually lived around 1000 BCE but the Deuteronomic theologians gave the books of Samuel their present form about 400 years later, after the exile. When David was anointed monarch (2 Sam. 5:1–25), to centralize the government and consolidate the power of the monarchy, he moved the ark from Shiloh to Jerusalem, where it continued to sit in a tent (6:1–23). David wanted to build a house (a temple) for God (7:1–3). However, the prophet Nathan received a message from God explaining that God does not require a house (*bayit*) to dwell with the people and to work actively in their behalf. Operating without ark, tent, or temple, God had liberated the people from bondage in Egypt. Represented only by the ark and the tent, God protected the people (7:4–9).

To be sure, David's successor (Solomon) would build a temple (7:13), but in mentioning this fact, the writers want not only to explain why David did not build a temple but to make the deeper point that the God of Israel operates freely. The claim that God is sovereign and did not require an earthly house assured the exilic community whose temple was destroyed that they could still trust in the promises of God.

Through Nathan God makes an unconditional promise. In a dramatic reversal of an earlier theme, God promises to give David a house (*bayit*) that will last forever—a lineage. The promise implies that David's dynasty and also the larger community of Israel will endure forever (7:11–16). Divine love is the sole reason for this promise (7:15). Christian preachers sometimes speak as if unconditional love originated with Jesus Christ, but this passage reminds us that God expressed such love to the house of David.

Given this promise, how could the Jewish community make sense of the exile? While the promise to David is unconditional, it comes with the stipulation that the monarch rule and that the people live according to God's provisions for a covenantal community outlined in Deuteronomy: free of idolatry, following the Ten Words, and providing for the poor and alien (e.g., Deut. 5:6–21; 10:12–22; 15:7–11; 17:14–20). When the monarch and the members of the community abrogate these stipulations, God will punish them (2 Sam. 7:14). The implication is that God used the exile to punish the descendants of David for violating the covenant. In the Deuteronomic theology punishment is not an end in itself but aims to provoke the community to repent and return to blessing (e.g., Deut. 4:30).

When today's Gospel reading says that Jesus is born "of the house of David" (Luke 1:27), the ancient readers were to hear Luke say that despite the destruction of the Temple by the Romans in 70 CE, the promise of God to David was still in effect. Luke and many other early followers of Jesus made two innovations. First, they believed that through Jesus Christ, God began to adopt Gentiles into the community descended from David. That is why Christians today worship the God of Israel and not a latter-day Zeus. Second, those early folk expected Jesus to keep God's promise to David by returning on the clouds with the angels in a dramatic interruption of history, finally and fully to manifest the realm of God. That event has not happened. The church today is in a situation much like that which the exiles faced in the days of Deuteronomy: We are called to live in covenant as we await the time when human community will be disturbed no more (7:10). The preacher can use 2 Samuel 7 to show fundamental continuity between God's unconditional love for the house of David and the extension of that love through Jesus Christ for the church.

Christmas Day/Year B

For comments on the readings for Christmas Day/Years ABC, please see Christmas Day/Year A.

First Sunday after Christmas Day/Year B

Isaiah 61:10–62:3

Further background on today's reading is found on the Third Sunday of Advent/Year B, Isaiah 61:1–4 (pp. 126–27) and in connection with the reading for Christmas Day 2/Years A, B, and C (pp. 9–10).

God's salvific intent for the people Israel, present in the Scriptures as God's original intent in electing Israel as God's pilot project for the whole world ("in you all the families of the earth shall be blessed," Gen. 12:3), is represented in today's opening verses as Third Isaiah's promise to Judea of its salvation in a time of gloom for the returned exiles. God's compassionate justice, of which Israel is to be a light to the Gentiles, will be richly bestowed upon the people. "I will greatly rejoice in the LORD, my whole being shall exult in my God; for he has clothed me with the garments of salvation, he has covered me with the robe of righteousness" (61:10). This is the righteousness that will bring good news to the oppressed, bind up the brokenhearted, proclaim release to the captives, and comfort those who mourn (61:1–2). It is a righteousness from the heart of God's love for each and all.

But it is not for Israel alone: "the Lord GOD will cause righteousness and praise to spring up before all the nations [Gentiles]" (61:11). By manifesting the communal characteristics of life and well-being, Israel will be a light and blessing to the Gentiles.

Chapter 62 returns to the theme about the rebuilding of Jerusalem and Judea articulated in 61:4: "They shall build up the ancient ruins, they shall raise up the former devastations; they shall repair the ruined cities, the devastations of many generations."

Third Isaiah copes with the misgivings of his strife-ridden and insecure community. They have found their homes burned to the ground, their crop lands wiped out by war, their institutions in shambles and their infrastructure wrecked. Life is unsafe, poverty rampant, and the Temple not rebuilt. Not only is the rebuilding critical to their well-being, it is also terribly uncertain. Many exiles have not returned and the surrounding countries still prey upon the defenseless Judeans.

Theirs is a question of theodicy. Is God true to God's promises? Has God got what it takes to pull off the reconstruction of Judea? Does God care? Third Isaiah again takes up Second Isaiah's proclamation: "For Zion's sake I will not keep silent, and for Jerusalem's sake I will not rest, until her vindication shines out like the dawn, and her salvation like a burning torch" (62:1). God declares that the people will be given a new name: "You shall no more be termed Forsaken, and your land shall no more be termed Desolate; but you shall be called My Delight Is in Her" (v. 4). God is not the "unmoved Mover" of Aristotle, but the most moved Mover of the Torah and the prophets. God cries out for Israel "like a woman in labor" (Isa. 42:14).

The new names signal a sharp turn in the course of historical events from the prophet's point of view. The time of desolation and defeat is in the past and YHWH calls Israel forward to a new future as God had called Moses and Abraham into a new future.

In this new future, through Israel God "will cause righteousness and praise to spring up before all the nations [Gentiles]" (61:11). Israel will be a light to the Gentiles and the blessings of God's loving-kindness will be shared by all the world. Today's passage is fittingly paired with the song of Simeon: "my eyes have seen your salvation, which you have prepared in the presence of all peoples, a light for revelation to the Gentiles and for glory to your people Israel" (Luke 2:30–32). In Jesus Christ we Gentiles see the light and in doing so give glory to the people Israel, recognizing that Christ is a gift to us from the God of Israel and the Israel of God.

Today's passage ends with the forth-telling that God will "rejoice" over Israel. In Ephesians 2:12–13, Paul reminds us Gentiles that before Christ "you were . . . aliens from the commonwealth of Israel, and strangers to the covenants of promise, having no hope and without God in the world. But now in Christ Jesus you who once were far off have been brought near." Now even we are "citizens with the saints [Israel] and also members of the household of God" (Eph. 2:19). We, too, should rejoice over Israel.

Second Sunday after Christmas Day/Year B

For comments on the readings for Second Sunday after Christmas Day/Years ABC, please see Second Sunday after Christmas Day/Year A.

Epiphany of the Lord/Year B

Isaiah 60:1–6

For comments on this passage, please see Epiphany of the Lord/Year A.

First Sunday after the Epiphany/Year B

Baptism of the Lord

Genesis 1:1–5

For comments on this passage, please see Trinity Sunday/Year A.

Second Sunday after the Epiphany/Year B

1 Samuel 3:1–10, (11–20)

As backdrop for this passage, see Proper 28 and First Sunday after Christmas/Year C. The note that Samuel was young when this call took place implicitly contrasts the wisdom and obedience of the youthful Samuel with the foolishness and disobedience of the older sons of Eli— Hophni and Phinehas. Since the word of God and visions were "rare in those days" the coming of such a word to Samuel testifies to Samuel's trustworthiness as the recipient of such an important occurrence (1 Sam. 3:1–2).

Samuel slept near the ark, a physical reminder of the divine presence, perhaps to fulfill a priestly duty. The "lamp of God" refers to the lamp in the tabernacle that burned all night (Exod. 27:20–21), meaning that this event took place before dawn. However, the postexilic community reading the text knew that the Temple had been destroyed, that is, that the light had gone out. The Deuteronomic editors want the community to believe the lamp had been quenched by the Babylonians because the community had not heeded the word of God as interpreted by the Deuteronomic theologians (1 Sam. 3:3–4).

Three times God called, "Samuel, Samuel," but the young person did not recognize the voice as God's until interpreted by Eli. Even Samuel had to be instructed in the ways of God in the manner of Deuteronomy 6:1–6 (1 Sam. 3:5–9).

When God came a fourth time, Samuel said, "Speak, for your servant is listening," thereby responding faithfully and receiving the blessing of the revelation from God (1 Sam. 3:10). In 1 Samuel 3:11, God says, "I am about to do something in Israel that will make both ears of anyone who hears of it tingle," that is, will give the listeners an earache because the message is painful (cf. 2 Kgs. 21:12; Jer. 19:3). God rephrases 1 Samuel 2:27–36 saying that God will end the priesthood of the house of Eli. So severe is the misbehavior that nothing can make expiation (2 Sam. 3:12–14). The fact that the sons of Eli cannot be forgiven impresses upon the postexilic community the importance of revitalizing the priesthood and the Temple in ways that honor Jewish liturgical practice and through which the priests participate fairly as members of the covenantal community in taking only their share of the offerings (see First Sunday after Christmas/Year C).

The story of the call of Samuel is sympathetic to one of the great themes of Epiphany—helping the congregation understand the purposes of God. However, this passage adds a sober note. The message that God gives Samuel is one of judgment. Samuel must bear this news to Eli who, despite his own faithfulness, will share in the calamity about to befall his family.

Eli, for his part, models how congregations should receive such news. "Do not hide it from me." Upon hearing the message, Eli accepted. At this point, however, the situations of Eli's family and of most contemporary communities differ. The judgment on Eli's house was irreversible. Most communities today have the opportunity to repent and to begin to walk in God's ways toward blessing.

The Gospel reading for today, John 1:43–51, does not have a direct literary or theological connection to the reading from 1 Samuel.

Third Sunday after the Epiphany/Year B

Jonah 3:1–5, 10

For comments on this passage, please see Proper 20/Year A.

Fourth Sunday after the Epiphany/Year B

Deuteronomy 18:15–20

The reading for today addresses two popular misconceptions regarding prophets. One is that the prophet was the epitome of the angry figure blasting the congregation with condemnation. The other is that prophets did not appear in Israel's story until after the Pentateuch in figures such as Elijah, Elisha, and Amos. Deuteronomy 18:15–20 corrects both misperceptions. Indeed, Torah presents several figures as prophetic (e.g., Gen. 15:2; 20:7; Exod. 7:1; 15:20; Num. 11:26–30; 12:6; Deut. 18:15–20; 34:10). The Deuteronomists want readers to think that prophetic ministry was rooted in Israel's oldest traditions. The text for today is the fullest reference to a prophet in Torah and presents Moses as the archetype of the prophets in the Deuteronomic literature.

Deuteronomy 18:9–20 deals with the issue, What kind of leader can Israel trust? This matter was important to the postexilic audiences of the Deuteronomic theologians. Deuteronomy 18:9–14 declares as "abhorrent practices" a list of customs found among Israel's neighbors—child sacrifice, soothsaying, auguring, sorcery, casting spells, consulting ghosts or spirits, and seeking oracles from the dead.

Moses announced God would "raise up for you a prophet like me from among your own people." Moses stood between the people and God because the people feared that they could not bear the intensity of exposure to God and the "great fire" at Horeb (Sinai; Deut. 18:16). God gave Moses messages for the people, something God promised to do for the prophets who came later (18:18). The Deuteronomists have in mind messages that reflect the theology and community practice advocated by Deuteronomy. God will hold accountable (i.e., will condemn) people who do not need these messages (18:19). The community is to kill prophets who speak in the name of other deities (18:20).

The text raises a haunting question: How can we recognize a word that God speaks? Deuteronomy poses a criterion. If a message "*takes place* or proves true," the community could believe the message was from God

(Deut. 18:21). While preachers often say that prophecy is less about predicting the future and more about speaking for God (the word "prophet" is from two parts: "to speak" and "for"), the Deuteronomic criterion for the trustworthiness of a prophet sometimes involves a future element.

The authors of this book have no doubt that God continues to speak through prophets and other media. However, congregations must often make decisions regarding how to respond to particular messages that purport to be prophetic without the advantage of knowing whether a message will actually come to pass. Given human finitude, it is more theologically honest to think that we seek the most *adequate interpretations* of God's purposes for the world than that we deal with pure, unquestionable messages from God. We therefore suggest a supplementary criterion for interpreting the adequacy of a prophetic message: the degree to which a prophet's message coheres with the community's deepest understanding of God's purposes. A prophet is similar to an ombudsperson whose work is to measure how well a community lives out its values, and to call attention to points at which the community needs to amend its behavior and to points at which the community embodies its deepest understanding of the divine purposes. Of course, the community needs to have conversation about such matters. Thinking together often brings to the surface questions and perspectives that do not come to individuals reflecting alone.

While the Gospel reading for today, Mark 1:21–28, does not refer explicitly to Deuteronomy 18:15–20, the picture of Moses in Deuteronomy does provide a generic frame within which to understand Jesus as an agent of God.

Fifth Sunday after the Epiphany/Year B

Isaiah 40:21–31

Chapter 40:1–11 is a message of comfort addressed to the people in exile in Babylonia. The rest of the chapter is a dispute with the people as to the credibility of this promise. It takes little imagination to understand the questions that a long-exiled people would put to a prophet who had just spoken what to them appeared to be an outrageous promise. Everything in their immediate experience argued to the contrary: YHWH's people had been defeated in war by Babylon and the god Marduk; the people were in exile among Babylonians who were doing quite well, particularly as compared to the poverty in devastated Judea. And these Babylonians could point to Marduk as having defeated YHWH and YHWH's people.

Today's reading is an argument in which Isaiah debates with the people, responding to their reservations and fears. They wanted to know whether YHWH could deliver on Isaiah's promise, whether YHWH's providential care for the people Israel could be evident in a world ruled by warlords. Such questions are seldom far beneath the surface of the minds of most parishioners. We pastors should take them seriously and respond in ways appropriate to the good news of God's grace and credible in the uncertainties of history.

Verses 21–26 discuss YHWH's competitors—the princes (national kings) and "rulers of the earth" (their national idols), and the stars in the sky that were claimed to be the celestial powers represented by the gods and princes (see vv. 18–20 for an argument against the idols). The aim of the debate is to reassure the people that their original trust in God could be restored in a new if no longer naïve way. Isaiah appeals to God's splendor in creation and God's redeeming efficacy in history, which never are separated in the Scriptures.

"Who has measured the waters in the hollow of his hand and marked off the heavens with a span, enclosed the dust of the earth in a measure, and weighed the mountains in scales, and the hills in a balance?" (v. 12). "It is he who sits above the circle of the earth . . . who stretches out the heavens like a curtain" (v. 22). YHWH "brings princes to naught, and makes the rulers of the earth as nothing" (v. 23). The Israelites have nothing to fear from these blowhards. Like the grass, "they wither, and the tempest carries them off like stubble" (v. 24). When we look "on high and see" the stars, "who created these?" (v. 26). The mighty and ruthless are nothing but stubble and not to be feared.

Verses 27–31 turn from debate to testimony. Isaiah addresses two matters. The people fear that the Lord does not know their plight and does not care about justice for them (v. 27). And, perhaps because of long exposure to idolatry, they forget that "the LORD is the everlasting God, the Creator of the ends of the earth" (v. 28). Perhaps they are looking for the kind of god who promises a quick fix to their deep problems. But that is not what Isaiah offers. Instead, he speaks of a God who "gives power to the faint, and strengthens the powerless" (v. 29). "Those who wait for the LORD shall renew their strength, they shall mount up with wings like eagles" (v. 31).

Isaiah does not promise that God will do everything for the people; God will empower them to cooperate with God as God's covenant people in bringing life and well-being to light. God is not a tool that we may use to meet whatever needs we have. God is the One whom we are to love with all our selves and on whom we may rely to do for us everything that it is appropriate for God to do. But there are things appropriate for us to do, one of which is to find the courage to take Isaiah's words to heart.

Sixth Sunday after the Epiphany/Year B

2 Kings 5:1–14

For comments on this passage, please see Proper 9/Year C.

Seventh Sunday after the Epiphany/Year B

Isaiah 43:18–25

Today's reading and that of the Fifth Sunday in Lent/Year C overlap two distinct segments of Isaiah 43 in which verses 16–21 constitute a declaration of redemption and verses 22–28 a discussion of the weightiness of Israel's sins. Hence we treat the two together.

The first unit (vv. 16–21) ends where our last reading from Isaiah (43:1–7) began and ended: with an affirmation that God is the creator of Israel, "the people whom I formed for myself so that they might declare my praise" (v. 21). In verses 16–21 Isaiah still urges the people to trust that the Lord will lead them from exile to restoration in Judea.

A considerable number of Israelites did not return to Judea. Hillel, around whom the school of Hillel gathered, was an older contemporary of Jesus who had come from Babylon. That the Babylonian Talmud was written in Babylon makes it clear that a Jewish community flourished there well into the sixth century CE. Jews did well in Babylon and many were reluctant to heed Isaiah's plea to respond to God's new initiative to return to Judea, itself a destitute and destroyed land.

So Isaiah begins this passage with a reminder of the exodus: God is "the LORD, who makes a way in the sea, a path in the mighty waters" (v. 16). God is yet able to deliver the people safely to Judea in spite of the obvious risks of such a journey.

Oddly, just having evoked Israel's primary historical memory and awareness of its identity, Isaiah then says: "Do not remember the former things, or consider the things of old" (v. 18). Yet, immediately after saying "forget all that stuff I just mentioned," he elicits the same memories: "I will make a way in the wilderness and rivers in the desert" (v. 19). How are we to understand this complex set of statements?

We always remember "the things of old" with all the certainty and clarity of hindsight. It is easy to be confident that the American war for independence will turn out the same way every time we read another history of it. What is hard to be confident about is that we can see our way through the fog of the present when we do not benefit from knowing how it will turn out. Isaiah appeals to the people to trust, now, that the Lord will deliver them and to act on that trust in spite of their very real fears that things might not work out well.

So the Lord says: "I am about to do a new thing" (v. 19). God is "the God of the call forward," as God has been ever since God called Abraham and Sarah forward to a promised future.[39] God is never simply the God of the past; God is the One who ever and again beckons God's covenant partners to live forward in hope toward a future that will be a source of light and blessing. Trust in the past is easier than hope in the future, because the latter requires us to act in spite of our lack of certainty as to outcomes and our fears as to what might happen to us if we do live forward.

God's "new thing" will provide a way, water in arid land (a life-sustaining resource to the people traveling through it), and "drink to my chosen people" (v. 20). God invites them to exercise an audacious approach to this new option. Faith is openness to God's future.

The purpose of all this is so that the people, once again, "might declare my praise" (v. 21). What this means is that God's purpose of leading all creation to a life of *shalom* and justice and well-being is the end in view. Worship of God who is the creator and redeemer of the world is what alone makes it possible for us to give ourselves to the mission of enabling all people to participate in blessing and peace.

Verses 22–28 indict Israel for its sins: "you have wearied me with your iniquities" (v. 24). Among these is Israel's failure to bring "sheep for burnt offerings . . . sacrifices . . . sweet cane with money . . . the fat of your sacrifices" (vv. 23–24). Instead of dismissing these verses as perversely advocating sacrificial Temple rituals, and reassuring ourselves that surely Jesus rejected Temple sacrifices, Christians should consider the possibility that we're missing something.[40]

In any healthy relationship, we "waste time" on each other, just enjoying and reveling in each other's company. This is well-invested time that signals our commitment to and affection for each other. We need to "waste time" with God in activities that, to the uncomprehending, look like "mere ritual." But these are times of joy and self-understanding and practicing, becoming what God gives and calls us to be, times of getting to know God and ourselves in relation to each other.

"You have burdened me with your sins . . . wearied me with your iniquities" (v. 24). Nonetheless, God "blots out" and "will not remember your sins" (v. 25). The people that God leads out of exile is a sinful people. Here is one of the theological axioms of Scripture: God works through human sin and error. As God promised deliverance to those who did not merit it long ago, so God can work even with the likes of us in leading us to deliverance from our own self-induced snares and idiocies. This is good news indeed.

Eighth Sunday after the Epiphany/Year B

Hosea 2:14–20

For our introduction to Hosea, please see Proper 12/Year C. Today's reading is the conclusion to chapter 2, which began in verses 1–13 with the Lord's heartbroken request to the Lord's children, phrased as Hosea's heartbroken request to his children to "plead with your mother, plead— for she is not my wife, and I am not her husband—that she put away her whoring from her face . . . or I will strip her naked and expose her as in the day she was born, and make her like a wilderness, and turn her into a parched land, and kill her with thirst" (vv. 2–3).

Presupposed by verses 1–13 is something like a legal procedure in which pleadings are entered and witnesses invited to decide between the plaintiff, the Lord, and the accused, the people. The accusation is that Israel has forgotten the Lord and run after her lovers: "I will go after my lovers; they give me my bread and my water, my wool and my flax, my oil and my drink" (v. 5). Israel has run after Baal (vv. 8, 13) whom Israel mistakenly thinks has provided her with the rich produce of the land. She has forgotten Deuteronomy 26:8–10: "The LORD [YHWH] brought us out of Egypt with a mighty hand and an outstretched arm, with a terrifying display of power, and with signs and wonders; and he brought us into this place and gave us this land, a land flowing with milk and honey. So now I bring the first of the fruit of the ground that you, O LORD, have given me." Instead, Israel now worships Baal to secure the blessings of the land.

Three times in chapter 2 we find a "therefore." "Therefore I will hedge up her way with thorns; and I will build a wall against her, so that she cannot find her paths" (v. 6). "Therefore I will take back my grain in its time, and my wine in its season; and I will take away my wool and my flax, which were to cover her nakedness" (v. 9).

Our passage begins with the third: "Therefore, I will now allure her, and bring her into the wilderness, and speak tenderly to her. From there

I will give her vineyards, and make the Valley of Achor a door of hope. There she shall respond as in the days of her youth, as at the time when she came out of the land of Egypt" (vv. 14–15). It is as if the Lord decides to go with Israel to a marriage encounter weekend in which the married couple spends time recalling what it was that they loved about each other at the time that they sealed their marriage covenant. Even in the long accusation the Lord eases up on Israel, attributing her wandering off to Baal less to utter sinfulness than to ignorance: "She did not know that it was I who gave her the grain" (v. 8), she "went after her lovers, and forgot me, says the LORD" (v. 13).

We recall Abraham J. Heschel's comment (Proper 12/Year C) that of all the prophets it was Hosea who had the most intimate glimpse into the heart of God and into God's heartbrokenness. God's motive in dealing with Israel is God's love for Israel, as highlighted in today's reading. God promises Israel: "I will take you for my wife forever; I will take you for my wife in righteousness and in justice, in steadfast love, and in mercy. I will take you for my wife in faithfulness; and you shall know the LORD" (vv. 19–20).

The Lord pledges to renew the covenant, "a covenant with the wild animals, the birds of the air, and the creeping things of the ground, and I will abolish the bow, the sword, and war from the land, and I will make you lie down in safety" (v. 18). These themes go back to the covenant with Noah, which was not only with Noah and all of his descendants, all human beings, but with all the living things and to the prophets with the promises of universal disarmament and the end of war. The Lord will yet deal with Israel with compassion: "I will have pity on Lo-ruhamah [whose name means "not dealt with compassionately"] and I will say to Lo-ammi [not my people], 'You are my people'" (v. 23). Love and grace have the last word.

Ninth Sunday after the Epiphany/Year B

Deuteronomy 5:12–15

Today's passage begins the second of three long sermons of the Deuteronomic Moses. Deuteronomy 5:1–21 contains the "ten words" (a designation for the Ten Commandments, Deut. 4:13; 10: 4). The Deuteronomists want these words to shape the covenantal life of Israel for "well-being" that will be long-lasting (Deut. 4:40). Other commandments in Deuteronomy help put the basic ten words into practice. As Deuteronomy 5:6 notes, obedience to these words does not earn God's grace. To the contrary, God freely chose Israel and graciously brought them out of bondage without reference to Israel's worthiness. Living the commandments is a way for Israel to say yes to the covenant with God as well as to give social form to covenantal community.

The fourth word, appointed for today, focuses on the Sabbath. Although Christians sometimes think the Sabbath is a day of worship, Deuteronomy 5:12–15 sees it as a day for rest. The word "Sabbath" transliterates *shabbat* meaning to rest, to cease, or to desist. While at various times some Christians have tried to maintain the spirit of Sabbath by observing Sunday as a Christian Sabbath, the original Sabbath day is the seventh day, Saturday. Having a Jewish Sabbath on Saturday and a Christian Sabbath on Sunday muted what could have been a powerful combined witness to the importance of rest. In any event, Christians often turned Sunday observance into a legalism.

While the heart of the fourth commandment is similar in Exodus and Deuteronomy, there are differences. In Exodus 20:8–11, the reason for Sabbath keeping is that God worked on the first six days creating the world, and then rested on the seventh day, thus providing the decisive model for human life. By resting on the seventh day, human beings remember that they are made in the image of God, which means to rule in their smaller spheres in the same way that God rules in the cosmic sphere. The experience of the Sabbath is itself an experience of blessing (Exod. 20:11).

In Deuteronomy 5:12–15, the reason for Sabbath keeping is to help the community remember that God brought them up from slavery in Egypt with an outstretched arm (note esp. v. 15). As Deuteronomy unfolds, readers realize that Sabbath keeping is both end (rest) and means (remembrance). Elsewhere, the memory of deliverance from slavery motivates the community to live in covenant, especially through justice and abundance for the marginalized (e.g., Deut. 15:15; 16:12; 24:18, 22). To observe Sabbath is for self and community to recall God's purposes and to reinforce commitment to them.

The directive to rest applies to all in the community: parent, daughter, son, female and male slave, ox, donkey, livestock, and resident alien. "It is as if the entire household is required to rest so that there can be no occasion to make the servants work. This one day a week, a servant is treated as the master's equal."[41] Insofar as the Sabbath is a day that belongs to God, it embodies God's purposes. Thus, the practice of insisting on rest for slaves is a reminder that the community is to relate humanely with slaves (Deut. 12:8–12, 15–19; 16:9–12) and resident aliens (e.g., Deut. 1:16; 14:21, 28–29; 16:9–14; 24:17–22; 26:12; 27:19). For slaves, resting as equals with owners is an experience similar to the release from bondage in Egypt. Sabbath thus anticipates the remission of slaves (e.g., Deut. 15:12–18; 23:15–16).

In connection with Proper 4/Year B, Deuteronomy 5:12–15 is paired with two stories that take place on the Sabbath in Mark 2:23–3:6. Unfortunately, Mark shaped these stories to justify tensions between the Markan community and the traditional Jewish community.

Last Sunday after the Epiphany/Year B

Transfiguration Sunday

2 Kings 2:1–12

For comments on this passage, please see Proper 8/Year C.

Ash Wednesday/Year B

Joel 2:1–2, 12–17 (Alternate)

For comments on this passage, please see Ash Wednesday/Year A.

Isaiah 58:1–12 (Alternate)

For comments on this passage, please see the Fifth Sunday after the Epiphany/Year A.

First Sunday in Lent/Year B

Genesis 9:8–17

Today's lection recalls how God made a second beginning with the human family (see Proper 4/Year A). In Genesis 9:1, God restates the purpose of human life as the same as in Genesis 1:26–28. According to Genesis 9:2, this vocation is necessary in the post-fall world because the relationship between humankind and animals is still under the curse of Genesis 3:14–19 (see Proper 5/Year B).

Because killing disrupts the divine purposes for life more than any other action, it receives detailed attention in verses 5–6. Only now, after the flood, does God explicitly permit the descendants of Noah to eat meat, and then only when the blood is drained (Gen. 9:3–4; see Lev. 17:10–14; Deut. 12:16, 23). Genesis 9:4 impresses upon the reader that the killing of animals is not to be indiscriminate, for all killing is now under divine scrutiny and regulation. Animals who take human life are to be killed, presumably to prevent them from further despoiling community. God forbids human beings from killing other human beings (Gen. 9:5), for they are made in the image of God. To kill a human being made in the divine image is to subvert the purposes of God for all to live together in mutuality and support and to turn the social world into chaos.

Killing so corrupts human community that God commands that killers be put to death, perhaps to remove the reminder of the possibility of killing (9:6). A principle of limitation applies here: the killer may be put to death but no further retribution is authorized to the killer's community. Opponents of capital punishment object that even the legal presence of such violence defaces the image of God and subtly reinforces a culture of violence, so they seek means other than legalized murder to deal with killers. Peace movements note that the step is very short from capital punishment to legalized killing through war. Simply finding authorization for a practice in the Bible does not automatically mean that the practice is desirable.

In 9:8–17 God articulates an explicit covenant with the descendants of Noah and with all living creatures. God promises never again to use a flood to return the earth to chaos. To people in the Near East where rainfall can quickly and dangerously create flood conditions, this promise assures that no matter how harmful future waters may be, they will not overwhelm the possibility of regeneration. To the stated covenant of 9:8–17 must be added the unconditional promise of Genesis 8:22 (Proper 4/Year A). God promises to continue the structures of creation that make life—and hence blessing—possible.

The sign of the covenant is a bow that God places in the heavens, presumably the rainbow. The Hebrew word bow *(keshet)* elsewhere almost always refers to a weapon. Hence, commentators often say that God uses the rainbow as a symbol of divine disarmament. Despite the fact that the immediate context of this bow applies only to the promise not to destroy the world by water again, the reader naturally hears 8:22 and 9:1–7 as part of the penumbra of the covenant. Thus when the reader of the Bible later encounters stories of killing in God's name (Holy War, etc.), the reader hears them not as celebration of violence but with the deep regret that such means were God's last resort to accomplish the divine purposes.

The Gospel reading for today does not echo Genesis 9. The letter for today, 1 Peter 3:18–22, directly recalls the flood story (though 1 Peter has in mind Genesis 6–8 more than Genesis 9). For Peter, the experience of baptism is a means to salvation similar to passing through the flood.

Jewish theologians in the Hellenistic age and later pondered the question of how to interpret the fact of faithful people among Gentiles who do not convert to Judaism. In the Hellenistic age, some Jewish thinkers derived the "Noahide laws" from this passage (and from wider reflection). These laws identified qualities through which Gentiles manifest the spirit of Judaism and live faithfully. These seven laws are: (1) avoiding idolatry, (2) not profaning the name of God, (3) not shedding blood, (4) establishing courts of justice, (5) not robbing, (6) not engaging in perverse sexual behavior, and (7) not eating meat from a live animal (*b. Sanhedrin* 56a; cf. *Jubilees* 7:20–33; *t. Abodah Zarah* 8:4–8; *Genesis Rabbah* 34:8). While the Noahide laws probably were not fully formulated by the first century CE, Luke picks up on prescient impulses in the report of the Apostolic Council in Acts 15:19–21 and 28–30.

Second Sunday in Lent/Year B

Genesis 17:1–7, 15–16

God cut covenant with Sarai and Abram in Genesis 15 (Second Sunday in Lent/Year C). By omitting Genesis 17:9–14, the lectionary cuts the heart out of Genesis 17, whose fundamental point is to explain the origin and meaning of the distinctive Jewish male sign of the covenant: circumcision. Scholars often point out that Genesis 17:1–27 is similar in language and theology to Genesis 9:1–17, thus indicating that the covenant with the ancestral couple takes place (and sets the mission of Israel) within the larger covenant that God made through Noah with the whole human race.

Like the covenant itself, the sign of circumcision is an act of grace. Neither Sarai nor Abram do anything to earn the covenant. The promises of the covenant are the same as in Genesis 15:1–6: a great community and the land in perpetuity (Gen. 17:3–7, 8). God now changes the name of the central male character from Abram ("exalted ancestor") to Abraham ("ancestor of a multitude"), for the name Abraham better embodies the content of the covenant.

In Genesis 17:9–14, God gives circumcision as a sign of the covenant. The great Jewish scholar Nahum Sarna interprets the theological significance of this sign as "an outward, physical reminder of the existence of the covenant, like the rainbow after the flood."[42] On a day-to-day basis, circumcision reminds the Jewish community of the steadfast presence and promises of God, and of the calling of the community to live in the ways of God. In bad times the community was tempted to forget the promise of blessing. In good times, the inverse temptation could occur: the community could forget that *God* was the source of blessing and that blessing brought with it responsibility to "walk in [God's] ways" (Gen. 17:1). The physical sign of circumcision functioned as a reminder. Colossians 2:8–15 interprets baptism as a form of circumcision for Gentiles who come to the God of Israel through Jesus Christ.

God changed Sarai's name to Sarah. While the text gives no specific etymological reason for this change, the narrator is clear that God will bless her and she will bear the heir. The narrator describes her role in bringing about the great nation in the same terms used for Abraham (Gen. 17:5–6, 16). Indeed, J. Gerald Janzen describes her as "mother of nations."[43] The promise is to both Sarah and Abraham, and they *together* are the parents of the coming progeny.

Objections are sometimes made (a) that circumcision is related to male superiority and (b) that there is no rite corresponding to circumcision for women. While it is regrettable that an overt sign is given only to the male, the sign itself is intended to symbolize a covenant that involves women and men equally. While it is also regrettable that women do not receive a sign, many women are grateful that Israel did not take up mutilating female genitalia, a practice that has been commonplace.

Genesis 17 does not contribute significantly to understanding Mark 8:31–38 or Mark 9:2–9. Genesis 17 is paired aptly with Romans 4 as Paul evokes Genesis 17 in Romans 4:11, 19 and quotes Genesis 17:5 in Romans 4:17.

Beyond Romans 4, Genesis 17 is widely cited in the New Testament. Luke alludes to 17:7 in Luke 1:55, 72–73, to Genesis 17:8 in Acts 7, to Genesis 17:10–14 in Acts 7:8, and to Genesis 17:12 in Luke 1:59 and 2:21. Paul draws on Genesis 17:7 in Galatians 3:16 and the Fourth Gospel refers to Genesis 17:10–13 in John 7:22 with Hebrews 11:11 invoking Genesis 17:19.

Third Sunday in Lent/Year B

Exodus 20:1–17

For comments on this passage, please see Proper 22/Year A.

Fourth Sunday in Lent/Year B

Numbers 21:4–9

Today's reading is cited in 1 Corinthians 10:9 as an example not to be emulated and in John 3:14 where Moses' lifting up of the bronze serpent, which enabled those who looked upon it to live (Num. 21:9), is likened to Christ's being "lifted up, that whoever believes in him may have eternal life." Numerous biblical stories are cautionary tales, and God's intent is to save all God's people.

The Numbers story of the bronze serpent is complex. The serpent played various symbolic roles in the religions of Israel's neighbors as it came to do in Israelite tradition. The serpent first appears as "crafty" (Gen. 3:1), not to be trusted. The serpent is the first actor to commit the sin of "evil speech," tempting Adam and Eve not to trust in YHWH but to put their trust in the illusory promise "you will be like God" (Gen. 3:5), encouraging them to trust ultimately in themselves.

According to Karen Randolph Joines, the serpent was "a strange synthesis of life and death, an object of both intense animosity and reverence."[44] The serpent's venom could kill but its annual shedding of its old skin and growing a new one accounts for how it became a symbol of life; "its penetrating eyes sparkle with unusual luster—it signifies superhuman wisdom."[45] Hence, it could elicit awe and, as a local idol, lure the Israelites away from faith in the Lord and become a religious alternative to YHWH. As YHWH came to be seen as the One who provides water (symbol of chaos and death) for salvation and newness of life (1 Kings 18), in today's story, YHWH co-opts the serpent and makes it clear that the serpent is merely a creature, a thing made of bronze, and that YHWH is the Lord and giver of life, not the serpent. This story deals with the relation between faith and culture; it does this by transforming what in the culture is an idol into a servant and creature of the Lord. Israel's theology was a monotheizing theology, having to contend with polytheism and idolatry in each phase of Israel's history. So does the church ever have to contend with the temptation to polytheism and idolatry. This way of looking at the story gives the preacher another way of dealing with it and the opportunity to ask how today's idols might be transformed.

The redactors of Numbers put the serpent story in the context of a complaint story in which the Israelites "become impatient" with the Lord and Moses. They were being led on a detour around Edom, actually a smart move on the order of giving sleeping dogs a wide berth (Edom always harassed Israel). We easily become grumpy when faced with detours. The Israelites trot out their standard gripes: no food, no water, and this miserable manna (see Pentecost/Year A). The Lord sends poisonous snakes among them as punishment, as a result of which "many Israelites died" (v. 6). At this point, Moses prays for the people, and the Lord instructs him: "Make a poisonous serpent, and set it on a pole; and everyone who is bitten shall look at it and live" (v. 8–9).

Numbers makes a pun in "serpent of bronze" (*nehash nehoshet*); the terms are closely related. The bronze serpent was later set up in the Temple. Second Kings 18:4 says that Hezekiah "broke in pieces the bronze serpent that Moses had made, for until those days the people of Israel had made offerings to it; it was called Nehushtan." Hezekiah regarded it as in violation of the commandment against images. That is another way to deal with idols: say no to them.

Fifth Sunday in Lent/Year B

Jeremiah 31:31–34

This passage occurs in the part of Jeremiah that was spoken during the exile as a Book of Consolation. The prophet looks forward to God returning the people from exile in Babylon and to restoring the life of the community in Palestine in every respect. Today's text introduces the best known concept (in Christian circles) from the book of Jeremiah, the new covenant.

When the people return home, Jeremiah foresees God repopulating the house of Israel (the northern part of the land) and the house of Judah (the southern part of the land) with generous numbers of people and animals who together can work the land and make it fruitful (Jer. 31:27). They can count on God to keep this promise because the exile itself is witness to the fact that God controls history (31:28).

The community has had a saying, "The parents have eaten sour grapes, and the children's teeth are set on edge," meaning that the effects of the sins of one generation are passed to the next. The sins of an earlier generation (e.g., idolatry, injustice) caused the exile, but the children of that generation (who did not sin to the same degree) had to bear the exile as well. However, in the new world, God will make that principle disappear. "All shall die for their own sins; the teeth of everyone who eats sour grapes shall be set on edge" (Jer. 31:29–30). Each generation will rightly suffer the consequences of its own sin, but consequences will not be passed to the next generation. The community can rebuild without being hog-tied by the sins of the previous generation (Jer. 31:34b).

In this context of renewal, Jeremiah anticipates a new covenant with both Israel and Judah, that is, with a newly reunited nation (Jer. 31:31).The covenant "will not be like the one that I made with their ancestors" whom God led out of Egypt. The ancestors broke the covenant, even though God was related to the community with the same bond that binds husband and wife (31:32).

What is *new* about the new covenant? Not very much. Even a casual reading of Jeremiah 31:33–34 reveals that the *content* of the covenant is not changed. According to Jeremiah, God says, "I will put my law *within* them, and I will write it *on their hearts*." This emphasis is similar to Deuteronomy 30:11–14, when Moses says that the commandment "is not too hard for you, nor is it too far away. . . . Neither is it beyond the sea. . . . No, the word is very near to you; it is in your mouth and in your heart for you to observe." The new element is that in the restored land, "No longer shall they *teach* one another, or say to each other, 'Know the LORD,' for they shall all know me, from the least of them to the greatest" (especially the monarch, priests, and prophets who have come under withering criticism in the book of Jeremiah) (Jer. 31:33–34, italics ours). With Jeremiah the new element is mainly a matter of emphasis.

The terms of the covenant will continue with life-shaping power. It will be inscribed on the hearts of the community. The people will no longer need human teachers (whose misinterpretations of Torah contributed to the downfall of Judah and Israel).

The passage from Jeremiah is paired with John 12:20–33 and Hebrews 5:5–10. These pairings can only be described as mystifying, for the motif of the "new covenant" does not appear in them. Christians sometimes say that the "new covenant" through Jesus Christ replaced the "old covenant" that God made with Israel. From an *exegetical* point of view, some texts do seem to fall into this category (e.g., Heb. 8:1–10:39, esp. 8:8–12; 10:16–17). However, from a *theological* point of view such a bald statement is problematic, for it would mean that God had abandoned the promises to the Jewish community. If God would abandon such promises, then God would no longer be trustworthy. Other texts from the New Testament are more in line with Jeremiah's vision, while implying the added dimensions of the covenant eventuating in the eschatological rule of God and including Gentiles (e.g., Luke 22:20; 1 Cor. 11:25).[46]

In any event, Jeremiah's hope is still unfulfilled. Judaism still ordains rabbis and the church still ordains ministers to teach Torah in community.

We long for the day when Torah will in fact be written on the heart in the way the prophet envisions.

Palm/Passion Sunday/Year B

Please see Palm/Passion Sunday/Year A, B, and C.

Good Friday/Year B

Isaiah 52:13–53:12

For comments on this passage, please see Good Friday/Year A.

Easter Day/Year B

Isaiah 25:6–9 (Alternate)

Because portions of this text are used elsewhere in the lectionary (All Saints/Year B, and on Proper 23/Year A), we contextualize verses 6–9 by dealing with the whole passage.

Isaiah 25:1–5 is a psalm of thanksgiving followed by an eschatological banquet (vv. 6–8), a hoped-for occasion of thanksgiving. It is addressed to "the LORD . . . my God" (v. 1) in the language of praise. It is spoken by an individual on behalf of the congregation of the people. It praises God for having done "wonderful things" (v. 1). What wonderful thing(s) has God done? God has "made the city a heap, the fortified city a ruin; the palace of aliens is a city no more, it will never be rebuilt" (v. 2). Thanksgiving for victory over enemies is familiar from the psalms. While the writers of this book do not hold God accountable for the destruction of cities and the many innocent people in them, we do recognize the importance of the Scriptures' understanding of salvation as concrete and down-to-earth. We should allow this passage to curb our tendency to regard salvation as so spiritual a thing that it is heedless of the course of this-worldly events. God's purpose to spread life and well-being entails involvement in the mess of history.

The city is not named and much scholarly ink has been spilled trying to identify it. That the city is unnamed may be intentional. Over the span of time during which the text of Isaiah was transmitted and redacted, quite a few different cities would have been in the minds of its readers and hearers and appropriately so. The namelessness of the city enables the text to find new pertinence down to the present.

While we do not think that God is the cause of the downfall of our enemies (other factors adequately account for the rise and fall of empires), we appreciate the fact that the psalmists frequently "pray through" their attitudes to their enemies. They do not piously assure themselves that they are too moral to have enemies, which may be only a form of self-deception. Rather, they accept that they have hostile attitudes toward enemies and take those attitudes into their conversations with the Lord. We should pray that the Lord transform our hearts and minds as well as those of our enemies. God's aim that reconciliation replace estrangement and hostility can transform our attitudes if we are honest and willing to work through them.

Verse 4 praises the Lord for having been "a refuge to the poor . . . to the needy in their distress, a shelter from the rainstorm and a shade from the heat." Here the Lord is praised for caring for the vulnerable, the last, the lost, and the least of society, central concerns of the Torah and the Prophets and of Jesus' ministry to the lost sheep of the house of Israel (Matt. 10:6; 15:24). It is particularly the vulnerable whom the Lord protects from "the blast of the ruthless" and "the noise of aliens" (v. 5). In our world it is still the most vulnerable who need protection from the ruthless, those women and their dependents, both the aged and children, on the bottom of the socioeconomic ladder.

Verses 6–8 describe an eschatological feast that the Lord "will make for *all* peoples" (italics ours). It is to be a sumptuous meal of rich food and fine wine. In this hoped-for future, "the shroud that is cast over all peoples" will be destroyed (v. 7); war, death, and the famine that comes with war will be taken away. The Lord will "swallow up death forever" and "wipe away the tears from all faces" (vv. 7–8). "Blessed are you who weep now, for you will laugh" (Luke 6:21) will in the end be true, when "God . . . will wipe every tear from their eyes [and] death will be no more" (Rev. 21:4).

What Advent looks forward to arrives in Jesus Christ fragmentarily and proleptically and what Easter celebrates, the triumph not only over death but also over death-dealing, is hardly yet on the scene. Evil still stalks the world and the nations still imagine vain things in war (Ps. 2:1), but in hope and faith God's covenant people can work and witness to a hope that the world might yet reflect the glory of God.

As Isaiah puts it: "on that day" it will be said, "This is the LORD for whom we have waited; let us be glad and rejoice in his salvation" (25:9).

Day of Pentecost/Year B

Ezekiel 37:1–14

For comments on this passage, please see the Fifth Sunday in Lent/Year A.

Trinity Sunday/Year B

Isaiah 6:1–8, (9–13)

Today's reading is referred to as Isaiah's call or commission or his Temple vision. The text of Isaiah has been redacted so extensively that it is point-less to treat it as straightforward autobiography. In its canonical context, we have to see today's passage as Isaiah's commissioning for a particular political mission in relation to an invasion from Syria/Samaria in or about 734 BCE. Chapters 6–8 have to do with precisely such an invasion. Although the text begins "in the year that King Uzziah died" (v. 1), we do not know the exact date of Uzziah's death.

Because the Lord instructed Isaiah to say to the people "do not com-prehend . . . do not understand . . . stop their ears . . . shut their eyes . . . that they may not . . . listen . . . and comprehend . . . and turn and be healed" (vv. 9b–10), the text does two things: it validates Isaiah's mission and explains why it did not work, why the people did not respond under-standingly to Isaiah's prophecy. Alternatively, if we see the mission as the text intends, we see that it did succeed: its purpose was to ensure that the people would not understand and turn and be healed.

The theological conundrum raised by the text is this: why would God foreordain that the hearts of the people be hardened against the message of God's prophet? The historical answer might be that Isaiah's mission did fail and that this passage is an after-the-fact explanation of the reason for the failure—God determined ahead of time that it would fail. This state-ment still leaves open the question, why would God do that?

In the anti-Jewish tradition that runs so strongly through the history of the church, this text has frequently been abused by putting it into the ser-vice of a displacement theology which argues that the Jews are a stubborn, obdurate people who never listened to God and that, as a consequence, the covenant has passed to us and we replace Jews in God's affections. This is a works-righteous argument that makes God's unconditional grace dependent on the condition that its recipients respond appropriately. Its self-contradictory nature is transparent.

Our text opens in the Temple (v. 1) with the Lord sitting on an elevated throne surrounded by six seraphs. The "LORD of hosts" (v. 3) is YHWH of whom Isaiah speaks more than sixty times as "YHWH of the [heavenly] hosts" (v. 3). Seraphs means "burning ones," which would explain the "live coal" in verse 6. Probably this text is selected for Trinity Sunday because of the threefold hymn of praise "Holy, holy, holy is the LORD of hosts"

(v. 3), which the seraphs sing to one another. Verse 4 alludes to an earthquake ("the pivots on the thresholds shook"), a typical description of a theophany (see Exod. 19:18 on the theophany at Sinai).

Because Isaiah was commissioned to speak for God, his lips were purified with the live coal; this was his preparation for his mission. The Lord asked: "Whom shall I send, and who will go for us?" (v. 8). The "us" refers to the heavenly host, not to the Trinity, although given the fact that texts have a reservoir of meaning, Christians have taken it in that sense. Isaiah immediately responds: "Here am I; send me!" (v. 8). Whereupon God tells Isaiah to say to the people that they will not hear, see, comprehend, or repent and be healed.

Isaiah asks, "How long, O Lord?" (v. 11). His question might ask how long he must proclaim this negative message or how long the predicted devastation of Judah might last. The text claims that the devastation will last "until the LORD sends everyone far away" (v. 12), that is, until the Judean community is in exile in Persia or Babylon (depending on how one locates the passage historically).

Matthew 13:14–15, Mark 4:12, Luke 8:10; 19:42, and Acts 28:26–27 refer to verses 9–10 of today's reading to explain why the message of Jesus or Paul falls on deaf ears. This is an explanation to be used carefully. There are those who simply will not hear, but there are also times when we who speak fail to make ourselves understood.

Proper 4 [9]/Year B

1 Samuel 3:1–10, (11–20)+ (Semicontinuous)

For comments on this passage, please see Second Sunday after the Epiphany/ Year B.

Deuteronomy 5:12–15* (Paired)

For comments on this passage, please see the Ninth Sunday after the Epiphany/Year B.

Proper 5 [10]/Year B

1 Samuel 8:4–11, (12–15), 16–20, (11:14–15)+ (Semicontinuous)

Today's passage is the most concise and direct criticism of the idea of monarchy in the Deuteronomic literature. The Deuteronomists were suspicious of monarchy and thought that a less structured covenantal community under the leadership of a prophet would have better served Israel. However, each generation is responsible for its own faithfulness, and on this point, the Deuteronomists were not myopic, as we see from 1 Samuel 8:1–3, where they report that the children of the great prophet Samuel (Joel and Abijah) "did not follow in [Samuel's] ways, but turned aside after gain; they took bribes and perverted justice." Prophetic DNA does not ensure faithfulness.

The elders of Israel recognize the corruption of Joel and Abijah and seek to replace judicial and prophetic leadership of the community with that of a monarch (1 Sam. 8:4–5). The theological editors had prepared listeners for this request in Deuteronomy 17:14–20. Although the elders acknowledge the perverse behavior of Joel and Abijah, the primary reason the elders give for wanting a change of government is *to be like other nations* (v. 5). A reader should remember that God sought to make Israel different from other nations so that Israel could demonstrate God's way of blessing.

Samuel is displeased and consults God who is also displeased, but who accedes. According to God, in this particular instance, the people are only repeating a pattern that has characterized them since being delivered from slavery in Egypt: forsaking God and turning to other gods. In an act of pastoral care, however, God instructs Samuel to warn the people regarding the negative effects of monarchial rule (1 Sam. 8:6–9). God is willing to work with the people's preference, but (to speak anachronistically) God wants them to make a critically informed choice.

By emphasizing that the *people* wanted the monarch, the Deuteronomist implies that the problems that ensued in the united and divided monarchies came not from God but from the community's own choice.

Samuel confronts the people with the negative consequences of monarchy. The characteristic activity of such a ruler is to "take" from the congregation (note that this verb appears six times in this short section and is the only verb characterizing the sovereign's activity). Samuel lists key ways the king will *take* from the people: sons to be warriors (implication: many will be killed), daughters to be perfumers, land and crops to go to courtiers and generals, slaves and animals to go to work for the ruler. The community will become slaves, and cry out, but God will not answer (1 Sam. 8:10–18). Although, according to Samuel, this is what it means to be "like other nations," the community redoubles its cry for a change of government (8:19–22).

The church continues to be vexed with a problem similar to that described in this passage. At what points are the life and witness of the church strengthened by accommodating, even adopting, the values and practices of the culture? And at what points is the church compromised by doing so? When the congregation, figuratively speaking, asks for a monarch, the preacher can follow the model of Samuel and help them think critically about such situations.

Luke places the only direct mention of this passage in the New Testament in Acts 13:21 on the lips of Paul, preaching to the synagogue in Antioch of Pisidia (Acts 13:21).

Genesis 3:8–15 (Paired)*

Genesis 2:4b–3:7 explains through the medium of myth *why* the world is no longer the superabundant, just, and covenantal realm of Genesis 1: the first two human beings ate of the tree of the knowledge of good and evil (see Trinity Sunday/Year A, Lent 1/Year B, and Proper 22/Year B). Today's reading, which must extend from 3:8 through 3:24 to honor the literary and theological integrity of the text, describes the *consequences*.

Genesis 3:8–13 sets the stage for the climax of the passage in verses 14–19. The narrator presents God anthropomorphically walking in the garden (Gen. 2:8). By hiding, the couple indicates they are aware of the boundary of 2:16–17. To make matters worse, in 3:10–13, first the male attempts to pass responsibility for the transgression onto the woman (and indirectly onto God) and then the woman attempts to pass responsibility to the serpent.

An effect of this early part of the text is to prompt the reader to ask, Do I attempt to pass off my responsibility for violating the purposes of God in the manner of the first woman and the first man?

God cursed the people and the earth in eight ways. First, the serpent no longer walks upright but loses its legs and must crawl (v. 14). Second, whereas the couple previously lived in harmony with the animals, that relationship became more distant, and was even marked by enmity (v. 15c). While Christians sometimes take 3:15c to refer to a messianic figure, nothing in the text itself supports such an interpretation. Third, the woman will suffer intense pain in childbearing (v. 16ab). The significance of the fourth part of the curse (v. 16c) is debated, but we take it to mean that despite the pain caused by childbirth, sexual yearning becomes potentially corruptive of personal and corporate life. Fifth, the male can rule over the female. Sixth, the ground itself is cursed. The earth was previously unabated in its effortless capacity to vegetate, but now it brings forth thorns and thistles and the human being must work very hard for the earth to produce (vv. 16–18). Seventh, human labor now becomes anxiety producing and physically draining (v. 19a). Eighth, each human being will eventually die (v. 19b).

The male's first act of ruling over the woman is to name her and thus to gain a measure of control (3:20). While Eve is the "mother of all living," this status brings with it the dangerous possibilities that come with sexual desire and the pain of childbearing.

God did not abandon or destroy the couple, but made garments out of skins to cover their nakedness in a way more substantial than the fig leaves of 3:7 that they had made for themselves and to help protect them as they made their way into the harsh environment in which they will now live (3:22–24).

This passage is interpreted in two ways. Jewish theologians note that while the story does describe the first act of disobedience and consequences, the story does not directly teach original sin as something that from Genesis 3 forward infects each human being. The text does not suggest that the capacity of Adam and Eve to make moral decisions was changed by the disobedience nor that their sin enfeebled the moral wills of their children. This story, then, illustrates the fact that women and men will ever struggle with the inclination to good or evil (*yetzer hatob* or *yetzer hara*). However, according to one rabbinic tradition *God forgave Adam*. After recounting the creation of Adam as if it took place in the first ten hours of New Year's Day, the rabbi says,

> In the eighth, [God] brought [Adam] into the Garden of Eden; in the ninth [Adam] was commanded [against eating the fruit of the tree of knowledge], in the tenth [Adam] transgressed, in the eleventh [Adam] was judged, in the twelfth [Adam] *was pardoned*. "This," said the Holy One, blessed be He, to Adam, "will be a sign to your children. As you stood in judgment before Me this day and came out with a free pardon, so will your children in the future stand before Me on this day and will come out from my presence with a free pardon."[47]

Another approach is nascent in the Hellenistic age through such writings as Wisdom of Solomon 2:21–24 (esp. vv. 23–24); 2 Esdras 3:4–36, esp. 20–27; 7:10–16, 45–48, 116–26; and 2 Baruch 48:42–43; 54:13–19. This strain begins to move in the direction of using Genesis 3 to explain that sin affects the entire human family. While this movement does not go as far as later Christian teaching on total depravity, it does hold that all human beings and the world itself are inherently impaired by the power of sin. Paul intensifies this second interpretation (e.g., Rom. 5:12–21; 8:18–25, 1 Cor. 15:20–28).

For other allusions to Genesis 3, see 2 Corinthians 11:3; Ephesians 5:22; Colossians 3:18; Hebrews 6:8; 1 Timothy 2:14; Revelation 22:3.

Proper 6 [11]/Year B

1 Samuel 15:34–16:13+ (Semicontinuous)

For comments on this passage, please see the Fourth Sunday in Lent/Year A.

Ezekiel 17:22–24* (Paired)

As we note on Proper 9/Year B, Ezekiel's prophecies during the exile had a dual focus of helping the community understand why the exile took place (as divine discipline for violating the covenant) and also encouraging the community to believe that God would be faithful to the promise to return them to the land and to restore the community.

Today's text is preceded by a vision that is interpreted allegorically. In allegory, a speaker uses one set of images to speak about another reality. Ezekiel 17:2–6 describes a first eagle (the eagle often represented military power in the ancient Near East) who came to Lebanon and carried off the top shoot of the cedar tree and carried it to another city and who then planted a seed from the land that became a small plant. Ezekiel 17:7–8 describes a second eagle toward whom the low plant stretched its foliage. God suggests through questions that the transplanted vine will not survive (17:9–10).

The cedar is the rebellious house of Israel. The first eagle is the ruler of Babylon, Nebuchadnezzar, who deports many leaders of the community to Babylon (17:11–12). The ruler of Babylon allowed the monarch of Israel, Zedekiah, to continue in power while serving Babylon (17:13–14). The second eagle is a pharaoh to whom Zedekiah turned while abandoning Babylon (17:15a). The Babylonians will attack Jerusalem again to punish Judah for the alliance with Egypt: Zedekiah will die in exile without help from the Egyptians, and listeners should understand these things as directed by God (17:15b–21).

Ezekiel uses many of the same visual elements in 17:22–24 but in the service of a vision of coming salvation. Some elements of this vision are parallel to those of the previous vision, but different characters, actions, and words show how God can transform a situation from judgment to restoration. God, instead of an eagle, now takes a sprig—tender but full of potential for growth—from the top of the cedar, and plants it in the land (17:22).

God plants the sprig on the mountain height of Israel so that it will "bear fruit" and become a thriving tree (17:23). Scholars agree that Ezekiel here speaks of God restoring the rule of the Davidic house (e.g., Isa. 11:1–10; Jer. 23:5–6; 33:15).

Strikingly, Ezekiel says, "Under it every kind of bird will live; in the shade of its branches will nest winged creatures of every kind" (Ezek. 17:23), echoing the full array of birds (clean and unclean) entering the ark in Genesis 7:14 for the judgment by flood. Scholars often observe that Ezekiel is here reminiscent of the vision of Isaiah and others of animals and humankind living together in peace in a restored world (Isa. 10:33– 11:9). Elsewhere, the prophet speaks of birds in ways that associate them with Gentile enemies (e.g., 31:6, 13; 32:4; 39:4, 17). William H. Brownlee points out that Ezekiel 47:21–23 promises shelter for Gentiles equal to that of Israel, and that Isaiah 2:2–4 (cf. Mic. 4:1–4) looks forward to the day when Gentiles will come to Jerusalem to learn from the God of Israel.[48] Thus Ezekiel envisions a world in which Israel lives in peace with the animal world and other nations while also becoming a shelter for Gentiles who seek to know the living God.

The passage concludes that this action will demonstrate to the other "trees of the field," that is, the other nations, that the God of Israel is sovereign. For the events around the exile and restoration demonstrate that God can make low the high, make high the low, wither the tree that is green, and cause the withered tree to revegetate (17:24).

This passage from Ezekiel is one of the best pairings in the lectionary with Mark 4:26–34, parables comparing the apocalyptic coming of the realm of God to a seed growing secretly (Mark 4:26–28) and the growth of a mustard shrub (4:29–32). Not only do the parables pick up the contrast between the small beginning (sprig, seed) and large conclusion (tree, bush), but the latter parable directly alludes to Ezekiel 17:23 (and Daniel 4:12) by saying that "the birds of the air can make nests in its shade" (Mark 4:32). Mark uses the reference from Ezekiel to affirm that repentant Gentiles will be in the eschatological realm (cf. Mark 1:15; 13:10).

Proper 7 [12]/Year B

1 Samuel 17:(1a, 4–11, 19–23), 32–49;
17:57–18:5, 10–16+ (Semicontinuous)

The story of David and Goliath (1 Sam. 17:1–58) shows that the spirit of God is "mightily upon David" (1 Sam. 16:13). The armies of Israel and the Philistines were camped on either side of a valley near Socoh, about fourteen miles west of Bethlehem. As their champion the Philistines put forward Goliath, about ten feet tall, covered in armor with only his forehead exposed, and holding a massive weapon (1 Sam. 17:1–11).

The Israelites feared Goliath and no one came forward to fight him. The young David was initially not even on the battlefield but was summoned (17:12–23). David asks a question, "Who is this uncircumcised Philistine that he should defy the armies of the living God?" With this, David surpasses the theological understanding of all others on the battlefield (17:24–30). After hearing David's record in killing lions and bears, Saul consents to David confronting Goliath (17:31–37). David takes only a staff, a sling, and five smooth stones to confront Goliath. He dispatches Goliath with one stone and the Philistines flee, leaving Israel to plunder their camp (1 Sam. 17:38–58).

Preachers often apply this text to personal life circumstances by pointing out that in partnership with God, individuals can overcome the repressive giants that confront them. The same is true for communities, a point that may be especially pertinent for struggling congregations. The church itself is increasingly a David-like presence for God's values in a Goliath-like culture of idolatry, exploitation, and violence.

Saul spoke with David, after which "the soul of Jonathan [Saul's heir] was bound to the soul of David" (1 Sam. 18:1). Although some interpreters think this expression refers to a same-gender sexual relationship, we are not persuaded by that argument and think instead that it refers more generally to a deep sense of commitment to one another. Today's culture might call them soul mates. They made a covenant, and Jonathan gave David a robe and weaponry. Some scholars conclude that with this gesture, Jonathan surrendered the throne of Saul to the former shepherd (18:2–4). While this incident is not so important in its own right, the narrators use it to establish the relationship between David and Jonathan that is later significant because of the shifting loyalties among Jonathan, Saul, and David. A preacher might develop a sermon that traces the relationship of David and Jonathan through the books of Samuel (e.g., 20:1–42; 23:16–18; 31:2; 2 Sam. 1:1–27; 4:4; 9:1–13; 16:1–4; 19:24–30; 21:7–14).

Saul initially approves David's success in battle (1 Sam. 18:5), but he grows angry when some Israelite women declare that Saul has killed thousands but David tens of thousands (18:6–9). The next day, under the influence of an evil spirit, Saul tried to kill David with a spear, but David got away. Saul, afraid and wanting to be rid of David, gave the younger person a commission in the army, but God was with David so that David enjoyed such success that "all Israel and Judah loved David" (18:10–16). The Deuteronomists did not write a manual of group organization, but leaders in today's church would do well to contemplate the destructive consequences of Saul's reaction to David, and to imagine modes of leadership in community that have less to do with popularity and control and more with leadership through prophetic covenantal community.

This last incident shows readers how right Samuel was to resist the idea of monarchy. For here we have an internecine conflict over the possession of the throne that will bring about social chaos and many deaths. Even though David has talent superior to Saul as warrior, administrator, and public persona, David's rule will also result in struggle for succession and attendant chaos.

The New Testament gives no overt attention to the particular stories told in today's reading.

Job 38:1–11 (Paired)*

After the collapse of his life, although Job repeatedly asks to speak directly with God in order to present his case and hear God's reply (Proper 22/Year B), God has been silent. God speaks for the first time in the lesson for today, a reading that should include Job 38:1–40:1 and 40:6–41:34. In these addresses, God puts one question after another to Job. When interpreting this material, the preacher should exercise what Charles R. Blaisdell calls "tone of voice exegesis," that is, noticing that the way one inflects the text—the tone of voice—makes a significant difference in the meaning that one assigns to the text.[49] The reader can intone the divine speeches with feelings as different as anger, arrogance, impatience, disdain, humor, or compassion.

God appears out of an overpowering windstorm, which sometimes accompanies theophanies, and states that Job does not have enough knowledge to speak perceptively about the matters raised by this book (Job 38:1–3). God then asks questions that urge Job (and the listening community) to acknowledge that Job did not make the world and hence cannot understand how it operates (38:4–7). Job did not observe when God created the present boundaries of the sea (thus limiting the power of chaos). What, then, can Job know about justice and injustice, blessing and suffering?

God never directly takes up the questions that Job has raised in the preceding chapters. Indeed, God never addresses the question of Job's innocent suffering or why the disobedient sometimes prosper and the obedient do not, and neither here nor in Job 42:1–6 does God offer a constructive statement of how to interpret these matters.

Despite this, however, two biblical theologians call attention to implications in the divine speeches that offer constructive paths for preaching. J. Gerald Janzen interprets God's speech in an ironic mode,[50] noting that God does not downgrade Job, but seeks to prompt Job to realize that God approves of Job's questions. Janzen also discovers echoes of Psalm 8 and Genesis 1:26–27 in the text, thus suggesting that God urges Job to continue the human calling to rule creation as interpreted in those texts.

Carol Newsom, who teaches at Candler School of Theology, notices that God's addresses to Job presuppose a dimension of moral order in the language "of place, limit, and nonencroachment." Newsom expands, "If one realizes that each thing, each person, has place, purpose, and limit, then there are places where I must not tread, places where the energy and vitality, indeed, the violence of my being must meet its limit."[51] According to this point of view Job and other members of the human family should honor the boundaries of our own knowledge and figure out how to live creatively within them.

The lectionary pairs this text with the story of Jesus calming the storm-tossed sea in Mark 4:35–41. While Mark does not allude specifically to Job 38, the latter passage does remind the reader of God's ability to work through water forces. Indeed, as God's creative presence in Job calmed the watery chaos and transformed it into a world capable of supporting life, so the presence of God through Jesus in Mark does the same in a setting of social chaos (e.g., Mark 13:3–23).

Proper 8 [13]/Year B

2 Samuel 1:1, 17–27+ (Semicontinuous)

Although conflict between Saul and David is rife in 1 Samuel 6:1–31:13, Saul maintains the crown and David respects Saul as God's anointed (1 Sam. 24:6; 26:9), twice sparing Saul's life. In a fierce battle in 1 Samuel 31:1–7, the Philistines killed Saul's three sons (Jonathan, Abinadab, and Malchishua) after which Saul fell on his own sword so that Philistines would not make sport of him and shame him.

David returns from Ziklag (2 Sam. 1:1–10) not knowing Saul and Jonathan are dead. An Amalekite describes Saul's death. The Amalekite saw Saul leaning on his spear. Whether Saul was attempting suicide or had been wounded and was using the spear as a crutch is not clear. Saul sought death at the hand of the Amalekite. The visitor presents David with Saul's crown and armlet.

David immediately rips his garments and begins to fast in traditional gestures of mourning. He learns that the messenger is a resident alien—a non-Israelite who lives in Israel and receives the benefit of protection from Israel but who is to live according to the same values as Israel. David has the Amalekite killed because the people of Israel are to respect (and certainly not to kill) God's anointed (2 Sam. 2:11–16).

David then intoned 2 Samuel 1:19–27 as a lament over the deaths of Saul and Jonathan and ordered that it be taught to all in Judah (1:17–19). David wants Israel to mourn the loss of its glory (Saul) but wishes that the Philistines would not hear of it and rejoice (1:19–20). Nature itself is to mourn because the shield of Saul will no more be rubbed with oil (1:21). The people of Israel are to mourn as they remember Jonathan and Saul as valiant warriors and as they recall Saul's gifts to them (1:22–25a). David names his grief about Jonathan in a brief but moving first person statement (1:25b–27).

A refrain, "How the mighty have fallen" occurs three times in the poem, and recalls similar themes in Hannah's song with its subtle inference that monarchy would bring difficult times upon Israel (1 Sam. 2:1–10). The death of Saul and Jonathan demonstrates the truth of her song.

Four things are noteworthy for preaching in these readings. First, although the Deuteronomists did not think about issues around suicide in the same way as communities today, the story of Saul taking his own life could provide the preacher with a point of entry into a broader theological consideration of that issue. Second is a reservation about David killing the Amalekite. Community members need to be accountable to community standards, but murdering the Amalekite (even if the Amalekite killed Saul) only increases the level of violence in community. Third, public lamentation—including the rituals of tearing the garment and fasting—encouraged people in antiquity to name their grief directly and to deal with it in a communal setting in which they had the support of other people. These attitudes and practices were much healthier than the ways in which many people in North America attempt to deny grief and hide displays of it. Fourth, while David and Saul were at loggerheads (and Saul even tried to kill David), David treated Saul respectfully according to the standards of covenantal community. David thus provides a useful model in a church and world in which conflicts continually increase, and in which increasingly vicious attitudes and behaviors are commonplace.

Lamentations 3:23–33
or Wisdom of Solomon 1:13–15; 2:23–24* (Paired)

While these alternate readings interact little with one another, they make interesting pairings with the complex reading from the Gospel.

Most scholars place the date of the Wisdom of Solomon in the middle of the Hellenistic age (circa 250 BCE to 50 CE). The author intertwines elements of the wisdom tradition in Judaism (see Second Sunday after Christmas Day/Years A B C and Proper19/Year B) and Hellenistic philosophy, with a smattering of apocalypticism. The book reinforces Jewish identity in a setting that pressured Jewish people to move away from Jewish tradition and practice and toward more Hellenistic ways. Moreover, in Alexandria (a likely setting for the book) the Jewish community experienced considerable tension with Greeks, and in 38 CE some Greeks destroyed synagogues and harassed Jewish people. The Wisdom of Solomon contrasts the just (typically Jewish people) and their fate of immortality with the unjust (typically representatives of the broader Hellenistic culture) and their fate of condemnation.

Wisdom 1:1–15 invites readers to live in righteousness (that is, according to God's designs) through wisdom and thereby to avoid the condemnation that awaits the unrighteous. Wisdom 1:12–15 encourages readers to avoid death that comes to people who "bring on destruction by the works of their hands," that is, idolatry and other failings to live according to God's designs (1:12). God did not create death and does not delight in it; rather, human beings brought it on themselves (1:13). God "created all things so that they might exist" and initially made them with "no destructive poison" (1:14). Indeed, "Righteousness [those who live righteously] is immortal" (1:15).

In Wisdom, "immortality" is not entirely defined but seems to refer to a Hellenistic notion of the soul continuing after death (e.g., 3:1–13), with a touch of apocalypticism (e.g., 4:20–5:23). Notions such as resurrection of the body and immortality of the soul were not always neatly demarcated in the syncretism of antiquity.

Whereas virtually all other texts in Lamentations (for background on which, see Proper 22/Year C) are unceasing lament over the destruction of Jerusalem at the time of the exile, today's reading voices confidence that the faithfulness of God to the covenant means that God will end the exile and restore the community (Lam. 3:22–24). In the meantime, the community should recognize that the exile is just punishment for their idolatry and injustice, and should therefore abide quietly while awaiting salvation (3:25–30). The community should remember that while God causes the grief of the exile, God is also compassionate and will ultimately act according to *hesed*, God's steadfast love, covenantal loyalty, loving-kindness. God afflicts the community with exile only when the people of the community bring it on themselves (3:31–33). Of course, this reading calls for singing the hymn "Great Is Thy Faithfulness."[52]

The texts from Lamentations and Wisdom are paired with the story of the raising of Jairus's daughter (Mark 5:21–24a), within which is the story of the courageous woman with the issue of blood (5:24b–34). On the one hand, in accord with Lamentations, both the courageous woman and Jairus trust in the faithfulness of God for restoration. On the other hand, neither "waits quietly" in the style of Lamentations 3:25–26; each approaches God assertively for help. The preacher might ruminate on conditions that call for waiting quietly and those that call for assertion.

Proper 9 [14]/Year B

2 Samuel 5:1–5, 9–10+ (Semicontinuous)

After the savage intrigue of the preceding chapters, the people of Israel come to David at Hebron with the declaration of solidarity that "we are your bone and flesh." They acknowledge David's occasional leadership over them even when Saul was alive, and recall God saying that David would be shepherd over Israel. The elders of Israel make a covenant with David and anoint him king over Israel, thus making David ruler over both Judah and Israel. David's first act is to move against Jerusalem, which is occupied by Jebusites (2 Sam. 5:6–10). Though they taunt David by saying, "Even the blind and the lame will turn you back," David's army quickly takes the city, and David establishes Jerusalem—central to both Judah and Israel—as the capital.

The characters who speak in 2 Samuel 3:26–39 absolve David of Abner's murder. The reader, however, knows that as a faithful ruler, David should have kept control over his house to avoid murder. Readers recognize further that the deaths of Ishbaal and his assassins and the bloody conflict between Abner and David resulted from the people's choosing monarchy, against Samuel's advice (1 Sam. 8:1–22). Although the narrator says David becomes "greater and greater," the cost to the community is immense, and only grows greater in later chapters in David's life.

The public anointing of David as sovereign of Israel provides a natural occasion to reflect more broadly on his role in the New Testament, which speaks directly about David fifty-seven times (twenty-four of which occur in Luke–Acts, seventeen in Matthew, six in Mark, and ten elsewhere). These passages typically use the figure of David in one of the following ways. David is an authority who interprets aspects of Jewish tradition (Rom. 4:6; 11:9; Heb. 4:7), who interprets Jesus or the Jesus movement (e.g., Acts 1:16; 2:25–31; 4:25), and whose behavior helps justify that of Jesus or his followers (e.g., Matt. 12:3; Mark 2:25; Luke 6:3). Yet Jesus is a greater authority than David (e.g., Mark 12:36–37; Matt. 22:42–45; Luke 20:42–44). David was an ancestor of Jesus, meaning that Jesus is successor to David (e.g., Matt. 1:1, 6, 17; Luke 3:31). Some in the first-century Jewish community envisioned a David-like warrior leader who would overthrow Rome (e.g., Matt. 2:6—the only direct citation from today's lection in the New Testament; Mark 11:10). The New Testament writers tend to define what it means to be David's heir in terms of apocalyptic eschatology: the coming realm of God succeeds Davidic rule (e.g., Luke 1:32; Acts 13:22–41; Rev. 3:7; 5:5; 22:16), which includes welcoming Gentiles (e.g., Acts 15:6) and the end of Rome. From this latter perspective, many of the New Testament authors are sympathetic to the Deuteronomists, who eschewed conventional monarchy in favor of prophetic leadership in covenantal community (see Proper 28/Year B).

Ezekiel 2:1–5 (Paired)*

Ministers sometimes cast the roles of priest and prophet as opposites, as if the priest is a comforter and the prophet a denouncer, but Ezekiel exposes the falsehood of such a dichotomy. Ezekiel was both. Priests oversaw regular community processes to help the community live in covenant and blessing through such things as teaching Torah, overseeing the Temple, and distributing resources for the poor. Judaism included rites to help community members recognize violations of the covenant (including priestly failures) and ways to make things right, and priests sometimes had to confront people with their sin.

Prophets functioned in a role similar to quality control officers today, monitoring community life and pointing out where the community was failing to live up to its vocation and, as possible, calling for restorative action. When the community failed to believe in the promises of God, the prophet typically called for hope. The roles of priest and prophet existed not in opposition but in complementarity.

Ezekiel helps listeners interpret why the exile took place. Probably reflecting a loss of confidence in God and exiles, the prophet assures the community that God will end the exile and restore their life in the promised land. Not surprisingly, Ezekiel the priest envisions the restoration climaxing in the building of a new Temple that includes awareness of the presence of God in a fresh way that would make it less likely that the people would disobey (Ezek. 40:1–48:35, esp. 43:7–13).

The passage assigned for today is part of the prophet's call. The purposes of a call narrative were to (1) assure the listener that the prophet is actually called by God and (2) reveal the character of the prophet's mission. In Ezekiel 1:4–28, the prophet receives a dramatic vision of a storm in whose center is a chariot containing the glory of God, which as Jon L. Berquist notes, assures the community that God is not limited to Jerusalem but is present with them in exile.[53]

God speaks to Ezekiel as "Mortal." The phrase in Hebrew, *ben adam*, sometimes translated "son of man" or "son of a human being," can mean a representative of a class, so that God's words to Ezekiel are for the wider community. The reference to the spirit entering Ezekiel assures readers that Ezekiel operates as representative of God (Ezek. 2:1–2).God sends Ezekiel to prophesy to a "nation of rebels," a community that in past and present generations has violated the covenant. Ezekiel is to say to them, "Thus says the Lord," that is, the prophet is to speak in God's behalf to them (Ezek. 2:3–4).

In a statement that should be of enormous encouragement to today's minister, God does not insist that Ezekiel succeed in changing the people. "Whether they hear or refuse . . . , *they shall know that there has been a prophet among them*" (our italics; Ezek. 2:5). Ezekiel is called to be faithful by carrying out the commission from God, who prepares the prophet for the fact that some in the community will resist the message and tells Ezekiel not to let fear of them inhibit the preaching (2:6–7).

God then gives Ezekiel a scroll to eat. The scroll contains the message that Ezekiel is to give; eating it indicates that it becomes a part of Ezekiel's own being. Although the scroll contains words of lamentation and woe (explaining that the community is in exile because of its sin), the scroll itself is sweet as honey because the exile is discipline preparatory to restoration (Ezek. 2:8–3:3).

This passage is paired with Mark 6:1–13, the rejection of Jesus at Nazareth (Mark 6:1–6) and the mission of the Twelve (6:7–13). Mark does not specifically presuppose this passage from Ezekiel, but thematic similarities occur between the readings. Both Ezekiel and Jesus face challenges from their own communities (Ezek. 2:6–8; Mark 6:1–6). Ezekiel is commissioned to minister, as are the disciples (Ezek. 1–5; Mark 6:7–13).

Proper 10 [15]/Year B

2 Samuel 6:1–5, 12b–19+ (Semicontinuous)

The ark, because it represented the immediate presence and power of YHWH, was one of the most potent physical symbols in Israel. The ark was a box containing two stone tablets of the covenant (Deut. 9:11; 10:5) on which were two cherubim—figures with the bodies of animals, the heads of human beings, and wings. Although God was said to be enthroned in the space between the cherubim (e.g., 1 Sam. 4:4; 2 Sam. 6:2), at its best, Israelite theology believed that God was present at all times. The ark was a physical reminder of that conviction, but it remained where it had been placed after capture by the Philistines (1 Sam. 4:1b–11; 5:1–12; 1 Sam. 6:1–7:2).

In last week's reading, David was anointed ruler over all of Israel and moved the capital of the newly unified monarchy from Hebron to Jerusalem (2 Sam. 5:1–10). Now the monarch seeks to bring the ark itself to Jerusalem. Presumably, David wants to be aligned with the power of YHWH as represented by the ark, and in its new location it will serve the political purpose of indicating the union of Judah and Israel.

At Baale-judah (another name for Keriath-jearim), the people place the ark on a new cart to replace the one they broke up and burned as part of the sacrifices of joy when the Philistines returned the ark (1 Sam. 6:13–16), and they bring the ark in a joyous procession that included dancing, singing, and instruments (2 Sam. 6:1–5).

The lectionary omits the part of the passage that raises a profound theological issue. Uzzah sees that the ark is about to fall off the cart and reaches a hand to steady it, whereupon God immediately killed Uzzah (1 Sam. 6:6–7). Scholars usually explain that Uzzah had not prepared in the proper ritual way to touch the ark. His immediate death even while doing something helpful reinforces the importance of obedience and the consequences of disobedience—vintage Deuteronomic themes (see Proper 17/Year B). David names the place Perez-uzzah, "Bursting Out Against Uzzah" (NRSV note) and is so fearful that the traveling group leaves the ark with Obed-edom, a Gittite. Only after David saw that the ark blessed the household of Obed-edom for three months did David bring the ark to Jerusalem (6:8–11).

Arriving in Jerusalem, the entourage engages in a typical ancient Near Eastern ritual of welcoming a new national deity to the city: a procession with pageantry, sacrifices along the way, dramatic rituals as the statue was installed in its new cultic home, and distribution of food to the people (6:12–19). David wears a linen ephod—a simple white linen garment associated with the priesthood.

The preacher might help the congregation name symbols that function similarly to the ark to awaken awareness of the divine presence. For instance, in our tradition (Disciples of Christ) the Communion table often has this quality. The preacher should also help the people recognize that while the text is intended to impress readers with the importance of following God's directives, from today's perspective it is theologically inappropriate to claim that a God of love would strike a person dead for trying to do something helpful, even if that person had not followed the typical prescriptions for being around the ark.

This text does not appear in the New Testament.

Amos 7:7–15* (Paired)

Amos 7:1–8:3 describes four images as the sources of Amos's prophetic inspiration; between the third and the fourth image is the account of his confrontation with "Amaziah, the priest of Bethel" (vv. 10–17). The four prophet-inspiring experiences are perfectly ordinary events: the Lord showed Amos locusts (7:1), fire (7:4), "a plumb line" (7:7), and "a basket of summer fruit" (8:1).

Locusts could devastate farms and meadows, bringing famine on animals and people (Joel 1:19–20). Amos sees the locusts eat all the grass of the land (v. 2), prompting him to beg the Lord to forgive because "Jacob . . . is so small" (v. 2). The Lord concedes to Amos's prayer. When the Lord shows Amos fire "eating up the land" (v. 4), Amos again prays to the Lord to "cease, I beg you!" (v. 5), and the Lord says, "This also shall not be" (v. 6).

Today's reading makes a different move. Amos sees the Lord "standing beside a wall . . . with a plumb line in his hand" (v. 7). The Lord said, "'Amos, what do you see?' And I said, 'A plumb line.' Then the Lord said, 'See, I am setting a plumb line in the midst of my people Israel; . . . the high places of Isaac shall be made desolate'" (vv. 8–9). This time Amos does not intercede on behalf of Israel. Using a plumb line to determine if a wall was properly built was standard practice in the ancient world. An out-of-plumb wall will collapse. Amos uses the plumb line to measure Israel's situation in relation to God: Israel's behavior is not an appropriate response to God's gracious love. Israel was to love the neighbor and take especial care of the widow and the orphan on whose behalf Amos waged a prophetic campaign, but Israel lacked concern for the least in society and therefore its "high places . . . shall be made desolate, and the sanctuaries . . . laid waste" (v. 9).

In verses 10–17, the story of Amos and Amaziah (Amaziah was priest of Bethel and supporter of the king and his regime), Amaziah reports to King Jeroboam that Amos has said that "Jeroboam shall die by the sword, and Israel must go into exile," accusing Amos of conspiracy against the king (v. 10). Amaziah misleads the king by claiming that Amos, rather than the Lord, has said these things and by avoiding any explanation as to why Amos said what he did.

Amaziah addresses Amos as if the prophet were an outside agitator— go back to Judah where you came from (v. 12). He says that Amos should not prophesy at Bethel because "it is the king's sanctuary, and it is a temple of the kingdom" (v. 13). This is striking! One would expect a priest of YHWH to know that it is the Lord's sanctuary and Temple. But because the king worships there, however inauthentically, it is not "decent" to remind listeners of the gift and claim of God upon the people. The northern kingdom had its house prophets, willing to live off the largesse of Jeroboam and say what he wanted to hear. This explains Amos's denial: "I am no prophet, nor a prophet's son; but I am a herdsman, and a dresser of sycamore trees" (v. 14) to whom the Lord said "Go, prophesy to my people Israel" (v. 15). Amos again prophesies, this time to Amaziah: "You say, 'Do not prophesy against Israel, and do not preach against the house of Isaac.' Therefore thus says the LORD: '. . . you yourself shall die in an unclean land, and Israel shall surely go into exile'" (vv. 16–17).

The criterion for authentic preaching is not whatever the powers-that-be deem appropriate. It is whether what is preached is appropriate to the grace and command of God. Genuine prophecy came from one who refused to call himself a prophet. He was willing to trust that decision to others. Amos had a prophetic modesty that we should emulate.

The lectionary pairs this text with the story of another king and another prophet, Herod and John the Baptist; each story is appropriately critical of a king who has turned his back on the covenant.

Proper 11 [16]/Year B

2 Samuel 7:1–14a+ (Semicontinuous)

For comments on this passage, please see the Fourth Sunday of Advent/ Year B.

Jeremiah 23:1–6 (Paired)*

Jeremiah, like others in Israel and Judah, speaks figuratively of the monarchs of Israel as shepherds (e.g., Jer. 3:15; 10:21; 22:22; 25:3–4), a way of speaking suggested by the fact that shepherds were responsible for the flock. The shepherd led the sheep to food and water, tended them when they were sick or hurt, and disciplined them to help them learn to stay with the flock.

By saying "Woe to the shepherds" Jeremiah means that God invoked a curse upon the monarchs because instead of keeping the flock together by insisting on the sound teaching of Torah and practice of justice, they let the people turn to idolatry and injustice and scattered the flock into exile. Because the shepherds did not attend to the flock, God will remove them from office (Jer. 23:1–2).

God plans to gather the faithful remnant from the exile and reunite Judah and Israel in the land of Israel so that they can "be fruitful and multiply," that is, carry out the deepest purposes of God for human life in covenantal community (see Trinity Sunday/ Year A). God will "raise up shepherds over them who *will* shepherd them." The people will not live in fear or be dismayed, nor "shall any be missing" (Jer. 23:3–4).

God promises to raise up a new ruler from the line of David, "a righteous Branch" who will "deal wisely and shall execute justice and righteousness." He will reunite Judah and Israel, see that the priests and prophets teach Torah rightly, lead the community in practicing justice, and avoid idolatry and unholy alliances with Egypt or others (23:5–6a). This ruler will be called "The LORD is our righteousness," meaning that the community will live according to the *torah* of God, which leads to right (covenantal) relationships and a life of blessing (23:6b).

Although Christians sometimes think of Jesus as this righteous branch, Jeremiah had in mind a leader who would rule in postexilic Palestine. Strictly speaking, the conditions that Jeremiah envisioned never unfolded after the exile as Palestine became a colony of Persia. Nor has Jesus recreated the world as the kind of flock-living-in-blessing-and-safety that Jeremiah hoped. Nevertheless, this text is a lure to today's church to offer to join with the synagogue in seeking to nurture such a world.

This text is paired today with Mark 6:30–34, in which the Gospel writer says of the hungry crowd of five thousand in the wilderness, "[Jesus] had compassion for them, because they were like sheep without a shepherd" (6:34). Jesus then carries out some of the quintessential works of the religious leader/shepherd in Israel by teaching them rightly and implies a contrast to the false teaching/shepherding of the scribes and other Jewish authorities who oppose Jesus (e.g., 1:21). The reading from Jeremiah is paired with Luke 23:33–43, the death of Jesus on the cross, on Reign of Christ Sunday (Proper 29/Year C). Luke neither cites nor echoes the reading from Jeremiah. The lectionary apparently places Jeremiah and Luke together to suggest (as does Mark) that Jesus is a faithful shepherd, whereas those who brought about his death (Jewish and Roman leaders) are not. A preacher can certainly affirm Jesus as a trustworthy shepherd. But a part of a preacher's responsibility as a faithful shepherd is to help the congregation recognize that the way in which Mark and Luke equate Jewish authorities with false shepherds is itself false shepherding and has contributed to the persecution and slaughter of many Jewish people.

Proper 12 [17]/Year B

2 Samuel 11:1–15+ (Semicontinuous)

The spring of the year was the season for war. The worst of the winter weather was usually over and troops could move more easily than in winter. David sent his army forth under the leadership of Joab while remaining in Jerusalem (2 Sam. 11:1).

One day, David was on the roof because the roof was often cooler than the interior of the house. He sees a beautiful woman, Bathsheba, bathing as a rite of purification in connection with her menstrual period (2 Sam. 11:4), meaning that at the time of her first encounter with David, she is not with child. David has Bathsheba brought to his house where they have a sexual relationship and she becomes pregnant (11:4–5). She is the spouse of Uriah, a soldier in David's army who turns out to be faithful to David and to the Deuteronomic traditions concerning warriors (2 Sam. 11:2–3). The ruler of Israel, in contrast, commits adultery in violation of Deuteronomy 5:18 and 5:21.

David brings Uriah home from the front and tells him, "Go down to your house, and wash your feet," which is probably a way of speaking about having sexual intercourse. David hopes that Uriah will have conjugal relations with Bathsheba so that he (and the community) will think the child is Uriah's. David is thus implicated in a lie. The soldier, however, did not go home to Bathsheba but slept near the entrance to David's house (1 Sam. 11:6–9). When David questioned Uriah about this matter, Uriah asserted that while the army was still in the field, he would maintain the purity required of the warrior in battle by practicing abstinence (1 Sam. 11:10–12;

cf. Deut. 23:9–14; Josh. 3:5; 1 Sam. 21:5). David got Uriah drunk, but still Uriah was faithful to the vow of the warrior (2 Sam. 11:13).

In a cruel touch, David wrote a letter that Uriah himself carried to Joab instructing the field commander to place Uriah at "the forefront of the hardest fighting and then to draw back" so that Uriah would be killed (2 Sam. 11:14–15). In this, David violates the spirit of Deuteronomy 5:17. To his discredit, Joab cooperates with this plan, and events unfold in just the way David hoped, but with a twist. Joab sends the soldiers too near the city wall so that "some of the [additional] servants of David from among the people fell." Joab composes the report of his failure of leadership in such a way as to highlight Uriah's death and hence to win David's favor (11:16–25).

Today's incident demonstrates the veracity of the statement of the prophet Samuel to the people that they should not seek a monarch to replace government by judges and prophets (1 Sam. 8:1–22). David here is the paradigmatic example of the monarch who *takes* from the people (see Proper 5/Year B).

Insofar as the behavior of a leader functionally legitimates behavior in community, by choosing monarchy the people themselves brought certain attitudes and behaviors into the center of their common life. As we see in 1 Samuel 11:16–25, when the leader deceives and kills, deception and death multiply. Such perspectives would cause the postexilic community to ask, What kind of leadership do we want as we rebuild our world? Leaders in the congregation (and in the broader world) could well ask, Am I a leader in the pattern of David in this text? What kinds of attitudes and behaviors in community do I authorize by my own attitudes and behaviors?

The writers of the New Testament do not refer to this text.

2 Kings 4:42–44* (Paired)

Today's reading is the last three verses from a chapter that tells stories about Elisha, prophet of the Lord, bringing life and well-being to people in a situation in which the wealthy and the royal have turned to idolatry and apostasy and practiced injustice against the poor. The stories deal with everyday matters—the elimination of a widow's debt and saving of her children from being sold into slavery (vv. 1–7); the raising of a faithful woman's son from the dead (vv. 8–37); removing the poison (or rancid taste) from a pot of stew (vv. 38–41); and the feeding of a hundred people with twenty loaves of barley (vv. 42–44).

These stories are remarkably like the "miracle" stories of Jesus in the Gospels and vice versa. In them, little or nothing is said about religious or spiritual matters, explicitly, except for the obvious fact that what God is all about in the Bible is making life and well-being available to God's creatures and opposing all that brings death and curse. This has to do with being out of debt and free of its consequences, being well instead of sick, alive instead of dead, having food to eat in an economy of scarcity and destitution, in which the rich and the royal look away from hunger as the kings of Israel often do; being free from suffering and pain.

In the first story Elisha works with what the woman has in the house: a jar of oil (v. 2). He asks her to borrow all the "vessels" she can find and pour the oil into them; she does and it does not run out until they are all full. He then tells her to sell the oil, pay her debts, and "you and your children can live on the rest" (v. 7). See 1 Kings 17:8–16 for a parallel story of Elijah and the widow of Zarephath. In the story of Elisha's raising of the son of the Shunammite woman, he uses a ritual of healing and prayer used by Elijah in reviving the widow's son (1 Kings 17:17–24). In the story about Elisha's removing "death" from the pot of stew, he uses flour: "and there was nothing harmful in the pot" (v. 41).

In today's reading, Elisha used the twenty loaves of barley and fresh ears of grain brought by "a man . . . from Baal-shalishah" (v. 42). Like Jesus, who used the "five barley loaves and two fish" that a boy had with him (John 6:9), Elisha works with what is available. Although usually treated as miracle stories, these accounts are remarkably matter-of-fact and do not stress the miraculous. They stress that God is at work in the ordinary, everyday, and run-of-the-mill matters of life: bread, fish, oil, prayer, and possibilities—the possibilities available by God's grace in the good creation which is God's gift to God's creatures.

Compassionate people with imagination; this is one way to think of prophets. Prophets not only empathize with God's pain at idolatry and injustice; they also empathize with the suffering and vulnerability of the little people, the nobodies of the world, in a situation of famine (see 2 Kings 2:19–22), hardship, early death, and royal indifference. Amid all of these, God is committed to bringing life and well-being into reality, particularly for the lost, the least, and the last.

The same theme is struck in the feeding of the five thousand at a time when Herod Antipas was feasting in his castle with his courtiers, generals, and the wealthy plantation owners of Galilee. (See our commentaries on Herod's banquet and the feeding of the five thousand in *Preaching the Gospels without Blaming the Jews*, pp. 137–40 [Mark 6:30–44], 62–63 [Matt. 14:13–21], 140–41 [John 6:1–21].)

Proper 13 [18]/Year B

2 Samuel 11:26–12:13a+ (Semicontinuous)

Today's lesson continues the story from last week. David violated the covenant by committing adultery with Bathsheba and by having her husband, Uriah, killed (2 Sam. 11:1–25). Bathsheba mourned the death of Uriah for seven days, as was the custom, at the end of which (wasting no time) David brought her to the palace where she became his wife and gave birth to a child (11:26–27).

In Deuteronomic theology, the prophet is to serve as an ombudsperson who monitors the faithfulness of the monarch in carrying out the royal responsibility of leading the community in covenantal life (Deut. 17:14–20). Nathan thus comes to David and tells the story in 2 Samuel 12:1b–5. Upon hearing the story, David is incensed, and declares that the wealthy person "deserves to die." That person should restore fourfold the lamb stolen from the poor person (2 Sam. 12:5–6). Nathan then pronounces the chilling words, more penetrating in the King James Version than in the more recent translations, "Thou art the man!" (12:7). David indicted himself in 12:5–6. Nathan only made explicit David's self-implication.

Nathan explains that God had providentially directed David's life and had been ready to do even more (1 Sam. 12:7b–8), yet David despised the word of God and did what was evil in God's sight by striking down Uriah and taking Bathsheba as a spouse (12:9). Consequently, because David engaged in such violation of relationship, David's future will be marked by repeated violence. Some of David's own wives will be given to David's neighbors. Although David had acted in secret, God will do these things in the open so that all can see them and learn from them (12:10–13).

David plaintively admits, "I have sinned." He remembers that he has pronounced a death sentence upon himself (12:5–6). In keeping with the promise of 2 Samuel 7:13 that David's house would go on, Nathan announces that David will not die. However, 2 Samuel 7:14 is also in the background: God will discipline David "with blows inflicted by human beings." The narrators subsequently report death visited on David's house (e.g., 1 Sam. 13:23–29; 18:9–15; 1 Kgs. 2:19–25) and the violation of David's wives (2 Sam. 16:21–22). The narrators imply here a principle that recurs in Jewish literature: punishment for a sin sometimes takes place by means of that very sin. David engaged in violence, and so he experiences violence.

While the New Testament does not cite the specific content of this text, some of the parables attributed to Jesus operate on the same literary principles as the parable that Nathan told David. Instead of confronting the hearer with the main issue of the text, and risking an immediate rejection on the part of the hearer, they first establish sympathetic identification among the listeners and the setting, characters, and beginning of the plot in the story. The storyteller then introduces a startling development into the plot, a twist that catches the listeners off guard. By the end of the parable hearers are faced with an unexpected possibility about which the congregation needs to make a decision about how to think, feel, or act. A preacher could adopt this model for sermons on such texts.

Exodus 16:2–4, 9–15* (Paired)

For comments on this passage, please see Proper 20/Year A.

Proper 14 [19]/Year B

2 Samuel 18:5–9, 15, 31–33+ (Semicontinuous)

This passage requires the larger narrative context. Absalom is the third of David's six sons (each from a different mother). In a story that turns the stomach, Amnon (Absalom's older brother) feigned an illness that brought their sister Tamar to care for him. Amnon raped her, and David did not punish him (2 Sam. 13:1–23). Setting a trap similar to the one by which Amnon deceived Tamar, the enraged Absalom had Amnon murdered. Absalom then stayed in exile at his mother's house for three years. David, in the meantime, mourned Amnon's death and grieved Absalom's absence, but did nothing (13:23–39).

Joab, David's nephew and commander of the army, used a wise woman from Tekoa to get David to bring Absalom back from exile (2 Sam. 14:1–32), but Absalom soon began to undermine David's rule. The narrator ironically presents Absalom winning the hearts of Jerusalem by posing as a wise judge who imparts justice to the community in contrast to David who provides no mechanism for such matters (15:1–14). The reader naturally thinks, Would that such wise judges were still at the center of our common life.

Fearing Absalom, David fled Jerusalem (15:15–16:14). Absalom entered the city supported by Ahithophel, one of David's advisors. Ahithophel wanted Absalom to murder only David, but David sent the spy Hushai into Absalom's court and persuaded Absalom to reject Ahithophel's plan. Dejected, Ahithophel hanged himself. Hushai advised David of Absalom's imminent attack so that David was prepared (16:15–17:29). David's disciplined army met Absalom's guerrilla force. More than twenty thousand died as David's army was victorious (18:6–8), but David instructed the generals to deal gently with Absalom (2 Sam. 18:1–5).

Absalom was riding a mule (a typical animal for royalty) and his head became caught in the branches of a tree; the mule walked away, leaving Absalom dangling. A soldier in Joab's army reported Absalom's condition to Joab, who was frustrated that the soldier had not killed the rebel. The soldier explained his dilemma: even if Joab himself wanted Absalom dead, if the soldier had killed Absalom, Joab would have punished the solider for disobeying David. Many readers today can identify with the impossible situation of this solider. Impatient, Joab thrust three spears into Absalom, ended the battle, buried Absalom, and set up a heap of stones (2 Sam. 18:9–15).

The grief of David's mourning quivers on the page even today (2 Sam. 18:19–33, esp. 33), so that Joab said, "You [David] have made it clear today that commanders and officers are nothing to you; for I perceive that if Absalom were alive and all of us were dead today, then you would be pleased." David then needed to restore relationships with his own supporters (19:1–15).

This story shows again the consequences of the community's preferring the rule of monarchy to leadership by judges. While David's personal exploits of military strategy were often breathtaking, his leadership did not maintain the practice of covenant in community, which could have prevented the multiple deceptions that led to Absalom's initial alienation from him. Indeed, without the monarchy, Absalom would have had no reason to embark on the violent quest to dislodge David from power and might well have lived. This painful story is an anti-model of the life in community envisioned by Deuteronomy.

When faced with alienation of households or competition for leadership in the congregation such as that between Absalom and David, can the preacher and congregation envision ways of resolving the conflict that have greater likelihood of constructive outcome?

The New Testament does not attend to this passage.

1 Kings 19:4–8 (Paired)*

Please see Proper 7/Year C for our commentary on this reading.

Proper 15 [20]/Year B

1 Kings 2:10–12; 3:3–14+ (Semicontinuous)

Today's reading tells of the death of King David and of Solomon's conversation with God in which Solomon asks for "an understanding mind" or a heart that listens to God (3:9) and God's gift of "a wise and discerning mind" (3:12). Stripped from the context of 1 Kings 1–3:14, it risks presenting a naïve view of Solomon, not unlike the one we learned in Sunday school where matters of sex, intrigue, and political shenanigans were not discussed. In context, however, today's passage is intriguing.

An apt theological adage claims that God works through human sin and error (*errore hominum providentia divina*). Those in the past with whom God worked were ambiguous and so are we; we should be less judgmental of them and more ready to accept that God can work even through us. So it was with Solomon, who eventually will be at cross purposes with God; 1 Kings 1–3:14 sets the stage for that eventuality.

First, some context. The story begins with an old, sexually impotent King David whom even a "very beautiful" girl was unable to help (1:1–5). Knowing of David's age and weakness, Adonijah seeks the kingdom for himself, recruits allies (1:5–10), and hosts them at a dinner. But the prophet Nathan and Bathsheba alert David to the situation (1:11–27) and to Bathsheba's fears that if Adonijah succeeds, she and Solomon "will be counted offenders" (1:21) and in all likelihood killed. David installs Solomon as king and charges him to walk in God's ways and keep God's statutes (2:3). Solomon then has Joab, Shimei, and Adonijah killed (2:5–38), cannily (wisely) securing his own position. First Kings 3:1 notes that Solomon marries Pharaoh's daughter, a comment presaging the later troubles Solomon will get into because his foreign wives bring other gods into the royal house (11:1–8).

Solomon visited a high place (shrine) at Gibeon (v. 4), at the time an authentic place for the worship of YHWH. God appeared to Solomon in a dream, a frequent means of divine revelation in the Scriptures (see Matt. 1:20), and invited him to "ask what I should give you" (3:5). Solomon's answer discloses that he is already rather wise (not just shrewd). He refers to his father David as "your servant" (v. 6) and to himself as "your servant" (vv. 7, 8, 9). At this stage, Solomon wishes to govern YHWH's people, whom he knows to be God's people, not his own (vv. 8–9), as God's servant (compare Mark 10:41–45; Matt. 20:25–28; Luke 22:24–27).

For this reason, Solomon asks for "an understanding mind" (v. 9); more precisely, a listening heart, to be open to hearing (*shema*) God's word; a constant reminder in Israel's worship then and now. God is pleased that Solomon did not respond with petitions for longevity, wealth, or the slaughter of his enemies (Solomon had already taken care of the latter), but for a heart to do the right thing. And so God grants him what he had asked plus all the things for which he did not ask—"riches and honor all your life" (v. 13; compare Matt. 6:25–34; Luke 12:22–31).

Because we already know how the story proceeds, with Solomon's failure to remain faithful to his opening prayer for wisdom—he does not retain a listening heart—we see that he sets himself a high standard to live up to in his prayer. God gives Solomon everything he asks for, as God does us—God always gives us everything that it is possible and appropriate for God to give us. But that remarkable grace in no way frees us from the requirement to use these remarkable gifts in trustworthy ways. Solomon teaches us both lessons.

Proverbs 9:1–6 (Paired)*

Proverbs 9:1–6 is an invitation from woman wisdom to attend a banquet, while 9:7–12 provides reasons for accepting the invitation of wisdom and 9:13–18 is an invitation from woman folly. (For background on wisdom and on the personification of wisdom as a woman, see Proper 19/Year B.)

Proverbs 9 uses an image familiar in Jewish literature: participating in a meal which is a figure of speech for a way of life. The figure and the meaning are connected organically. The way of life directed by wisdom is as important to individuals and the community as food for the body.

According to Proverbs 9:1, wisdom has built her house with seven pillars. While the meaning of the seven pillars is much debated, it seems logical to see this image as an extension to the pillars on which wisdom, working with God, set the earth above the primeval sea (Prov. 8:29b). Those who dwell in woman wisdom's house and eat at her table will not be overwhelmed by chaos.

The mention of slaughtered animals and mixed wine imply an exceptional feast (Prov. 9:2). Woman wisdom takes the initiative by sending servant women to call from "the highest places in the town," from which people are most likely to hear them (9:3). The invitation is to the simple (those who do not know wisdom) to come into the banquet hall. Those who accept wisdom's invitation will eat of her bread, drink of her mixed wine, and in the process "lay aside immaturity, and live, and walk in the way of insight," the way of God (9:5–6).

Proverbs 9:7–12 underscores why it is important to respond to wisdom's invitation. "The wise will love you" and will become wiser (9:7–9).

Given this situation, the writer underscores the point that the fear of God (i.e., reverence for God and seeking after God's ways) is "the beginning of wisdom" (9:10). Wisdom herself will multiply the days and years of those who follow her (9:11).

The writer warns the congregation against the feast of the foolish woman (on whom see Proper 19/Year B). Note that she imitates woman wisdom in almost every respect: sitting at the high places, inviting people in, even speaking specifically to the simple (Prov. 9:14–16). The foolish one teaches things that violate practices that are necessary for maintaining vital community. When the foolish woman says that "stolen water is sweet" (9:17a) she probably recalls the use of water imagery to speak of sexuality in Proverbs 5:15–19 and here refers to adultery. To "eat bread in secret" (9:17b) may invoke a secret, illicit liaison as in Proverbs 7:6–23. While such terminology can, of course, refer to actual sexuality (and its misuse outside the covenant of marriage), Jewish writers sometimes use the language of adultery to speak figuratively of the unfaithful life. Fools commit adultery. Those who join woman folly in such activities effectively send themselves to the realm of the dead (9:18). The author here reveals an essential aspect of folly: it offers as life-giving that which leads to death. If the community learns to distinguish wisdom's feast from that of folly, they will find instead that "years will be added" to their lives (9:11b).

The text puts a choice to listeners: which invitation will I accept?

Proverbs 9:1–18 uses the picture of a feast to represent a way of life, whereas John 6:51–58 (the Gospel reading for today) refers to actual participation in the bread and cup. Nevertheless, on the positive side Jesus' followers enjoy something akin to a Johannine version of wisdom's feast by eating the flesh and blood of Jesus, for that gives life in a way similar to wisdom's feast (John 6:57/Prov. 9:6). On the negative side, as a part of justifying the tensions between the synagogues of Jesus' followers and those who did not follow Jesus, John polemicizes that the bread that the Jewish ancestors ate in the wilderness led to death (John 6:58). The latter, of course, is Johannine polemic.

Proper 16 [21]/Year B

1 Kings 8:(1, 6, 10–11), 22–30, 41–43+ (Semicontinuous)

Most of chapter 8 consists of Solomon's prayer (vv. 22–53) to God at the dedication of the Temple. It contains seven supplications: for persons who sin (vv. 31–32), for Israel when it sins (vv. 33–34), for periods of drought

(vv. 35–36), for times of famine (vv. 37–40), for foreigners who pray (vv. 41–43), for those whom the Lord sends out in battle (vv. 44–45), and for captives taken in battle (vv. 46–51). These appeals cover a wide range of situations in which Israel would need to pray. Before and after his prayer, Solomon asks God to bless the assembly gathered for the dedication (vv. 14–21; 54–61). These prayers begin as do all Jewish blessings: "Blessed be the LORD" (vv. 15, 56). The whole is bracketed with liturgical worship of God and a communal meal (vv. 1–13; 62–66).

Verse 1 describes the bringing up into Jerusalem of the "ark of the covenant" from the "city of David," the lower city, south of the Temple. "Up" refers to the fact that Jerusalem was on higher ground. The ark is moved into the Temple and placed in "the inner sanctuary of the house" (v. 6). The ark was carried on "poles" (vv. 7–8). In spite of having a house in which to dwell, YHWH is not confined to the Temple but capable of being anywhere, of moving.

Verses 10–11 speak of the "cloud" that filled the house of the Lord, a symbol of the "glory" of the Lord. Solomon mentions (v. 12) that God had said that God "would dwell in thick darkness." The Lord remains a mystery, no more trapped in the Temple than in having a name that can be contained by a definition (see Proper 17/Year A).

Verses 22–26 begin with praise and appeals to God, particularly to God's "keeping covenant and steadfast love for your servants" (v. 23). God keeps the promises that God has made: a God "abounding in steadfast love and faithfulness, keeping steadfast love for the thousandth generation" (Exod. 34:6–7). Israel can pray to God and be confident that God will hear and respond because it knows God to be a God of steadfast love and faithfulness. And because God has kept promises, Solomon can appeal to God to continue to keep the promises made to "your servant my father David" (v. 25). Verses 25–26 continue the prayer for the preservation of the Davidic monarchy.

Verses 27–30 reflect theologically on the idea of God's dwelling in the Temple. Solomon declares: "Even heaven and the highest heaven cannot contain you, much less this house that I have built!" (v. 27). YHWH is not confined to the Temple; nor is there any literalism involved in calling it "God's house." God is omnipresent, available to all who pray anywhere, and the "gates of prayer" are always open even though those of the Temple might be closed (as at night). Solomon asks that God's eyes "may be open night and day toward this house" (v. 29), that those who pray "toward this place" may be heard.

Verses 41–43 address a topic of perennial concern to the Torah—the situation of "strangers" or "foreigners" in the land. The Torah frequently reminds Israel to be attentive to the plight of foreigners, vulnerable in a land not their own. The *mitzvah* to "love the stranger as yourself" is the most frequently repeated of all commandments in the Torah. Israel trusts God to hear the prayers of the stranger because when Israel was a stranger God heard its prayers. This prayer is broader than much that passes for "ecumenical" in our time, where "ecumenical" usually refers to the movement for unity among Christians. This prayer asks God to hear the prayers of those who are not "of us." It assumes that God is the God of all peoples everywhere. Israel's faith gave it to understand that Israel and the Gentiles were to be a blessing to each other.

Joshua 24:1–2a, 14–18 (Paired)*

For comments on this passage, please see Proper 27/Year A.

Proper 17 [22]/Year B

Song of Songs 2:8–13+ (Semicontinuous)

Although the Song of Songs was once attributed to Solomon, its language is much closer to that of the late Persian or early Hellenistic eras, suggesting that an unknown author wrote it. It has frequently been interpreted as an allegory of the love of God for Israel, but biblical scholars recognize that it is about the romantic relationship between a male and female. The Song of Songs is one of only two books in the Tanakh not to explicitly mention the name of God (Esther being the other). However, as with Esther (Proper 21/Year B), the Song of Songs presumes an implied theology.

In biblical antiquity, the sexual relationship was intended to be an intense and expressive form of covenantal community between two partners. The intimacy of sex is an experience in its own right (especially in its pleasure) and a representation of the mutual support and responsiveness in community that God wills for all. Indeed, the closeness of two human persons who are so immediately responsive that they are as one flesh (Gen. 2:24) is the epitome of covenantal community.

The Song of Songs is about this kind of love. The sensual relationship between the two partners is a blessing in its own right. This relationship also expresses and forms some of the most intimate dimensions of community.

The incident in today's text takes place in the spring, a season that listeners associate with fertility. The woman is dark skinned (Song 1:5) and is apparently at her house. Her beloved comes to her with such intense desire that he leaps over mountains like a gazelle or a young stag—powerful, swift, agile animals. Outside her window he invites her into an intensification of experience by calling to her (2:8–10a).

The invitation uses evocative imagery that suggests generativity, growth, and security. The dormancy of winter is past. The rainy season is over—a season providing the water resources necessary for growth in a semiarid land but complicating transportation and sometimes creating danger (e.g., flash flooding). Singing is associated with sweet moments in life (though the same word in Hebrew, *zamir*, could be rendered "pruning" and thus could suggest that these moments are preparing for intimacy in the same way that pruning prepares plants for greater foliation). The turtledove appears in spring and, in ancient literature, sometimes represents endearment. The blooming of the fig tree and the vineyards reinforces an atmosphere of fruitfulness (2:10b–13). The associations evoked by this text suggest dimensions of the tone and meaning of the sexual experience.

People encounter sexuality in North America today in multiple ways: as a commodity for sale or voyeurism, a dirty little secret, nothing more than hormones, raw physicality, explosive, the content of fantasies, a means to conceive, an occasion for tension; as perversion, addiction, temptation; as part of controversy regarding exercise of free speech; as source of frustration, disappointment, occasion for the practice of premarital purity, source of confusion with respect to one's own identity (e.g., gay, lesbian, bisexual, transgendered, asexual, and questioning); as well as source of confusion regarding how to respond to others whose sexuality is different from one's own. The appearance of the Song of Songs in the lectionary gives the preacher an excellent entrée into a sermon that helps the congregation think theologically about such matters.

The New Testament does not refer explicitly to the Song of Songs.

Deuteronomy 4:1–2, 6–9 (Paired)*

Many scholars think that an early version of Deuteronomy was part of Josiah's reform in the sixth century BCE (2 Kings 22:1–23:27; 2 Chr. 34:1–35:37) but that the Deuteronomic tradition was later redacted to account for the exile and times afterward (e.g., Deut. 4:26–29; 28:49–57,

64–68; 29:28). The Deuteronomic theologians use a past setting (the story of Israel coming out of Egypt and wandering in the wilderness) to talk about the present situation of the community (interpreting the exile and living in the postexilic world). The purposes of Deuteronomy are to help the community understand why disaster fell upon them (they were unfaithful) and to encourage the community toward renewed faithfulness as the way toward community regeneration, security, and prosperity.

Most of the book is in the form of three sermons from Moses (1:1–4:43; 4:44–28:68; 29:1–30:20) with 31:1–34:24 recounting Moses' significant last words. When the writers picture Moses addressing the exodus and wilderness generations as "you," the later community at the time of the redaction of the text was to hear the passage addressed homiletically to them.

Christians sometimes read Deuteronomy as legalistic and works righteous. This perception is wrong. For Deuteronomy, Torah is a gift to help the community live in God's gracious love. Christians sometimes say that Deuteronomy teaches a wooden notion of obedience leading to blessing and disobedience to curse. This interpretation is caricature. Today's lection offers Deuteronomy's alternatives to these misperceptions.

In Deuteronomy 1:6–3:29, Moses recounts how the community arrived at the edge of the promised land. In today's reading, Moses teaches the congregation that the quality of life in the new land will depend upon the degree to which they live in accord with God's instructions. Many scholars see this chapter as the core of the Deuteronomic theology that is found also in Joshua, Judges, the Samuels, and the Kings.

The text gives four reasons for living in accord with God's designs for community.[54] (1) According to Deuteronomy 4:1–4, the incident involving Baal at Peor shows that the community suffers grievously when it allows people to add to, or subtract from, the divine commandments. At Peor, all Israelites who "yoked themselves to" the local deity, the Baal at Peor, were to be put to death (Num. 25:1–18). (2) According to Deuteronomy 4:5–8, Israel's neighbors will recognize both the greatness of the God of Israel and that following the statutes has made Israel "a wise and discerning people" whose justice is greater than any other people's. (3) According to Deuteronomy 4:9–31, the community is to avoid idolatry because the revelation at Mount Horeb (Mount Sinai) prohibits it. Furthermore, when the congregation traffics with idols, they can expect the community to collapse, and, indeed, even for people to be uprooted from the land and scattered among the peoples. This statement is, of course, a theological interpretation of the exile. (4) According to Deuteronomy

4:32–40, Israel has had an unparalleled encounter with the Transcendent. Moreover, no other people know a God who is like the God of Israel. The relationship between God and the people is the result of God's grace.

The benefit of following the statutes, commandments, and ordinances is "for your own well-being and that of your descendants after you, so that you may long remain in the land that the LORD your God is giving you for all time" (Deut. 4:40). To a community looking forward to a renewed life after the exile, the commandments offer pastoral guidance in how to put into practice attitudes and behaviors that result in peace, love, justice, and abundance.

Although Mark 7:1–23 does not quote Deuteronomy 4, the two texts are paired. The theology in Deuteronomy 4 contains a wisdom that is not found in the typical Christian reading of Mark 7, for Mark caricatures some Jewish people of Mark's time as legalistic and ethically empty. Deuteronomy, by contrast, pictures Torah as rich and powerful and life-giving.

Proper 18 [23]/Year B

Proverbs 22:1–2, 8–9, 22–23+ (Semicontinuous)

Proverbs 22:1–16 is part of a general collection of sayings that begins in 10:1. These pithy recommendations for how to live typically result from the community's reflection on real-life experience as a source for determining God's purposes for life, as explained on Proper 19/Year B. Proverbs 22:17–24:22 is similar in spirit and content to a well-known wisdom text in Egypt called *The Instruction of Amenemope*, though the material in Proverbs incorporates Jewish theological concerns.

In Proverbs 22:1 by "a good name" the writer means reputation, long-standing evidence of a faithful life, honoring God by fulfilling one's responsibilities to household and community, including giving support to the poor. The same verse also claims that "favor is better than silver or gold." This proverb recollects Proverbs 3:3–4, which notes that "favor" with the community results from expressing loyalty (*hesed*).

When Proverbs 22:2 indicates that both the rich and poor were created by God, the implication is that they are bound together in community. The rich are to share material resources with the poor so that the poor are relieved of the anxiety of struggling every day for survival. Indeed, as 22:22–23 indicates, the wealthy are responsible to God for the ways in which they relate to the poor.

Proverbs 22:8 states an important principle: those who "sow injustice will reap calamity." Injustice in Proverbs has particular application to the mistreatment of the poor. People who are complicit in denying the good life to the poor will find that their behavior has set in motion forces that will bring calamity upon themselves. Furthermore, when the writer says that "the rod of anger will fail," the writer borrows an image from using a stick at the harvest to separate the grain from the stalk. The anger of the unjust person will not bring about what the unjust person desires but will fail.

Proverbs 22:9 is a counterpoint to 22:8: "Those who are generous are blessed, for they share their bread with the poor." Responsible relationship with others, represented here by sharing bread with the poor, is the way to blessing.

Proverbs 22:22–23 puts into forceful legal terms the call to support the poor. Some people with power "rob the poor because they are poor" (the poor do not have the power to resist). The powerful "crush the afflicted at the gate," and they take advantage of the poor through the legal system (the gate being the place where legal issues were settled in antiquity). God is the legal representative of the poor (22:23).

According to Proverbs, the good life is possible only through participation in community in ways that support others. This thinking is so different from our world, which teaches us "to look out for Number One." From the Proverbs perspective, that will eventuate in social calamity. Even if calamity does not happen in every individual case (many exploitative rich persons die thinking they are happy), such behavior sets in motion social forces that will eventually cause a social world to collapse on itself.

The preacher might reflect on the fact that many of the proverbs (especially those found in 22:17–24:22) are similar to wisdom sayings from other cultures and religious groups, which suggests that the Jewish and Christian traditions do not have a monopoly on understanding the meaning of life. Other communities can have insight that enriches Jewish and Christian perspective.

The New Testament contains some passages that are similar in theme to those found in Proverbs 22 such as 2 Corinthians 9:6–7 and Ephesians 6:2.

Isaiah 35:4–7a (Paired)*

Please see the Third Sunday of Advent/Year A for commentary on this passage.

Proper 19 [24]/Year B

Proverbs 1:20–33+ (Semicontinuous)

An important question is how the human community arrives at an interpretation of the nature, presence, and purposes of God. Scholars sometimes say that the Bible puts forward three modes whereby human beings learn about God: (1) through God's actions in history, for example, the exodus from Egypt; (2) through direct revelation from God, such as God's giving the commandments to Moses; (3) by observing life and drawing conclusions from it. The first two modes involve special moments of revelation, whereas the third derives from interaction with everyday life experience. These three modes all involve interpretation on the part of the receiver or observer, and they overlap in practice.

Much Wisdom literature, such as the book of Proverbs—along with Job, Ecclesiastes, Sirach (also known as Ben Sira or Ecclesiasticus), and Wisdom of Solomon—falls generally into the third category. The underlying theological presupposition is that God has created the world to reflect the divine purposes. By paying close attention to what happens in the world, we can deduce the character and aims of God (e.g., Prov. 6:6–11; cf. Proper 18/Year B on 22:1–2, 8–9, 22–23).

The term "wisdom" (*hokmah*, a feminine term) is used in two related but different ways. First, in a general sense wisdom is the awareness of God's presence and aims in the world and the act of responding appropriately. Foolishness is misperception of the divine presence and aim, and the fool lives accordingly. Second, wisdom is more than a body of awareness; it is also an agent of God and is active in the world. This literature often personifies wisdom as a woman. Today's lesson offers a general portrait of Woman Wisdom, while Proverbs 8 focuses more specifically on wisdom as agent and sustainer of creation (Trinity Sunday/Year C).

Wisdom appears in Proverbs 1:20–33 as a woman calling in the streets. She stands at the city gates or on the public square where the economic and social life of the community is centered and where orators sometimes stood to gain an audience (1:20–21). She implicitly offers the awareness of God's designs for community, but many people (e.g., simple ones and scoffers) reject God's hopes (1:22). Despite this rejection, this woman continues to invite the city dwellers to partake of wisdom (1:23).

Wisdom does not actively harm people who do not listen to her call, but the consequences of their foolishness fall upon them (Prov. 1:24–26). Panic besets them like a storm and calamity like a whirlwind (1:27). In desperation they will seek but not find her (1:28). Because they did not listen to Wisdom, "they shall eat the fruit of their way and be sated with their own devices" (1:29–31). Indeed, their own complacency in ignoring Wisdom "destroys them" (1:32). How much better to listen to Wisdom, for they "will be secure" (1:33).

This text puts a question before the congregation: Do we recognize and respond to wisdom, or do we pay attention to foolishness and live accordingly? The preacher might invite the congregation to listen for Woman Wisdom calling in the streets today. The preacher might particularly help the congregation think about ways that the experience of women opens windows into God's nature and purposes.

The New Testament does not take up this passage. As we note in connection with Proverbs 8:1–8, 22–31 (Trinity Sunday/Year C), however, the New Testament draws on the notion of wisdom to help interpret the relationship of God and Jesus.

Isaiah 50:4–9a (Paired)*

Please see Palm/Passion Sunday/Years A, B, and C for our commentary on this passage.

Proper 20 [25]/Year B

Proverbs 31:10–31+ (Semicontinuous)

The passage for today pictures a woman who is hardworking and creative and who is variously called capable, ideal, excellent, valorous, or strong. By placing the poem at the climax of the book, the writer implies that this woman models the vision of life commended throughout the book. This poem uses the woman as a model for all to live wisely. The woman does not transcend all roles and restrictions typical of women in antiquity. She is, after all, identified as a spouse, though her unnamed husband does not play a major role in the text; she takes initiative without referring to him. However, her characteristics and behavior point toward egalitarianism and independence.

Commentators agree that the opening question does not mean that a good spouse is impossible to find but that she is rare and valuable (Prov. 31:10a). Right relationships are more important than excess wealth such as jewels (31:10b). She is trustworthy, and her work will bring gain to the household (31:11–12). The qualities associated with this courageous woman are typical of ancient women. She clothes the family (31:13) and like a ship making arduous journeys, brings food from faraway places and arises early to prepare meals. She manages the household servants well (31:14–15).

She exercises authority in more ways than most women in the ancient world, buying a field without consulting her husband, operating the vineyard herself, and engaging in negotiation and management (31:16). Indeed, she is "girded" and "strong" like a military leader (31:17). Confident that her work is valuable, she works late into the night (31:18–19). She cares for the poor and needy (31:20). She prepares her husband for challenges, represented by her making clothing for snow as well as fine clothing for community celebrations (31:21–22). While practicing solidarity with the poor (31:20), she enables her spouse to sit at the gates where elders enact justice (31:23).

More important than the garments she sells outside the home (Prov. 31:24) are her strength and dignity. Moreover, she speaks wisdom and teaches the practice of kindness (31:24–26). She is vigilant with regard to the needs of her household so that children and spouse honor her (31:27–29). Charm and beauty deceive, but the woman who fears God, that is, who lives wisely, is honored, and receives a share of the work of her own hands. Her life invites all to participate in wisdom as it is lifted up at the city gates (31:30–31).

A preacher should avoid using this text to reinforce repressive roles for women. A sermon could not only call for removing limitations on women but for empowering women toward creativity, initiative, and choice. More than that, the sermon could hold up this wise woman as a model for all to live wisely in community.

The New Testament does not directly invoke this passage. It does, however, put forward pictures of strong, creative, independently functioning women in line with pictures of women in the Old Testament, and also in the New Testament (e.g., Gen. 1:26–28; Exod. 1:15–2:10; 15:20–21; Num. 12:1–15; Josh. 2:1–21; 6:15–25; Judg. 4:1–5:31; 2 Sam. 14:1–20; 20:14–27; 2 Kgs. 22:14–20; Ruth 1:1–4:22; cf. Jer. 31:15–22; Matt. 1:18–25; 28:1–10; Mark 5:25–34; Luke 7:11–17, 36–50; 8:1–3; 10:38–42; 24:1–11; Acts 9:32–42; 12:12; 16:12–40; 18:1–3; 21:1–10; Rom. 16:1, 3, 6, 12, 15; Gal. 3:28, though contrast Col. 3:18–19 and 1 Pet. 3:1–6).

Jeremiah 11:18–20; Wisdom of Solomon 1:16–2:1, 12–22* (Paired)

Although the readings from Jeremiah and Wisdom are offered by the lectionary as alternate readings and come from different communities, their emphases are compatible in ways that make it logical to consider them at the same time. For background on the books of Jeremiah and Wisdom, see the Fourth Sunday of Epiphany/Year C, and Proper 8/Year B.

Jeremiah's sermons on judgment made some people so uncomfortable that, in today's short lesson, Jeremiah laments that some people in Judah plotted to assassinate him. Until God made this known to Jeremiah (Jer. 11:18), he was like a gentle lamb being led to the slaughter, innocent and unaware of the plot against him (Jer. 11:19a). The prophet quotes those involved in the conspiracy as saying they want to destroy him and see to it that his name is no longer remembered so that the memory of his ministry would not trouble subsequent generations (11:19b). Jeremiah, however, knows that God judges righteously. In the minds of many in antiquity, this quality included God's punishing perpetrators of injustice. When Jeremiah says, "To you I have committed my cause," Jeremiah means that the prophet trusts God to carry out retribution (Jer. 11:20).

The Wisdom of Solomon invites readers to live in a godly way and thereby attain immortality while cautioning readers against ungodliness that leads to death. In Wisdom 1:16 the author introduces a speech from the mouths of the ungodly, assuring the reader that the ungodly make a covenant with death. In 2:1–20, the author uses the literary form of the Hellenistic diatribe to voice the viewpoint of the author's opponents, the ungodly. For them, death means the end of existence (2:1–5). Therefore, they should enjoy the pleasures of this present life to the maximum, even if such pleasure means that they oppress others, including the poor and righteous (2:6–11).

In Wisdom 2:12–16, the ungodly charge that the presence of the righteous is an inconvenience because they reproach the ungodly (2:12). The ungodly plan to kill the righteous to test whether the words of the righteous one are true (2:18). If so, God will deliver the righteous person from death (2:19). They condemn the righteous to "a shameful death" that includes insult and torture to find out how faithful and gentle that person is and whether God will protect (2:19–20).

The author then comments that the reasoning of the ungodly is mistaken. They are blind to the secret purposes of God which includes an afterlife. The writer is confident of immortality because God "created human beings for incorruption" by making them in the divine image which is "the image of [God's] own eternity" (2:21–23). At the end of earthly existence, the righteous do not die but pass into fullness of life with God and are truly "happy."

Although the Gospel reading for today, Mark 9:30–37, does not directly recollect the passages from Jeremiah or Wisdom, the latter illustrate a motif recurring in Jewish literature that illumines Mark's interpretation of the death of Jesus (Mark 9:30–32). A righteous person calls attention to unfaithfulness, which sometimes invokes the wrath of those to whom that person preaches.

Proper 21 [26]/Year B

Esther 7:1–6, 9–10; 9:20–22+ (Semicontinuous)

The narrative told in the book of Esther is set in the period when Persia ruled the Near East (circa 486–465 BCE). However, many scholars think the book was actually written in the Hellenistic age (circa 300 BCE) using the earlier setting to comment on Jewish life in the Diaspora culture that pressured ethnic groups to give up their identity and to assimilate. The book of Esther is a single narrative that is really the text for the sermon.

Ahasuerus, ruler of Persia, gave a lewd banquet exploiting women. When queen Vashti refused to parade before the males, Ahasuerus searched for a new queen. The beautiful Jewish woman Esther, cousin of Mordecai (a distant advisor to Ahasuerus) emerged as the new queen and Mordecai saved Ahasuerus's life (Esth. 1:1–2:23). Ahasuerus gave Haman administrative command over Persia, and when Mordecai refused to bow to Haman, Haman decided to destroy the Jewish people (3:1–15), or bring their own destruction.

At Mordecai's request, Esther agreed to intercede for the Jewish community, for she had come "to royal dignity for just such a time as this" (4:14). She invited Ahasuerus and Haman to a series of banquets during which Ahasuerus asked three times what he could do for Esther. During these events, he also decided to honor Mordecai for saving Ahasuerus's life, even as Haman was building a gallows to hang Mordecai (4:1–6:13). When Esther requested Ahasuerus to spare the Jewish people, Ahasuerus became aware that Haman was responsible for the order to exterminate them, and ordered Haman hung on the gallows intended for Mordecai (7:14–8:2).

Because, according to custom, Haman's edict could not be reversed, Ahasuerus gave the Jewish people the right to defend themselves and sent a proclamation urging Gentiles not to persecute the Jewish community (8:3–17). While most Gentiles followed this, members of the Jewish community were forced to kill some opponents (9:1–19).

Esther 9:20–32 authorizes the Jewish observance of Purim. Today's preacher could acquaint the congregation with this festival. The name

Purim is from the Hebrew word for "lots," in reference to Haman casting lots to set the date for the destruction of the Jewish people (Esth. 3:7; 9:24). On Purim, usually in March (on the day after Haman thought the Jewish people would be exterminated), the Jewish community sends food and gifts to the needy, and celebrates by reading of the book of Esther with plenteous food and drink, and entertainment that shows that enemies do not have final power over the community.

Interpreters sometimes complain that the book of Esther is religiously deficient because it does not name God. However, Jewish theology recognizes that, whether named or not, God is always present. The book of Esther implies that God worked through the courage of Esther. It implicitly encouraged the Jewish community in the Diaspora to maintain its identity against the challenges of Hellenism in the confidence that God would continue to work through Esthers. The book of Esther invites the community to act on their own courage and creativity as instruments through whom God works.

The only citation of Esther in the New Testament is in Mark 6:23.

Numbers 11:4–6, 10–16, 24–29 (Paired)*

For comments on this passage, please see Pentecost/Year A.

Proper 22 [27]/Year B

Job 1:1; 2:1–10+ (Semicontinuous)

The book of Job has given rise to an unusual number of interpretations. While scholars sometimes distinguish between its prose beginning and ending, and the great poem in the middle of the book, it is a whole. Complicating the preacher's tasks is the fact that the book of Job tells one long story. A preacher must take into account the entire narrative.

Interpreting the book of Job would be simpler if we knew more about the historical context that caused its unknown author to write it. Most scholars agree that a major task of the book of Job is to respond to the Deuteronomic theology. As we point out in discussing Deuteronomism elsewhere (e.g., Proper 17/Year B), a central conviction of the Deuteronomic corpus is that obedience to the covenant results in blessing, while disobedience brings about curse (e.g., Deut. 27:1–28:68). For the Deuteronomists, blessing and curse have to do with material dimensions such as family, land, and animals, as well as nonmaterial dimensions. The community that generated the book of Job protests the simple equation of obedience leading to blessing and disobedience leading to curse, and Jon L. Berquist refers to the book of Job as "literature of dissent."[55]

The prosperity of the character Job in chapter 1 leaves the impression that Job is obedient and therefore blessed. The horrid conditions that descend on Job's life result not from sin and curse but from God allowing Satan to conduct a testing program to determine whether Job would serve God even if his world was radically diminished (Job 1:6–12; 2:1–6). In the book of Job Satan is not the direct adversary of God as in later apocalyptic literature but serves as something like an attorney in God's' court. With God's approval, Satan destroys Job's livestock, servants, and children, and inflicts "loathsome sores" (Job 1:13–19; 2:7–8).

The lection raises penetrating issues but does not pose a theological resolution. Indeed, the issues are developed even further in Job 3:1–37:24 and brought to a head only in 38:1–42:6. Is the congregation ready for a sermon that raises questions but does not answer them? If so, a preacher could envision today's sermon as the first in a four-week series on Job that moves through the lections toward theological climax in 38:1–42:6. The message today could encourage the congregation to identify situations in the contemporary world that raise issues similar to Job's. If a multi-week series on Job does not fit the congregational context, a pastor might use today's reading (or any of the readings over the next weeks) as a point of entry into the entire story of Job.

Many ministers welcome the book of Job because it calls into question theological ideas that are still commonplace in many congregations, namely, notions that obedience does bring about blessing and disobedience curse. Job poses a sharp criticism of such formulaic approaches to life. However, preachers need to honor the complexity of such discussions. Sometimes obedient people do prosper, but sometimes they do not, and sometimes the disobedient prosper. Sometimes disobedience does result in suffering. But sometimes, the obedient suffer without apparent reason while the disobedient enjoy nothing but the high life.

Genesis 2:18–24* (Paired)

Genesis 2:4b–24 is a second story of creation. Its placement in the canon makes theological diversity a lens through which to engage the rest of the Bible. The First Testament contains several theological schools (e.g., Elohist, Yahwist, Deuteronomist, Priestly, Wisdom, apocalyptic). By including such diverse viewpoints, the Bible implicitly invites the community to compare, contrast, and enter into critical conversation with the different perspectives.

The biblical redactors used Genesis 2:4b–24 to supplement the majestic theology of creation in Genesis 1:1–2:4a and (as part of the literary unit Genesis 2:4b–3:24) to explain how the universe changed from covenantal community in Genesis 1:1–2:4a to the more unjust and even violent life of Genesis 4:1ff. (see Trinity Sunday/Year A and Lent 1/Year A).

As Genesis 2:4b–14 begins, the earth is bare, but as the text unfolds, God causes water to flow so that it becomes fertile. Working like a potter, God forms the first human being (*adam*) out of the dust of the ground (*adamah*). The human being and the ground are thus intimately interconnected. Verse 7 gives no explicit indication that the first human being was a male; sexual differentiation becomes explicit only in verse 23. The four rivers that flowed from Eden watered the whole earth, thus revealing that God intended for the entire creation to manifest the fecundity of Eden. God placed one limitation on the human being: not to eat of the tree of the knowledge of good and evil (see Lent 1/Year A).

In 2:18–20, God forms the nonhuman creatures. In antiquity, to know the name of another was to have a certain power over the other; the fact that the human being names the nonhuman creatures demonstrates this fact. However, with Genesis 1:26–28 in the background, the reader realizes that this power is for the purpose of helping all creatures live in covenant (see Trinity Sunday/Year A).

Genesis 2:18 gives the reason for the creation of woman: "It is not good that the human being should be alone." Human beings most fully manifest the purposes of God when living together in covenant with one another and nature as in Genesis 1:1–2:24.

The New Revised Standard Version moves toward the character of the relationship between the two human beings in the phrase "a helper as [the human being's] partner" (2:18). The term "helper" does not imply secondary status, for elsewhere it refers to the help that God gives Israel (e.g., Exod. 18:4; Deut. 33:7, 29) and to forms of assistance in which the helper has the superior resources of the two (e.g., Ezek. 12:14; Dan. 11:34).

None of the animals are "a helper as [the human being's] partner." To make such a helper, God puts the human being to sleep. The human being has no say in the creation of this partner. There is nothing in symbolism of the rib in antiquity or in the narrative itself to suggest that the second human being is subordinate to the first.

In verse 23a, the first human being explains the relationship between the two human beings. God made the second human being not from the dust (from which God made the nonhuman creatures) but from the actual human being. They are of the same stuff, thus suggesting primeval equality. Verse 23b contains the first direct indication of gender difference, even as it reiterates the theme of similarity-and-connection-with-difference expressed in the designations Woman (*ishshah*) and Male (*ish*).

Scholars almost universally see God bringing the couple together in verse 22 as indicating that marriage is instituted by God. In the world of biblical Israel, marriage involved the female leaving her home to join the male and his family. However, some interpreters think that verse 24 preserves the memory of an earlier time when the male left his home and joined that of the woman.

In its present form, the key affirmation of the latter part of the text is that male and female "become one flesh." This statement does not mean that difference between the two is eradicated. The phrase has a sexual overtone: in the sexual relationship, male and female can become so responsive to one another that they function as one. The phrase thus signals that the two human beings work together in singularity of purpose (making use of their differences) to fulfill together the role of exercising dominion (Gen. 1:26–28).

The text concludes by noting that in this pristine period of existence, they did not know shame. Shame results only from the fall.

This text is ideally paired today with Mark 10:2–11, for Mark asserts its viewpoint to explain why divorce is not possible in the community of those awaiting the final apocalyptic manifestation of the realm of God. This passage is also directly or indirectly cited in 1 Corinthians 6:16 and 11:8–9, in Ephesians 5:3, and in 1 Timothy 2:13.

Proper 23 [28]/Year B

Job 23:1–9, 16–17+ (Semicontinuous)

Intending to give Job pastoral care, friends visit Job on the ash heap of life and offer what they take to be appropriate theological interpretations of his situation. By oversimplifying, we can summarize Eliphaz (Job 4:1–5:27), voicing the popular idea still heard today that obedient people succeed while the disobedient suffer (e.g., 4:6–7) and that circumstances such as Job's are divine discipline (5:17). Bildad (8:1–22) thinks that God is just and punishes sin. The suffering of Job must, therefore, reveal that Job has sinned and should prompt Job to repent. Zophar (11:1–20) reprises the notion that God is fair and points out that God knows more than Job about sin. In a second series of speeches, the friends expand on such themes (Eliphaz: 15:1–35; Bildad: 18:1–21; Zophar: 20:1–29). Eliphaz sets the context for today's reading by repeating the idea that Job's plight demonstrates that Job has done something evil (22:5–9): if Job will repent, God will restore his fortunes (22:15–30). In six speeches, Job replies to each friend by claiming innocence and noting that a false admission of guilt would compromise his integrity (Job 6:1–7:20; 9:1–10:22; 12:1–14:22; 16:1–17:6; 19:1–29; 21:1–34).

The passage assigned for today, from the larger literary unit of Job 23:1–24:25, expands on the notion that God permits injustice. According to Job, God often hides from the human family. If Job could find God, Job would present his case to God and could hear an explanation of his situation directly from God—and surely God would judge him innocent (23:1–7). Although Job cannot see God, God surely knows that Job has walked in God's ways (23:8–12). But when God is in hiding, the just suffer, a circumstance that causes Job to be terrified of God and to wish to vanish into darkness (23:13–17).

Job lists several examples of unjust people whose success is bought by the price of the suffering of the innocent (24:1–4). Such people are "like wild asses in the desert," taking food that others have prepared and engaging in crude behavior (24:5–8). They take infants as pledges of debt and force the poor to go about naked and carrying food for the wealthy even though they themselves are hungry. Yet God does not notice (24:9–12). Murderers and adulterers go unpunished (24:13–17). Drought, natural disaster, and infertility curse the innocent (24:18–20); God supports and prolongs the lives of unjust people. "If it is not so," Job asks, "who will prove me a liar?" (24:21–25).

Preacher and congregation should not miss the fact that in the midst of his suffering what Job most wants is a *theological interpretation* that makes sense of what is happening to him and to others who suffer unjustly. Without discounting the importance of sitting silently with those in similar situations, there comes a time when the preacher needs to help people name—in theological terms—their feelings, questions, and issues, and to seek a vision of God that adequately accounts for, and helps them understand, their experience.

Job grumbles that God hides (Job 23:1–9, esp. 8–9). In contrast, the authors of *Preaching the Old Testament* believe that God is ever present and, by definition, cannot hide. Job's problem is one of perception: Job does not *perceive* God, but that does not mean *God* is hiding. A sermon could help the community explore ways we could become conscious of God's presence, especially in situations similar to Job's. Nor do we believe that God willfully inflicts (or allows) evil to befall people or nature. A God of unconditional love would not act in that way. That such things happen raises a question about divine power that we take up in connection with Proper 25/Year B.

Amos 5:6–7, 10–15 (Paired)*

Amos prophesied during the reigns of Jeroboam in Israel and Uzziah in Judah, a period of calm and prosperity in these two kingdoms. From Tekoa in Judah, Amos worked in the northern kingdom, of which he was sufficiently critical that Amaziah, priest of Bethel, said to him: "O seer, go, flee away to the land of Judah, earn your bread there, and prophesy there; but never again prophesy at Bethel, for it is the king's sanctuary, and it is a temple of the kingdom" (7:12–13).

Amos's first group of prophecies (1:3–2:3) are directed against Israel's neighbors over their war-making activity and their reliance on stout means of defense as a way of wreaking havoc on others while dwelling in safety. Damascus, Gaza, Tyre, Edom, the Ammonites, and Moab are targets of prophetic critique. Amos's concern is not limited to the people Israel.

Since 2:4, however, Amos has been roundly criticizing the northern kingdom, because it ignores the instructions of Torah to be committed to compassionate justice for the most vulnerable in society. Instead, "they sell the righteous for silver, and the needy for a pair of sandals—they . . . trample the head of the poor into the dust of the earth, and push the afflicted out of the way" (2:6–7). Powerful and at peace in its time of prosperity, Israel ignores its responsibility to distribute the goods of life fairly among all its people. It violates the covenant by turning its back on the well-being that YHWH intends for all people.

Today's reading laments the sins of Israel: "Hear this word that I take up over you in lamentation, O house of Israel: Fallen, no more to rise, is maiden Israel; forsaken on her land, with no one to raise her up" (5:1–2). Amos mourns what will happen to Israel, not what has happened: "Seek the LORD and live, or he will break out against the house of Joseph like fire, and it will devour Bethel, with no one to quench it" (v. 6). This is the logic of life and blessing or death and curse that runs throughout the Torah and the Prophets. The condition of blessing is that it be received as a gracious gift from God and shared by all; it cannot be grabbed, possessed, or hoarded for oneself and denied to others. Blessing is profoundly relational. We may derive temporary advantages for ourselves by denying food and shelter to some so that we may have more than we need, but in dealing out curse and death to others, we eventually bring it upon ourselves.

Further, Amos points out that the Israelites regard themselves as above criticism: "They hate the one who reproves in the gate, and they abhor the one who speaks the truth" (v. 10). The prophetic principle is that anyone or anything can and must be criticized; to put oneself above criticism is tantamount to idolatry. But the Israelites feel free to "trample on the poor" on whose grain they impose heavy taxes (v. 11). They pervert justice through bribery "and push aside the needy in the gate" (v. 12). The gate was a square between the inner and outer walls of the city where court was held, but instead of doing justice, says Amos, the Israelites "afflict the righteous . . . take a bribe, and push aside the needy in the gate" (5:12).

Returning to the choice between "life and death, blessings and curses" (Deut. 30:19), Amos exhorts his listeners: "Seek good and not evil, that you may live; and so the LORD, the God of hosts, will be with you . . . establish justice in the gate; it may be that the LORD . . . will be gracious to the remnant of Joseph" (vv. 14–15).

This reading is aptly paired with Mark's story of the "rich young ruler." Set in a time of widespread destitution, it is a story about the conflict between wealth and the kingdom of God: "It is easier for a camel to go through the eye of a needle than for someone who is rich to enter the kingdom of God" (Mark 10:25). This story is also about the conditions of life and well-being.

Proper 24 [29]/Year B

Job 38:1–7, (34–41)+ (Semicontinuous)

For comments on this passage, please see Proper 7/Year B.

Isaiah 53:4–12 (Paired)*

For comments on this passage, please see Good Friday/Year A.

Proper 25 [30]/Year B

Job 42:1–6, 10–17+ (Semicontinuous)

Job 42:1–6 is Job's reply to God's speeches in 38:1–40:2 and 40:6–41:34. Job asserts that God "can do all things" (42:2), and takes God's words as reflecting Job's own perspective (42:3). Job goes along with God's earlier statement that he does not have God's perspective on such matters (42:4–5). Unfortunately, Job 42:6 is difficult to interpret.[56] Some scholars think that Job recognizes that both the Deuteronomic viewpoint on blessing and curse (represented in the book of Job by the friends) and Job's persistent demands to understand this notion in another (but unnamed) framework of meaning come up short. Having been addressed directly by the awesome God, Job recognizes that chaos is innately a part of creation and that neither chaos nor prosperity can be neatly explained. While chaos is powerful, God's speeches in chapters 38 through 41 assure Job that it will not destroy the patterns of life through which God supports the world.

J. Gerald Janzen poses an inspired interpretation of the phrase "dust and ashes" as referring to God's image in Job.[57] To "repent in dust and ashes," therefore, is for Job to recognize the limits on being human (and not knowing all that God knows) but also to accept the purpose of the divine image, namely, to rule or to help the many pieces of the created world live together with as much possibility as can occur in a universe still infused with chaos.

In 42:10–17, God restores Job's life. Interpreters struggle to make sense of this part of the text.[58] A persuasive suggestion is that the book of Job here presumes the Jewish notion that those who deprive others of property or other means of life should pay the injured person double the loss (Exod. 22:4). God's restoring the fortunes of Job would be restitution for causing the losses in Job's life.

Given finitude, human beings cannot understand all things. However, if God is omnipotent in the way assumed by the book of Job, then God is responsible for everything that happens. God either initiates or permits all things. God, then, is not only responsible for all suffering, but has the power to end suffering.[59] The authors of this book are among those convinced that God is unconditionally loving and just. Such a God could not initiate or permit suffering. We conclude, with other relational theologians, that God is not unqualifiedly omnipotent. God does not have the power simply to change situations. Instead, God is ever present in every situation seeking to lure participants into decisions that promise blessing. When people (and elements of nature) make choices that do not promise blessing, God works with those reduced possibilities to try to draw us to as much blessing as they offer. Conditions that communities today associate with curse and blessing typically result from people making choices that move in the direction of such conditions. However, because the elements of life are systemically interrelated, the choices that people make may have effects on other people very far away. I may personally live an upright life but live in a condition associated with curse because of choices made by people in other parts of the life system. A part of what it means to live as "dust and ashes" is to name God's presence in offering us choices for blessing.

Although the circumstances of Job's life are not greatly different in Job 1:1 and Job 42:17, Job's point of view has changed. Readers learned in 38:1–41:34 that God has structured the world in such a way as to provide resources for human beings to make our way through chaos. Beneath the chaos are elements of providence on which human beings can rely. Although *situations* may not improve, the *perception* that God is with us can tilt the scale when we have the option of yielding to chaos and living bitterly, or of making our way through difficult situations aware of the capacity of God through creation to sustain.

Proper 26 [31]/Year B

Ruth 1:1–18+ (Semicontinuous)

In its canonical context in the Old Testament, the book of Ruth is placed between Judges and the first book of Samuel, breaking the flow of the narrative from Judges to Samuel. However, the Jewish Bible places Ruth among the Writings, where it more naturally fits, and where the lectionary wisely assigns the reading. Because the story of Ruth is a single, unbroken narrative, a preacher focusing on the book of Ruth should consult the comments both today and next week, Proper 27/Year B.

Because of famine in Judah, a Jewish woman, Naomi, moved with her husband to Moab, a land directly east of the Dead Sea. Her husband died as did her only two sons, leaving Naomi a widow, as were her Moabite daughters-in-law, Ruth and Orpah (Ruth 1:1–5). In those days, a woman's security came from being related to a male—father, husband, sons, or other male relatives, and the text does not mention other males who were responsible for Naomi. Hence, she decided to return to Judah where she had heard that God provided food for widows in her state of abandonment (Ruth 1:6). Presumably Naomi had in mind the practice of gleaning in the fields (e.g., Deut. 24:19; Lev. 19:9; 23:22).

Although her daughters-in-law start the journey to Judah with Naomi, she exhorts them to remain in Moab and go to the families that would provide for them (Ruth 1:7–9). When they object, Naomi points out that she

is too old to find a husband or to have children. Orpah kissed her mother-
in-law good-bye but Ruth clung to Naomi (1:10–14), and said she would
live as an Israelite and would worship YHWH (1:16–17). Phyllis Trible
characterizes Ruth's decision:

> From a cultural perspective, Ruth has chosen death over life. She has
> disavowed the solidarity of family; she has abandoned national iden-
> tity; and she has renounced religious affiliation. In the entire epic of
> Israel, only Abraham matches this radicality, but then he had a call
> from God (Gen. 12:1–5). Divine promise motivated and sustained his
> leap of faith. Besides, Abraham was a man, with a wife and other pos-
> sessions to accompany him.[60]

Trible points out, further, that Ruth had no possessions and stood by herself as she made her promise to Naomi. God did not speak to her as God
spoke to Abraham. She had no pledge of help from other human beings.
"And there is more," Trible continues. "Not only has Ruth broken with
family, country, and faith, but she has also reversed sexual allegiance. A
young woman has committed herself to the life of an old woman rather
than to the search for a husband, and she has made this commitment not
'until death do us part,' but beyond death."[61]

Commentators often call attention to the fact that the book of Ruth
contains little explicit theological interpretation of the story, but implicit
theological themes are at work. Covenantal community is a means
whereby YHWH makes it possible for all in the community to experience
security. Ruth enters into covenantal commitment with Naomi. Indeed,
this story twice uses the famous Hebrew term *hesed* (loving-kindness,
covenantal loyalty) to describe a relationship among women (Ruth 1:8;
3:10). Since this term often refers to YHWH's relationship with Israel,
these occurrences suggest that the interaction of the women was a means
whereby divine *hesed* came to expression. A third instance of *hesed* (2:20),
in reference to Boaz, reinforces the idea of human relationship as mode
through which divine *hesed* operates. The story thus alerts the congregation to look for ways that *hesed* is embodied through human beings who
are different in ethnicity, and, by extension, in other ways.

The preacher could help the congregation identify ways that women
provide covenantal support for one another today. In the name of expressing *hesed* for one another, where are women today making commitments
such as the one Ruth made to Naomi? What would it take for today's congregation to make a Ruth-like commitment to the Naomis of the world?

The New Testament does not refer directly to the book of Ruth. However, we discuss New Testament references to Ruth 4 on Proper 27/Year B.

Deuteronomy 6:1–9 (Paired)*

This passage, which contains the *Shema* (from the Hebrew word for "hear" in Deut. 6:4), has become a defining text for Judaism. Beginning in antiquity and continuing to today, the Jewish community recites it in daily and weekly worship (*m. Ber.* 1:1–3:6) where it continues to function much as it did in the time of the Deuteronomists. As we note in discussing the historical context of the book of Deuteronomy (Proper 17/Year B), while Moses appears to direct these words to the people who arrived at the border of the promised land, the redactors designed this material to admonish the exilic or postexilic community to live faithfully so that the days of the congregation "may be long" and so that "it may go well" with the community in the years following the exile (Deut. 6:1–3).

Scholars disagree about how to interpret the main theme of the *Shema* in Deuteronomy 6:4. It could be rendered: "The LORD is our God, the LORD alone" (NRSV). In this case, the meaning is that God alone is God of Israel. Given the multiple opportunities the people had to worship other gods, they were to maintain complete fidelity to God and were to do all that God said. Another possibility is, "The Lord our God, the Lord is one" (or slight variants). In this case, the meaning is that God is undivided and has integrity ("the Lord is one"), and, therefore, the community can count on God to keep God's promises. This affirmation would be important to a community whose confidence in God's trustworthiness had been challenged by the exile. It asserts that the occupation of the nation and the deportation do not call God's integrity and trustworthiness into question. God can work through such circumstances to keep the divine promises.

In Deuteronomy, love always involves actions for the good of another. God's love is expressed through God's actions (4:32–40; 5:8–10; 7:7–11; 10:12–22; 23:5). Members of the community love God by walking in God's ways, by living in covenantal love in mutual support, peace, and justice (10:12–22; 11:1–7, 13–17; 13:1–6; 19:9; 30:1–6, 15–20). While for us the heart is the seat of feeling, in the ancient world the heart was the center of the will, the center of thought and discernment. The soul was a place of feeling, even of passion.

The combination of heart, soul, and might speaks of the passionate totality of the self actively expressing love for others in the community and even for those outside (e.g., aliens). The self becomes one in response to the oneness of God. The integrity of God begets integrity within the human being and in the human community.

The community is perpetually to teach the *Shema* and, by implication, the whole of Deuteronomy (6:6–9). The home is to be a classroom. Community members are to "bind them [Moses' words] as a sign" on the hand and to fix them on the decorative forehead band. People were to write them on their doorposts (giving rise to the Jewish custom of mounting a small container with the Ten Words, called a mezuzah, at the entrance to the house). Copies were also placed at the city gates so that people entering and leaving would remember to walk in God's ways. "The idea [is that] the habit of observing God's laws has the long term effect of instilling reverence for God" and of helping those habits become a faithful way of life.[62] Many congregations today could recover this emphasis on teaching as an antidote to theological amnesia.

Deuteronomy 6 is half of an ideal pairing with Mark 12:28–34. When asked to identify the commandment that is first of all, the Markan Jesus responds by adapting Deuteronomy 6:4–5 with the text that would complete the ideal pair for today, Leviticus 19:17–18 (see Seventh Sunday after the Epiphany/Year A). Similar points come out in Matthew 22:34–40 and Luke 10:25–28, Romans 3:30, 1 Corinthians 8:4, and Ephesians 4:6.

Proper 27 [32]/Year B

Ruth 3:1–5; 4:1–17+ (Semicontinuous)

Although the narrative of Ruth is ostensibly set in the period of the Judges, it should be dated in the postexilic period as a voice in the conversation in the Jewish community regarding whether Jewish people could marry Gentiles. Ezra called Jewish people to divorce marriage partners who were not Jewish (Ezra 9:1–10:44; cf. Neh. 10:30; 13:1–3, 23–27). While this step sounds harsh today, the preacher should help the congregation realize that Israel's postexilic life was languishing as people drifted from Torah (e.g., Ezra 4:1–7; Neh. 1:3; 5:1–15; 9:1–37; Mal. 1:6–14; 2:1–9, 13–16; 3:5, 7–10). The Deuteronomic theologians counseled putting away foreign gods (e.g., Josh. 24:14–28) and avoiding intermarriage and otherwise keeping distant from the inhabitants of the land to maintain the blessing of YHWH (e.g., Deut. 7:1–4; 12:29–32; 13:12–18; 23:3–6; cf. Exod. 34:11–16). In the days of Ezra and Nehemiah, Jewish leaders sought to restore the vitality of the community. Intermarriage may have led some Jewish people to bring foreign gods and practices into Jewish homes, and some in the community sought to rid the community of such compromises with the culture and thereby to invoke God's blessing on the restoration of the land.

The book of Ruth offers an alternative viewpoint to Ezra-Nehemiah, but does so in the form of a story. On Proper 26/Year B, we considered the beginning of the story of the Jewish widow Naomi and the Moabite Ruth. Ezra 9:1 refers to Moabites (and others) as people from whom Israel should maintain separation (cf. Neh. 13:1). When the women returned to Israel, Ruth encountered Boaz while she was gleaning. Boaz was kin to Naomi's husband and was responsible for family security. Boaz ensured that Ruth would receive a generous portion of grain (Ruth 2:1–23), an action that Naomi interpreted as a means through which God's *hesed* was at work (2:20).

Naomi guided Ruth to meet Boaz on the threshing floor (3:5). While Boaz was sleeping, Ruth lay at his feet and when he awoke asked him to spread his cloak over her because she was kin, that is, she asked him to marry her. Boaz, an exemplary Israelite, declared that Ruth was a "worthy woman," a woman on a par with Israelite women as a candidate for a wife. Boaz's own integrity is verified by the fact that he consulted with a kin-protector who was more closely related to Ruth than is Boaz (3:1–18). When the other kin-protector yielded his right to Ruth, Boaz married her. Ruth gave birth to a child whom the women of the neighborhood named Obed (4:1–17). The narrator concludes with the pointed fact that Ruth was the grandmother of the great monarch David (4:18–22).

This story challenges the restriction on intermarriage mentioned in the first part of this comment in two ways. First, it shows a Moabite woman demonstrating *hesed* (covenantal loyalty) to the Jewish Naomi. Second, the exemplary Israelite, Boaz, brings the Moabite into his own household as if she were an Israelite. Throughout, Ruth manifests qualities of covenantal behavior. How could the community forbid relationship with the people of *David's* grandparent? An indirect message is that just as God manifested *hesed* through the relationship of Naomi and Ruth prior to Ruth's marriage to Boaz, so God will continue to manifest that quality through persons and relationships that are not officially acknowledged by the Jewish leadership.

Jon L. Berquist points out that the mother-in-law and daughter-in-law are the "relationship of highest significance" for much of the narrative, "a relationship relatively unidentified within the culture and [that] would not have been considered to be a family relationship that implied protection." As the story moves toward its conclusion, "the family includes Boaz and Ruth, an absent father and a foreign mother, whose child nursed at his grandmother's breast" and who was named by the women of the community (a surprise since naming was typically done by males). "The story in the process of solving the problems and lacks described at the beginning transforms the normal Israelite family at the start to something almost thoroughly unrecognizable as family at the end." Yet, Berquist concludes that "the book of Ruth senses God's activity within the world as people go beyond the limits placed upon them by society."[63]

The book of Ruth raises an interesting possibility in homiletical style. Instead of replying to the viewpoint represented by Ezra and Nehemiah with an argument made up of propositions and ideas, it tells a story that invites listeners to imagine the issues from the standpoint of the story. The preacher might identify a perception in the community that is analogous to that of Ezra and Nehemiah on intermarriage and divorce, and construct a reply in a narrative mode.

Ruth figures prominently in the genealogy of Jesus in the First Gospel (Matt. 1:5) to show that Jesus' lineage included a Gentile presence. Luke 3:31–33 mentions Boaz instead of Ruth, but the Gentile connection is still in the background.

1 Kings 17:8–16* (Paired)

For comments on this passage, please see Proper 5/Year C.

Proper 28 [33]/Year B

1 Samuel 1:4–20 (Semicontinuous)

The books of Samuel tell stories of events that took place in the years leading toward and eventuating in the monarchy in Israel (roughly 1020 to 920 BCE). However, they were edited in their present form as part of the Deuteronomic theology expressed in Deuteronomy, Joshua, Judges, 1 and 2 Samuel, and 1 and 2 Kings. The Deuteronomists shaped the books of Samuel to address the postexilic Jewish community, whose life languished and was often contentious. Two underlying convictions from the Deuteronomic theology are especially important for understanding these narratives. For one, the Deuteronomists believed that obedience to the covenant results in blessing while disobedience results in curse, a viewpoint that explains prosperity and calamity. For the other, the Deuteronomists preferred prophetic leadership like that of Moses, Joshua, the judges and Samuel to that of the monarchs, who were especially susceptible to theological and ethical compromise.

The books of Samuel and Kings, then, present the monarchs as ambiguous leaders whose strengths (and obedience) are nearly always accompanied by faults (and disobedience). The prophets were ombudspeople who monitored the degree to which the monarchs and the wider community were faithful to the covenant, and as necessary called for corrective action or interpreted the consequences of human misdeeds and YHWH's actions. Given the Deuteronomic atmosphere, the reader is not surprised when the monarchy later divides, or when the people go into exile. These books are as much cautionary tale as celebrations of the monarchs or monarchy, especially in implying that those returned from exile should avoid the actions that sent them to Babylon.

Today's lection is a part of the Deuteronomists' literary strategy to show that Samuel was a true prophet (though later we see Samuel himself somewhat compromised). Literature in the ancient Near East often uses birth stories to help authenticate the life and message of the one born. This story focuses on God graciously inspiring the life of Samuel from the beginning, and on Hannah as a model of a person or community who tenaciously seeks divine blessing and through whose faithfulness God guides the community.

Elkanah had two wives, Peninnah who had given birth and Hannah who was barren. To be barren was to have no future, for children represented a future. The relationship between Peninnah and Hannah was so tense that Hannah wept and would not eat (1 Sam. 1:3–8). While today's culture sees things differently, many people in antiquity considered barrenness a disgrace.

Hannah went to the place of worship to pray. The narrator mentions that Eli, the priest, was at the door, thus placing a male figure in the text to testify to the veracity of the subsequent events that center in the woman. Hannah asserts considerable initiative by pleading with God to grant her a male child whom she would give over to God for service as a Nazirite. The Nazirites were devoted completely to God, and did not cut their hair, abstained from wine, avoided contact with corpses, and often manifested charismatic gifts (cf. Num. 6:1–21) (1 Sam. 1:9–11).

Hannah prayed silently, moving her lips, an unusual mode of prayer in those days. The narrator portrays Eli as an uncomprehending male who mistakes Hannah's behavior for drunkenness (1 Sam. 1:12–13), but she becomes an instructor for the religious leader by theologically interpreting her own experience (1:14–15). Eli then truly functions as priest by assuring Hannah that God would answer her prayer. She named her male child "Samuel," the Hebrew meaning of which is "One from God" (1:16–20).

Many people today can identify with Hannah's circumstance, especially those with a limited sense of the future. Confronted with barrenness, Hannah took initiative to seek partnership with God to change her situation. To be sure, a preacher should not suggest to the congregation that they make deals with God (such as offering a child in exchange for an answer to prayer) but a sermon can hold up her initiative (especially as a woman) in taking action to secure a future. Furthermore, a sermon could consider points at which conventional religious leadership (represented by Eli) misperceives a situation and is instructed by people, groups, and ideas that are as unlikely as resources of insight today as people in antiquity would have perceived Hannah as being. Indeed, Hannah's initiative became the medium through whom God brought Samuel into the world as model judge and prophet.

Luke has Mary echo this text (as well as similar themes in Hannah's song, 1 Sam. 2:1–10) in Luke 1:15 and 48.

Daniel 12:1–3 (Paired)*

On Proper 29/Year B we discuss the historical setting and purpose of Daniel 7:1–12:13, the first fully developed apocalypse in the Torah, Prophets, and Writings. Some Jewish theologians generated quite a bit of literature similar to Daniel (e.g., *1 Enoch, 2 Baruch, Testaments of the Twelve Patriarchs*) but none of it is in the Protestant canon. The apocalyptic 2 Esdras (4 Ezra) 3:1–16:78 is in the Apocrypha. The passage assigned for today brings to a climax the apocalyptic hope of Daniel while offering an answer to one of the deepest questions facing any theological interpretation of life.

The apocalypse includes the end of the present evil age with emphasis upon the destruction of the powers of evil (that assume the form of social groups such as the rule of Antiochus Epiphanes IV) and the coming of the realm of God in which all things take place according to God's purposes. Daniel 12:1a presupposes the popular idea that God provided a guardian angel for each community. These angels were a means whereby God acted providentially for the community. When social circumstances become difficult God sends the angel Michael to help them through the season of suffering.

One feature of apocalyptic theology is the expectation of a "time of anguish" as the present age comes to an end. This period, called "the tribulation" by some writers, came about as the forces of evil retrenched to resist the coming of God to destroy them and replace their rule with the divine realm (Dan. 12:1b).

Daniel 12:2–3 is the first fully developed reference to the resurrection of the dead in the Old Testament. Many apocalyptic thinkers thought either that at death people lost consciousness and all forms of life, or that the dead went into a kind of holding tank (similar to Sheol) where they experienced neither joy nor sorrow. In connection with the apocalypse, God would raise everyone, that is, bring each person back to consciousness in a body, but one that would not wear out like the present earthly body. God would raise the righteous to everlasting life in the renewed cosmos (the realm of God) and the wicked to "shame and everlasting contempt." Daniel 12:3 compares the resurrection body of the righteous to the brightness of stars.

To Daniel and other apocalyptic theologians, the resurrection is not otherworldly pie in the sky. These theologians were profoundly troubled by the continuing prosperity of the wicked and the unjust repression of the righteous. Many of the wicked died without being punished, and their institutions prospered, while many of the righteous died while suffering and apparently bereft of the life of blessing that God promised. The apocalyptic theologians conceived of the resurrection as the means whereby God would act rightly for the righteous by giving them the life of blessing they had been denied during the evil age. Of course, God would visit curse and condemnation upon the wicked.

The apocalyptic thinkers used their vision as a way of helping people survive difficult circumstances in the present and of affirming that God can ultimately be trusted to act rightly in the future, even the future beyond death. Some preachers today do not fully accept the idea that God will end the present age and inaugurate a new one through an apocalypse, or raise the dead. Nevertheless a preacher could see the reading from Daniel as affirming that God is with the community as strengthening presence in present suffering and can be trusted to be as loving and gracious in any future life as God is in the present. Such awareness could empower individuals and congregations to live courageously in the face of forces ranging from cancer to exploiters who distort and repress.

This lection from Daniel is in the background of Mark 13:1–27 (and parallels) and many other passages in the New Testament (e.g., Matt. 28:1–10; Mark 16:1–8; Luke 24:1–43; cf. Matt. 13:36–43; 25:31–46, esp. 46; Acts 24:10–21, esp. 14; Rom. 6:4–11; 1 Cor. 15:12–47; Rev. 3:5; 7:13–14; 20:5–6).

Proper 29 [34]/Year B

Reign of Christ

2 Samuel 23:1–7+ (Semicontinuous)

The last recorded words of a major figure in antiquity were often important because they summed up major themes from that person's life (e.g., Propers 25/Year A, 27/Year A, and 16/Year B). Today's text presents the last words of David as interpreted by the Deuteronomic theologian (Proper 17/Year B).

In 2 Samuel 23:1 the authors remember that God appointed David by taking him from a shepherd's life and making him monarch of all Israel. David was anointed by Samuel at the behest of God, who raised David over Saul and preserved him on the throne despite challenges to his rule. As ruler, however, David should be responsible for fulfilling the obligations of the monarch set forth in Deuteronomy 17:14–20.

In 2 Samuel 23:2a, David uses language that usually comes from a prophet. The writers present David as implicitly acknowledging that the monarchy is responsible to prophetic evaluation, a perspective the writers would like for the postexilic community to incorporate into their reconstitution of the nation. These themes become explicit in 2 Samuel 23:3. When David describes God as a rock, he calls to mind the idea that God is a fortress or stronghold. If the community wants the security implied by living in a fortress, they need a sovereign who "rules over the people justly, ruling in the fear of God." The editors want the community to be led by one who practices the behaviors prescribed in Deuteronomy and who has the deep sense of religious awe described in that book. The narrators compare this rule to the light and sun of morning, gleaming from the rain on a grassy land (23:4), gently evoking the idea that the practice of justice in community restrains chaos and aims toward blessing for all.

There is an ironic dimension in 2 Samuel 23:5. While David may think of the promise of God triumphalistically, the reader recalls that in 2 Samuel 7 this everlasting promise is not only to sustain the Davidic lineage but to discipline the community in the hope that it will repent and embody justice (see Fourth Sunday of Advent/Year B). Indeed, David's statement in 23:6–7 foreshadows aspects of what will happen to the people of Israel and Judah as their behavior leads them toward exile.

Some Jewish authors in the first century CE believed that David spoke the psalms through the Spirit. Matthew 22:43 interprets 2 Samuel 23:2 in saying that the Spirit led David in Psalm 110:1 (quoted in Matt. 22:44) to say that David calls Jesus "Lord" so that Jesus cannot be "David's son," thereby suggesting the superiority of Jesus to earlier Jewish figures. Today's preacher can critique such use of this material, while still helping the congregation realize that Matthew found it instructive to engage the Davidic tradition, as did the Deuteronomists who were uneasy with the monarchy.

Daniel 7:1–3, 7–9, 13–14, 15–18 (Paired)*

The book of Daniel was written between 168 and 165 BCE. The community was under a repressive occupation when the Maccabean revolt broke out in 168 and liberated the nation in 165 (see 1 and 2 Maccabees). The Jewish community was divided as to whether to participate in military action. Daniel views history through the worldview of apocalypticism. Daniel 7:1–12:13 is the most fully developed apocalyptic theology in the Old Testament. Apocalyptists see history divided into a present evil age that God will destroy through an apocalypse and a new cosmos in which all things take place according to God's purposes (sometimes called the realm or kingdom of God).

Apocalyptic visions typically make use of vivid imagery in which animals, people, places, and events stand for historical realities. In today's reading, the sea represents the chaotic situation of the world at Daniel's time (Dan. 7:1–3), and the four beasts are the four most recent empires—Babylonia, the Medes, Persia, and Alexander the Great—with the Seleucids as ten horns, and Antiochus Epiphanes IV, ruling during Daniel's time (7:4–8) being the last horn. These beasts are described horrifically to represent the oppressive quality of life that they visited upon the community.

In Daniel 7:9–10 thrones are set in place in a cosmic judgment hall where the Ancient One (God) presides. God's appearance—clothing white as snow and hair like wool—bespeaks transformed life in the heavenly world. Fire is a frequent symbol for judgment, and its presence in this scene certifies that God is passing judgment on all names and deeds in "the books" (7:11), that is, on all things that have happened in history.

Daniel sees two things. First, the last horn (Antiochus Epiphanes IV) was put to death, though the other beasts were allowed to live for a time. Daniel thus foresees the end of the immediate rule of Antiochus but not the end of the present world with its evil empires. The complete transformation of the cosmos is yet to come (7:11–12).

Second, Daniel sees "one like a human being" (RSV: "one like a son of man") coming from the heavenly court to the Ancient One. This newcomer looks much like a human being but is of heavenly origin. God appoints this one as God's representative to rule the cosmos as judge and redeemer. God's realm of love and justice extends over "all peoples, nations, and languages." Unlike the reigns of Antiochus, the other horns, and the beasts, the rule of "the one like a human being" is everlasting (7:13–14).

The reign of the one like a human being is not yet fully manifest on the earth. That will occur after the apocalypse (7:15–18). This vision asserts God's sovereignty over history. It assures the struggling community of Daniel that despite repression and violence, God aims to re-create the cosmos as a place of blessing. People can live with courage now in the confidence that God has shown them what will happen in the future.

Even if the preacher is not apocalyptic in theological orientation, a sermon can help the congregation recognize an underlying message in this apocalyptic text. God always seeks to end the reign of evil and to lead the world toward ever greater manifestation of qualities associated with the realm of God—that is, love, justice, peace, and abundance. Today's community is advised not to simply wait passively for such a time but to join God in working actively for it.

The passage from Daniel is paired with John 18:33–37. In the latter passage, when Jesus is questioned by Pilate, Jesus says, "My domain [NRSV: kingdom] is not of this world." These readings are not well paired. Daniel is apocalyptic with its chronological dualism and conviction that God will *remake the cosmos*. The worldview of the Fourth Gospel, influenced to a degree by a modified metaphysical dualism, sees existence *divided into two spheres that exist at the same time*—heaven as sphere of God, life, love, light, and truth, and the world as that of death, hate, darkness, and falsehood. When John says that Jesus' domain is not of this world, it means that Jesus' domain is a sphere revealing God within the corrupt world. John places little emphasis on the end of this age. The preacher could develop a sermon comparing and contrasting these worldviews.

The passage from Daniel would be better paired with passages in the New Testament that directly refer to it, esp. Matthew 24:29–31; Mark 13:24–26; Luke 21:25–28; and Revelation 12:12–16.

All Saints/Year B

Isaiah 25:6–9 (Alternate)

Please see Easter Day/Year B for commentary on this reading.

Wisdom 3:1–9

As we note in introducing Wisdom on Proper 8/Year B, among other things we seek to show that the promises of God prove true for the righteous who continue to live faithfully even in the midst of difficulty and persecution. Faithful members of the community to which Wisdom was written may have died in the midst of social tension, in apparent contradiction to the promise of God that they would experience blessing. Many wicked people apparently profited from their wickedness and lived without reproach during this life. Wisdom 3:1–13 claims that at a point after death, God will provide a new life of blessing for the righteous (1–9) and punish the ungodly (1:10–12).

Wisdom 3:1 presupposes a somewhat platonic notion of the soul as an immortal part of the self that continues to exist after death (though some scholars think that an interlude, similar to Sheol, takes place between death and the beginning of the new life described in Wisdom 3:1–9). The righteous, who only seem to have died, are in the hand of God, beyond torment, and at peace (3:1–3). The foolish and wicked may have thought that the deaths of the righteous were punishment, but the hope of the righteous "is immortality," which the dead now enjoy and to which those who are still alive can look forward (3:2c–3a, 4).

When Wisdom speaks of the righteous being "disciplined" by their difficulty, the writer makes use of a notion, popular in Hellenistic circles, that maturity sometimes came about through suffering. The notion of God "testing" the people here is not a simple matter of God doing things to them to see if they would pass or fail but God giving them difficult circumstances in the same way that gold ore is put into the furnace so that the slag can burn away and the pure ore be left. God accepted their faithfulness in the same way that God accepts a burnt offering (3:5–6).

When God takes these souls into care (the "visitation" of Wis. 3:7), they will shine forth. Here the author uses language that echoes Daniel 12:3 and other apocalyptic texts that dealt with life beyond death. From their place with God in the heavenly world they operate as God's agents, much like angels, helping God rule the nations (3:8). The passage closes by drawing on covenantal language to affirm that God watches over the faithful with grace and mercy and that in the new life they will understand all things (including the reasons for their suffering) and will abide forever with God in love (3:9).

Today's congregation cannot know precisely what happens after death. The idea of immortality beyond the grave is Wisdom's way of showing that God is ultimately righteous and trustworthy, and is intended to empower the community to live faithfully in the present. All Saints' Day is an excellent occasion for the preacher to help the congregation remember some of its own members (and people beyond) who typify the qualities of the righteous in Wisdom 3:1–9.

The passage from Wisdom is read with Revelation 21:1–6a and John 11:32–44, neither of which directly draws from this text.

Thanksgiving Day/Year B

Joel 2:21–27

Please see Proper 25/Year C for commentary on this reading.

Year C

First Sunday of Advent/Year C

Jeremiah 33:14–16

The text for today is from Jeremiah's prophecy during the Babylonian exile. Jeremiah 33:1–9 indicates that Jerusalem, destroyed by Babylonian siege, will be rebuilt and made secure and prosperous. Jeremiah 31:10–11 pledges that life in the land, including in the world of nature, will regenerate. Jeremiah 31:12–13 looks forward to the renewal of flocks.

Jeremiah 33:14–16 adds to these salvation oracles the promise that God will fulfill the promises made to Judah and Israel, the reunited nation, by causing a righteous branch to spring up from David. The key is that this branch (a ruler) "will execute justice and righteousness in the land"; the monarch will guide the community in living according to the stipulations of the covenant. The righteous branch will not tolerate injustice and will insist on righteousness from the priests and prophets and from other members of the community. The emphasis is less on the personal identity of the monarch and more on the covenantal qualities of his rule (Jer. 33:15). Such leadership could save Judah from reverting to the conditions that led to exile, and the community will live in safety (33:16a). Indeed, the renewed *community* will be called "The LORD is our righteousness," a name that bespeaks the fact that the community lives according to God's values for living rightly (33:16b).

The sermon might ask the congregation to think about leaders—of the city, state, and nation, in the worlds of business and education, and yes, even the church. To what degree are such leaders today more like the corrupt figures of Jeremiah 22:1–23:4 or the leaders who seek for community to embody covenantal practices, as in Jeremiah 33:14–16?

The Gospel lesson for today is Luke 21:25–36, a part of the larger Lukan version of the conditions preceding the apocalypse—the return of Jesus from heaven to destroy evil and finally and fully to manifest the realm of God (Luke 21:5–28), with exhortation to live in such a way as to be prepared for that event. While this text does not directly mention Jesus as a descendant of David, Luke elsewhere makes this connection (e.g., Luke 1:27, 32; 2:4, 11; 3:31; 18:38–39, but note 20:42–44). For Jeremiah, the renewal of the Davidic line represented a renewal of covenantal life for Israel and Judah in a reunited monarchy. Luke envisioned the second coming as a means whereby God created a realm of covenantal life (often called the realm of God). That realm has not replaced the current world. Israel, the church, and the wider human family still live in conditions similar to those around the exile or described in Luke 21:5–24. However, a congregation could view Luke's apocalyptic vision as a way of saying that God, dissatisfied with the current world, is ever at work to encourage people to work toward a world that is more like the vision of Jeremiah or of the realm of God. No matter how fierce the repression and resistance, God works with *every* situation to maximize the possibilities for blessing within the limits of that situation.

Second Sunday of Advent/Year C

Baruch 5:1–9

The letter of Baruch purports to be written by Baruch, scribe of Jeremiah, and to refer to the exile and return. Many scholars think it was written in the Hellenistic age, perhaps shortly after the Maccabean revolt but prior to the start of the Common Era. Like much Jewish literature in this period, it makes use of the exilic setting to speak about the situation in the Hellenistic period. Also like many other Jewish writings, Baruch encourages the Jewish community to remain faithful amid the pressures of Hellenization.

The encouragement takes the form of leading the community to acknowledge that while they may have sinned in the past, they have done penance, experienced discipline (Bar. 1:10–3:8), and received wisdom (including Torah) for living now (3:9–4:4) in confidence that God will soon restore the fortunes of the community (4:5–5:9).

The passage for today is part of the poem of restoration. The day is coming when the communities of the Diaspora will end their mourning and will forever live in the immediate presence of God (5:1). They will "put on the robe of righteousness," that is, live in a community in which all things take place rightly according to God's purposes (5:2). The community will live in regenerated splendor as a witness to all other peoples of the power and possibilities that come with the God of Israel (5:3). Indeed, God will name the restored community "Righteous Peace, Godly Glory" (5:4).

The writer looks forward to the people of Israel coming from east and west, ending the Diaspora and regathering the community in Jerusalem (Bar. 5:5). God will carry the people home as if on a throne (5:6) and will transform nature by lowering the mountains, raising the valleys, and creating shade (5:7–8). In such ways God will be faithful to the covenant that God made with Israel (5:9). This future is one for which the community should want to live faithfully in the present.

This text is paired with Luke 3:1–6, the preaching of John the Baptist. While Luke makes no direct use of this passage from Baruch, John does anticipate the coming of a new age that is similar to the hope Baruch speaks in today's lesson. However, by assigning Malachi 3:1–4 (commentary below) as the alternate reading for today, the lectionary misses a significant opportunity to show how a tradition was interpreted in different settings for similar purposes but nuanced for different contexts. Luke 3:3b–6 quotes Isaiah 40:3–5 in the mouth of John the Baptist. The context of Luke's quote is Isaiah 40:1–11, which in turn is a rich resource for the author of Baruch who incorporates imagery from that passage into Baruch's consolation of Zion (4:1–5:9). A preacher might craft a lesson in hermeneutics as a sermon that moves from Isaiah to Baruch to Luke.

Malachi 3:1–4 (Alternate)

A postexilic prophet who worked in Jerusalem in the mid-fifth century, like Zechariah and Haggai, addressed a despondent and suffering people for whom the wonderful promises of Second Isaiah about returning to a land of peace and plenty had not come true. They had great difficulty trusting in and relying on the Lord and had come to doubt that the Lord loved them: "I have loved you, says the LORD. But you say, 'How have you loved us?'" (1:2). Verses 1:2–5 are a dialogue between the Lord and the people over this very question. The Lord had chosen Jacob over Esau, yet the Babylonians had ravaged Jacob (Israel), and Esau (Edom) had abetted the Babylonians and benefited from Israel's destruction. In 1:2–5 the Lord expresses anger at Edom and claims to "have made his hill country a desolation and his heritage a desert for jackals."

In this context, today's reading is the Lord's reassuring promise to the people of Judah/Jerusalem that the Lord YHWH is personally coming to be with the people and dwell in their midst in the Temple. The Lord's covenant with Levi, says the Lord, "was a covenant of life and well-being, which I gave him" (2:5). But the people have not enjoyed life and well-being. Rather, they ask, "How have you loved us?" The most decisive answer to that question is today's passage: by the Lord's presence with the people in the midst of their situation.

Verse 1 needs to be understood as being about YHWH. "See, I am sending my messenger to prepare the way before me, and the Lord [*Adon*] whom you seek will suddenly come to his temple." *Adon* is used to avoid pronouncing the divine name YHWH. The Lord is not the messenger and today's reading does not tell us who is, but Malachi 4:5 identifies the messenger as Elijah: "Lo, I will send you the prophet Elijah before the great and terrible day of the LORD comes." Once again God's glory will dwell in Jerusalem and the people will reflect that glory in the ways that they demonstrate considerate justice for the widow and the orphan and the stranger.

This passage appropriately appears in the lectionary in Advent (Second Sunday of Advent/Year C). In the Synoptic Gospels John the Baptist is regarded as an Elijah-figure who is the messenger preparing the way before Jesus (Mark 1:2 and parallels). The ministry of Jesus was one in which the lost sheep of Israel were urged to return to the Lord, and it became one in which all the Gentiles were urged to turn to the Lord for the first time. In traditional Trinitarian language, God the Son calls people to faith in God the Father. Remembering that God is One can help us avoid reading the Jesus story in anti-Jewish, supersessionist ways.

But how is this the appearance of the God of love, if God is "like a refiner's fire" (3:2)? The "refiner's fire" is a simile for speaking of the transformative love of God. We are so accustomed to speaking of God's justifying, forgiving, and redeeming grace that we sometimes forget the basic point that God has a purpose in all that God does, and the purpose is that all people should have life and well-being (2:5). Yet clearly they cannot as long as we insist on and persist in living in ways that lead instead to death and curse. God's love is freely given to each and all, but it is a love that gives and calls us to become people who love God with all our selves and our neighbors as ourselves and to act accordingly in relation to our neighbors. It is not a love that wants us to go on with making war and preying on the weak. God wants the neighborhood bully to change.

Third Sunday of Advent/Year C

Zephaniah 3:14–20

For an introduction to Zephaniah, see Proper 28/Year A. That passage was about the Lord's imminent judgment on Judah and all the world: "I will utterly sweep away everything from the face of the earth" (1:2). In today's passage, an altogether different note is struck: "Sing aloud, O daughter Zion; shout, O Israel! . . . The LORD has taken away the judgments against you" (3:14–15). God's disciplining of Israel and its enemies (2:1–3:7) has resulted in the cleansing of Judah: "the remnant of Israel . . . shall do no wrong and utter no lies . . . they will pasture and lie down, and no one shall make them afraid" (3:13).

Our reading begins in the imperative: "Sing aloud . . . ! Rejoice and exult!" Although Zephaniah uses warrior imagery to speak of God's judgment on Israel and its neighbors, in the end Zephaniah is all about the love of God graciously given and the grace of God lovingly bestowed. What Judah had to come to comprehend was that the only way it could understand itself in any ultimate sense was as freely loved by the God who freely loves all. Instead, it had wandered off into the worship of Baal and Milcom (1:4–5) and forgot the teachings of Torah about seeing to it that justice was compassionately directed to the care of the orphan and the widow. It committed "violence and fraud" (1:9).

But to understand that we are loved by the only God who is God is to understand that what YHWH wants is the creation of compassionate community, one that encompasses all human beings. To love YHWH is to love and do justice to the neighbor and the stranger as a grateful response to God's right-setting love freely given to us. So Zephaniah announces the most important news in his text: "The LORD, your God, is in your midst, a warrior who gives victory; he will rejoice over you with gladness, he will renew you in his love" (v. 17). The Lord frequently self-identifies the Lord as "the Holy One in the midst of you," whether in the ark of the covenant, in the Temple, or simply in the midst of the people. God will freely dwell again within the physical people Israel.

There will be singing and dancing, "as on a day of festival" (v. 18), and the Lord will be one of the participants. God is organizing a great party at which God the host will be present. Christians should resonate to this image; at every Eucharist we celebrate a meal called the Lord's Supper at which the Lord is present as the inviting host. The glory of Jerusalem will be that the Lord is present in it, the Lord who "will save the lame and gather the outcast" (v. 19).

This reading is appointed both for the Easter Vigil and for the Third Sunday of Advent/Year C. Advent and Easter are perfect seasons for reading Zephaniah's hymn of joy, seasons in which Christians "rejoice and exult with all . . . [our] hearts," singing, dancing, and feasting in the presence of the Holy One in our midst.

Frequently, on such occasions, Christians talk about how the forthtellings of the prophets are fulfilled in Jesus Christ; now has come what Zephaniah anticipated! And that is utterly appropriate, as long as we remember that what Zephaniah promised has not yet been actualized: "they shall do no wrong and utter no lies, nor shall a deceitful tongue be found in their mouths" (3:13). We still live in a world characterized by "violence and fraud" (1:9) on a scale far grander than Zephaniah could possibly have imagined.

Fourth Sunday of Advent/Year C

Micah 5:2–5a

For an introduction to Micah, see Proper 26/Year A. Micah 5:1–6 marks the third time that Micah speaks of imminent danger and then promises salvation. Each begins with the word "now." "Now why do you cry aloud? Is there no king in you?" (4:9) is uttered to the people as they are about to "go to Babylon." "Now many nations are assembled against you" (4:11) refers to armies encamped around Jerusalem. Today's reading begins: "Now you are walled around with a wall; siege is laid against us; with a rod they strike the ruler [king] of Israel upon the cheek" (5:1). This is the punishment that Micah had foreseen coming upon Jerusalem for the sins of its leaders, prophets and priests (3:12).

Each of the first two statements promised salvation from the pressing danger. "There [in Babylon] you shall be rescued, the LORD will redeem you" (4:10; see also 4:12–13). Our passage announces prophetic hope for the future of the people Israel: there will come from the city of David a ruler under whom the people "shall live secure, for now he shall be great to the ends of the earth; and he shall be the one of peace" (5:4–5).

Verse 2 speaks to Bethlehem: "But you, O Bethlehem of Ephrathah, who are one of the little clans of Judah, from you shall come forth for me one who is to rule in Israel." The expression "of Ephrathah" identifies which "Bethlehem" Micah intended. "Bethlehem" referred to a village (*beit*) *le-hem* (of bread), so-called because it had a mill for grinding flour. Joshua 19:15 mentions another Bethlehem in the territory of Zebulun. That Bethlehem is little reminds us that God's choice of the people Israel in the first place was of the most unlikely and insignificant people to accomplish God's purposes.

For a time the Lord will allow his people to stay in exile, but will deliver them "when she who is in labor has brought forth" (v. 3). As with a woman in labor, the exile will be painful but short-lived and assuredly result in the return of the people from exile. The "one who is to rule in Israel" (v. 2) will "stand and feed his flock in the strength of the LORD" (v. 4). He will be a good shepherd, in contrast to the wayward shepherds whom Micah earlier described (3:5–11).

What this promised ruler will do primarily involves bringing peace. Micah 4 speaks of "days to come" when all peoples shall come to the "mountain of the LORD's house" that they may learn the Lord's ways and walk in his paths (4:2). "For out of Zion shall go forth instruction, and the word of the LORD from Jerusalem" (4:2). The Hebrew terms for way, path, and instruction (*torah, halacha*) come to mind in reading this verse. This ruler will "arbitrate between strong nations far away; they shall beat their swords into plowshares, and their spears into pruning hooks; nation shall not lift up sword against nation, neither shall they learn war any more" (4:3). Micah agrees with Isaiah 2:2–4, to cite one of many passages, and the royal psalms, for example: "In his days may righteousness flourish and peace abound, until the moon is no more" (Ps. 72:7).

All this is caught up in 5:5a: "He shall be the one of peace." We mention this because of our Christian predilection, particularly in Advent and Christmas, to claim that in the Gospels all the prophetic hopes and forth-tellings are fulfilled. Jesus was born in Bethlehem as Micah foretold, and did many things which Matthew regards as having been done in order that the Scriptures might be fulfilled. But those who make such claims do not mention the fact that the anointed one (messiah) was to bring universal peace (*shalom*). They blame those who cannot see that Jesus fulfilled all the prophecies because their own desire was to have a military conqueror. Some probably did look for a conqueror. So did Micah (5:5–6). But what some cannot see, because it is not yet here to be seen, is universal peace. Jesus' followers should still seek and work for that outcome.

Christmas Day/Year C

For comments on the readings for Christmas Day/Years ABC, please see Christmas Day/Year A.

First Sunday after Christmas Day/Year C

1 Samuel 2:18–20, 26

In the context of 1 Samuel 2:11–36, today's lection is part of a vintage Deuteronomic explanation for the fall of the house of Eli as a priestly family and the rise of Samuel. While the narrator never criticizes Eli, the narrator depicts Eli's children (Hophni and Phinehas, 1 Sam. 1:3) as unfaithful, scoundrels who "had no regard for God." Samuel, in contrast, is the picture of obedience (on Deuteronomic thinking, see Propers 17/Year B and 28/Year B). The events take place at the community's center of worship at Shiloh, located about twenty miles north of Jerusalem. In a few years, Jerusalem would replace Shiloh as the primary place of worship.

The food for priestly families came from offerings that people brought to Shiloh. According to Deuteronomy 18:3, the priests were allotted specific portions of the meat, but Eli's sons simply poked a three-pronged fork into the meat while it was boiling. According to Leviticus 3:16–17 (cf. Num. 17:18; Deut. 32:38), the fat belongs to God, and so the priests should not take the fat from an offering but should place it in the fire (perhaps to burn as incense). Hophni and Phinehas kept the fat, compelling the narrator to say they treated the offerings "with contempt" (1 Sam. 2:12–17).

The passage assigned for today, 1 Samuel 2:18–20, depicts Samuel in direct contrast to Hophni and Phinehas. Hannah made Samuel a linen ephod, a simple, white linen garment (perhaps a loincloth) that was characteristic dress for priests (cf. 1 Sam. 2:28; 22:18; 2 Sam. 6:14). Samuel faithfully carries out priestly duties. Eli acknowledges the validity of Samuel's ministry by praying for Elkanah and Hannah to have more children as a sign of blessing (2:20–21).

The people brought negative reports about Hophni and Phinehas to Eli. When Eli heard that his sons had engaged in sexual misconduct by lying with women "who served at the entrance to the tent" (cf. Exod. 38:8), he called them to return to faithful behavior, but they would not, for "it was the will of [God] to kill them" (1 Sam. 2:22–25). By contrast, Samuel "continued to grow . . . in favor with [God] and with the people" (2:26).

A holy person brought a message from God to Eli. While God had revealed to Eli's ancestors that they would be priestly, God is now displeased with Eli's children (2:27–29). Consequently, God would cut off Eli's household so that "no one in your family will live to old age" (vv. 30–32). Abiathar will survive but grieve (v. 33; cf. 1 Kgs. 2:26–27). Hophni and Phinehas die on the same day (v. 34).

In place of Eli's family, God will raise up "a faithful priest" who will "do what is in my heart and mind," and for whom God will build "a sure house" (v. 35). Many commentators understand this priest as Zadok. However, Robert Polzin points out that the literary context, and a number of verbal clues point to Samuel.[64] For the Deuteronomist, Samuel is a better representative of the faithful priest, though Samuel himself is not always faultless.

Luke 2:52 directly recalls 1 Samuel 2:26 in wanting listeners to recognize that Jesus is a religious leader in the line of the Deuteronomic Samuel, who resisted conventional monarchy (with the dangers cataloged in the books of Samuel and Kings) and who sought blessing for all through prophetic leadership in covenantal community.

Second Sunday after Christmas Day/Year C

Jeremiah 31:7–14 or Sirach 24:1–12

For comments on the readings for Second Sunday after Christmas Day/Years A B C, please see Second Sunday after Christmas Day/Year A.

Epiphany of the Lord/Year C

Isaiah 60:1–6

For comments on this passage, please see Epiphany of the Lord/Year A.

First Sunday after the Epiphany/Year C

Baptism of the Lord

Isaiah 43:1–7

Today's reading is as pure a statement of God's unconditional love for Israel and all people as can be found in the Scriptures. Its center is in verse 4: "Because you are precious in my sight, and honored, and I love you."

The people Israel, together with "everyone who is called by my name" (v. 7), is the apple of God's eye. This is the constitutive or priestly axiom of the Scriptures: the proclamation that we are the apple of God's eye. Sometimes the emphasis is so strong that the claim is made: "you only have I known of all the families of the earth" (Amos 3:2), as if Israel were the only people whom God loves and chooses. But the prophetic axiom, that we are to love and do justice to all our neighbors for they, too, are God's children, is equally important: "Did I not bring Israel up from the land of Egypt, and the Philistines from Caphtor and the Arameans from Kir?" (Amos 9:7). Are they not, too, my people? God loves each and all of us as if we were the apple of God's eye. And we are to love and serve one another because the neighbor is the one whom God gives us to love.

Today's reading is preceded by a chapter that speaks of God's judgment against Israel for not having done justice: "So he poured upon him [the people Israel] the heat of his anger and the fury of war" (42:25). Wrath and love are not two opposing character traits of YHWH. Rather, love is opposed to whatever is opposed to love and justice is the form love takes. Love should lead to justice in relationships, just as achieving greater justice in relationships should lead to more love. Wrath is God's "strange" work; love is God's "proper" work. It misrepresents God's love when we presume upon it and hence neglect to see that kindhearted justice is done.

That is the context of today's passage. Just having preached God's judgment, Isaiah changes course: "*but now* thus says the LORD" (v. 1, italics ours). Our reading is a psalm singing the good news. It takes the form of a chiasm in which verses 1 and 7 sing of God's creation. It begins: "But now thus says the LORD, he who created you, O Jacob, he who formed you, O Israel" (v. 1). And it ends with: "everyone . . . whom I created for my glory, whom I formed and made" (v. 7). The God who redeems Israel and us is the God who made us.

Verses 1b–3 and 5–6 begin: "Do not fear," a frequent admonition in Scripture found often in the New Testament. "Do not fear" signals God's presence as savior: "I have redeemed you" (v. 1b). God promises to be with Israel when it passes through water and rivers, fire and flame, the hazards of the journey out of exile into Judea. God will be with Israel because God is Israel's "savior" who gave "people in return for you, nations in exchange for your life" (v. 4).

The center and the point are in the statement of God's unmerited, unconditional love for Israel (v. 4). This is at the heart of the Scriptures. "It was not because you were more numerous than any other people that the

LORD set his heart on you and chose you. . . . It was because the LORD loved you and kept the oath that he swore to your ancestors" (Deut. 7:7–8). God's love for Israel is a decision of unfathomable grace. When the church understands its faith appropriately, it confesses that it stands only on the unconditional grace of God made known to it in Jesus Christ. It perverts and denies God's grace when it claims, as too often it has, to displace Israel in God's love because it did the right thing—believed in Jesus as the Christ—when Israel largely did not. To say that is to take the gift of God's unconditional love and turn it into a condition apart from which God is not free to love. That is the heart of what Luther called "works-righteousness." It contradicts the good news of God's free and gracious love.

We celebrate the manifestation of that same loving grace in the season of Epiphany. That is the pertinence of this passage to this spot in the liturgical year.

Second Sunday after the Epiphany/Year C

Isaiah 62:1–5

For comments on this passage, please see the First Sunday after Christmas Day/Year B.

Third Sunday after the Epiphany/Year C

Nehemiah 8:1–3, 5–6, 8–10

The book of Nehemiah, with its companion book Ezra, was written after the exile when some leaders of Israel had returned there to find cities in disrepair, the Temple in ruins, the wall unfinished (meaning that security was compromised), and the residents who had remained behind unhappy with having to accommodate the returning exiles into the lives they had developed while these exiles were in Babylon. Persia, which liberated the exiles, made Israel a colony. Jewish men who married non-Jewish women had children who spoke the languages of their mothers (rather than Aramaic or Hebrew) and thereby made it easier for foreign influence to upset the local economy and social arrangements. Therefore, Nehemiah urges Jewish men to divorce their Gentile spouses.[65]

Nehemiah 8:9 describes Ezra as priest and scribe (cf. Ezra 7:6) and Nehemiah as governor. However, both were approved by Persia and both sought to help members of the Jewish community maintain their Jewish identity while making their way through the requirements of being a Persian colony. The rebuilding of the Temple and the wall and other economic reforms sought to stabilize the nation for two simultaneous social purposes: to improve the quality of life in the Jewish community and to fulfill their responsibilities to the Persian Empire.

At the time of the new moon festival, people assembled before the Water Gate (on the east side of Jerusalem near the Temple). Women were included as were "all who could hear with understanding," that is, mature young people. In its present context, this event in today's reading took place after the reconstruction of the wall to instruct the community in how they should live in their newly secured city for all to enjoy blessing (Neh. 7:73b–8:2; cf. 6:15–19).

Ezra read from the Torah from early morning to midday while standing on a platform, perhaps a precursor to the pulpit. When he unrolled the Torah, the people stood, and after the scribe blessed God, they prostrated themselves in worship and in commitment to practicing Torah in revitalized community (Neh. 8:3–6). The Levites passed among the people giving "the sense" so that the community "understood the reading" (8:7–8). Presumably these interpreters were helping listeners apply the teaching of Torah to the issues discussed at the beginning of this comment.

The people initially wept, probably in mourning as an act of repentance for not having walked in the ways of Torah. But Ezra instructed them not to weep but to celebrate and feast for the new moon festival as they originally planned, and to send portions of their food to the poor and to strangers as the Torah said (Neh. 8:9–12; cf. Deut. 14:22–29; 26:12–15). Ezra thus points to consistent obedience to Torah as the path toward a stable, responsible, and just future.

A preacher could use this passage to help a congregation understand what should happen in preaching by pointing to the minister as a kind of scribe and Levite making sense of sacred tradition. Going beyond, the books of Ezra-Nehemiah raise the question of the degree to which it is acceptable for a congregation to cooperate with the interests of social forces beyond the congregation (e.g., government, transnational corporations).

Today's lection is paired with Luke 4:14–20. Nehemiah 8:1–12 tells of Ezra interpreting a sacred text to help revitalize the community. Luke pictures Jesus as a faithful Jewish interpreter in a similar effort.

Fourth Sunday after the Epiphany/Year C

Jeremiah 1:4–10

Jeremiah's ministry took place in Judah from 626 to 587 BCE, the years leading to the exile and its early phases. Jeremiah is sometimes known as the "weeping prophet" because his message is heavier on judgment than on restoration. Our expression "jeremiad" comes from this characterization.

Prior to the exile, Jeremiah announced that the community's unfaithfulness (evidenced by idolatry, seeking security through political alliances, and social injustice) would bring about God's judgment. During the exile, Jeremiah sought to help the community make theological sense of what had happened and how to respond. The prophet believed that faithfulness to the covenant creates a community of blessing but unfaithfulness invokes curse (Proper 17/Year B).

The reading for today concerns Jeremiah's call as prophet. Call stories were a stylized form in Jewish literature whose purposes were to authenticate the message and mission of the prophet. Jeremiah 1:4 is a standard formula in such calls. Jeremiah 1:5 indicates that YHWH had envisioned Jeremiah's ministry even before his conception in the womb. His mission is to be a "prophet to the nations," a theme expanded in 1:9–10.

The prophet's hesitation to accept the call and God's assurance in Jeremiah 1:6–8 are also standard elements in call stories. Jeremiah does not know how to speak because he is too young. God responds that since God is with the prophet, Jeremiah's youth is not a problem. YHWH's words "I am with you" typically occur in the Jewish tradition in antiquity to signal that God is present and active, to deliver, judge, or redeem. God's words, "Do not be afraid," are the opening expression of a salvation oracle, another stylized expression promising that God will act providentially for persons and communities in distress. God will deliver Jeremiah from those who oppose him.

Touching Jeremiah's mouth, God anoints the prophet's speech. When God appoints Jeremiah "over nations and dominions [NRSV: kingdoms]," God means that Jeremiah's prophetic word, and not the decisions of monarchs, will determine what takes place in history. Jeremiah's prophecy will point to both condemnation and restoration (1:10c; cf. Jer. 30:1–31:40). Jeremiah will even identify Babylon as agent of God's judgment on Judah.

The lection for today is an ideal opportunity for preacher and congregation to reflect on the mission to which they believe they are called. However,

today's community would do well not to drift into arrogance for we can easily mistake our own biases for divine leading. The congregation should think
critically about how to *interpret* God's call. The book of Jeremiah implies useful criteria. A community's interpretation of its call has a high degree or prob-
ability of authenticity when it seeks to move the community in the direction
of covenantal blessing, but has a less likely degree of claim when the community's self-understanding legitimates acts of unfaithfulness, such as idolatry, alliances that work against God's purposes, and injustice.

The call of Jeremiah is paired with Luke 4:21–30. Although Luke does
not directly invoke the call of Jeremiah in Luke 4, and a passage from
Isaiah would have been a better pair with today's Gospel, the choice of
Jeremiah can help the preacher. In ways similar to Jeremiah (and other
prophets) the Lukan Jesus pronounces judgment and salvation, encounters hostility (Luke 4:18–21), and experiences God's support (Luke
4:29–30). Paul draws on the calls of Jeremiah and Isaiah to interpret his
own vocation as missionary to Gentiles (Gal. 1:15). Luke draws on the
same prophetic calls to authenticate Paul's ministry to Gentiles in Acts
(Acts 9:15–16; 22:14–15; esp. 26:16–17). From the perspective of Luke
and Paul, then, the ministries of Jesus and Paul are not breaks with
Judaism, nor even dramatic innovations, but continue the traditions of
Jeremiah, Isaiah, and other prophets.

Fifth Sunday after the Epiphany/Year C

Isaiah 6:1–8, (9–13)

For comments on this passage, please see Trinity Sunday/Year B.

Sixth Sunday after the Epiphany/Year C

Jeremiah 17:5–10

After the exile, a redactor likely inserted Jeremiah 17:1–4 and 5–13 into
the part of the book of Jeremiah that portrays the prophet's early ministry,
to help explain why the exile took place. The redactor hopes that the postexilic community will avoid the mistakes that led to the exile.

The prophet claims that the sin of Judah is "written with an iron pen,"
that is, that the people had become so accustomed to the life of idolatry
that it was an indelible part of their lives. This life is evident not only in
their participation in fertility religion (e.g., "sacred poles beside every

green tree," etc.) but in their false use of the "horns of their altars" (17:1–3a). The horns were extensions on the corners of ancient altars on which the blood of sacrifices was applied and to which people seeking safety could cling. The horns no longer offered protection but were instead evidence of the people's indictment. As a result, the prophet says, God will give Judah's treasure as a spoil to invaders and will "make you serve your enemies in a land that you do not know" (17:3b–4).

Jeremiah 17:5–8 has the flavor of Wisdom literature, prompting some scholars to think that it originally came from a sage. With the memory of the exile incited by 17:1–4, verses 5–8 prompt the congregation to consider whether they would like to live under a curse (similar to 17:1–4) or blessing. God intended life to be an experience of blessing, that is, mutual support, shalom, justice, and material abundance in community. To be cursed is to be denied blessing. Curse is manifest through fractiousness in community, injustice, and scarcity.

According to Jeremiah 17:5–6, communities are cursed when they trust in human beings whose plans are not informed by God and when their hearts turn away from God and toward idols. Then they will be like shrubs in the desert that receive no water; they will live in parched wilderness, indeed, in uninhabited salt lands. These images recollect the drought of Jeremiah 14:1–10 (Proper 25/Year C) and imply that the drought resulted from idolatry.

In contrast are those who trust in God. In this setting trust is not only an act of the mind but refers to living in God's covenantal ways (Jer. 14:7–8). To trust God is actively to turn away from idols, false alliances, and injustice, to worship the living God, and to practice justice. Such communities then and now are like a tree planted by a stream of water, a source of life that will not dry up. When the heat (adversity) comes, its leaves stay green even in the drought.

The human heart, unfortunately, is devious; that is, human beings have a hard time discerning God's purposes and living according to them (17:9). Nevertheless, readers can be assured that God will eventually deal with all people and situations justly (17:10). God will apportion curse or blessing according to the fruit of their doing, that is, according to the degree to which they have walked in God's ways.

The Gospel lection is Luke 6:17–26, the first section of the Sermon on the Plain with its beatitudes and woes. Although there is no direct literary relationship between the passages from Jeremiah and Luke, hearing the curses (woes) and blessings (beatitudes) in Jeremiah reminds the listener of the Jewish character of the Sermon on the Plain.

Seventh Sunday after the Epiphany/Year C

Genesis 45:3–11, 15

For comments on this passage, please see Proper 15/Year A.

Eighth Sunday after the Epiphany/Year C

Sirach 27:4–7

The book of Sirach was written about 200 to 180 BCE when the Jewish community was struggling with increasing pressures of Hellenization (see Proper 17/Year C for additional information). Sirach urges the community to practice its Jewish heritage within the larger Hellenistic culture. The author sets the stage for this discussion by stressing that wisdom dwells in the Jewish community (Sir. 24:1–22; cf. Second Sunday after Christmas Day/Years ABC). The Torah is an expression of wisdom so that walking in the way of Torah expresses wisdom (24:23–34). The author then uses everyday life situations to illustrate people living wisely or foolishly (25:1–27:3).

Today's lesson comes as a warning to pay careful attention to what people say because what they *say* reveals what is in their minds and hearts. The writer uses three examples to make this point. The first is the refuse that remains when a sieve is shaken. At harvest, grain was placed on a floor and stepped on to separate the kernels from the husks. The kernels and husks were then run through a sieve that collected the husks but let the kernels drop through. In the same way, a person's faults will shake out of the sieve of that person's mind when he speaks (27:4). Second, when a potter puts a pot into a kiln, the kiln reveals whether the pot is strong or has faults. Similarly, what a person says discloses the character of that person's life (27:5). Third, the quality of the fruit discloses the quality of the tree. In like manner, a person's talk discloses what is in her mind (27:6). Consequently, the community should praise people only after they speak, for what one says reveals the degree of wisdom with which one operates.

A congregation can be wary of people and groups who advocate ideas and behaviors that are contrary to the values of wisdom as Torah. One would like to think that a person or group calling for the practice of Torah and its values in community is trustworthy. However, as we see today, speech and public communication can be manipulative and sophisticated in its deviousness. Taking a cue from Sirach 27:22–29, a preacher could urge a congregation to explore the degree to which the actual life of a person or community is consistent with what is said. Most of the time, "whoever sets a snare will be caught in it" (Sir. 27:26). Correspondence of speech and action indicates trustworthiness.

Luke 6:39–49, the end of the Sermon on the Plain, is the Gospel lesson for today. The image of the fruit revealing the quality of the tree (Sir. 27:6 and Luke 6:43–45) is a point of connection between the lessons. However, the two writers use this image in different ways. For Luke it means that the *actions* of a person's life (fruit) indicate whether the person is faithful or unfaithful.

Isaiah 55:10–13 (Alternate)

For comments on this passage, please see Proper 10/Year A.

Ninth Sunday after the Epiphany/Year C

1 Kings 8:22–23, 41–43

For comments on this passage, please see Proper 26/Year B.

Last Sunday after the Epiphany/Year C

Transfiguration Sunday

Exodus 34:29–35

In chapter 34 YHWH reestablishes the Sinai covenant with Moses and Israel after Israel's sin with the golden calf and Moses' intercession on its behalf; chapter 34 contextualizes today's reading. After instructing Moses to bring two stone tablets up the mountain (vv. 1–4), YHWH explicates the meaning of God's name "The Lord [YHWH, *adonai*]" (v. 5). "The LORD, the LORD, a God merciful and gracious, slow to anger, and abounding in steadfast love and faithfulness, keeping steadfast love for the thousandth generation . . ." (vv. 6–7). God's compassion (*rahamim*) is a term derived from the word for "womb," *rehem*. God loves Israel with a "womblike love," as a mother loves her children. God's love is *hesed*, loyalty, and *emet*, faithfulness. It is this God with whom Moses speaks. God is all these things "freely"; the adjective is from the noun *hanan*, "grace."

God is "slow to anger"; that is, does not have a low flash-point. Yet God "by no means" clears "the guilty," but rather visits the sins "of the parents upon the children . . ." (v. 7). God's great forgiveness does not overlook sin and its destructive consequences. It is a fact, for example, that the sins of abusive parents are sadly visited upon the children and the children's children. But God's fundamental disposition caresses these children in God's motherly love and seeks always to bring good out of evil.

Then, after a not quite literal repetition of the "ten words" in verses 11–18, today's passage begins. When Moses talked with God "his face shone" (v. 29), as the appearance of Jesus' face "changed, and his clothes became dazzling white" (Luke 9:29) when he went up the mountain to pray and appeared with Moses and Elijah (Luke 9:30). "All the Israelites saw" that Moses' face was shining, just as Peter and his companions "saw his [Jesus'] glory and [that of] the two men who stood with him" (Luke 9: 32).

What are we to understand from the statement that Moses' face shone when he spoke with God and that "whenever" Moses spoke with God (v. 34) or for God to Israel (v. 34), "the skin of his face was shining" (v. 35)? And what are we to understand from Luke that Jesus' face reflected the glory of God? There is an immediate connection between the Hebrew term for "shine" and the word "horn," suggesting that Moses is the genuine leader of Israel instead of the bull that the Israelites had demanded of Aaron.

Terence Fretheim has suggested that the shining of Moses' face indicates that Moses not only speaks for God but that "in some sense he *embodies*" the word of God, bodies it forth.[66] Moses is as inseparable from *torah*, the call and claim of YHWH, as Jesus is inseparable from the Gospel. Each embodies the word that God gives and calls him to proclaim. When they interact with Moses, the Israelites have to do with God, and when we Christians commune with Jesus, we are laid bare before the One who creates and redeems the world. Jesus does not replace Moses; he represents Moses, as both represent God. And as they were transformed by God's presence, so we may be transformed into newness of life by God's grace and justice.

When we "hear" the word of God, which we may do in study or prayer or listening to authentic preaching and teaching, we are not merely to give intellectual assent to truth or trust in and rely upon God's steadfast love and compassion. We are called to embody that word, body it forth, in how we present our living bodies: "present your bodies as a living sacrifice . . . which *is* your spiritual worship" (Rom. 12:1; emphasis ours). How we throw ourselves into the world embodiedly is our true worship.

Ash Wednesday/Year C

Joel 2:1–2, 12–17 (Alternate)

For comments on this passage, please see Ash Wednesday/Year A.

Isaiah 58:1–12 (Alternate)

For comments on this passage, please see the Fifth Sunday after the Epiphany/Year A.

First Sunday in Lent/Year C

Deuteronomy 26:1–11

The authors of Deuteronomy shaped Moses' sermons to Israel as they were about to cross into the promised land so as to speak to people in the years after the exile (see Proper 17/Year B). This phenomenon is clear in today's text, as it prescribes practices for liturgy that are to shape community life. The community symbolically acts out in ritual how they are to live in covenant with God and one another. The liturgical action takes place in three parts—the offering of the first fruits (26:1–4), recalling God bringing the people into the promised land (26:5–10), and eating some of the first fruits in a festal setting (v. 11).

In Deuteronomy 26:1–5a, the people are instructed to present the first fruits (*reshit*) of the harvest in a basket at the Temple to the priest. Giving the first fruits, often considered the best, was a symbol acknowledging that the harvest (and all things that made for life) resulted from God's grace. In a larger sense, making this offering was a way of committing oneself to use the harvest and other gifts of God in ways consonant with God's purposes in covenantal community. The offering was also a down payment or pledge on the full tithe. Furthermore, the offerings served as a practical channel for God to provide food for the Levites (who had no land) as well as the alien, orphan, and widow.

The words of the worshiper to the priest when presenting the basket voice a distinctive understanding of history: "Today I declare to the LORD your God that *I have come into the land* that the LORD swore to our ancestors to give us" (Deut. 26:3). Worshipers, even at the time of the exile and to the present day, speak as if *they* themselves were among the people who entered the promised land (cf. Deut. 6:20–25).

Upon making the offering, community members are to recite Deuteronomy 26:5b–10, an ancient creed used here as a summary of God's providence to the wandering Arameans (Sarah, Abraham, and their descendants) who lived as aliens in Egypt and were harshly enslaved. God delivered them with signs and wonders and brought them into the land flowing with milk and honey. According to the understanding of history in 26:4, this story is the worshiper's own experience.

In Deuteronomy 26:10 the worshiper places the basket before God, bows down, and acknowledges that God brought the community into the land. By this simple action the worshiper affirms that God is indeed one, for God works for one purpose through both history and nature (Deut. 6:4; Proper 26/Year B). To people returning from exile to a desolate Judah, these affirmations demonstrate that God has the power to control, redeem, and regenerate. If they do their part (as Deuteronomy repeatedly insists), they can live in confidence and hope.

The people are then to eat some of the first fruits in a festal meal (26:11; cf. 12:7). This meal is not only an occasion of thanksgiving but a physical symbol of assurance of God's power to redeem from slavery and to use nature to serve the divine purposes. This festal meal illustrates the abundance that God wants for all people all of the time.

By ending the reading at 26:11, the lectionary bypasses an important custom mentioned in verses 12–15. Every third year, households were to put their tithes into local hands so that the poor of the immediate community could "eat their fill" and thereby experience a measure of providential care and blessing (26:12–13; cf. 14:28–29).

Insofar as Lent is a season for reflection on the degree to which the congregation is living out the divine aims for community, this text prompts two questions. First, how can we put our first fruits in the service of God's purposes of covenant; how can we not only give our best efforts but dedicate all our efforts to covenantal community? Second, can the congregation tell the story of its theological identity with the precision of Deuteronomy 26:5b–9? If not, the preacher could help the congregation learn to do so in Lent.

Only vague similarities connect Deuteronomy 26:1–11 and Luke 4:1–13, the Gospel lection for the day. A sermon would be better served by pairing the story of the temptation with readings to which Luke makes explicit reference: Deuteronomy 6:13, 16; 8:3; compare Psalm 91:11–12.

Second Sunday in Lent/Year C

Genesis 15:1–12, 17–18

In Genesis 13 and 14, Abram appears to be at the pinnacle of success, beholding the land that will come to the ancestral pair (Genesis 13) and rescuing his nephew Lot (Genesis 14), but Sarai is barren (Gen. 11:30). And without an heir, the promise of Genesis 12:1–4 to make the couple a great nation could not be fulfilled. The situation of Sarai and Abram is similar to that of Israel during the exile and after the return to a homeland in disrepair, when Genesis was given its final form: their future as a people was in doubt.

God came to Abram in a vision, just as God came to many prophets. The first words that God spoke reveal that the promises and call of God can be disturbing: "Do not be afraid." These words frequently begin oracles of salvation when the people felt imperiled and need assurance. Despite the fact that God points out that God is Abraham's shield (Gen. 15:1), the human progenitor questions whether God can keep the promise of an heir (v. 2), pointing out that a slave child could be the heir in the absence of a child to Sarai (v. 3). If Abram was bold enough to question God in the very presence of the Holy One, we should do so as well. In Genesis 15:4, God stated flatly that the slave child will not be the heir. Sarai and Abram will have a biological child together (Gen. 15:4).

The usual translation of Genesis 15:6 puts the emphasis on Abram's trust in the promise: "he [Abram] believed the LORD; and he [NRSV: the LORD] reckoned it to him [Abram] as righteousness." However, another translation is grammatically possible and theologically preferable: "he [Abram] believed the Lord, and he [Abram] reckoned it to him [the Lord] as righteousness."[67] "Righteousness" (*sedaqah*) is a relational term that refers to doing what is right. The latter rendering is preferred because Abram *has* trusted God, but to this point in the story, God has not fulfilled the promise. God's righteousness, not Abram's, has been in question. Abram, however, declared that God is, indeed, righteous. God coming to Abram has as much as made the promise certain.

When Abram sought a sign to demonstrate God's righteousness, God told Abram to cut animals in two (Gen. 15:8–11). This action was employed in covenant-making ceremonies in the ancient Near East and gave birth to the expression "to cut covenant," a synonym for making a covenant.

In the same "deep sleep" as the first human being was in when God created woman (Gen. 2:21), Abram envisions the future offspring as aliens and prisoners in Egypt and also foresees divine judgment on (and the offspring's liberation from) Egypt (Gen. 15:12–16).

The divine presence is represented by the smoking fire and flaming torch passing between the animals (Gen. 15:17–20). Verse 18 makes the meaning of the scene explicit: God has cut covenant with Sarai and Abram. Henceforth, the couple (and their descendants) and God are conjoined. "When covenanting parties pass through the halves of sacrificial animals, they bind themselves to one another in such a way that covenant disloyalty will tear each of them in two as the animals lie cut in two."[68]

In Genesis 15:18–21, God gives the land to Sarai and Abram. However, their descendants will not possess it until four generations have passed. Nevertheless, the couple experiences a prolepsis: they live in the land as if it is already theirs. What would happen in our churches if we lived in the present as if it were a promised land?

Genesis 15 does not inform Luke 9:28–36, Luke 13:31–35, or Philippians 3:17–4:1. However, Paul cites or alludes to Genesis 15:5 in Romans 4:18 and to Genesis 15:6 in Romans 4:3, 6, and 22, and in Galatians 3:6, with James 2:23 referring to the passage. Luke makes use of Genesis 15:13–14 in Acts 7:6–7.

Third Sunday in Lent/Year C

Isaiah 55:1–9

For comments on this passage, please see Proper 10/Year A.

Fourth Sunday in Lent/Year C

Joshua 5:9–12

The season of Lent includes reflection on the degree to which the congregation manifests faithful witness. Although the larger literary setting of this reading is immediately after the Israelites cross the Jordan into the promised land (see Proper 26/Year A), Joshua 5:1 introduces a theme that fits the season of Lent. When the leaders of the peoples inhabiting the promised land (Amorites and Canaanites) heard that YHWH had dried up the Jordan when the Israelites crossed over, the hearts of these leaders melted, and "there was no longer any spirit in them, because of the Israelites."

Circumcision was a sign of God's promise and faithfulness (see Second Sunday in Lent/Year B). The Israelites who had come out of Egypt had been circumcised in accord with God's directive in Genesis 17:1–16, but the generation who wandered in the wilderness did not listen to the voice of YHWH and did not circumcise their children (Josh. 5:6). As one of the first acts in the promised land, Joshua ordered circumcision for the new generation that had crossed the Jordan and was about to occupy the promised land (Josh. 5:2–9).

Commentators disagree on the meaning of the "disgrace of Egypt" that God rolled away by having the new generation circumcised (Josh. 5:9).

Was the disgrace having been enslaved, or the disobedience in the wilderness, or something else? Whatever it was, the text presents the act of circumcision as assuring the people of Israel that they had been re-created for life in the new land.

In Joshua 5:10–12 they keep the Passover, the meal that not only commemorates their deliverance from Egypt but that makes the power of that event present to each new generation (e.g., Deut. 6:20–25). This meal has such identity-forming power that it is to be constitutive of the community in the new land. The covenantal life they are to embody is described in detail in the book of Deuteronomy. By eating the meal, they commit themselves to embody that life.

The day after the Passover, they ate of the produce of the land (including unleavened cakes and parched grain), and the manna ceased that had accompanied them through the wilderness wandering. God's providence and faithfulness previously expressed in the wilderness through manna would now be expressed through the generativity and abundance of the land. The people were prepared for the next stage in their new life; their part was then to follow God's directives through Joshua in the subsequent chapters.

Joshua 5:1–15 has only a vague literary or theological relationship with the other readings for the Fourth Sunday in Lent. The vision of Joshua 5 of the re-creation of the people Israel does fit with the motif of new creation in 2 Corinthians 5:16–21, and even with the re-entry of the prodigal son into the household of the loving parent in Luke 15:11b–32. From this perspective, Paul and Luke envision the God of Israel re-creating people through Christ and the church (especially Gentiles) in a way similar to God's re-creation of Israel in Joshua. A hermeneutic of continuity is at work.

The lectionary does the church a disservice by not including any lections from Joshua or Judges that describe the Israelites taking the land by violence (e.g., Josh. 6:1–27). Such passages would give the congregation dramatic opportunities to learn about the notion of holy war (a timely concern), to reflect on the roles of God and the people in holy war, and to think critically about the appropriateness of violence in Christian life and witness, especially violence whose goal is a more just world.

Fifth Sunday in Lent/Year C

Isaiah 43:16–21

Please see the Seventh Sunday after the Epiphany/Year B for our comments on this passage.

Palm/Passion Sunday/Year C

Please see Palm/Passion Sunday/Years A, B, and C.

Good Friday/Year C

Isaiah 52:13–53:12

For comments on this passage, please see Good Friday/Year A.

Easter Day/Year C

Isaiah 65:17–25 (Alternate)

Today's reading from Isaiah is a marvelous text. It follows Third Isaiah's pronouncement of judgment on the sinful in Israel and stands in dialectical tension with that pronouncement (see Proper 7/Year C). The prophet is saying that the way forward into God's promised future for the people is through facing our sins and errors with honesty and dreaming of what might be. We are reminded of faithful people like Martin Luther King Jr., who knew all too well the difficulties faced in the struggle for equality but in spite of them proclaimed "I have a dream" and described a future when that dream would be realized.

Anyone with a clear-sighted assessment of the situation in which we live should be depressed. With millions suffering because of natural disasters, victimized by war and genocide, dying because of destitution and starvation; with the poor getting poorer and with militarism constantly on the rise, what hope is there that God's order of kindhearted justice for everyone will ever happen?

There are several options in the face of such realism. One is gnostic: to give up on the salvation *of* this world and live on the hope to be saved *from* this world. Another is to satisfy ourselves with doling out charity in the form of free clothes for the homeless, free food for the destitute, blankets and tents for victims of natural disasters, and to regard God's compassionate justice as in effect something that will never be realized. A third possibility is to escape into the kind of apocalyptic thinking that leaves it to God to do all the heavy lifting while we wait passively for the reign of God and the return of Jesus.

The prophets, the Gospel writers, and Paul will have none of these. They set forth a grand vision of what might be and insist that by walking the way of faith and doing deeds of loving-kindness we can mend the world (*tikkun olam*; see pp. xxi). They make it clear that there is no earthly force, no matter how self-interested or destructively powerful, that can obstruct God's will to bring about a world in which God's creatures enjoy life and well-being. Before the fall of the Berlin Wall, Martin Luther's hymn "A Mighty Fortress Is Our God" rang out in the churches of East Germany as a song of defiance. The underlying conviction is that as compared to God the destructive rulers of this world are "like grasshoppers . . . [God] brings princes to naught and makes the rulers of the earth as nothing" (Isa. 40:22–23).

Not for the first time, the book of Isaiah sings of a time when there will be universal peace: "The wolf and the lamb shall feed together, the lion shall eat straw like the ox . . . they shall not hurt or destroy on all my holy mountain" (65:25). Even predatory animals will be vegetarians! All killing shall cease.

God will create "new heavens and a new earth" (v. 17). Jerusalem will be "a joy and its people a delight" (v. 18), a prophecy that would be good news indeed to all the inhabitants of present-day Jerusalem. No more weeping and distress will be heard in Jerusalem (v. 19), neither Palestinian nor Israeli. They will do the work of peace: build houses and plant vineyards (v. 21). Children will not die in infancy (v. 20) nor grow up to experience calamity (v. 23). God will be present, the people will do justice and love mercy, and all will be well. While these promises are specific to Israel, Isaiah's universal horizon is always present.

In praising Eleanor Roosevelt, Adlai Stevenson said: "She would rather light a candle than curse the darkness." That is what preachers can do with this passage. And we can remember how she put it: "The future belongs to those who believe in the beauty of their dreams."

When this text is paired on Proper 9/Year C with Jesus' foretelling of the Temple's destruction in Luke 21:5–19, at a time when Jesus' followers were being "brought before kings and governors because of [Jesus'] . . . name," its message is even more apropos.

Day of Pentecost/Year C

Genesis 11:1–9

Today's text is the climax of the primeval history written by the Priestly theologians to explain why God decided to supplement God's attempt to bless all human societies through nature and general instruction by calling *one* family as a model for the path to blessing for *all* (Gen. 12:1–3).

The Table of the Nations in Genesis 10 indicates that after Noah, the human family divided into different ethnic groups and geographical dwelling places. The Table includes nations from the world known to the Priestly theologians—the Middle East, Africa (e.g., 10:6–7, 13), and perhaps Indo-Europe (e.g., 10:3–4).

As Genesis 11 begins, all the peoples of the world speak one language (Gen. 11:1). They settle at Shinar, a name for Babylon (11:2; cf. 10:10). Initially the inhabitants of Shinar are a model of cooperation and industry, making high-quality bricks (11:3). However, they soon built a city with "a tower with its top in the heavens." Many Mesopotamian cities contained such a tower—a ziggurat, a building wide at the base with increasingly smaller stories. Deities visited or dwelled at the top of the towers where priests and other rulers could ascend and confer with the deities. To the Priestly readers, of course, such efforts were idolatrous. Moreover, the people built this tower so they could "make a name" for themselves, an expression referring to the fact that Near Eastern monarchs often affixed their names and those of their deities to such buildings as long-lasting monuments.

As the scene shifts to God in 11:5, the text exhibits a little humor. Despite the fact that the builders sought to erect a tower "with its top in the heavens," God had to come *down* to examine it. God recognized that the people were cooperating in an endeavor that could further undermine God's purposes for creation (11:6). Consequently, God confused their language so that they could no longer understand one another (11:7–8), and scattered them to different places on the earth. God called that place "Babel" (which means "to confuse").

At one level, this story explains why the peoples of the earth speak so many languages. At another level, it offers a theological interpretation of Babylon. Indeed, according to another Priestly theologian, the rulers of Babylon ascended "to the tops of the clouds" (on a ziggurat) to "make [themselves] like the most high" (Isa. 13:14). The tower thus represents Babylon's attempt to claim for itself power that belongs only to God. By extension the story applies to other nations that behave like Babylon. The story indicates that God will cast down, scatter, and confuse those who manifest attitudes and behaviors like the Babylonians. Very likely, by the time text was given its present shape, Babylon had been overpowered and its name besmirched, thus underlining the folly of 11:4b.

The lectionary is short-sighted in assigning this text as an *alternate* reading for the Day of Pentecost. For Luke views the story of Pentecost in Acts 2:1–42 as a reversal of the events of Genesis 11:1–9.

Trinity Sunday/Year C

Proverbs 8:1–4, 22–31

As we note on Proper 19/Year B, the Jewish tradition uses the notion of wisdom to refer both to the content of awareness of God's purposes for the world and to Woman Wisdom, who is active in the world as an agent of the divine presence and purposes.

Proverbs 8:1–4 depicts wisdom in a way similar to Proverbs 1:20–23 (Proper 19/Year B). She is on the heights, at crossroads, beside the gates of the city, and at the portals calling to people to heed her. She wants all in the community to "learn prudence, acquire intelligence," that is, to live according to God's design in ways that will bring blessing to all (8:5). Her instruction is trustworthy (8:6–9) and worth more than silver, gold, and jewels (8:10–11). Those who follow her live with knowledge and discretion, but distance themselves from evil such as pride, arrogance, and perverted speech (8:12–14). She is manifest through rulers who govern justly (8:15–16) and, ideally, those who love her will live in her ways and thereby find security, righteousness, and justice (8:19–21).

The community can trust the words of Woman Wisdom because God created her when God began to create the world (8:22–23). While wisdom is one of God's closest agents, wisdom is not herself God. God brought her forth even before the deep existed (8:24). The language "brought forth" usually refers to the act of giving birth, thereby imaging God as a woman whose womb birthed wisdom.

Woman Wisdom was present in the world before the creation of the mountains, hills, earth, fields, and soil (Prov. 8:25–26). Wisdom was on hand before God made the heavens, shaped the horizon, gave the sky its form, established the deep, and limited the power of the sea by setting the boundaries beyond which it could not go (8:27–29). In a key assertion, Woman Wisdom describes herself as beside God like a "master worker," that is, working as an accomplished builder (8:30a). Such work brings God delight, causes wisdom herself to rejoice, and further brings delight to the human family who benefit from this work (8:30b–31).

The Wisdom literature assumes that the world itself reveals the character and purposes of God. The idea that Woman Wisdom was an agent of creation is one way of explaining how the divine intentions became implanted in the world: wisdom put them there. Now, people can discover God's design for the good life by paying attention to what we learn from life itself.

Awareness of these themes is important to understanding aspects of the New Testament. Although John 16:12–16 (the Gospel passage for today) does not directly evoke Proverbs 8, the notion of wisdom from Proverbs (and other sources in Jewish literature) helps explain Jesus in the Fourth Gospel. In John 1:1–5, for instance, the preexistent Jesus functions as God's agent at creation.[69] Furthermore, in the Fourth Gospel Jesus comes down from heaven to reveal the nature and purposes of God in a way similar to wisdom. Wisdom similarly appears elsewhere in the New Testament, for example, Matthew 11:25–30; 1 Corinthians 1:18–31; 8:6; Ephesians 3:8–10; Colossians 1:15–20; Hebrews 1:1–4; Revelation 3:14. Living wisely is a value in some texts, such as Colossians 4:5; Ephesians 1:17; 5:10; and James 1:5–11.

Proper 4 [9]/Year C

1 Kings 18:20–21, (22–29), 30–39+ (Semicontinuous)

Verses 1–17 set the scene for the dramatic contest between the lone Elijah and the 450 prophets of Baal and the 400 prophets of Asherah (the "Lady of the Sea"), a goddess who appears here as the wife of Baal. The drought (see 17:1) has taken a severe toll, and Ahab enlists Obadiah, a faithful follower of YHWH (18:13), to find water to save the horses and mules of the kingdom.

At Elijah's demand (v. 19), Ahab assembled "all the Israelites" and the prophets at Mount Carmel (v. 20). At issue is the effectiveness of Baal, a fertility god, in making fertility possible or whether YHWH, who created heaven and earth and graciously covenanted with Israel, can end the drought and make possible life and well-being as YHWH through Elijah had done three times in chapter 17.

Ahab is the culprit who introduced Baal worship into Israel (16:29). He was not like politicians who respond to popular demands as registered in polls; 1 Kings never intimates that the people requested this action from Ahab. Nonetheless, Elijah addresses "all the people" and asks: "How long will you go limping with two different opinions? If the LORD is God, follow him; but if Baal, then follow him" (v. 21). While talking to them he refers to Baal as "your god" (v. 24). Yet previously he accused Ahab of having "troubled Israel" (v. 17). The apparent confusion may be due to the redaction of the text. (Paul faces a similar problem in the reading for today from Galatians.)

Elijah sets the terms for the contest. Eight hundred and fifty prophets of Baal and Asherah are pitted against one lone prophet of YHWH; the scene is set for dramatic effect. These prophets have all day in which to plead with Baal to provide lightning to set fire to their sacrifice. The significance of lightning is its connection to thunderstorms and rain. Baal's prophets called on his name "from morning until noon" and from noon until midday and "until the time of the offering of the oblation" (vv. 26, 29). The entire day passes, "but there was no voice, and no answer" (vv. 26, 29).

Then Elijah constructed his altar of twelve stones, one for each "of the tribes of the sons of Jacob" (v. 31). He dug a deep trench around the altar, placed wood on it, and butchered the bull to be offered to the Lord. Dramatically, he drenched the whole thing in water three times (vv. 33–34), so much that even the trench was filled. He prayed to God to "let it be known this day that you are God in Israel . . . so that this people may know that you, O LORD, are God, and that you have turned their hearts back" (vv. 36–37).

In spite of Israel's having followed Ahab into the worship of Baal, Isaiah speaks only of God's making God's lordship known again to Israel and turning back their hearts to God. He asks God to act graciously and God immediately does so. In the blink of an eye, "the fire of the LORD fell and consumed the burnt offering" along with the altar and water that was in the trench.

Our reading ends with the people Israel declaring that "the LORD indeed is God; the LORD indeed is God" (v. 39). The text goes on to say that "in a little while the heavens grew black with clouds and wind; there was a heavy rain" (v. 45).

Far more than a miracle story, our text raises questions of how we think and speak of God, whether what we mean by "God" is one like Baal who provides "no voice and no answer" or whether God is the One who is companion of all, vulnerable to relations, affected by prayer, and who interacts with God's people and God's world. Christians often traditionally talked of God as impassible. Here it is Baal who is impassible and YHWH who is passible and moved to respond.

1 Kings 8:22–23, 41–43 (Paired)*

For comments on this passage, please see Proper 16/Year B.

Proper 5 [10]/Year C

1 Kings 17:8–16, (17–24)+ (Semicontinuous)

Chapter 17 consists of Elijah stories. Ahab appears in 17:1 and only reappears in 18:1. Today's reading introduces Elijah as faithful to YHWH (his name means "YHWH is my God"), in contrast to Ahab, who introduced into Israel the worship of Baal and built an altar to him in Samaria (1 Kgs. 16:31–32).

First Kings 17:1–6 presents Elijah as sent by God to Ahab to announce: "there shall be neither dew nor rain these years, except by my word" (v. 1). This put Ahab on notice that it is YHWH and not Baal who provides fertility, life, and well-being. At God's direction, Elijah hid from Ahab at the Wadi Cherith (a wadi is a typically dry riverbed where life can flourish in the rainy season). There ravens fed him "bread and meat" and he drank from the wadi until it "dried up because there was no rain in the land" (vv. 6–7). God uses even ravens (birds of prey) for God's purpose of providing life.

Today's reading contains two Elijah stories (vv. 8–16 and 17–24). The first has to do with the widow of Zarephath to whom the Lord sends Elijah when the wadi runs dry. Preachers should note that Elijah and Elisha, northern prophets, enjoy free and open relations with women and perform miracles of feeding and raising the dead, and that Jesus as a Galilean northerner frequently acts in the mode of these northern prophets.

Elijah asks the widow for water (v. 10) and bread (v. 11) only to receive the reply: "I have nothing baked, only a handful of meal in a jar, and a little oil in a jug; I am now gathering a couple of sticks, so that I may go home and prepare it for myself and my son, that we may eat it, and die" (v. 12). The widow fears, in the drought, that she and her son are on the precipice of death. Elijah utters words often found on the lips of Jesus: "Do not be afraid" (v. 13), asks for a "little cake" and suggests that she prepare food for herself and her son. He tells her that God has promised that "the jar of meal will not be emptied and the jug of oil will not fail until the . . . LORD sends rain on the earth" (v. 14). God and God's creatures, Elijah and the widow, act together to make possible life and well-being. Elijah depends on both God and the widow, who in turn depends upon both God and Elijah. In a land where Baal is worshiped, it is YHWH who gives life to this family and its prophetic guest. This feeding miracle involves divine-human interaction.

The second story (vv. 17–24) has to do with raising the dead. The Gospel writers often use Elijah as a model for Jesus' ministry; preachers may wish to link this story with Luke 7:11–17, where Jesus raises the son of the widow of Nain. In today's reading, the widow's one remaining family member, her son, became so ill that "there was no breath left in him" (v. 17). Her fears have been compounded and she accuses Elijah: "You have come to me to bring my sin to remembrance, and to cause the death of my son!" (v. 18). Elijah does not respond but instead takes the boy to his room, places him on his bed, and cries out to God: "Have you brought calamity even upon the widow with whom I am staying, by killing her son?" (v. 20). Then he lay upon the boy and prayed to God "let this child's life come into him again" (v. 21). The Lord heard; not only Israel is supposed to "hear" (*shema*); YHWH also hears Israel. And because God heard, life returned to the boy and Elijah presented him to his mother: "See, your son is alive" (v. 23).

The woman's bad theology—her son's illness is caused by her sin—is set aside as empty of significance and YHWH acts on behalf of life and blessing. Like Moses (Exod. 33:12–23), Elijah prays to God with chutzpah, using the imperative to demand (v. 21) the child's life. The child's life is not restored without Elijah's prayer or without the rite of healing that he performs. Nor is it accomplished without God's action; God and God's servant interact to bring about life and blessing.

This story is about the little people and things—a prophet hiding from a powerful king, a starving widow and her ill son, carrion birds, complaints born out of fear and doubt—through which God's purposes are accomplished.

1 Kings 17:17–24 (Paired)*

For comments on this passage, please see the passage immediately above (Proper 5/Year C).

Proper 6 [11]/Year C

1 Kings 21:1–10, (11–14), 15–21a+ (Semicontinuous)

Today's reading is the story of Naboth's vineyard and Ahab's attempt to buy it. Understanding the story requires seeing it in the light of the Torah's teachings on land (property). The concern of the Torah is for the well-being of all people, particularly the vulnerable. In an agricultural economy, land is the basis of all well-being. Being thrown off it for whatever reason (poverty, unpayable taxes, greedy neighbors getting richer by buying up the one source of economic productivity) brings homelessness and destitution.

YHWH proclaims: "The land shall not be sold in perpetuity, for the land is mine; with me you are but aliens and tenants" (Lev. 25:23). In the jubilee year every family was to be restored to its property (Lev. 25:10,

13). Land could not be sold "in perpetuity." Land could be sold between one jubilee year and another, but "it is a certain number of harvests that are being sold" (Lev. 25:16); the land itself belongs to God, and the family that originally owned it was to be restored to it. This was key to the Torah's antipoverty campaign.

Ahab and Jezebel violate Torah in their confiscation of Naboth's vineyard. Ahab has already introduced apostasy into Israel; now we see that apostasy leads to social injustice. Naboth's vineyard was "beside" Ahab's palace in Jezreel. Reflecting the values of a money-economy, Ahab offers to give Naboth the vineyard's "value in money" or swap it for "a better vineyard" farther away (v. 2). Naboth's refusal (v. 4) was in line with the teachings of Torah, and he was sagely reluctant to deal with Ahab. Ahab is "resentful and sullen" (v. 4), and Jezebel is incensed: "Do you now govern Israel?" (v. 7). That is: "you're the king; you can do what you please." So she cooks up a scheme to have Naboth charged with cursing God and the king, as a result of which he is stoned to death (v. 13). One injustice is compounded by another: murder. The "spilling of blood" was also taking what was the Lord's: "Whoever sheds the blood of a human, by a human shall that person's blood be shed; for in his own image God made humankind" (Gen. 9:6). God is the giver of life and life was understood to be in the blood (Gen. 9:4); not even the blood of animals belonged to human beings.

With Naboth conveniently out of the way, Ahab takes possession of his vineyard (v. 16). Once more, God's word comes to Elijah who receives a commission to say to Ahab: "Thus says the LORD: Have you killed, and also taken possession?" (v. 19). He is told to follow that remark with this prophecy: "In the place where dogs licked up the blood of Naboth, dogs will also lick up your blood" (v. 19). Ahab asks: "Have you found me, O my enemy?" Elijah answers: "I have found you. Because you have sold yourself to do what is evil in the sight of the LORD, I will bring disaster on you" (vv. 20–21).

The themes of this story resonate throughout the Gospels' accounts of the ministry of Jesus: the unfairness of the wealthy and the royal, the haughtiness of the powerful who can never have enough. See Luke's parable of the Rich Fool (12:13–21), who built bigger barns to hold his crops amid an economy of scarcity. As the Torah makes clear, this is an offense not just against other human beings but against God, to whom the land and its produce belong and whose will is that no one is homeless and hungry.

Naboth steadfastly resists Ahab's proposal and does so in the name of the Lord (v. 3). He and Elijah are faithful to YHWH, to the Torah, and to YHWH's demand that we act justly in relation to each other. Although Ahab's punishment is delayed because of his contrition at hearing Elijah's words (vv. 27–29), he will later repent of his repentance and receive his comeuppance (2 Kings 9:25–26; 10:17).

Meanwhile we have a wonderful text on the relationship between faithfulness and social justice. It raises a question that troubles many in our times of unlimited greed: is there ever any limit to how much of the world's riches the wealthy can commandeer for themselves while others live on the street?

2 Samuel 11:26–12:10, 13–15 (Paired)*

For comments on this passage, please see Proper 13/Year B.

Proper 7 [12]/Year C

1 Kings 19:1–4, (5–7), 8–15a+ (Semicontinuous)

Immediately after his triumph over the prophets of Baal and Asherah at Mount Carmel, Elijah becomes a hunted man. Jezebel heard from Ahab that Elijah had killed the prophets of Baal (18:40) and sent a message to him: "So may the gods do to me, and more also, if I do not make your life like the life of one of them by this time tomorrow" (19:2). In the books of Kings God works with people in spite of their doubts and fears. In chapter 19 God works with Elijah to overcome his fears in the pursuit of his prophetic vocation.

On hearing Jezebel's message, Elijah fled in fear beyond Beer-sheba, quite a ways south in the land of Israel, and "sat down under a solitary broom tree" (v. 4) in the wilderness, hiding away from Jezebel's hit squad. But an angel, a messenger of God, roused him from sleep saying: "Get up and eat" (v. 5). YHWH's messenger gave him bread and water; Jezebel's messenger, who was also Baal's messenger, delivered a death sentence.

Elijah walked for forty days and nights to Horeb (Sinai), "the mount of God" (v. 8) where he confessed his failure: "the Israelites have forsaken your covenant, thrown down your altars, and killed your prophets with the sword. I alone am left, and they are seeking my life, to take it away" (v. 10; see Rom. 11:3). Then he witnessed "a great wind," an earthquake, and a fire, but the Lord was not in any of them (v. 11). After the fire "there came a voice to him that said, 'What are you doing here, Elijah?'" (v. 13). After the noise of wind and earthquake, God spoke in a "sound of sheer silence." In response Elijah makes the same confession of failure as before. Clearly, he wants to be released from his vocation as a prophet.

But God is having none of it. Instead, God says to go to "the wilderness of Damascus" (v. 15) and make some appointments: Hazael will be king over Aram, Jehu will be king of Israel (instead of Ahab), and Elisha will be Elijah's successor, "prophet in your place" (vv. 15–16). Elijah will no longer be carrying on alone; he will have help. Implicitly there is another promise from God: I will be with you. Elijah is brought back to faithfulness at Sinai after Israel's apostasy, as Moses earlier was after Israel's murmuring (Exod. 17:5–6). And YHWH points out to Elijah that there are "seven thousand in Israel . . . that have not bowed to Baal" (v. 18; see Rom. 11:4 on the faithful remnant).

Elijah calls to mind the story of the rich young ruler who, amid the terrible conditions of the people Israel in exile in their own land under Roman domination and suffering from economic deprivation, spoke to Jesus exclusively about himself: "what must *I* do to inherit eternal life?" (Luke 18:18; Mark 10:17; Matt. 19:17; emphasis ours). Amid the widespread apostasy of Israel, Elijah still focuses on himself even after his rescue by the angel, and after God spoke to him in the still, small voice.

God does not become disgusted with Elijah, nor does God deny Elijah's fears or his right to express them; God simply keeps Elijah on course. God's love keeps after us; God does not give up on us, although it would be easy to do so.

Responding to the call and claim of God is a risky business, and defeat and despondency are often the companions of those who do so. We should not wallow in such feelings, although Elijah did just that, but be open to the God who ever calls us forward as Elijah, in spite of himself, was called. God's adamant love gets us through the hard times.

Isaiah 65:1–9* (Paired)

Today's reading is a proclamation of judgment and salvation to "a nation that did not call on my name" (v. 1), "a rebellious people" (v. 2). It looks like a judgment on the whole of Judea, but the likelihood is that its prophetic critique is directed against those who engage in the practices that the proclamation lists (vv. 2b–4, 7).

Our text begins with God's self-description as a gracious God seeking a covenantal relationship with God's people. "I was ready to be sought out by those who did not ask, to be found by those who did not seek me. I said, 'Here I am, here I am,' to a nation that did not call on my name" (v. 1).

God will remain steadfast to God's self-identification and in spite of the judgment that follows is committed to the salvation of the people (vv. 8–9). The passage opens and closes on the note of grace.

The first two verses respond to the question posed three times in the preceding lament: "Where is the one who brought them up out of the sea?" "Where is the one who put within them his holy spirit?" "Where are your zeal and your might?" (63:11bc, 15b). God replies: I am always with you. It is your alienation from me that is the issue, not mine from you. The people need to turn (*shuv*) to God in repentance, always a possibility in the theology of Israel. Third Isaiah summons them to encounter honestly their own sinfulness and take up again the covenantal responsibility involved in the worship of God, deeds of loving-kindness toward the vulnerable.

Our text lists the sins that brought the prophetic indictment: the people were "following their own devices" (v. 2), not living according to God's covenant of considerate justice but according to their own ideas of how life should be lived. They were "sacrificing in gardens . . . offering incense on bricks" and sitting "inside tombs" (vv. 3–4). They passed the night "in secret places" and ate "swine's flesh" (v. 4). They "offered incense on the mountains, and reviled me on the hills" (v. 7). These are the religious behaviors of the local fertility cult and of attempting divination by communicating with the dead. Eating swine's flesh violated the ban on pork and was important to Third Isaiah because it went against Mosaic instruction and because it symbolized the abandonment of faith in YHWH of which the other sins were evidence.

What is worse, to these sins they add another: "do not come near me, for I am too holy for you" (v. 5). This is like the student who plagiarizes a paper and, upon being found out, reacts with high moral dudgeon and a refusal to accept that he or she can be called to account. This is self-centeredness run amok. God finds such people nauseating: "These are a smoke in my nostrils" (v. 5).

God reacts to this array of sinful behavior: "See, it is written before me: I will not keep silent, but I will repay; I will indeed repay into their laps their iniquities and their ancestors' iniquities together, says the LORD" (vv. 6–7). "It is written before me" alludes to the metaphor of the book in which the deeds of sinners and of faithful people are noted. It means that what we do matters ultimately because and only because it matters to the One who is ultimate. Otherwise, we would be condemned to live life with no idea that it might be ultimately important. It is a point that Jesus makes in the parable of the Last Judgment: "just as you did it to one of the least of these who are members of my family, you did it to me" (Matt. 25:40). The God of relational love is affected by our behaviors; they matter to God.

In spite of the promise of judgment, God will not destroy God's people who are likened to "wine . . . in the cluster" of which "they say, 'Do not destroy it, for there is a blessing in it'" (v. 8). God's chosen will inherit Judea and God's servants "shall settle there" (v. 9). Like the Gerasene demoniac (Luke 8:26–39), also unclean, the Judeans will return to their home and declare how much God has done for them (Luke 8:39).

Proper 8 [13]/Year C

2 Kings 2:1–2, 3–5, 6–14+ (Semicontinuous)

Note: Because this reading largely overlaps with that for the Last Sunday after the Epiphany, Transfiguration Sunday/Year B (2 Kings 2:1–12), we comment here on 2:1–14.

This passage has to do with the transition of prophetic leadership from Elijah to Elisha. Unlike Second Isaiah, who said "The LORD called me before I was born, while I was in my mother's womb he named me" (Isa. 49:1), our passage tells a careful story of inheritance from one prophet to another. God is the primary actor, ever since God instructed Elijah to "appoint Elisha . . . as prophet in your place" (1 Kings 17:16). The lectionary stops this reading with verse 14, but it culminates in verse 15, where the "company of prophets who were at Jericho . . . declared, 'The spirit of Elijah rests on Elisha.'" It is this which our passage wants to make clear to its readers.

Verses 1–6 are a travel narrative by which Elijah and Elisha arrive at Jericho. At each stop along the way, Elijah says to Elisha: "Stay here; for the LORD has sent me as far as Bethel," then Jericho, then the Jordan (vv. 2, 4, 6). Each time Elisha responds by taking an oath on the Lord and says: "I will not leave you" (vv. 2, 4, 6). Elisha is determinedly faithful to Elijah and repeatedly resists the older prophet's command to "stay here." His loyalty to Elijah speaks to the character of Elisha.

They arrive at the Jordan where it flows by Jericho, and Elijah takes his mantle, rolls it up, and strikes the river, with the result that the waters part and they walk across "on dry ground" (v. 8). Later, after Elijah's ascent into "heaven," a term that pious Jews used as a roundabout way of referring to God, whose name they increasingly hallowed by not pronouncing it, Elisha takes up Elijah's mantle and again strikes the water, which parts once more, so that Elisha can cross on dry ground (v. 14).

Two significant reverberations of older scriptural themes ring out here. One is that of Moses' parting the waters of the Sea of Reeds so that the Israelites could cross on dry ground (Exodus 14). The other is that of Joshua, who crossed into the land of promise across the Jordan from the east (Joshua 4). Moses was leading the people away from the oppression of Pharaoh, and the mission of Elijah and Elisha is to lead the people back to faith in YHWH in spite of the oppression of Ahab and his successor Ahaziah, who, like pharaohs in Israel, had introduced the apostasy of worship of other gods and brought injustice into Israel. Coming back into the land of Israel across the Jordan also reenacts Joshua's entry into the land of promise. And there are connections to the story of John the Baptist, who baptized people in the Jordan; their coming out of the Jordan back into Israel in a time of Roman oppression was a symbolic reentry into the land (Mark 1:4–5). Our passage is intertextually opulent with significance: the faithfulness of YHWH in spite of unfaithfulness, the legitimacy of Elisha, his faithfulness to Elijah and Elijah's prophetic vocation, the oppression of faithless rulers, YHWH's intent to liberate the people.

Before Elijah's departure he asks Elisha: "Tell me what I may do for you." Elisha responds: "Please let me inherit a double share of your spirit" (v. 9). As Elijah ascended, Elisha "kept watching" until he "could no longer see him" (v. 12). "Spirit" refers primarily to God, who is spirit, and whose spirit in creation breathes life into all living creatures; spirit is also, hence, possessed by human beings; prophets are those who are aware of God's spirit, God's empathy and vulnerability to the misadventures and faithlessness of the people. Elisha asks for and receives the spirit to be God's prophet in the manner of Elijah. Both prophets have theologically loaded names: Elijah means "YHWH is my God" and Elisha, using another term for God, means "God saves."

Verse 11 speaks of the "chariot of fire and horses" that separated Elijah and Elisha from each other and the "whirlwind" in which Elijah ascended into heaven. Elijah's ascent led to later views that he would return to herald the "days of the Messiah" or reign of God. "Lo, I will send you the prophet Elijah before the great and terrible day of the LORD comes" (Mal. 4:5). The Gospels associate Elijah with John the Baptist (Mark 6:14–15// Matt. 14:1–2//Luke 9:7–9; Mark 8:27–28//Matt. 16:15–16//Luke 9:19–20). He appears in the story of the Transfiguration (Mark 9:2–8//Matt. 17:1–8//Luke 9:28–36).

Delightfully, at every Passover Seder the front door is opened, in case Elijah returns. This liturgical act reminds us that the world is not yet redeemed, that Elijah and Elisha still have work to do.

1 Kings 19:15–16, 19–21* (Paired)

For comments on this passage, please see Proper 7/Year C.

Proper 9 [14]/Year C

2 Kings 5:1–14+ (Semicontinuous)

Today's text picks up the story of Israel's covenant going back to Abraham, to whom YHWH promised: "in you all the families of the earth shall be blessed" (Gen. 12:3). The blessings that Israel is to receive from God are shared with Gentiles. Blessing is available only as a gift from the Lord as shared in mutuality with others who are different from us. Blessing is freely available to Israelites and Gentiles in relationships of difference from and mutuality with each other.

Many Gentiles feature prominently in the story of Israel: Abraham and Sarah, Melchizedek, Abimelech, Jethro, Balaam, Rahab, Ruth, Ittai the Gittite, Hiram, Cyrus, and Naaman, the Syrian commander of the army in today's passage. On the surface, the story of Naaman's healing is a miracle story. More profoundly, it is a theologically sophisticated story of well-being graciously available to each and all from the God of each and all who is the God of Israel.

Naaman "suffered from leprosy" (v. 1). The Torah-teachings concerning leprosy in Leviticus 13–14 show us that what the Scriptures call "leprosy" is not Hansen's disease. The indications of leprosy in Leviticus "do not correspond to any known skin disease."[70] That a "leprous disease" can appear in wool or linen or "anything made of skin" (Lev. 13:47) or on the walls of a house (Lev. 14:34–53) make this obvious. Jacob Milgrom suggests the term "scale disease" as an alternative to leprosy and argues that it was regarded as an impurity because it bore the appearance of death, the antithesis of life and well-being in which the body seems to be wasting away.[71]

Naaman, commander of the army to which the Lord gave victory over Israel (v. 1), fears for his life. An Israelite girl, taken captive after the battle, is the first agent of God's blessing: she directs Naaman's wife to "the prophet in Samaria" who can cure his leprosy (v. 3). Throughout Kings, God works through the little people. The kings of Aram and Israel proceed to make a royal mess of things (vv. 5–7), but Elisha reminds the king of Israel that "there is a prophet in Israel" (v. 8) and that Naaman (and perhaps Israel's king as well?) will learn of this.

Naaman arrives at Elisha's house "with his horses and chariots," only to be told by Elisha's messenger: "Go, wash in the Jordan seven times, and your flesh shall be restored and you shall be clean" (vv. 9–10). Naaman was insulted that Elisha did not "come out" and pull off what Naaman would regard as a miracle—a waving of the hand, a calling on the name of "his God," and an instantaneous curing of his leprosy (v. 11). Why, he wants to know, are the waters of Jordan any better than those of the rivers of Damascus (v. 12)?

Naaman misunderstands. Elisha is a prophet who speaks the word of God, a word of promise and command. The promise is well-being in the form of healing; the command is to wash in the Jordan. Its waters are not the bearers of supernatural power or superior to any of God's waters anywhere; the cure is available through God's grace and obedience to God's word.

When Naaman's servants convinced him to do what the prophet said (v. 13), he "immersed himself seven times in the Jordan." "His flesh was restored like the flesh of a young boy, and he was clean" (v. 14). He then confesses that "there is no God in all the earth except in Israel" (v. 15), a confession that strikes the two notes of particularity (in Israel) and universality (in all the earth).

Naaman tries to express his appreciation by offering a present to Elisha (v. 15), but it is not accepted—God's gift of well-being is graciously available. Accepting Naaman's gift would obscure that point, a point that Elisha's servant Gehazi later misses and lives to regret when Naaman's leprosy clings to him (v. 27). The Gentile Naaman receives God's gracious healing and the Israelite Gehazi suffers God's judgment. Who is the outsider and who the insider?

Isaiah 66:10–14* (Paired)

Today's promise that Jerusalem and Judea shall prosper follows a description of the worship that is appropriate to offer to YHWH. The chapter opens with the Lord's definition of "the one to whom I will look, to the humble and contrite in spirit, who trembles at my word" (66:2). What this means is made clear by statements about those whom the Lord will "mock" (v. 4a). Who are they? "Whoever slaughters an ox is like one who kills a human being" (v. 3) is the answer. Third Isaiah reflects Torah teachings concerning which animals could be eaten and which could not; killing any animal not on the list of the few that could be eaten was equivalent to the killing of a human being (Lev. 17:3–4).[72] Violence and killing are to be curbed and avoided (Isa. 66:3c). The only appropriate worship is that accompanied by deeds of loving-kindness (*mitzvoth*). "All these things my hand has made . . . are mine, says the LORD" (v. 2). They are not ours to kill. True worship involves doing justice, loving-kindness, and walking humbly with God (Mic. 6:8). Micah and Third Isaiah share a discomfort with the Zadokite priesthood and its approach to the Temple and Temple worship.

Then Third Isaiah moves with verse 5 into the theme of today's reading: the promise that Jerusalem shall rejoice and be vindicated. "Yet as soon as Zion was in labor she delivered her children. Shall I open the womb and not deliver? says the LORD" (vv. 8–9). No: "Rejoice with Jerusalem, and be glad for her, all you who love her; rejoice with her in joy . . . that you may nurse and be satisfied from her consoling breast" (vv. 10–11).

Throughout the Scriptures of Israel, the eschatological vision is always intimately connected with down-to-earth matters. Blessing was a matter of concrete, everyday well-being. It involved "prosperity" (v. 12), because well-being is incompatible with hunger and homelessness. Blessing means that the "bodies" of the people would "flourish like the grass" (v. 14). A vindication that left Jerusalem gaunt with famine would be no vindication. When our understanding of salvation is not world-affirming, we have failed to comprehend the biblical witness.

Salvation is available from a gracious God, which is the good news of Isaiah. But God's grace is not cheap. God wants proper worship, not idolatry, and worship that liturgically reflects and reinforces a life of faithful living. God's mercy does not mean that God will not "execute judgment . . . on all flesh" (v. 16). Nor does it mean that God will tolerate "those who sanctify . . . themselves to go into the gardens . . . eating the flesh of pigs, vermin, and rodents" (v. 17); they "shall come to an end together" (v. 17).

The chapter ends on two apparently discordant notes. The first (vv. 22–23) is the familiar universalism of the Isaianic vision of salvation: "all flesh shall come to worship before me, says the LORD" (v. 23). The second is at first strange: "And they shall go out and look at the dead bodies of the people who have rebelled against me; for their worm shall not die, their fire shall not be quenched, and they shall be an abhorrence to all flesh" (v. 24). And so, Isaiah ends with worms crawling in and out of the dead bodies of those who did not heed God's call to live a life conducive to sharing of life and blessing.

This is utter realism. The Torah and the prophets make clear that we have a choice between a way of life and blessing or, alternatively, a way of death and destruction. If the nations do not make for peace, they get war, lots of corpses and worms. There is, however, a choice, and we could, thanks to God's grace, live lives conducive to peace and well-being. We should allow God, not the worms, to have the final say as to how we live. Today's Gospel reading, Luke 10:1–11, equally makes clear that rejecting the kingdom (reign) of God and its peace brings negative consequences.

Proper 10 [15]/Year C

Amos 7:7–17+ (Semicontinuous)

For comments on this passage, please see Proper 10/Year B.

Deuteronomy 30:9–14 (Paired)*

As we point out on Proper 17/Year B, most interpreters think that Deuteronomy addressed a community stinging from the exile, a circumstance to which the Deuteronomic writer makes direct reference in 29:10–29, especially in 22–27. The reading for today seeks to help the congregation embrace God's plan to restore the community and to persuade community members to walk in God's ways.

Deuteronomy 30:1 shifts the reader's attention from the fact and pain of exile (29:10–27) to the means for restoration. According to Deuteronomy 30:1–5, when the people are "among all the nations where the LORD your God has driven you," they are to "return to the LORD your God" and to obey with heart, mind, and soul (a phrase so important to this chapter that it recurs repeatedly; on it see Proper 26/Year B). The word "return" translates the Hebrew *shuv* and refers to repentance, that is turning *away* from idolatry, injustice, and other violations of God's purposes and turning *toward* walking in God's ways.

For those who repent, God will "circumcise the heart" so they will love God with heart and soul (Deut. 30:6–10). Circumcision is a classic sign of Jewish covenantal identity indicating God's promise to the community, the community's embrace of that promise, and commitment to walk in God's ways. To circumcise the heart is to implant these qualities in the deepest reaches of self and community. The covenant and its instructions are internalized. Obedience arises from identity. The community that lives according to God's ways of love and justice will prosper. As a corollary, however, God will curse the enemies who "took advantage" of Israel.

God's ways are "not too hard for you" nor are they "too far away" (Deut. 30:11–14). The commandment with its possibilities for life is not removed from the community in heaven, as if someone needs to go and get it. Nor is it "beyond the sea," so that someone would need to make a sea voyage. "No, the word is very near to you; it is in your mouth and in your heart for you to observe." The community assists in internalizing the commandments by teaching them constantly (see Proper 26/Year B).

The Deuteronomic theologians do not use the term "prevenient grace," but something like that notion is indicated here. God has already placed the resources for obedience and blessing within the community. The community needs only to act on these things.

On the one hand, this text invites idolatrous communities today to repent. On the other hand, real-life experience is often more ambiguous; these themes do not always work out as cleanly as the Deuteronomists suppose. Further, while God's general designs are "not too hard" to understand, identifying the most faithful way to put them into practice in particular situations is not always easy. Communities need to struggle together in conversation to determine what appear to be more and less adequate attitudes and behaviors.

Leviticus 19:17–18 (Seventh Sunday after the Epiphany/Year A) or Deuteronomy 6:4–6 (Proper 26/Year B) would be better readings to go with Luke 10:25–37, the Gospel for today. Elsewhere, Matthew and Mark adapt the notion of regathering of exiles (Deut. 30:4) to the eschatological ingathering the apocalypse (Matt. 24:31; Mark 13:27): as God was faithful to Israel in exile, so God will be faithful at the time of the apocalypse. First John 5:3 echoes Deuteronomy 30:11 to make the point that following the Commandments is not burdensome. In Romans 2:29 Paul cites Deuteronomy 30:6 to show that Gentiles share a mode of circumcision with their Jewish companions.[73] In the same vein, in Romans 10:6-8, the apostle interprets Deuteronomy 30:12–14 to say that "God's character remains the same as in the time of Moses."[74] By coming to the God of Israel through Jesus Christ, Gentiles do not supersede Israel but join Israel as witnesses to God's faithfulness.

Proper 11 [16]/Year C

Amos 8:1–12+ (Semicontinuous)

Today's text falls into three parts. Verses 1–3 present the fourth imaginative experience that was the source of Amos's prophecy to the northern kingdom; verses 4–8 sharply criticize the way in which the well-to-do merchants of Israel fleeced the poor; and verses 9–12 announce the com-

ing day of the Lord that will be "like a bitter day" (v. 10) to Israel. It is a
fitting summary of Amos's prophecy.

In verses 1–3 we are told that the Lord showed Amos "a basket of summer fruit [*qayits*]" and then said to Amos, "The end [*qets*] has come upon
my people Israel." YHWH is not above making a pun on the Hebrew term
for fruits. God repeats the statement "I will never again pass them by"
(v. 2; see 7:8) and adds "the songs of the temple shall become wailings in
that day" (v. 3; emphasis ours). "That day" was standard prophetic talk for
the day of the Lord, in this case not a day for God's purposes to be con-
summated but for Israel to be punished for its violation of those purposes.
In the third section of today's reading, Amos returns to this theme.

The end that the Lord and the prophet have in mind for Israel is bleak
indeed: "the dead bodies shall be many, cast out in every place" (v. 3). How
do we interpret such a teaching as this? If death and curse are diametri-
cally opposed to life and blessing, God's announced purposes (Deut.
30:19–20), how does God's dealing out death and destruction for violating God's purposes make any kind of sense? God is in the position of violating God's self-declared intent. Some might ask: with friends like this,
who needs enemies? Further, Christians have long been tricked by such
texts as this into describing the God of Israel as harsh and vindictive, and
contrasting YHWH unfavorably with the God of Jesus and Paul.

We suggest a manner of interpretation that insists that God's purpose
is that life and well-being are to be shared by all and that God makes clear
the conditions necessary to spreading life and well-being. These conditions are the teachings of the Torah and the prophets that announce God's
free gift to us of love and justice and God's call to us to respond with heartfelt love and justice to the neighbor. The hard reality is that these are
real conditions and violating them creates other conditions that lead to
death and curse. For example, if we wreak havoc on other peoples, we can
expect at some point to have havoc wreaked on us, our self-deluding myth
of innocence notwithstanding. It is not that God deals out death and
destruction; it is that we receive the consequences of our willing refusal
to follow the way of life instead of the way of death. Anger and wrath are
not attributes of YHWH, but indications of how deeply pained God is at
our sin.

In verses 4–8, Amos details how the upper class of Israel sets up the condition for its own destruction. They "trample on the needy, and bring to
ruin the poor of the land." This charge claims more than that the poor are
mistreated; they are, or they would not be poor. To "bring to ruin" means

to eliminate. They are so thoroughly ground down as to be on the verge of dying. The businessmen of Israel are formally religious but impatient for the new moon and the Sabbath to end so that they can get back to swindling their customers. Specifically, they did three things: (1) they used a small *ephah* (basket) but charged for a full-sized one; (2) they used a heavier *shekel* (weight) on the scales, swindling their customers; (3) they "sold the sweepings of the wheat" (imagine finding sawdust in your breakfast cereal). They bamboozle the widow and orphan instead of protecting them. God is not happy.

Hence, in verses 9–12, "On that day . . . I will turn . . . all your songs into lamentation. . . . I will send a famine on the land . . . [a famine] of hearing the words of the LORD." Samaria (the northern kingdom) will fall "and never rise again" (v. 14).

This text accords well with the concluding paragraph of the parable of the Dishonest Manager (Luke 16:1–13) with which it is paired in Proper 20/Year C.

Genesis 18:1–10a (Paired)*

For comments on this passage, please see Proper 6/Year A.

Proper 12 [17]/Year C

Hosea 1:2–10+ (Semicontinuous)

The book of Hosea begins by mentioning four kings of Judah and "King Jeroboam" of the northern kingdom. Hosea lived in and pronounced his message to the northern kingdom. The time of Uzziah in Judah and Jeroboam in Israel was one of calm for the two kingdoms, but after Jeroboam died the picture changed drastically, and by 722 BCE the northern capital, Samaria, had fallen to the Assyrians and its people had been taken into captivity. Hosea's teachings address this and subsequent calamities.

In addition to the drastic ups and downs of Israel's political and economic situation, there was a second calamity: the people committed idolatry in worshiping Baal (2:8, 13, 16). Hosea's first oracle (1:2–9) pronounces judgment on them for their idolatry, followed by an announcement of grace (1:10). For all the threat in the oracle of judgment, that God would withdraw God's compassion for and election of Israel, the covenantal and redeeming grace of God prevails as the basic message.

The Lord (YHWH) instructs Hosea to "take for yourself a wife of whoredom and have children of whoredom, for the land commits great whoredom by forsaking the LORD" (1:2). Apparently, given the account of Israel's unfaithfulness that constitutes chapter 2, Hosea's wife, Gomer, was a "prostitute" involved in the worship of Baal, although the text does not make this explicit. Hosea's relationship with Gomer is an acted parable of the life of God with the people Israel, in which the relationship of God with the people is described as a relationship between husband and wife. Hosea's metaphors for God are many: God is a parent and the people an ungrateful child (11:10); God is a physician, the people an ailing patient (14:4); God is a bear whose cubs have been stolen (13:7–8), to name but a few. Preachers could discuss why it is important to explore many metaphors for talking about our relationship with God.

Hosea is told to give his children symbolic names. The firstborn, a son, is named Jezreel, because in the valley of Jezreel, Jehu killed all the worshipers of Baal (2 Kgs. 9:18–31). In Hosea 1:4, God announces that "I will punish the house of Jehu for the blood of Jezreel, and I will put an end to the kingdom of the house of Israel." The second child is a daughter who is named "Lo-ruhamah" (v. 6), a name drawn from the root word for compassion to which a negative prefix has been added to mean "one for whom I have no compassion." The third child, a son, is named "Lo-ammi," a name drawn from the word for "people" plus the negative prefix to mean "not or no longer my people."

The three names constitute a mounting crescendo of threats: the people will first lose their kingdom, then God's compassion, and finally their relationship with God altogether. But this is not the whole story, and God's apparent rejection is more a prophetic warning than a decisive rejection of the people (as was often claimed in the Christian tradition of the displacement of Israel in favor of the church). Hosea speaks frequently of God's tender love for Israel and in so doing uses for "love" a verb (*aheb,* 11:1) used in the Baal cult to signal God's warm and heartfelt love. Abraham Joshua Heschel says: "It is Hosea who flashes a glimpse into the inner life of God as He ponders His relationship to Israel. In parables and lyrical outburst the decisive motive behind God's strategy in history is declared. The decisive motive is love."[75]

This unconditional love first came to expression in God's promise to Abraham and Sarah and their descendants that God would fashion with them an utterly gracious covenant. Hence our reading ends on the note of promise: "Yet the number of the people of Israel shall be like the sand of the sea . . . and in the place where it was said to them, 'You are not my people,' it shall be said to them, 'Children of the living God'" (1:10). God's grace is the first and last word. God's loving grace is beautifully expressed in Jesus' parabolic teaching about prayer (Luke 11:5–13).

Genesis 18:20–32* (Paired)

The literary unit should be Genesis 18:16 through 19:29. This thematic whole shows that God is righteous (18:16–33), reveals wrestling with God as a trait prized in the Old Testament (Gen. 18:16–33), invites a discussion on the identification of the sin of Sodom (19:1–11), renews the idea that sin has consequences (19:12–28), and reinforces the divine intention to fulfill the promises to Sarah and Abraham (19:29).

In Genesis 18:16–20, Abraham joined God and the other two visitors to Mamre (Gen. 18:1–15) as the latter were on the way to Sodom and Gomorrah, where God would investigate those cities because the outcry concerning their sin had reached God. God decided to speak to Abraham about the city so Abraham could help the household of Sarah and himself (and thereby help "all the nations of the earth") walk in righteousness and justice and avoid the judgment on Sodom and Gomorrah. Abraham was a prophet, that is, one who helps the community discern God's vision of righteous community and the degree to which the community is living into that vision (cf. Gen. 20:7).

Anticipating that God would find the cities sinful, Abraham wrestled with God in behalf of the community. "Will you indeed sweep away the righteous with the wicked?" It would be unjust for God to destroy the righteous (Gen. 18:21–25). God responded positively to Abraham's request by saying that if Sodom contained fifty righteous persons, God would not only spare them but would "forgive the whole place for their sake" (18:26). Abraham pressed God repeatedly to reduce the number until the ante was down to ten righteous persons (18:27–33). Abraham's boldness with God is a model, reminding us that God is not immovable but continues to respond to calls for justice.

Genesis 19:1–11 reveals that Sodom was depraved. Lot (Abraham's nephew) took two angels (who evidently looked like human beings) into his house for the night, and offered them sumptuous hospitality (vv. 1–3; on hospitality, see Proper 6/Year A). A group of men from Sodom surrounded the house and insisted on "knowing" the guests (vv. 4–5). Lot interceded, even offering to bring out his daughters saying, "Do to them [the daughters] as you please, only do nothing to these men for they have come under the shelter of my roof" (vv. 6–8). The angels saved those on the interior of the house by causing the outsiders to become blind and "unable to find the door" (vv. 9–11).

While some Christians assume that homosexuality was the sin of Sodom, critics point out that the text does not directly mention homosexuality (though the verb "to know," *yada*, could refer to sexual relationships, 19:5, 8). Such interpreters argue that the sin of Sodom was inhospitality. These scholars point out that later passages in the Old Testament that refer to Sodom as a general example of a city condemned and do not specify its sin as sexuality (e.g., Deut. 29:23; 32:32; Isa. 1:9–10; 3:9; 13:19; Jer. 23:19; 49:18; 50:40; Lam. 4:6; Ezek. 16:43b–58; Amos 4:11; Zeph. 2:9). In any event, Lot offering his own daughters to the mob—even to save angels—is reprehensible.

Evidently Sodom did not contain even ten righteous people, for God destroyed it with sulfur and fire (Gen. 19:12–28). Whatever the sin of Sodom, the implication of the text is bracing: such violation of God's purposes completely destroys community. God did act righteously by saving those in the city who were not implicated in sin. When Lot's spouse disobeyed, God turned her to salt (vv. 17, 26).

The passage concludes with the stirring affirmation that even when raining down sulfur and fire, "God remembered Abraham" (Gen. 19:28). God will keep the promise even when confronted by flagrant sin such as that of Sodom and Gomorrah.

Although Luke 11:1–13 contains no direct inference from the text in Genesis, Abraham's request that God spare Sodom loosely exemplifies Luke's promise that when the community prays for a good thing, God will grant it. Passages from the New Testament that directly invoke Genesis 18:16–19:26 tend to use the destruction of the two ancient cities as a warning that even greater punishment awaits sinners at the apocalypse.

Given the high profile of conversations about homosexuality in today's church, preachers should note that the New Testament only once (Jude 7) names sexuality as a sin of Sodom and Gomorrah and instead refers to inhospitality (e.g., Matt. 10:15; Luke 10:12), lack of repentance (Matt. 11:20–24; Luke 17:28–33), and idolatry. Revelation 11:7–10 pictures Sodom as type of the Roman Empire. In 2 Peter 2:6–10 the writer sees the rescue of Lot as showing that God preserves the righteous while destroying the wicked (compare Rom. 9:29). The image of God raining sulfur and fire on Sodom and Gomorrah may have contributed to the notion of hell as a place of punishment characterized by these elements (e.g., Rev. 14:9–11; 19:20–21; 20:7–15).

Proper 13 [18]/Year C

Hosea 11:1–11+ (Semicontinuous)

Hosea's prophecy has to do with the political and military chaos that reigned between Israel and Judah and between the two of them and Assyria after the time of the reign of Jeroboam in Israel and Uzziah in Judah. Today's reading speaks to a situation in which some citizens of Israel, the northern kingdom, have been taken into exile. Military conflict is going on in the cities of Israel: "The sword rages in their cities, it consumes their oracle-priests, and devours because of their schemes" (v. 6); soon they will be taken captive: "They shall return to the land of Egypt, and Assyria shall be their king" (v. 5). "Egypt" functions symbolically to point to a place of oppression, much as "exile" or "Babylon" would later serve as stand-ins for Roman occupation.

Our passage follows a diachronic movement in four parts: (1) deliverance from Egypt in the exodus (vv. 1–4); (2) return to "Egypt . . . because they have refused to return to me" (vv. 5–7); (3) YHWH's "tender compassion" for the people (vv. 8–9); and (4) the ingathering of scattered Israel (vv. 10–11).

Verses 1–4 metaphorically refer to YHWH as a tender mother who loves her child, Israel. The compassionate yearning of a husband for a straying wife, Hosea's earlier way of talking about God and Israel, is replaced with the image of a mother who was "like those who lift infants to their cheeks. I bent down to them and fed [suckled] them" (v. 4). YHWH's profoundly personal love for Israel is emphasized: "I loved him . . . I called my son . . . it was I who taught Ephraim to walk, I took them up in my arms . . . I led them with cords of human kindness . . . I bent down to them and fed them" (vv. 1–4). Hosea sees into the heart of God's womblike love for Israel ("compassion," *rachamim*, derives from *rehem*, "womb"). Hence, "out of Egypt I called my son" (v. 1), a line memorably cited by Matthew in the story of the return of the Holy Family from Egypt (Matt. 2:15).

Verses 5–7 tell of how the warfare initiated by Israel in alliance with Assyria against Judah has resulted in the exile of the northern kingdom. The subjects of the sentences are now the people, not God: "they shall return to the land of Egypt . . . my people are bent on turning away from me" (vv. 5, 7). Hosea indicts them for their refusal to be faithful to the Lord and indicates that return to a land of oppression is the consequence of their option for war and conflict. Now, in their extremity, they remember God: "To the Most High they call, but he does not raise them up at all" (v. 7b).

Verses 8–9 return to Hosea's theme of the trauma in the heart of YHWH, whose everlasting covenant with Israel means that God is stuck with this people by God's free decision. Unlike the "unmoved mover" of Aristotle and classical Christian theism, YHWH is the "most-moved mover" of the Torah, the prophets, and the rabbis. God cries: "How can I give you up, Ephraim? How can I hand you over, O Israel?" (v. 8). In travail, God declares: "My heart recoils within me; my compassion grows warm and tender" (v. 8c). God identifies God's self as "the Holy One in your midst" (v. 9). This is an incarnational statement: God dwells within the people Israel.

In Israel's theology, God is the God of the past (the exodus and deliverance), the God of the future who calls Israel forward onto a journey through history, the God of the above whom Israel is given and called to adore, and the God of the below, the ground of Israel's being. But God is also "God with us," God who pitches a tent among, dwells with Israel. If Israel goes into exile, the Holy One in Israel's midst goes with Israel. When John wants to talk about Jesus Christ as God with us, he speaks the language of Israelite faith: the Word "lived among us," pitched a tent among us (John 1:14). God's nature is relational, not one of dwelling in impassible perfection.

Verses 10–11 speak of God's womblike love leading Israel home: "They shall come trembling like birds from Egypt, and like doves from the land of Assyria; and I will return them to their homes, says the LORD" (v. 11). Again, God's gracious love has the last word; God's heart yearns for Israel's turning again to the Lord.

Ecclesiastes 1:2, 12–14; 2:18–23 (Paired)*

The main body of Wisdom literature (Proverbs, Wisdom of Solomon, and Ecclesiasticus) derives from people whose lives are comfortable and for whom wisdom (coming from observation of life; see Proper 19/Year B) provides principles by which to live a meaningful and satisfying life. Job and Ecclesiastes belong to wisdom, but their observations of life lead them to dissent from the perspectives of typical wisdom teaching (on Job, see Propers 22–25/Year B).[76]

Scholars agree that the main theme of Ecclesiastes' interpretation of life is 1:2: "Vanity of vanities. . . . All is vanity." In 1:12–14, the author reports engaging in the quintessential activity of wisdom teachers by observing "all that is done under heaven" and then naming what was learned. "It is an unhappy business that God has given to human beings to be busy with." Life is "vanity and a chasing after wind."

The term *hebel*, vanity, can also be translated as breath, wind, or vapor. While scholars debate its connotation in Ecclesiastes, we take it to indicate that human life is not only as transient as the passing of a vapor but that its significance is no more apparent. The pieces do not fit neatly together in a single tapestry of meaning. Indeed, contradictions abound (thus undercutting the neat principles of Proverbs), and death ends the significance of all that human beings have done. This author voices a deep longing to know the meaning of life, and yet in this life human beings cannot possess this knowledge. Ecclesiastes does not envision a future life.

Ecclesiastes 2:18–23 expresses this attitude. The author works hard under the sun, but then, at death, leaves the results of a whole life's work to heirs. "Who knows whether they will be wise or foolish?" (2:19). This circumstance is a "great evil," that is, it is manifestly unjust for people who work hard to die and not to get the results of their own toil (2:21–22). All the pain and vexation that comes with labor comes to nothing (2:23).

Nevertheless, human beings can have limited fulfillment. In Ecclesiastes 2:24, the teacher acknowledges, "There is nothing better for mortals than to eat and drink, and find enjoyment in their toil. This also, I saw, is from the hand of God." This comment is not a statement of hedonism but an assertion that while human beings cannot know the ultimate meaning of life, God has structured existence so that everyday human activities can bring limited—if fleeting—feelings of satisfaction. This is "what mortals get from all the toil and strain" (2:22). However, people need to take note when such pleasures occur because such joys can come and go as God takes from one and gives to another (2:26).

Ecclesiastes is painfully honest. In fact, human beings cannot *know* how lives ultimately count. Hearing this viewpoint in the Bible can be a point of identification for those in the congregation who share Ecclesiastes' reticence. This reading presses the preacher to raise questions that gnaw at many in the congregation. What is the point of my life? What can we expect in life? What sense can we make of life? We join most Jewish and Christian theologians in believing that the community can have a greater sense of possibility and optimism than does Ecclesiastes. Nevertheless, every good theology manifests a certain pastoral agnosticism.

The passage from Ecclesiastes is paired with Luke 12:13–21, the parable of the Rich Fool (Luke 12:16–21) set in the context of a warning against greed (12:13–15). The reading from Ecclesiastes for today should include 2:24–26 given the fact that the barn builder makes a statement in Luke 12:19 that sounds much like Ecclesiastes 2:24. Although similar in wording, the statements differ in intent. However, Luke 12:19 is a statement of hedonism and greed for which God condemns the barn builder. The preacher needs to clarify these different nuances of meaning.

Proper 14 [19]/Year C

Isaiah 1:1, 10–20

Isaiah opens his book with the announcement that it is his "vision" (*ḥāzon*), and in 6:1 relates his first vision "of the Lord sitting on a throne" and his call to go and speak to the people of Judah. This vision came to him in the year of Uzziah's death (6:1) and in 1:1 Isaiah says that his vision concerned Judah and Jerusalem from the time of King Uzziah to that of King Hezekiah, a time span of roughly thirty-five years ending in about 701 BCE. Isaiah (and the later prophets in this long Isaian tradition) worked in a period of virtually unremitting hostilities between Syria and Israel in which Judah was on-again, off-again involved. Always in the wake of the larger and more well-to-do northern kingdom, Judah was tugged one way and the other as different powers sought to engage it in their side of the ongoing conflict.

In 1:1, Isaiah also tells us his name, *yĕsa'yâ*, "may YHWH save." Isaiah 1–12 ends with a hymn of thanksgiving to YHWH for salvation.

In Isaiah 1:2–31, YHWH presents a case against Judah, a complaint against its disloyalty to God. God "reared children and brought them up, but they have rebelled against me" (1:2). Even the ox and donkey know their owners, "but Israel does not know, my people do not understand" (1:3).

This is the context for 1:10–20, which begins as did 1:2 with the imperative "hear," pay attention. "Hear the word of the LORD, you rulers of Sodom! Listen to the teaching [*torah*] of our God, you people of Gomorrah!" In Isaiah's time Sodom and Gomorrah symbolized injustice to the poor and needy and social chaos (see 3:9; 13:19). Isaiah says nothing about homosexual behavior in this connection. This reading is framed by Isaiah as torah-instruction.

Verses 11–15 constitute a prophetic critique of the Temple cult. Prophetic passages such as this have been dealt with ideologically in the past by Protestant interpreters who used them to take a swipe at Roman Catholicism or Judaism, often at both. We should instead read them as a comment on ritual and worship as such, ours included. In all the regions where the people Israel lived in the eighth century, whether Bethel, Dan, Samaria or Jerusalem, prophets inveighed against the Temple cult. We should not forget that the cult was a state cult and embroiled in all the entanglements and compromises that come with established religion. Further, such cults imposed significant financial hardship on the people: they gave religious legitimacy to the state and its bureaucracy, economic support of them was required of the people, and the state-cult personnel were tax-exempt.

"What to me is the multitude of your sacrifices? says the LORD; I have had enough of burnt offerings of rams and the fat of fed beasts . . ." (v. 11). "Your new moons and your appointed festivals my soul hates . . ." (v. 14).

The end of verse 15 discloses the deeper concern: "your hands are full of blood." Bloodstained hands point to the need for a conversion of the people to genuine morality and compassionate justice: "Wash yourselves; make yourselves clean; remove the evil of your doings from before my eyes; cease to do evil, learn to do good; seek justice, rescue the oppressed, defend the orphan, plead for the widow" (vv. 16–17).

Verses 18–20 lay out the options for Judeans: they can practice compassionate justice and receive the blessings that come with it: "If you are willing and obedient, you shall eat the good of the land" (v. 19). Or they can "refuse and rebel" and "be devoured by the sword" (v. 20). It is a choice between the way of life and blessing or that of curse and death (Deut. 11:26–28). It is a choice for all of us to ponder.

Genesis 15:1–6* (Paired)

For comments on this passage, please see the Second Sunday in Lent/ Year C.

Proper 15 [20]/Year C

Isaiah 5:1–7+ (Semicontinuous)

For comments on this passage, please see the Proper 22/Year A.

Jeremiah 23:23–39* (Paired)

Jeremiah complained that Judah suffered a failure of leadership. Civil authorities (including the monarch), priests, and prophets supported idolatry and unfaithful political alliances with Egypt, and they condoned and even profited from the exploitation of the poor and other social injustices. Such leadership set the course toward the exile and must be avoided in the rebuilding of the community after the return from Babylon.

God is the speaker quoted by Jeremiah in the lesson for today. The people, including the false prophets, can hide nothing from God (Jer. 23:23–24). The false prophets claim to have received dreams from God (dreams were a way whereby God communicated with prophets) but they lied (23:25). They have deceitful hearts and encourage the populace to forget God (23:27). Such prophets have wandered so far from God's purposes that instead of calling the monarch and the people to turn back to God they need to turn back to God themselves (23:26).

Prophets who know God's word should preach it forcefully, for it is like fire, and like a hammer that shatters a rock (Jer. 23:28–29). God, indeed, opposes the false prophets who pass off their own words supporting idolatry and injustice as messages from God (23:30–32).

People will ask, "What is the burden [*masa*] of [God]?" Commentators typically point out that the Hebrew *masa* can be rendered either burden or oracle. The people want to know, "What is the oracle or word from God?" Jeremiah is to reply, "You are the burden" that God must bear, so God will "cast you off" (Jer. 23:33). God will cast off all priests and prophets who misrepresent God's oracles (23:34). Such people will talk among themselves about how to interpret God's oracle but they will continue to pervert the divine message (23:35–36). People will ask the prophets for clarification concerning God's purposes, but when the false prophets substitute their own oracles for those of God, God will send them into exile and bring everlasting disgrace and shame upon them (23:37–39).

It is easy for today's preacher to inveigh against false prophets. But how does a congregation distinguish true and false prophecy? According to Deuteronomy 18:15–22, false prophets preach in the names of idols, never raise the specter of judgment but only approve of what the community is doing, deceive people into thinking their messages represent God when in fact they shape their messages to support idolatry and injustice, and, of course, they predict things that do not come true. These themes are stated or implied in Jeremiah 23:23–39. True prophets help the community turn from idolatry and injustice, and they identify points at which it can live more fully in covenant with God and one another, even when such messages run against the grain of community preference and even when (as in the case of Jeremiah) they must announce judgment. Their predictions come true.

Sometimes today's congregation can (or should be able to) clarify true and false prophecies with relative ease. But that demarcation is sometimes more apparent in hindsight than in the roil of immediate circumstances. Preachers and communities may indeed think that we have identified true prophecy only to find, with distance and critical reflection, that we have not. When that occurs, a lesson from the false prophets of Jeremiah's day is in order. They had the opportunity to repent, but did not, and were destroyed. Today's congregation probably still has time to repent.

The lection from Jeremiah is paired with Luke 12:49–56. While the passage in Luke does not directly invoke the reading from Jeremiah, Luke 12:54–56 does highlight the importance of being able to interpret the signs of the times correctly (in ways similar to those of the true prophets like Jeremiah) and speaks harshly of those who do not know how to interpret those signs of the times (perhaps like the false prophets of whom Jeremiah speaks).

Proper 16 [21]/Year C

Jeremiah 1:4–10+ (Semicontinuous)

Please see the Fourth Sunday after the Epiphany/Year C for commentary on this passage.

Isaiah 58:9b–14 (Paired)

For comments on this passage, please see the Fifth Sunday after the Epiphany/Year A.

Proper 17 [22]/Year C

Jeremiah 2:4–13+ (Semicontinuous)

As noted in introductory remarks on the book of Jeremiah (Fourth Sunday after the Epiphany/Year C), this part of Jeremiah was spoken prior to the exile at a time when Judah was unfaithful in various ways. The form of today's passage recalls that of a lawsuit (Hebrew: *riv*) in which a plaintiff brings charges against a defendant. A lawsuit typically contains: summons, charges, recollection of God's love, accusation, rhetorical questions, witnesses, announcement of verdict, and punishment. While all elements of the lawsuit formula are not present in Jeremiah 2:4–13, the text evokes the lawsuit spirit.

Jeremiah 2:1–3 frames the lawsuit as if the relationship between God and the community is a marriage gone bad (2:2–3). God summons the party being charged to hear the charges (Jer. 2:4), and then asks rhetorical questions to get readers to recall what God has graciously done for Judah (2:5–8). God wants to know what the ancestors found wrong with God, so that they went after "worthless things," idols (e.g., Jer. 8:19; Deut. 32:21). By going after idols, the people have "become worthless themselves," and their community life has taken on the character of the idols (2:5). Jeremiah 10:1–16 satirizes idols as "like scarecrows in a cucumber field," unable to speak or walk, impotent, false, worthless, works of delusion, soon to perish (cf. 14:22; 16:18; 51:17). The people did not remember God delivering them from slavery in Egypt, and sustaining them in the wilderness, nor did they remember how God brought them into the promised land. By engaging in idolatry they defiled the land (2:6–7). In a comment that today's ministers should find sobering, the priests and other leaders bear special responsibility for the community's lapse into idolatry. The prophets, who should have functioned as ombudspersons and helped the people recognize they were departing from God's purposes, became instruments of Baal (2:8).

The accusation is summarized in 2:9–11. The term "I accuse" is *riv*, a technical term for bringing charges (2:9). With rhetorical questions, God urges the community to look to Cyprus and to Kedar to see if any other people have abandoned a deity who loved them as much as YHWH loved Judah. (Cyprus is an island sixty miles west of Israel; Kedar was a large area approximately a hundred miles east of the Jordan.) Can the defendants cite another people who gave up their deities for beings who are "no gods," who have changed their glory for "something that does not profit"?

God calls witnesses, the heavens, to verify the truth of the charges in 2:12. So flagrant are the violations that God can call elements of nature (whom the Jewish tradition often viewed as animated) to testify against the community. Heaven and earth were original witnesses to the making of the covenant (Deut. 30:19).

The verdict is made public in 2:13. The people have committed two evils. While scholars debate just what those two evils are, a natural interpretation from the context is that they are (a) forsaking God, who is a fountain of living water, and (b) digging out cisterns for themselves that are cracked and can hold no water, that is, turning to idols that are made by hands. The contrast between living, fresh water and stagnant cistern water that leaks out of the cistern is vivid. Later, Jeremiah will specify the consequences of this disobedience.

The contemporary preacher could ponder whether the congregation or others today are exchanging the purposes of God with their power to bless community for the ends of idols that, we will soon learn, bring about social collapse. Inspired by the lawsuit form, the preacher could develop a message that makes the case that the congregation (or others) is abandoning God in ways analogous to those of people in the text.

The writers of the New Testament do not make explicit use of this passage.

Proverbs 25:6–7 and Sirach 10:12–18 (Paired)*

Although the readings from Proverbs and Sirach are listed as alternate lections as pairs for the Gospel today, we discuss them at the same time because Proverbs 25:6–7 is such a short text and some of its themes are expanded in Sirach 10:12–18.

The ancient world had a more hierarchical view of the social world than we do today. People were generally expected to stay within their places in the social pyramid unless invited by persons above them to interact in ways that differed from the usual social expectation. Subordinates who went beyond the level of their station could bring shame upon themselves and their families.

Proverbs 25:1–27:27 appears to be a series of admonitions concerning how to behave in the presence of the royal court and similar upper-level social situations. A number of scholars think that the short lesson for today is directed to young people who might like to become officials of the court not to push themselves forward. They should wait to hear the invitation, "Come up here" (25:6–7a; cf. 27:1–2). If they put themselves forward they may be put lower and even shamed (25:7b).

In this reading we see, as Jon Berquist has observed, proverbs functioning to maintain the existing social order.[77] On the one hand, a preacher can certainly commend humility and prudence in relationships, and seasons in life when maintaining social stability encourages the purposes of God. On the other hand, occasions certainly come when maintaining hierarchical modes of relationship actually works against God's aims.

Sirach, also known as Ben Sira or Ecclesiasticus, is considered canonical by the Orthodox and Roman churches but by few Protestants. Sirach was assembled in the Hellenistic age, perhaps around 200 to 180 BCE, by a teacher, Ben Sira, in Jerusalem. Like other writers of this period, Ben

Sira, combining elements from the wisdom and Torah traditions, wrestled with how the Jewish community should respond to Hellenism. Ben Sira urges the community to practice Jewish values in personal and home life and within the Jewish community while living peacefully with the various occupying powers, even while criticizing those powers and reminding the Jewish community that God will eventually topple them.

Today's reading from Ben Sira warns readers against pride, which in Jewish tradition is esteeming oneself and one's power more highly than is deserved, especially in comparison to God's power. Pride begins when the human being does not have a respectful sense of the divine (Sir. 10:12–13a). God will bring such calamities upon the prideful—especially rulers and nations—that they will be destroyed. In their place, God will enthrone the lowly and plant the humble in place of the prideful. The lowly and humble are those who have a proper sense of themselves as created beings whose purpose is to cooperate with other created beings in living according to God's aims (12:13b–18). This passage encourages readers to avoid pride and live humbly according to the principles of Torah and, thereby, avoid being completely annihilated and forgotten.

The readings above are wisely paired with Luke 14:1, 7–14. The Lukan Jesus counsels that instead of seeking places of honor, people should follow the wisdom of the Jewish tradition (represented in the readings from Proverbs and Sirach) and take the lowest places at the table. By doing so, the guests, having taken a high seat, will avoid the shame of being asked to take a lower one. As he does so often, Jesus commends classic Jewish tradition while bringing it into a new situation.

Proper 18 [23]/Year C

Jeremiah 18:1–11+ (Semicontinuous)

The key picture from this passage—God as a potter—is one of the best-known images from the Bible. A popular hymn in many Protestant congregations captures associations that people tend to have with God as the potter and the singing congregation with the clay. The congregation invites God to mold them and make them after God's will while they wait quietly.[78] Even those with little acquaintance with this hymn sometimes think of God as a potter, gently shaping them. However, Jeremiah's comparison of God to a potter moves in quite a different direction.

Jeremiah believed God was about to punish Judah for idolatry, injustice, and other crimes against covenant, by sending Babylon to conquer them. In Jeremiah 17:1–18, the prophet made one of many such announcements (see Sixth Sunday after the Epiphany/Year C). In Jeremiah 17:19–27, aware that members of the community have not kept Sabbath, the prophet urges the community to honor the Sabbath day or face the fact that God will kindle a fire in the gates that will devour the palaces of Jerusalem.

To reinforce these points, Jeremiah recounts the word from God (18:1). God took Jeremiah to a potter's shop (18:2–3). Nearly every village had such a workplace. The potter mixed mud and shaped it on a wheel turned either by feet or by hand. Jeremiah saw a spoiled vessel on the wheel, that is, one that did not assume the form the potter intended. The potter, then, reshaped it (18:4).

God can do to the community what the potter did to the clay (18:5–6). In this context in Jeremiah the focus is on God as sovereign over community. On the one hand, when a community is unfaithful, God can pluck it up, break it down, and destroy it (18:5–7a), but if that community turns from evil, then God will cancel the disaster that God had planned (18:7b–8). On the other hand, when a community begins by living in God's ways but then turns away, God can change God's mind about the good that God intended to do (18:8–10).

The chilling conclusion is in Jeremiah 18:11. God commissions Jeremiah to tell the people of Judah that God is a potter "shaping evil against you." God had planned good for Judah, but they have become unfaithful, and so God is about to punish them (18:11a). However, that is not what God wants. In 18:11b, God pleads with the community to turn from their evil so they can then be spared the judgment. Unfortunately, they refuse (18:12).

This text raises two important issues. One is the extent and nature of divine power in the affairs of communities and individuals. Preachers often try to say that God is simultaneously all powerful, all loving, and all just. Jeremiah assumes that God as potter can do anything to the world God wants at any time God wants. However, the continued presence of unpunished evil and of unrewarded faithfulness suggests either that God is not altogether loving and not altogether just or that God is not altogether powerful. We side with the latter in thinking that God is indeed completely loving and just but that while God is more powerful than any other entity, God cannot shape individual and corporate lives in the singular way of a potter fashioning a pot. Instead God works in every situation by offering individuals and groups options for maximum faithfulness with which they can choose to cooperate (or not). Cooperation moves them in the direction of blessing. Rejection means that they set in motion consequences that eventuate in lower quality of life and perhaps even in destruction. God helps shape us by offering opportunities on the path to blessing. We join the potter's work by accepting or denying what the potter has done.

Paul makes use of the image of the potter and the clay in Romans 9:21. Whereas Jeremiah 18:1–11 uses the image to speak exclusively of God the potter shaping judgment against Judah, the apostle uses the figure more generally to establish that the pot cannot question the potter.

Deuteronomy 30:15–20 (Paired)*

For comments on this passage, please see the Sixth Sunday after the Epiphany/Year A.

Proper 19 [24]/Year C

Jeremiah 4:11–12, 22–28+ (Semicontinuous)

If the community does not repent of its violations of the covenant, God will bring "evil from the north," invasion by a power as yet unnamed but later identified as Babylon (Jer. 4:5–10). Babylon was the epitome of an idolatrous culture, thus reinforcing a notion that was common in ancient Jewish theology that a people who sinned (e.g., idolatry) were punished in ways congruent with the sin (in this case, being overrun by idolaters). The people should sound the alarm that an invasion is coming, and those in villages and rural areas should take refuge in the safety of fortified cities, and engage in communal lament by putting on sackcloth (Jer. 4:5–8).

Jeremiah compares this situation to the coming of a sirocco, an extra hot wind from the north that blasts across the land and that was too strong to help with winnowing. At harvest, farmers would beat the stalk and toss it in the air, separating kernels and stalk, with a good wind carrying away the refuse. This wind, however, simply blows away everything in its path (Jer. 4:11–12).

The judgment comes with incredible force (4:13). Jerusalem, however, could "wash your heart clean of wickedness," that is, could repent (4:14). As it is, a siege will be laid against Jerusalem (4:15–17). The prophet soberly explains to Judah, "*Your* ways and *your* doings have brought this upon you" (4:18).

Jeremiah 4:19–22 illustrates why Jeremiah is sometimes called "the weeping prophet," for Jeremiah is moved to visceral anguish. Contemporary preachers can sometimes take a clue from Jeremiah. The ancient prophet speaks not in self-righteous anger but in anguish over the calamity the people bring upon themselves. The former tends to put off listeners and destroy communication whereas the latter tends to build identification and keep alive the possibility of communication and change.

Using language that echoes Genesis 1:1–2:4a, Jeremiah hauntingly depicts the results of invasion and siege (4:22–28). Creation will be reversed and Judah will revert to chaos, much as it was before God spoke the words of creation: a waste, a void, without light, the mountains and hills quaking as they come apart, no human beings present, birds fleeing, the land a desert, cities in ruin (4:22–26). However, the destruction will not be complete; God will leave open the possibility of regeneration (4:27).

The preacher can help the congregation consider whether the future depicted in this text is one they want for their households, the congregation, the nation, and the world. If not, the preacher can help the congregation identify actions that bespeak repentance and that help others come face to face with the coming consequences of a way of life based on idolatry, falsehood, and injustice. Such consequences are more immanent for some than for others. But even if collapse is months, years, even generations removed, the preacher can ask whether people want their children, grandchildren, or great-grandchildren to live in the chaos set in motion today.

The New Testament does not refer to this passage.

Exodus 32:7–14 (Paired)*

Please see Proper 23/Year A for our commentary on this passage.

Proper 20 [25]/Year C

Jeremiah 8:1–9:1+ (Semicontinuous)

This passage continues the theme from the reading last week of Judah being invaded by Babylon as God's judgment on Judah's unfaithfulness. Showing respect for the dead was a key value in the ancient Near East. Imagine the community's shock that invasion will bring the disinterment of the corpses of many leaders and inhabitants of Jerusalem. Their remains will be spread before the heavenly gods the people had served—sun, moon, and stars—and will lie like dung on the surface of the ground before the empty deities impotent to end this disrespect (Jer. 8:1–2). The prophet is relentlessly straightforward: this outcome is what the people chose (Jer. 8:3).

Jeremiah 8:4–13 is an oracle of judgment, a typical form in prophetic speech announcing that God has condemned the people, giving reasons for the judgment, and indicating what the people can expect. The prophet is astonished that Judah, faced with the evidence that the prophet has mentioned in the previous chapters, does not repent. It should be as natural for the people to repent as for someone who falls to get up again (8:4–5a). Even birds know what to do when the seasons change, but the Judahites fail to repent and therefore become "like a horse plunging headlong into battle" (8:5b–7).

The scribes were interpreters and teachers. According to Jeremiah, the scribes of his day professed to be wise, but lied about the meaning of the Torah and, from prophet to priest, were greedy and false, committed abomination, and acted shamefully. They "treated the wound of my people carelessly, saying, 'Peace, peace,' when there is no peace," that is, they did not help the community realize points at which it had violated covenant, and when the Babylonian threat became imminent, they assured the community that all would be well ("Peace, peace") (8:8–12). Like a vineyard owner, God comes to gather grapes and figs, but the vines and trees are bare (8:13). As a result, they will be put to shame, carried off, lose their spouses to conquerors, and "shall fall among those who fall" (8:9a, 10a, 12b).

The prophet laments that the community is resigned to its fate and unwilling to repent. They think that God has doomed them to perish in their besieged cities (Jer. 8:14–15). They can already hear the snorting of the Babylonians' horses in the region of Dan in the north. The invasion is like letting adders loose that cannot be charmed but will bite (8:16–17).

Jeremiah feels the suffering of the people in his own body (8:18, 21), especially because they do not understand the situation. They continue to think that God will save them: "Is [God] not in Zion?" Failure of teaching is so complete in Judah that they do not recognize that they provoked God to anger with their idols (8:19–20).

In 8:22, then, the prophet asks, in a line that inspired a famous African American spiritual, "Is there no balm in Gilead?"[79] Gilead was an area east of the Jordan known for balm (a resin for healing made from balsam trees). The possibility of healing for Judah does exist (repentance), but the people will not take advantage of it. This double awareness of the resource for healing but people's refusal to use it causes the prophet to speak one of the most poignant passages in the book in Jeremiah 9:1.

If the preacher would like to urge today's congregation to avoid a fate similar to that of Judah, Jeremiah himself suggests an approach. A key reason Judah fell is that they did "not know the ordinance of the LORD" because the scribes, prophets, and priests had not carried out the teaching dimension of their ministries that the book of Deuteronomy regards as fundamental (Deut. 6:1–6). Today's passage (and others in Jeremiah) calls preachers to help the congregation become a teaching community.

Amos 8:4–7* (Paired)

For comments on this passage, please see Proper 11/Year C.

Proper 21 [26]/Year C

Jeremiah 32:1–3a, 6–15+ (Semicontinuous)

When the Babylonians laid siege to Jerusalem, Jeremiah was imprisoned by the monarch Zedekiah because the prophet claimed that God directed the Babylonian onslaught and that Zedekiah would be exiled. Zedekiah charged Jeremiah with treason (Jer. 32:1–5; cf. 37:11–21). In today's passage, Jeremiah enacts a prophetic gesture or symbolic action—a physical gesture or action whose meaning symbolizes the prophet's message. Jeremiah often enacted such symbols, for example, Jer. 13:1–11 (loincloth), 12–14 (wine jar); 16:1–13 (celibacy and marriage); 19:1–11 (broken jug); 27:1–11 (yoke); cf. 18:1–12 (potter).

In the midst of double calamity (national disaster and personal imprisonment), Jeremiah received a vision that Hanamel would come and ask him to buy a piece of family land in Anathoth—Jeremiah's home about seven miles north of Jerusalem, occupied by the Babylonians. According to Leviticus 25:25–28, family members had the first right to buy land held in a family. This provision was a means of helping families maintain stability and security as a limitation on exploitation. When Hanamel came as envisioned, Jeremiah believed that God wanted him to buy the land.

The sale took place and was documented (Jer. 32:9–14). The city was about to be overrun. Jeremiah was confined. More people could be exiled. Yet, while many Judahites were yielding to despair, Jeremiah bought the land as a sign that God could be trusted to bring Judah into a renewed future. He envisioned the time when people would again buy houses and fields and vineyards as a part of everyday life in a restored land (Jer. 32:15).

A preacher could explore with the congregation symbolic actions that it could take to act out an aspect of the purposes of God. What could the congregation do to represent hope and renewal in a way that is as expressive as Jeremiah buying a field in the midst of siege? The preacher might further envision a sermon that is itself a prophetic symbol (or that employs elements of prophetic symbolism).

Matthew 27:9–10 purports to quote Jeremiah to interpret the thirty pieces of silver and the buying of a potter's field as a burial place for strangers. The quote in Matthew recalls instead Zechariah 11:7–14 (esp. v. 13). Perhaps by mis-citing Zechariah as Jeremiah, Matthew intends for the reader to hear Jeremiah 18:1–12 and 32:6–15 as lenses through which to interpret Matthew 27:3–10. If so, Matthew may mean to use the image of the potter reshaping a pot to bespeak the judgment of Judah (Jer. 18:1–11; Proper 18/Year C) as a way of indicating that the leaders who sold Jesus are under judgment, and to use the field bought as a sign of promise in a season of judgment (Jer. 32:6–15) to point to Jesus' ministry and resurrection as signs of hope even as the world careens toward apocalyptic judgment.

Amos 6:1a, 4–7 (Paired)*

For an introduction to Amos, see Proper 23/Year B. Today's reading follows Amos's announcement of YHWH's rejection of inauthentic worship devoid of any concern for the needy, widows, and orphans (5:1–27). Our text is composed of two utterances of affliction, each beginning with "Alas" (vv. 1, 4).

The first (vv. 1–3) is addressed to "those who are at ease in Zion . . . who feel secure on Mount Samaria," a reference to the northern kingdom (see 7:10–13). Earlier, Amos gave voice to the Lord's judgment on countries who were under the illusion that they dwelt in security behind their defensive barriers: "the strongholds of Ben-hadad . . . the gate bars of Damascus" and Gaza's strongholds (1:4–5, 7) will not protect them from God's judgment for their war-making and taking of peoples into exile (1:6, 9). Military superiority cannot be counted on to provide security for nations that commit transgressions against other peoples; the only true security comes from a people's readiness to carry out compassionate justice.

In our first saying of affliction, Amos asks the house of Israel whether it is "better than" these kingdoms. Addressing an Israel that allows itself to "feel secure" in its prosperity and power, Amos claims that it is only putting off "the evil day," that day of the Lord that will be "darkness, not light" (5:18, 20) because Israel engages in "a reign of violence" (6:3). The punishment of those "who are at ease in Zion" is that "they shall now be the first to go into exile" (v. 7).

But Amos has not yet, in this passage, said why this is to be the case. That is the issue of verses 4–6. Here he returns to his earlier theme of judgment on those "who oppress the poor, who crush the needy, who say to their husbands, 'Bring something to drink!'" while ignoring the covenantal obligation to engage in active justice for the vulnerable (4:1). Behind their fortress walls, the Israelites "lie on beds of ivory, and lounge on their couches, and eat lambs from the flock, and calves from the stall" but "are not grieved over the ruin of Joseph!" (6:4, 6). Israel haughtily trusts its fortifications to keep it secure while it ignores injustice and revels in partying. The overconfidence of Israel's "notables" (6:1) is matched by its upper-class lack of empathy for the plight of the poor and the destitute. Their utter lack of concern and coldness toward the hungry and the homeless will bring their downfall.

Amos is talking about the sins of a comfortable people. They eat meat (lambs and calves), a clear indication of wealth in the economy of Amos's time; for ordinary people meat was a food that they could seldom afford. They "drink wine from bowls" (v. 6), copiously, not even bothering with a cup or glass. They "anoint themselves with the finest oils, but are not grieved over the ruin of Joseph!" (v. 6). Their lack of concern for the suffering of the widow and the orphan evokes Amos's critique. "They shall now be the first to go into exile" (v. 7).

This reading is well paired with the parable of the Rich Man and Lazarus (Luke 16:19–31). The behavior of the rich man in the parable exactly parallels the behavior of the upper classes whom Amos condemns. He "was dressed in purple and fine linen and . . . feasted sumptuously every day" (Luke 16:19). Meanwhile Lazarus lay just outside his gated community "covered with sores" (16:20), attended only by dogs. The well-dressed, magnificently fed rich man ignored him. When the rich man begs Abraham to raise Lazarus from the dead and send him as a warning to the man's brothers, Abraham's remarkable retort is: "If they do not listen to Moses and the prophets, neither will they be convinced even if someone rises from the dead" (16:31).

It is said of our society that in it the poor are invisible. In how many ways do we manage to be oblivious to them?

Proper 22 [27]/Year C

Lamentations 1:1–6+ (Semicontinuous)

Although many in the past thought Jeremiah wrote Lamentations, the book itself does not make that claim, and some of its material has a different tone from that of the book of Jeremiah. Most scholars think

Lamentations came from an anonymous prophet who spoke in Judah during the exile. Some scholars think that these laments were used in public liturgies mourning the destruction of the Temple.

The book is made up of five laments. Three laments are in the form of acrostic in which each verse (1:1–22; 2:1–22; 4:1–22) or group of verses (3:1–66) starts with a successive letter of the Hebrew alphabet. (The fifth lament, 5:1–22, does not follow this pattern.) Many scholars think that in addition to serving as a memory device, "The use of all the letters of the alphabet may imply fullness of expression—everything from A to Z—thereby symbolizing the completeness of the devastation being described and also of the mourning being expressed."[80] The lament is a medium that gives grief a healthy theological form.

This first lament describes the desolation of Jerusalem after the Babylonians had destroyed the Temple in 586 BCE. The first word of the book is the Hebrew *eka*, ("how," "alas"), and it is frequently used in laments to signal a tragic change of circumstance from joy to sorrow: "How lonely sits the city that once was full of people!" (Lam. 1:1). Judah was recently a great presence among the nations but is now like a widow. The comparison with the widow invokes for the city the range of feelings that were attached to the widow in ancient culture: widows were considered to be some of the most vulnerable people in the community, often living on the edge of survival and dependent upon God's care as expressed through structures of provision in the community.

Like a widow in mourning, Judah weeps bitterly in the night. Listeners imaginatively feel both the "tears on her cheeks" and her emptiness in which she has "no one to comfort her." Other nations, once friends, joined with the Babylonians and "dealt treacherously with her" and became her enemies (Lam. 1:2). Judah feels betrayed. The community is suffering in exile, which brings with it "hard servitude," and it has no standing among the nations, and no rest (1:3).

Reflecting an ancient Jewish view that nature itself was animated, "the roads to Zion mourn" because the Temple is destroyed and people no longer come for the major religious observances. The priests groan not only because of the loss of vocation but because they depended upon the Temple offerings for food and livelihood. Even young women grieve (Lam. 1:4).

The exile is punishment for "the multitude of her transgressions" (especially idolatry and injustice). The children (representing the future of the community) are in Babylon (Lam. 1:5). Daughter Zion has lost her majesty. The young male rulers have become like stags without pasture, that is, without sources to sustain fullness of life and procreation (1:6).

While the lamentations are especially suited to major occasions of public tragedy when the community as a whole needs to mourn, it is unlikely that such a tragedy will occur just at the time this text appears in the lectionary. However, North American culture often has difficulty dealing with grief in either individual or communal circumstances. People often deny grief or respond to it in ways that frustrate individual lives and community. The preacher might take the occurrence of this passage in the lectionary as an occasion to help prepare the congregation to deal with such grief by naming and expressing personal and public grief in a theological framework that helps individuals and communities move forward in ways consistent with God's hope for all to live in covenant, in which all are fully responsible for one another and make optimum contributions to community.

This passage does not appear in the New Testament.

Habakkuk 1:1–4; 2:1–4 (Paired)*

In this passage Habakkuk asks questions (1:2–4; 1:12–2:1) and God answers (1:5–11; 2:2–4). Habakkuk is a thinking prophet to whom God's punishment of the people with foreign armies does not make sense. Like Abraham and Moses, Habakkuk takes his questions directly to God and God responds with no show of displeasure. God welcomes Habakkuk's questions.

Habakkuk prophesied in Judah in the late seventh and early sixth centuries. His initial question is: "How long shall I cry for help, and you will not listen? Or cry to you 'Violence!' and you will not save?" (v. 2). He is aghast at the "destruction and violence" (v. 3) that Judeans commit against each other. Shortly after the religious reform under the reign of Josiah, the Judeans have again abandoned their tradition; "the law [*torah*] becomes slack and justice [*mishpat*] never prevails" (v. 4). *Torah* here stands for Torah-teachings, prophecy and wisdom, the heritage of the people Israel. *Mishpat* is God's intended order of kindhearted justice of actively seeing to the well-being of widows, orphans, and the destitute. Society is wracked by trouble and violence. And Habakkuk agonizes over the fact that his prayers to God apparently go unheeded: "you will not listen" (v. 2). He has prayed and nothing has changed.

In verses 5–11, the Lord answers his agonizing question about the turmoil in Judean society and about God's silence. God is in fact active amid the disarray; "a work is being done in your days that you would not believe if you were told" (v. 5). In spite of Habakkuk's suspicions, God knows what is happening. God proposes to rouse "the Chaldeans, that fierce and impetuous nation . . . they all come for violence . . . they gather captives like sand" (vv. 6–9). God is prompting the Babylonians under Nebuchadnezzar (ca. 605–562) to swift and terrible (vv. 7–8) actions; they will capture every fortified city (v. 10). They worship their own armored power (v. 11). The Judeans want violence and God will let them have violence. God lets us deal with the consequences of our sins.

Habakkuk addresses his second "complaint" (1:12–2:1) to the Lord. "Your eyes are too pure to behold evil, and you cannot look on wrongdoing. . . . You have made people like the fish of the sea, like crawling things that have no ruler" (vv. 13–14). God is not the God of might and power whom Babylonians worship: "their own might is their god!" (v. 11). Habakkuk longs for God's *torah* and *mishpat*, God's considerate justice, to come to pass. Habakkuk knows that God's intent is that we receive life and well-being, but God proposes to counter violence with violence, injustice with injustice. How does this advance God's purpose of *shalom*? God will wipe out an unjust society with an even more unjust society. Is the enemy to "keep on . . . destroying nations without mercy?" (v. 17).

In 2:2–4, God again answers Habakkuk. "Write the vision; make it plain on tablets, so that a runner may read it." Like many of the early Jesus-communities living in the tension between the revelation of God in Jesus and the delay in his return (the Parousia), Habakkuk lives in the in-between time. God reassures Habakkuk that the goal remains the same: "there is still a vision for the appointed time" (v. 3). Persistence and patience, the dynamic waiting that commits itself to a life of deeds of loving-kindness amid the otherwise chaotic world, are required.

Then the conclusion: "the righteous live by their faith [*emunah*]" (v. 4). Faith, trust in and reliance on God, is the opposite of pride (v. 4a), which relies on its own resources to solve all the problems of injustice. We are to walk in the way of life and blessing, trusting in God, in the midst of the madness of the world.

There are other theological responses to Habakkuk's question, several of which stress in one way or another that God is a covenantal God who does not do everything but relies on God's covenantal partners to carry out their responsibilities. But whatever the answer, preachers can use Habakkuk to help parishioners wrestle with questions that they most likely have but to which they seldom give voice.

This reading is paired with Luke 17:5–10, the parable of the Mustard Seed and a saying about discipleship, probably because of the point about "faith the size of a mustard seed." Such faith can accomplish great things.

Proper 23 [28]/Year C

Jeremiah 29:1, 4–7+ (Semicontinuous)

By the time of today's reading, Babylon had conquered Judah and sent many of its leading citizens to exile. Jeremiah 27:1–28:17 reports a conflict that took place among community members who were left in Judah. The conflict centered on whether the community left behind should organize a revolt against Babylon (a viewpoint Jeremiah identifies with the false prophets), or as Jeremiah recommended, the community should submit patiently to the yoke of Babylon in the confidence that God would eventually liberate them; revolt, the prophet believed, would lead to the annihilation of the community. Whereas the false prophet Hananiah announced that the exiles and the Temple treasures the Babylonians had taken as booty would be returned to Judah within two years, Jeremiah countermanded Hananiah. God would keep the leaders of Judah in exile for a long though indeterminate time (see Proper 8/Year C).

In the lection for today, the prophet writes a letter in the name of God to the exiles in Babylon (Jer. 29:1–3). God through the prophet counsels the exiles to settle in Babylon and create a new life there instead of constantly being on edge by planning revolt or thinking that their return will be imminent. They should take the time and resources to build houses and plant gardens. Like the Hebrews in Egypt, they should marry and have children so that their number will increase rather than decrease (29:4–6). During this phase of the exile, they should "seek the welfare of the city where I have sent you . . . , and pray to [God] on its behalf, for in its welfare you will find your welfare"; that is, they should cooperate with economic, social, and political forces that would help Babylon be a place of peace and prosperity that provided abundantly for all (Jer. 29:7).

The preacher needs to speak carefully about this aspect of Jeremiah's letter. The prophet does not urge readers to incorporate *Babylonian* values and practices into the Judahite community in exile or the Judahites to assimilate into Babylonian culture. The prophet offers a practical guide for the survival of the Jewish community as Jewish, given the political and military realities of Babylon as the international superpower and Judah as a conquered community that Babylon could utterly and finally pulverize. Jeremiah advises creating a Jewish community with the power to sustain itself over a long period as *Jewish* in identity by building homes and institutions that foster that identity in the midst of an alien culture.

Jeremiah offers a model that has some possibility for Christian community in North America. Churches could build communities to nurture and witness to *Christian* identity within the larger North American culture with its Babylonian style idolatry and injustice. Indeed, such churches can pray and work for the welfare of *all* in the larger culture so that all will experience peace, justice, and abundance. From such a position, congregations might even be able to work for systemic change in the larger world. Yet, a congregation can easily cross the line from being a community with a distinct identity and mission living within the larger culture to becoming a community shaped by the assumptions and values of that culture and, indeed, co-opted by the culture. A preacher might reflect with the congregation on where their life falls on a spectrum whose poles are maintaining identity for witness and being shaped by the larger culture.

Jeremiah's advice was contextual, of course. Not only were the exiles not immediately threatened by extermination but in many respects they had a comfortable life. In more urgent situations, a congregation might need to take more dramatic action.

While the New Testament does not refer directly to this passage, we do hear a thematic resonance between Jeremiah and the New Testament in the call to pray for one's enemies (e.g., Matt. 5:43–48; Luke 6:27–36; Rom. 13:8–10; Gal. 5:13–15; Jas. 2:8–13).

2 Kings 5:1–3, 7–15c (Paired)*

For comments on this passage, please see Proper 9/Year C.

Proper 24 [29]/Year C

Jeremiah 31:27–34+ (Semicontinuous)

For comments on this passage, please see the Fifth Sunday in Lent/Year B.

Genesis 32:22–31 (Paired)*

For comments on this passage, please see Proper 13/Year A.

Proper 25 [30]/Year C

Joel 2:23–32+ (Semicontinuous)

Please see Ash Wednesday/Year A for the context of today's reading. Joel has just declared the end of the famine caused by a plague of locusts: "You shall eat in plenty and be satisfied . . . and my people shall never again be put to shame" (2:26). Our reading begins with YHWH's promise: "Then afterward I will pour out my spirit on all flesh; your sons and your daughters shall prophesy, your old men shall dream dreams, and your young men shall see visions. Even on the male and female slaves, in those days, I will pour out my spirit" (vv. 28–29).

"Afterward" refers to some future time that Joel does not specify. He has just promised (2:27) that the people Israel "shall know that I am in the midst of Israel, and that I, the LORD, am your God and there is no other." Verses 28–29 expand the promise into one with universal scope: "all flesh," not just all Israel. This is in keeping with the original promise to Abraham and Sarah and their descendants that in them all the Gentiles would be blessed. We note the all-inclusive character of this promise in Joel in other respects as well: sons and daughters, old men and young men, male and female slaves—on all of them God will pour out God's spirit.

God's spirit (*ruach* YHWH) is not just any spirit. The term "spirit" is free-floating and can refer just as well to the spirit of the Delta Chi sorority as to the spirit of the Nazi party. "Spirit" is always defined by what follows the "of." The spirit of the Lord is the spirit of the God of considerate justice. Usually biblical scholars associate spirit with "power," specifically the power to do impressive deeds or to prophesy. Yet spirit is more than power; it is the union of power with meaning. Understanding the meaning is good, but having the spirit or heart to act it out is also available from God as gracious gift. Power separate from meaning is chaotic.

In this future time, Joel comments: ". . . everyone who calls on the name of the LORD shall be saved" (v. 32). His reference is to those who will be saved from some future calamity, a calamity that he does not identify, and it is a promise to the people Israel—in Mount Zion and Jerusalem there will be survivors (v. 32b).

Today's reading is quoted extensively in Acts 2:14–21, Peter's sermon at Pentecost. Unfortunately the sermon manifests the theology of accusation, twice accusing the "men of Judea and all who live in Jerusalem" of having crucified Jesus (2:23, 36). This is a major theme of the early section of Acts, repeated in 3:13 and 4:10. It is immensely sad that the precious gift of Jesus Christ to the church, a gift that would not have been possible apart from the people Israel in whom Jesus took shape, is received in a spirit of hostility.

That this spirit involves a good bit of theological distortion is evident when we note that Acts 2:21 quotes Joel 2:32: "Then everyone who calls on the name [YHWH] of the Lord shall be saved." Yet in Acts 4:11–12 we read: "Jesus is 'the stone that was rejected by you, the builders; it has become the cornerstone.' There is salvation in no one else, for there is no other name under heaven . . . by which we must be saved."

Here is the hermeneutical issue: Is Acts self-contradictory or do we usually read Acts 4:11–12 wrongly? We suggest the latter, noting that the name "Jesus" means "YHWH saves." If we remember this, then Acts is not self-contradictory. But then neither does Acts 4:11–12 limit salvation to those who call on the name of Jesus Christ.

Jeremiah 14:7–10, 19–22 or Sirach 35:12–17 (Paired)*

The readings from Jeremiah and Sirach occur in the lectionary as alternates. While Jeremiah helps interpret Mark 9:30–37, the reading from Sirach coordinates a little better with Luke 18:1–8, the parable of the Widow and the Unjust Judge (Proper 24/Year C). On Jeremiah and Sirach, see Fourth Sunday after the Epiphany/Year C, and Proper 17/Year C.

Jeremiah 14:1–6 pictures Judah in drought. The ground is cracked; cisterns are empty; farmers are dismayed; the doe forsakes the newborn fawn because there is no grass; the wild asses pant because there is no vegetation. The Judahites believed that God had brought the drought upon them. Acknowledging that their iniquities testify against them, they pray for God to end the drought "for your name's sake," that is, to restore God's reputation by ending their plight (14:7, 9b). They say God acts like a stranger who is in the land but is not a member of the community. God is like a traveler asleep for the night (14:8). God behaves as if confused, like a helpless warrior (14:9a). God replies that God will not accept them and will punish them because they "have not restrained their feet" (14:10).

The people pray again in Jeremiah 14:19–22, asking in anguish whether God has rejected and loathed Judah. They seek peace and healing but find terror (14:19). They acknowledge their wickedness and plead for God not to spurn them. By ignoring them, they claim, God dishonors God's name and breaks covenant (14:20–21). They admit that only God and not the idols can give rain, and set their hope on God (14:22). Some commentators think that their remarks do not come from the deepest reaches of the heart and that they are not fully repentant.

This text raises two immediate issues for the preacher. First, some people today believe that God sends particular natural disasters upon communities. The preacher needs to point out that while many people in antiquity believed that, few theologians today agree. While the human family's ecological abuse contributes to failures in nature, we believe that natural disasters are outside divine control. Second, Jeremiah indicates that God simply turns away some people, especially the unrepentant. We do not agree. Of course human beings often suffer the consequences of misdeeds. However, even within the limitations of such circumstances we believe God is ever present to offer individuals and communities as many possibilities of restoration, healing, fulfillment, and alignment with the divine purposes as the circumstances allow.

The reading from Sirach should be 35:14–26. Sirach 35:1–5 indicates that faithfully keeping the commandments functions similarly to observing ritual. Nevertheless, Sirach 35:6–13 reminds the community that ritual is important. The best life is the one in which ritual represents symbolically the faithful life.

Sirach 35:14–26 stresses that God is not partial but always does what is right, so people should behave accordingly by not offering bribes or dishonest sacrifices (35:14–16a). God listens to the prayers of the wronged and pays particular attention to the orphan and widow (35:16b–19). God will accept and act on the prayers of the faithful for justice (35:20–22a). God will not delay in crushing the unmerciful and repaying sinners "according to their deeds" while pouring out mercy on the faithful (35:33b–36).

The readings from Jeremiah and Sirach are paired with Luke 18:9–14, the parable of the Pharisee and the Tax Collector. The lectionary may have turned to Jeremiah to interpret the Pharisee. Sirach 35:12–13, 16a (as well as 35:21) relates loosely to the tax collector. In any event, the preacher needs to handle the parable with care because Luke has shaped that story as a negative caricature of many Pharisees to validate separation taking place between the Lukan congregation and other Jewish communities and to encourage the congregation to welcome repentant persons such as the tax collector.

Proper 26 [31]/Year C

Habakkuk 1:1–4; 2:1–4

For comments on this passage, please see Proper 22/Year C.

Isaiah 1:10–18* (Paired)

For comments on this passage, please see Proper 14/Year C.

Proper 27 [32]/Year C

Haggai 1:15b–2:9+ (Semicontinuous)

Haggai worked in Jerusalem in 520 BCE. His period of prophesying and Zechariah's occurred in the same year (Zech. 1:1). He dates his book by telling us when he received each of his prophetic visions. He says of the first one: "In the second year of King Darius, in the sixth month, on the first day of the month, the word of the LORD came by the prophet Haggai to Zerubbabel . . . governor of Judah, and to Joshua . . . the high priest" (1:1). Haggai's last words from the Lord came to him four months later (2:10, 19).

Haggai has only one concern, a distinctly odd one for a prophet in Israel. He wants the Judeans to rebuild the Temple that the Babylonians had destroyed. Four times in the first chapter he refers to the "house" of the Lord (vv. 4, 8, 9, and 14). Previous prophets had little positive to say about the Temple, although they cannot be said to have wanted to do away with it. They desired that its worship be authentic, a liturgical celebration of a genuine life of faith committed to YHWH's considerate justice and not an ersatz substitute for actively seeing to the needs of the widow and the orphan. Yet their comments, in the un-nuanced manner of prophetic speech, spoke strongly against the Temple (e.g., Isa. 1:10–17; Jer. 7:1–15; Ezek. 24:15–24).

All of a sudden here comes a prophet who strongly urges Zerubbabel, the governor of Judah under the authority of Darius the king of Persia, and Joshua, the high priest, to: "Go up to the hills and bring wood and build the house" (1:8). He is insistent on this point. How is it that the people can live in "paneled houses, while this house lies in ruins?" (1:4). "My house lies in ruins, while all of you hurry off to your own houses" (1:9). Thus Zerubbabel and Joshua and the people "came and worked on the house of the LORD of hosts, their God, on the twenty-fourth day of the month, in the sixth month" (1:14–15), little more than three weeks after Haggai's initial prophecy.

When the church construction boom took place in the mid–twentieth century, it was said that some pastors had an "edifice complex." There is enough iconoclasm in many of us to lead us to look askance at an emphasis on buildings. Haggai's text is precisely pertinent to us because it leads us to question our biases.

We have already, in the liturgical year, been aware of Zephaniah's promise to Zion, upon its return from exile, that the Lord will be "in your midst . . . he will rejoice over you with gladness, he will renew you in his love; he will exult over you with loud singing as on a day of festival" (Zeph. 3:17–18). "Festival" is the meaning of Haggai's name. Haggai works in that period which Zephaniah anticipated. He wants to house the festival with God in a Temple, as the Eucharist with God is housed in a church building with a table set with bread and wine, a cross, and a baptistery.

Pastors raise an eyebrow at church members who hint that being present when the community gathers for worship is not terribly important. After all, is not God everywhere? Can we not commune with God in a garden, on the golf course, or in the football stadium? But the point of the symbols, rituals and, yes, the architecture of worship is not that they capture and contain God, to whom access is nowhere else available. It is that in numerous ways they symbolize, point to, and remind us of the actuality of the living God who desires that we live in authentic community. Tangible, material, ecclesial things focus our attention on matters of ultimate importance; the football stadium and the golf course focus it on transient matters.

Job 19:23–27a (Paired)*

The story of Job is a single narrative so that a sermon on a text must set the passage in the larger narrative context (see Proper 22/Year B). A theme from Deuteronomic theology is in the background: obedience brings blessing while disobedience results in curse. The book of Job challenges this idea.

In Job 1:1–2:10, Satan set up an experiment to see whether Job would reject God if Job's prosperity ended. Job lost nearly everything. Job laments (3:1–26). Three friends interpret Job's suffering. Eliphaz says Job suffers because Job sinned (4:1–5:27). Job challenges the friends to show that Job deserves to suffer (6:1–7:21). Bildad says that Job should repent (8:1–22). Job replies that his situation is hopeless since God is prosecutor and judge (9:1–10:22). Zophar states that God could expose Job's guilt (11:1–20). Job accuses the friends of retreating into conventional wisdom: Job wants to confront God (12:1–14:20). Eliphaz returns to point out that Job cannot know the divine purposes fully (15:1–35), which calls for another statement of innocence from Job and the cry that Job has no hope (16:1–17:16). Bildad comes back to affirm that God punishes the wicked, so Job must be wicked (18:1–21).

Job protests the harsh verdict of the three friends (Job 19:1–6). By sending the calamities, God has dealt unfairly with Job (19:6–12). Job's family, friends, servants, and spouse are all estranged (19:13–19). His body is disintegrating (19:20). Job pleas for pity from the friends who harass him as God does (19:21–22). Job wanted a written record so that in the future, he could bring forth vindicating evidence. Indeed, Job would like to chisel his case into stone (Job 19:23–24).

Many Christians have so connected the notion of "redeemer" (*goel*) with Christ in Job 19:25–27a that it can be hard to interpret *goel* in the actual context in the book of Job. The language of redeemer comes from the family and refers to the closest male relation whose mission was to protect the interests of family members, especially when they were incapacitated from doing so. The *goel* would restore lost property, recover family sold as slaves, and punish people who harmed family members (e.g., Lev. 25:25, 28; Num. 5:8; 35:19; Deut. 19:6). The redeemer is not God. Instead, Job seeks a *goel* who will recover from God what Job has lost. While it is not clear whether Job has in mind a redeemer who is simply a human being or is a heavenly being, Job is certain that the *goel* is alive and will take Job's case to God in the future (Job 19:25b).

Unfortunately, the Hebrew of Job 19:26 is unclear. Most English versions imply that Job's vindication would take place in the resurrection life. However, the Jewish community at the time of the writing of Job may not have had such a notion. Consequently, some commentators think that Job 19:25–26a and 19:26b–27 make different statements, verses 25–26a as above, but verses 26b–27 referring to Job's insistence that he would like to confront God now.[81] From this perspective the Tanakh translation reads: "But I would behold God while still in my flesh, I myself, not another, would behold [God]."

From this point of view, the lection for today achingly states Job's longing to be vindicated but does not offer an immediate resolution. The preacher can certainly use this aspect of Job as a point of identification for those in the congregation who feel that they unjustly suffer or are unjustly accused. The sermon might help some folk name their feelings. The preacher must decide whether to propose a theological resolution by moving to the last chapters of Job or to the preacher's own theology.

The lectionary pairs Job 19:23–27 with a question to Jesus from the Sadducees (who did not believe in the resurrection) to Jesus concerning a woman who was widowed seven times and under levirate law became the seriatim spouse of seven brothers (Deut. 25:5–6). As we have seen, the book of Job does not presume the apocalyptic view of resurrection found in Luke. The preacher might use the confluence of these texts as a starting point for a sermon that considers different views of life and life beyond death in the Bible.

Proper 28 [33]/Year C

Isaiah 65:17–25+ (Semicontinuous)

For comments on this passage, please see Easter Day/Year C.

Malachi 4:1–2a (Paired)*

With this passage from Malachi (4:1–6), the church's canon of the First Testament comes to a close and shortly so will the three-year lectionary cycle. Malachi is primarily concerned with the keeping of the covenant, particularly as that applies to Temple worship: "I have sent this command to you, that my covenant with Levi may hold, says the LORD of hosts. My covenant with him was a covenant of life and well-being, which I gave him. . . . True instruction was in his mouth" (2:4–6). Yet the priesthood has violated the covenant "by offering polluted food on the altar" (1:7) and the people have violated it by being lured into worship of other gods by their foreign wives (2:10–12) as well as by the Judean males' willingness to divorce "the wife of your youth" (2:13–16), which Malachi also regards as faithlessness (2:16). Further, the people are not offering the tithes and offerings to the Temple, in effect robbing God (3:8–15).

The Lord keeps arguing a case against the people, letting them know that their troubles are due to their lack of trust in God. But they keep arguing back, asking: "How have you loved us?" (1:2); "Where is the God of justice?" (2:17); or "How shall we return [to the Lord]?" (3:7). Now they argue: "It is vain to serve God. What do we profit by keeping his command . . . ? Now we count the arrogant happy; evil-doers not only prosper, but when they put God to the test they escape" (3:14–15). They are rightly criticized in the commentary tradition, but they ask pertinent questions: How clearly is God's providential care for the world evident amid the general run of stupidity and violence that passes for ordinary life? Yet their case is severely weakened by their failure to live out the compassionate justice of the covenant.

The commandments of the covenant, which the Judeans so freely break, are Torah-teachings or illustrations of how those who trust in God should live: by walking the way of life and blessing rather than that of death and curse. "Law" illustrates how we are to love God by caring for the last and the least in society, widows and orphans; by being honest in business and seeing to it that justice is done in the courts; by guarding and protecting the well-being of the stranger; by being responsible for the world of nature as God's creation and recognizing God's covenant with all the living things; and by the proper worship of God.

But in spite of the fact that the Judeans have ignored the commandments, and argued against God, God's love for them remains steadfast (1:2). A remnant (3:16–18) will be saved from Judah. Our passage consists of this affirmation. "See, the day is coming, burning like an oven, when all the arrogant and all evildoers will be stubble; the day that comes shall burn them up, says the LORD of hosts, so that it will leave them neither root nor branch. But for you who revere my name [the remnant] the sun of righteousness shall rise, with healing in its wings."

"Sun of righteousness" is metaphorical talk about God's justification of the people. It is "righteousness" in the sense that Paul used it to talk of God's "setting-right" of the relationship between human beings and God and between the insiders and the outsiders of God's house—the creation of a worldwide community of life and blessing. This will be the "healing in its wings."

The good news in Malachi is that, although we sin long and hard, God never gives up on us. God's steadfast love is an adamant love, a love that will not let us go. That is surely a good note on which to end one lectionary year and move to the advent of the one through whom we Gentile Christians came to understand ourselves in relation to God and God's salvation.

Our passage is dialectically paired with Luke 21:5–19, in which Jesus speaks of the coming destruction of the Temple, the Temple that Malachi defended in his protests against the corruption of its worship by priest and people (Mal. 1:6–2:9; 3:8–15).

Proper 29 [34]/Year C

Reign of Christ

Jeremiah 23:1–6

Ancient readers would have assumed two motifs in the background of today's reading. One is that ancient people often described monarchs as shepherds. The other is that the monarch was responsible to the people and to the deity to protect and provide for the community. Jewish monarchs were to see that the community lived in covenant with God and one another and that the community provided for the poor (e.g., Ps. 72).

In Jeremiah 23, the prophet interprets the rulers of Judah during the years before the exile as "false shepherds." The prophet charged them with allowing idolatry (Jer. 2:11; 10:3–11; 14:22), with seeking protection against Babylon by alliances with Egypt (2:18), with failing the covenant by leaving the poor destitute (e.g., 5:28; 6:13), and with failing to practice other aspects of their religion (e.g., chap. 7; 8:8; 14:13–16; 17:22).

In the brief oracle of judgment in 23:1–2, Jeremiah begins, as occasionally elsewhere, with the word "Woe," which was commonly used at funerals. This word signals to the listeners that the message that follows is a kind of funeral homily for the false shepherds. God will dethrone them and send them into exile (vv. 1–2).

Exile and punishment, however, are not the last words. Jeremiah affirms that God will renew the community in the future. In 23:3–4 God promises to gather a "remnant" from the exile and return them to Israel. God will "raise up shepherds" who will lead the community in "being fruitful" and "multiplying," which will fulfill God's purposes for human life (Gen. 1:28).

In 23:5–6, the prophet specifies the character of the new line of shepherds. The new ruler will come from the house of David, but will be "a righteous Branch." The ruler will "deal wisely and shall execute justice and righteousness in the land." The latter qualities (justice and righteousness) indicate that the vocation of the renewed monarchy is to help the community order its life according to the stipulations of the covenant so that all live in accordance with the divine purposes. The name of the new leader will be "The LORD is our righteousness" (v. 6), that is, the new sovereign will rule by the principles of living according to covenant that graciously come from God. Jeremiah articulates a vision of the leader that could be a norm against which to measure any leader.

Jeremiah did not have Jesus in mind as the "righteous Branch." Nevertheless, today the Gospel lection intends for us to interpret Jesus as a descendant of David who rules by establishing justice and righteousness. By reading from the story of the death of Jesus (Luke 23:33–43), the lectionary reminds the community that Jesus' reign is not that of a self-serving Caesar but that of one who, according to Luke, is willing to become a martyr to demonstrate the depth to which to go to be faithful to God's purposes.

All Saints/Year C

Daniel 7:1–3, 15–18

For comments on this passage, please see Proper 29/Year B.

Thanksgiving Day/Year C

Deuteronomy 26:1–11

Please see the First Sunday in Lent/Year C for commentary on this passage.

Notes

Introduction

1. In Christian circles today, a discussion is under way regarding how to refer to the body of literature that the church has traditionally called the "Old Testament." We adopt this terminology as a sign of respect for the tradition and to avoid confusing readers. However, we do note the broad lines of this discussion. As far as we know, prior to the middle of the second century, the church did not distinguish between parts of the canon. Soon after Marcion (who dismissed the Old Testament as containing a picture of a wrathful second-class deity), many in the church began to speak of the "Old Testament" and the "New Testament" as bodies of literature corresponding with an old covenant that was superseded by the new. Cyril Richardson, distinguished professor of church history at Union Theological Seminary in New York, thus concludes that the "peculiar interest in a *New* Testament stems from rejection of the Old" (Cyril C. Richardson, "Introduction to Early Christian Literature," in *Early Christian Fathers*, Library of Christian Classics [Philadelphia: Westminster Press, 1953], vol. 1, 25. See further Clark M. Williamson, *A Guest in the House of Israel: Post-Holocaust Church Theology* [Louisville, KY: Westminster/ John Knox Press, 1993], 141–42). The very term "Old Testament" thus itself is theologically problematic. The theological problems associated with the term "Old Testament" are magnified in the early twenty-first century because the word "old" is often associated with that which is outdated and worn-out, especially in contrast to that which is new (and improved). Consequently some Christians seek language that is less freighted with negative associations, such as Hebrew Bible or First and Second Testaments. Unfortunately, each terminology has its own problems. Referring to the "Hebrew Bible" overlooks the facts that a small part of that material was actually in Aramaic and also that many in the early church knew this literature through the Septuagint (the translation of the Hebrew and Aramaic materials into Greek). "First Testament" has the virtue of reminding the reader of the chronological relationship between the First and Second Testaments but could subtly be taken to suggest not simply chronology but significance as in First Place in contrast to Second Place. The church prior to the time of Marcion offers us a solution: the Jesus movement simply referred to "the scriptures" by which the community meant the Bible of the Jewish community to which the church gradually added material

from Paul, the Gospel writers, and others. The early followers of Jesus understood the acts of God in Jesus Christ as continuous with the acts of God described in the earlier parts of the Bible. Rather than think of two covenants or two testaments, we suggest that Christians conceive of one biblical story. The Jewish community provides a model for distinguishing materials within the Scriptures when they speak of their canon as Tanakh. The word *Tanakh* is an acronym coming from the Hebrew words *torah* (instruction, guidance, or law), *nebiim* (prophets), and *ketubim* (writings). To these terms, we add the designations *Gospels* and *Letters* (including Acts with the Gospels, and the book of Revelation with the Letters). Thus, the full designation for the Christian Bible would be Torah, Prophets, Writings, Gospels, and Letters.

2. Most Protestant churches regard the first thirty-nine books in the typical Protestant copy of the Bible as the Old Testament. The Roman Catholic and Orthodox canons include, further, the books of Tobit, Judith, 1 and 2 Maccabees, Wisdom of Solomon, Sirach (Ben Sira or Ecclesiasticus), and Baruch. The Orthodox churches add 1 Esdras, 3 and 4 Maccabees, Odes, Psalms of Solomon, and Letter of Jeremiah. Some Orthodox communions bring even more books into the canon, such as 1 Enoch. In our view, the Roman Catholic and Orthodox canons serve the church better than the Protestant version. Most of the books of the Old Testament were completed about 400 BCE. (Daniel, written 168–165 BCE, is a definite exception.) Consequently, Protestant knowledge of Judaism, as far as the canon is concerned, effectively ends at 400 BCE. However, following that time, Judaism continued to generate significant theological literature—for example, the Apocrypha, the Pseudepigrapha, and early rabbinic writings such as the Mishnah and the Talmud. Protestant sermons can help congregations learn more about Jewish theology, life, and witness from 400 BCE through 200 CE by tracing themes from the thirty-nine books of the Protestant canon into these later works. In the Jewish canon, Tanakh, the Torah is made up of the same books in the same order in both Jewish and Christian Bibles. But in Tanakh the prophets come next and include Joshua, Judges, 1 and 2 Samuel, 1 and 2 Kings, Isaiah, Jeremiah, Ezekiel, Hosea, Joel, and the books Amos through Malachi. The Writings are then grouped at the end of the canon—Psalms, Job, Proverbs, Ruth, Song of Solomon, Ecclesiastes, Lamentations, Esther, Daniel, Ezra, Nehemiah, and Chronicles. Many Jewish communities think that revelation continues as subsequent generations study these materials.

3. For example, Clark M. Williamson, *A Guest in the House of Israel: Post-Holocaust Church Theology* (Louisville, KY: Westminster/John Knox Press, 1993), 139–66; Ronald J. Allen and John C. Holbert, *Holy Root, Holy Branches: Christian Preaching from the Old Testament* (Nashville: Abingdon Press, 1994).

4. More fully, see Clark M. Williamson, *When Jews and Christians Meet: A Guide for Christian Preaching and Teaching* (St. Louis: CBP Press, 1989), 1–14.

5. A more detailed exposition of theological misappropriation of the Old Testament is found in Allen and Holbert, *Holy Root, Holy Branches*, 15–31.

6. Empirical confirmation of sermonic neglect of the Old Testament comes from Joseph Faulkener, a researcher in communication at Pennsylvania State University. Faulkener studied the content of more than 200 sermons in typical congregations of the Christian Church (Disciples of Christ) and found that only 24 percent of sermons in these congregations were based on texts from the Old Testament. In these congregations, ministers preach 76 percent of their sermons from the New Testament. While we cannot quantify the importance of the Testaments to the church simply according to how often

ministers preach on them, the fact that preachers turn to the New Testament so much more often than to the Old Testament certainly leaves the congregation with the impression that the Old is of less significance. See Joseph Faulkener, "What Are They Saying? A Content Analysis of 206 Sermons Preached in the Christian Church (Disciples of Christ) in 1988," in *A Case Study of Main Stream Protestantism*, ed. D. Newell Williams (St. Louis, MO: Chalice Press, and Grand Rapids: Wm. B. Eerdmans Publishing Co., 1991), 417. We suspect that statistics are similar for denominations and movements that are similar to the Christian Church (Disciples of Christ).

7. Consultation on Common Texts, *The Revised Common Lectionary* (Nashville: Abingdon Press, 1992), 12.
8. James A. Sanders, "Canon and Calendar: An Alternative Lectionary Proposal," in *Social Themes of the Christian Year*, ed. Dieter T. Hessel (Philadelphia: Geneva Press, 1983), 257–63.
9. Consultation on Common Texts, *Revised Common Lectionary*, 112.
10. *Tikkun* = to mend, repair, heal, or transform; *olam* = world.
11. Taanith 22a, trans. J. Rabbinowitz, in *The Babylonian Talmud*, ed. I. Epstein (London: Soncino Press, 1938), vol. 14, 110.

Commentary

1. Jan Oberg, "The New International Military Order: A Threat to Human Security," in *Problems of Contemporary Militarism*, ed. Asjorn Eide and Marek Thee (New York: St. Martin's, 1980), 47.
2. *Torah from Our Sages: Pirke Avot*, trans. Jacob Neusner (Dallas: Rossel Books, 1984), 3:9, 106.
3. See Richard C. Austin, *Hope for the Land: Nature in the Bible* (Atlanta: John Knox Press, 1988).
4. *Torah*, 39–40.
5. *Sipra Qedosim* par. 1:1 as quoted in Jacob Milgrom, *Leviticus* (Minneapolis: Fortress Press, 2004), 219.
6. Ibid., 227.
7. Ibid., 230.
8. For a provocative consideration of how David is portrayed in the books of Samuel, Chronicles, and Psalms, see Marti J. Steussy, *David: Biblical Portraits of Power*, Studies on Personalities of the Old Testament (Columbia, SC: University of South Carolina Press, 1999). Steussy emphasizes that in Samuel, David is portrayed as deeply human and flawed.
9. Nahum Sarna, *Genesis*, JPS Torah Commentary (Philadelphia: Jewish Publication Society, 1989), 147.
10. See Lloyd Gaston, *Paul and the Torah* (Vancouver: University of British Columbia Press, 1987), 80–99, esp. 88.
11. Sarna, *Genesis*, 153.
12. J. Gerald Janzen, *Genesis 12–50: Abraham and All the Families of the Earth*, International Theological Commentary (Grand Rapids: Wm. B. Eerdmans Publishing Co., 1993), 128.
13. Richard B. Hays, *Echoes of Scripture in the Letters of Paul* (New Haven, CT: Yale University Press, 1989), 61, hears Rom. 8:32 echoed in Rom. 11:21, meaning that God did not spare Israel but allowed Israel to suffer for the sake of the Gentiles so that all (including Israel) could be gathered into the eschatological world.

14. Janzen, *Genesis 12–50*, 87.

15. Ibid., 91.

16. On primogeniture, see Janzen, *Genesis 12–50*, 94–98.

17. On hair as uncouth, see ibid., 96–97.

18. Janzen, *Genesis 12–50*.

19. On the latter suggestion, see ibid., 150–51.

20. Comment inspired by ibid., 151.

21. J. Gerald Janzen, *Exodus* (Louisville, KY: Westminster John Knox Press, 1997), 22.

22. J. Gerald Janzen, "And the Bush Was Not Consumed," *Encounter* 63 (2003): 119–27.

23. Catherine M. LaCugna, *God for Us: The Trinity and the Christian Life* (New York: Harper-Collins, 1991), 302.

24. Abraham Joshua Heschel, *The Sabbath: Its Meaning for Modern Man* (New York: Farrar, Straus & Giroux, 1951), 3.

25. We are indebted for the analysis in this paragraph to J. Gerald Janzen, *Exodus*, 108–9.

26. Sarna, *Genesis*, 348.

27. Janzen, *Genesis 12–50*, 199–200.

28. Ibid., 175; on vengeance, see 204.

29. Terence E. Fretheim, *Exodus*, Interpretation: A Bible Commentary for Teaching and Preaching (Louisville, KY: John Knox Press, 1991), 182.

30. Janzen, *Exodus*, 142.

31. For a complete discussion arguing that "you shall not kill' is the appropriate translation, see Wilma Bailey, *You Shall Not Kill or You Shall Not Murder? The Assault on a Biblical Text* (Collegeville, MN: Liturgical Press, 2005).

32. Fretheim, *Exodus*, 235.

33. See Anson Laytner, *Arguing with God: A Jewish Tradition* (Northvale, NJ: Jason Aronson, 1990), on argument in Jewish prayer.

34. We discuss this matter in Proper 24/Year A of *Preaching the Gospels without Blaming the Jews* (Louisville, KY: Westminster John Knox Press, 2004), 78–79.

35. For a survey of interpretive possibilities, see Jacob Milgrom, *Numbers*, JPS Torah Commentary (Philadelphia: Jewish Publication Society, 1990), 448–56.

36. Jeffrey H. Tigay, *Deuteronomy*, JPS Torah Commentary (Philadelphia: Jewish Publication Society, 1996), 40–42, 339.

37. Joseph R. Jeter Jr., *Preaching Judges*, Preaching Classic Texts (St. Louis, MO: Chalice Press, 2003), 53.

38. Tigay, *Deuteronomy*, 95.

39. John B. Cobb Jr. coined the expression "the call forward" in his *God and the World* (Philadelphia: Westminster Press, 1969), 45.

40. For the case that Jesus did no such thing, see E. P. Sanders, "Jews, Ancient Judaism, and Modern Christianity," in *Jesus, Judaism, and Christian Anti-Judaism*, eds. Paula Fredriksen and Adele Reinhartz (Louisville, KY: Westminster John Knox Press, 2002), 31–55.

41. Tigay, *Deuteronomy*, 69.

42. Sarna, *Genesis*, 125.

43. Janzen, *Genesis 12–50*, 50.

44. Karen Randolph Joines, *Serpent Symbolism in the Old Testament: A Linguistic, Archaeological, and Literary Study* (Haddonfield, NJ: Haddonfield House, 1974), vi.

45. Ibid.

46. For further discussion of the motif of "new covenant" in texts in the New Testament, see Ronald J. Allen and Clark M. Williamson, *Preaching the Gospels without Blaming the Jews: A Lectionary Commentary*, and idem, *Preaching the Letters without Dismissing the Law: A Lectionary Commentary* (Louisville, KY: Westminster John Knox Press, 2006), 126.

47. *Leviticus Rabbah* 29:1, trans. Judah J. Slotki, in *Midrash Rabbah*, ed. H. Freedman and Maurice Simon (London: Soncino Press, 1939), vol. 4, 369–70; our italics.

48. William H. Brownlee, *Ezekiel 1–18*, Word Bible Commentary (Dallas: Word Publishing Co., 1983), 275.

49. Charles R. Blaisdell, cited by Clark M. Williamson and Ronald J. Allen, *A Credible and Timely Word: Process Theology and Preaching* (St. Louis, MO: Chalice Press, 1991), 89, n. 34.

50. J. Gerald Janzen, *Job*, Interpretation: A Bible Commentary for Teaching and Preaching (Atlanta: John Knox Press, 1985), 225–27.

51. Carol A. Newsom, "The Book of Job," in *The New Interpreter's Bible*, ed. Leander Keck et al. (Nashville: Abingdon Press, 1996), vol. 4, 626.

52. Thomas O. Chisholm, "Great Is Thy Faithfulness," *Chalice Hymnal* (St. Louis, MO: Chalice Press, 1995), 86.

53. Jon L. Berquist, *Surprises by the River: The Prophecy of Ezekiel* (St. Louis, MO: Chalice Press, 1993), 20–28.

54. Tigay, *Deuteronomy*, 40–42.

55. Jon L. Berquist, *Judaism in Persia's Shadow: A Social and Historical Approach* (Minneapolis: Fortress Press, 1995), 207–15.

56. For a concise overview of possibilities in interpretation, see Newsom, "Book of Job," 628–29.

57. Janzen, *Job*, 255–57.

58. E.g., Newsom, "Book of Job," 636. For a dramatically different reading, see Janzen, *Job*, 267–69.

59. For discussion of how neo-process theology relates to such matters, see Clark M. Williamson, *Way of Blessing, Way of Life: A Christian Theology* (St. Louis, MO: Chalice Press, 1999), 131–56.

60. Phyllis Trible, *God and the Rhetoric of Sexuality*, Overtures to Biblical Theology (Philadelphia: Fortress Press, 1978), 173.

61. Ibid.

62. Tigay, *Deuteronomy*, 75.

63. Berquist, *Judaism in Persia's Shadow*, 224, 225.

64. Robert Polzin, *Samuel and the Deuteronomist: A Literary Study of the Deuteronomic History* (San Francisco: Harper & Row, 1989), 41–42.

65. For a more detailed reconstruction, see Jon L. Berquist, *Judaism in Persia's Shadow*, 108–19.

66. Fretheim, *Exodus*, 311.

67. Gaston, *Paul and the Torah*, 47.

68. Janzen, *Genesis 12–50*, 40.

69. We can only touch on this aspect of the complex discussion of the relationship of wisdom, word (*logos*) and Torah in the Gospel of John.

70. Milgrom, *Leviticus*, 127.

71. Ibid., 129.

72. Ibid., 102–3, 188–92.
73. Adapted from Stanley K. Stowers, *A Rereading of Romans: Justice, Jews and Gentiles* (New Haven, CT: Yale University Press, 1994), 155.
74. Ibid., 310.
75. Abraham J. Heschel, *The Prophets: An Introduction* (New York: Harper & Row, 1962), vol. 1, 47.
76. Berquist, *Judaism in Persia's Shadow*, 205–20.
77. Ibid., 172–73.
78. Adelaide A. Pollard, "Have Thine Own Way, Lord," in *Chalice Hymnal* (St. Louis, MO: Chalice Press, 1995), 588.
79. African American Spiritual, "There Is a Balm in Gilead," in *Chalice Hymnal* (St. Louis, MO: Chalice Press, 1995), 501.
80. Daniel Grossberg, "Lamentations," in *The Jewish Study Bible*, ed. Adele Berlin and Marc Zvi Brettler (New York: Oxford University Press, 2004), 1589.
81. Newsom, "Book of Job," 478.

Reference List of Ancient Sources
in English Translation

Athanasius. "Festal Letter 39." In *New Testament Apocrypha*, ed. Edgar Hennecke and Wilhelm Schneemelcher. Trans. R. McL. Wilson (Philadelphia: Westminster Press, 1963), vol. 1, 59–60.

Babylonian Talmud, ed. Rabbi Dr. I. Epstein (London: Soncino Press, 1938).

Charlesworth, James H., ed. *The Old Testament Pseudepigrapha: Apocalyptic Literature and Testaments* (Garden City, NY: Doubleday, 1983), vol. 1.

"Creation Epic, The," trans. E. A. Speiser. In *Ancient Near Eastern Texts Relating to the Old Testament*, ed. James B. Pritchard, third ed. (Princeton: Princeton University Press, 1969), 60–72.

"Epic of Gilgamesh, The," trans. E. A. Speiser. In *Ancient Near Eastern Texts Relating to the Old Testament*, ed. James B. Pritchard, third ed. (Princeton: Princeton University Press, 1969), 72–98.

Eusebius. *Ecclesiastical History*, trans. Kirsopp Lake. Books I–V. Loeb Classical Library (Cambridge, MA: Harvard University Press, 1984).

Eusebius. *Ecclesiastical History*, trans. J. E. L. Oulton. Books VI–X. Loeb Classical Library (Cambridge, MA: Harvard University Press, 1973).

Fathers According to Rabbi Nathan, The, trans. Judah Goldin. Yale Judaica Series (New Haven, CT: Yale University Press, 1955).

Irenaeus. *Against Heresies*. Ed. Dominic J. Unger. Ancient Christian Writers (New York: Paulist Press, 1992).

Leviticus Rabbah. In *Midrash Rabbah*. Ed. H. Freedman and Maurice Simon. Trans. Judah J. Slotki (London: Soncino Press, 1939), vol. 4.

Torah from Our Sages: Pirke Avot. Trans. Jacob Neusner (Dallas: Rossel Books, 1984).

Bibliography

African American Spiritual, "There Is a Balm in Gilead." In *Chalice Hymnal*, 501. St. Louis, MO: Chalice Press, 1995.

Allen, Ronald J. "A New Name for the Old Book." *Encounter* 68 (2007), forthcoming.

Allen, Ronald J., and Clark M. Williamson. *Preaching the Gospels without Blaming the Jews: A Lectionary Commentary*. Louisville, KY: Westminster John Knox Press, 2004.

Allen, Ronald J., and Clark M. Williamson. *Preaching the Letters without Dismissing the Law: A Lectionary Commentary*. Louisville, KY: Westminster John Knox Press, 2006.

Austin, Richard C. *Hope for the Land: Nature in the Bible*. Atlanta: John Knox Press, 1988.

Bailey, Wilma Ann. *You Shall Not Kill or You Shall Not Murder? The Assault on a Biblical Text*. Collegeville, MN: Liturgical Press, 2005.

Berquist, Jon L. *Judaism in Persia's Shadow: A Social and Historical Approach*. Minneapolis: Fortress Press, 1995.

———. *Surprises by the River: The Prophecy of Ezekiel*. St. Louis, MO: Chalice Press, 1993.

Brownlee, William H. *Ezekiel 1–18*. Word Bible Commentary. Dallas: Word Publishing Co., 1983.

Chisholm, Thomas O. "Great Is Thy Faithfulness." In *Chalice Hymnal*, 86. St. Louis, MO: Chalice Press, 1995.

Cobb, John B., Jr. "The Authority of the Bible." In *Hermeneutics and the Worldliness of Faith: Essays in Honor of Carl Michelson*, ed. Charles Courtney, Olin M. Ivey, and Gordon Michelson. *The Drew Gateway* 45 (1974–75): 188–202.

———. *God and the World*. Philadelphia: Westminster Press, 1969.

Consultation on Common Texts. *The Revised Common Lectionary*. Nashville: Abingdon Press, 1992.

Faulkener, Joseph. "What Are They Saying? A Content Analysis of 206 Sermons Preached in the Christian Church (Disciples of Christ) during 1988." In *A Case Study of Main Stream Protestantism*, ed. D. Newell Williams. St. Louis, MO: Chalice Press, and Grand Rapids: Wm. B. Eerdmans Publishing Co., 1991.

Gaston, Lloyd. *Paul and the Torah*. Vancouver: University of British Columbia Press, 1987.

Grossberg, Daniel. "Lamentations." In *The Jewish Study Bible*, ed. Adele Berlin and Marc Zvi Brettler. New York: Oxford University Press, 2004.

Hays, Richard B. *Echoes of Scripture in the Letters of Paul.* New Haven, CT: Yale University Press, 1989.

Heschel, Abraham Joshua. *The Prophets: An Introduction.* New York: Harper & Row, 1962.

———. *The Sabbath: Its Meaning for Modern Man.* New York: Farrar, Straus & Giroux, 1951.

Janzen, J. Gerald. "And the Bush Was Not Consumed." *Encounter* 63 (2003): 119–27.

———. *Exodus.* Westminster Bible Companion. Louisville, KY: Westminster John Knox Press, 1997.

———. *Genesis 12–50: Abraham and All the Families of the Earth.* International Theological Commentary. Grand Rapids: Wm. B. Eerdmans Publishing Co., 1993.

———. *Job.* Interpretation: A Bible Commentary for Teaching and Preaching. Atlanta: John Knox Press, 1985.

Jeter, Joseph R., Jr. *Preaching Judges.* Preaching Classic Texts. St. Louis, MO: Chalice Press, 2003.

Joines, Karen Randolph. *Serpent Symbolism in the Old Testament: A Linguistic, Archaeological, and Literary Study.* Haddonfield, NJ: Haddonfield House, 1974.

LaCugna, Catherine M. *God for Us: The Trinity and the Christian Life.* New York: Harper-Collins Publishers, 1991.

Laytner, Anson. *Arguing with God: A Jewish Tradition.* Northvale, NJ: Jason Aronson, 1990.

Milgrom, Jacob. *Leviticus.* Minneapolis: Fortress Press, 2004.

———. *Numbers.* JPS Torah Commentary. Philadelphia: Jewish Publication Society, 1990.

Newsom, Carol A. "The Book of Job." In *The New Interpreter's Bible,* ed. Leander Keck et al., vol. 4. Nashville: Abingdon Press, 1996.

Oberg, Jan. "The New International Military Order: A Threat to Human Security." In *Problems of Contemporary Militarism,* ed. Asjorn Eide and Marek Thee. New York: St. Martin's, 1980.

Pollard, Adelaide A. "Have Thine Own Way, Lord." In *Chalice Hymnal,* 588. St. Louis, MO: Chalice Press, 1995.

Polzin, Robert. *Samuel and the Deuteronomist: A Literary Study of the Deuteronomic History.* San Francisco: Harper & Row, 1989.

Richardson, Cyril C. "Introduction to Early Christian Literature." In *Early Christian Fathers,* Library of Christian Classics, vol 1. Philadelphia: Westminster Press, 1953.

Sanders, E. P. "Jews, Ancient Judaism, and Modern Christianity." In *Jesus, Judaism and Christian Anti-Judaism,* edited by Paula Fredriksen and Adele Reinhartz. Louisville, KY: Westminster John Knox Press, 2002.

Sanders, James A. "Canon and Calendar: An Alternative Lectionary Proposal." In *Social Themes of the Christian Year: A Commentary on the Lectionary,* edited by Dieter T. Hessel. Philadelphia: Geneva Press, 1983.

Sarna, Nahum. *Genesis.* JPS Torah Commentary. Philadelphia: Jewish Publication Society, 1989.

Steussy, Marti J. *David: Biblical Portraits of Power.* Studies on Personalities of the Old Testament. Columbia, SC: University of South Carolina Press, 1999.

Stowers, Stanley K. *A Rereading of Romans: Justice, Jews and Gentiles.* New Haven, CT: Yale University Press, 1994.

Tigay, Jeffrey H. *Deuteronomy.* JPS Torah Commentary. Philadelphia: Jewish Publication Society, 1996.

Trible, Phyllis. *God and the Rhetoric of Sexuality.* Overtures to Biblical Theology. Philadelphia: Fortress Press, 1978.

Williamson, Clark M. *A Guest in the House of Israel: Post-Holocaust Church Theology.* Louisville, KY: Westminster/John Knox Press, 1993.

———. *Way of Blessing, Way of Life: A Christian Theology.* St. Louis, MO: Chalice Press, 1999.

———. *When Jews and Christians Meet: A Guide for Christian Preaching and Teaching.* St. Louis, MO: CBP Press, 1989.

Williamson, Clark M., and Ronald J. Allen. *A Credible and Timely Word: Process Theology and Preaching.* St. Louis, MO: Chalice Press, 1991.

Index of Passages in Canonical Order

Joel 2:23–32	Proper 25/C
Amos 5:6–7, 10–15	Proper 23/B
Amos 5:18–24	Proper 27/A
Amos 6:1a, 4–7	Proper 21/C
Amos 7:7–15	Proper 10/B
Amos 7:7–17	Proper 10/C
Amos 8:1–12	Proper 11/C
Amos 8:4–7	Proper 20/C
Jonah 3:1–5, 10	Epiphany 3/B
Jonah 3:10–4:11	Proper 20/A
Mic. 3:5–12	Proper 26/A
Mic. 5:2–5a	Advent 4/C
Mic. 6:1–8	Epiphany 4/A
Hab. 1:1–4; 2:1–4	Proper 22/C
Hab. 1:1–4; 2:1–4	Proper 26/C
Zeph. 1:7, 12–18	Proper 28/A
Zeph. 3:14–20	Advent 3/C
Hag. 1:15b–2:9	Proper 27/C
Zech. 9:9–12	Proper 9/A
Mal. 3:1–4	Advent 2/C
Mal. 4:1–2a	Proper 28/C
Wis. 1:13–15; 2:23–24	Proper 8/B
Wis. 1:16–2:1, 12–22	Proper 20/B
Wis. 3:1–9	All Saints/B
Wis. 6:12–16	Proper 27/A
Wis. 10:15–21	Christmas 2/ABC
Wis. 12:13, 16–19	Proper 11/A
Sir. 10:12–18	Proper 17/C
Sir. 15:15–20	Epiphany 6/A
Sir. 24:1–12	Christmas 2/ABC
Sir. 27:4–7	Epiphany 8/C
Sir. 35:12–17	Proper 25/C
Bar. 5:1–9	Advent 2/C